the unbeatable Squirrel Girl

Ryan North
WITH **Chip Zdarsky** (#6)
WRITERS

Erica Henderson
ARTIST

Rico Renzi
COLOR ART

Joe Morris (#1), **Matt Digges** (#2), **David Robins** (#2), **Chip Zdarsky** (#2 & #6) & **Doc Shaner** (#3)
TRADING CARD ART

Joe Quinones
VAN ART (#6)

VC's Clayton Cowles (#1-2, #4) & **Travis Lanham** (#3, #5-6)
LETTERERS

Erica Henderson WITH **Joe Quinones** (#6)
COVER ART

--- **Howard the Duck #6** ---

Chip Zdarsky
WITH **Ryan North**
WRITERS

Joe Quinones
PENCILER

Joe Rivera, **Marc Deering** & **Joe Quinones**
INKERS

Joe Quinones & **Jordan Gibson**
COLORISTS

VC's Travis Lanham
LETTERER

Joe Quinones WITH **Erica Henderson**
COVER ART

Chris Robinson
WITH **Charles Beacham** (HOWARD THE DUCK #6)
ASSISTANT EDITORS

Wil Moss
EDITOR

COLLECTION EDITOR: **JENNIFER GRÜNWALD**
ASSISTANT EDITOR: **SARAH BRUNSTAD**
ASSOCIATE MANAGING EDITOR: **ALEX STARBUCK**
EDITOR, SPECIAL PROJECTS: **MARK D. BEAZLEY**

SENIOR EDITOR, SPECIAL PROJECTS: **JEFF YOUNGQUIST**
SVP PRINT, SALES & MARKETING: **DAVID GABRIEL**
BOOK DESIGNER: **JAY BOWEN**

EDITOR IN CHIEF: **AXEL ALONSO**
CHIEF CREATIVE OFFICER: **JOE QUESADA**
PUBLISHER: **DAN BUCKLEY**
EXECUTIVE PRODUCER: **ALAN FINE**

THE UNBEATABLE SQUIRREL GIRL VOL. 3: SQUIRREL, YOU REALLY GOT ME NOW. Contains material originally published in magazine form as THE UNBEATABLE SQUIRREL GIRL #1-6 and HOWARD THE DUCK #6. First printing 2016. ISBN# 978-0-7851-9626-6. Published by MARVEL WORLDWIDE, INC., a subsidiary of MARVEL ENTERTAINMENT, LLC. OFFICE OF PUBLICATION: 135 West 50th Street, New York, NY 10020. Copyright © 2016 MARVEL No similarity between any of the names, characters, persons, and/or institutions in this magazine with those of any living or dead person or institution is intended, and any such similarity which may exist is purely coincidental. **Printed in the U.S.A.** ALAN FINE, President, Marvel Entertainment; DAN BUCKLEY, President, TV, Publishing & Brand Management; JOE QUESADA, Chief Creative Officer; TOM BREVOORT, SVP of Publishing; DAVID BOGART, SVP of Business Affairs & Operations, Publishing & Partnership; C.B. CEBULSKI, VP of Brand Management & Development, Asia; DAVID GABRIEL. SVP of Sales & Marketing, Publishing; JEFF YOUNGQUIST, VP of Production & Special Projects; DAN CARR, Executive Director of Publishing Technology; ALEX MORALES, Director of Publishing Operations; SUSAN CRESPI, Production Manager; STAN LEE, Chairman Emeritus. For information regarding advertising in Marvel Comics or on Marvel.com, please contact Vit DeBellis, Integrated Sales Manager, at vdebellis@marvel.com. For Marvel subscription inquiries, please call 888-511-5480. **Manufactured between 4/1/2016 and 5/9/2016 by R.R. DONNELLEY, INC., SALEM, VA, USA.**
10 9 8 7 6 5 4 3 2 1

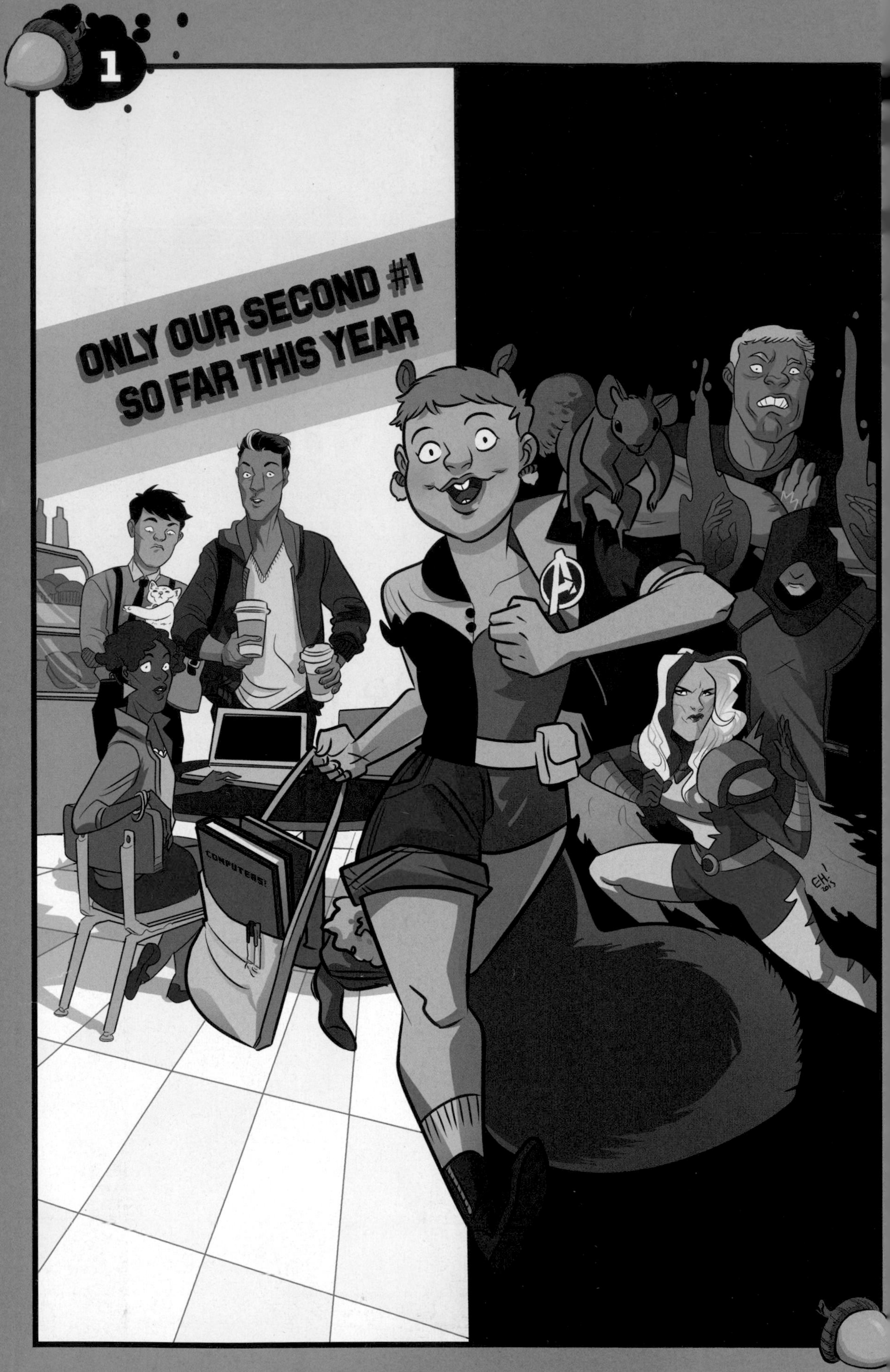
1
ONLY OUR SECOND #1
SO FAR THIS YEAR
COMPUTERS!

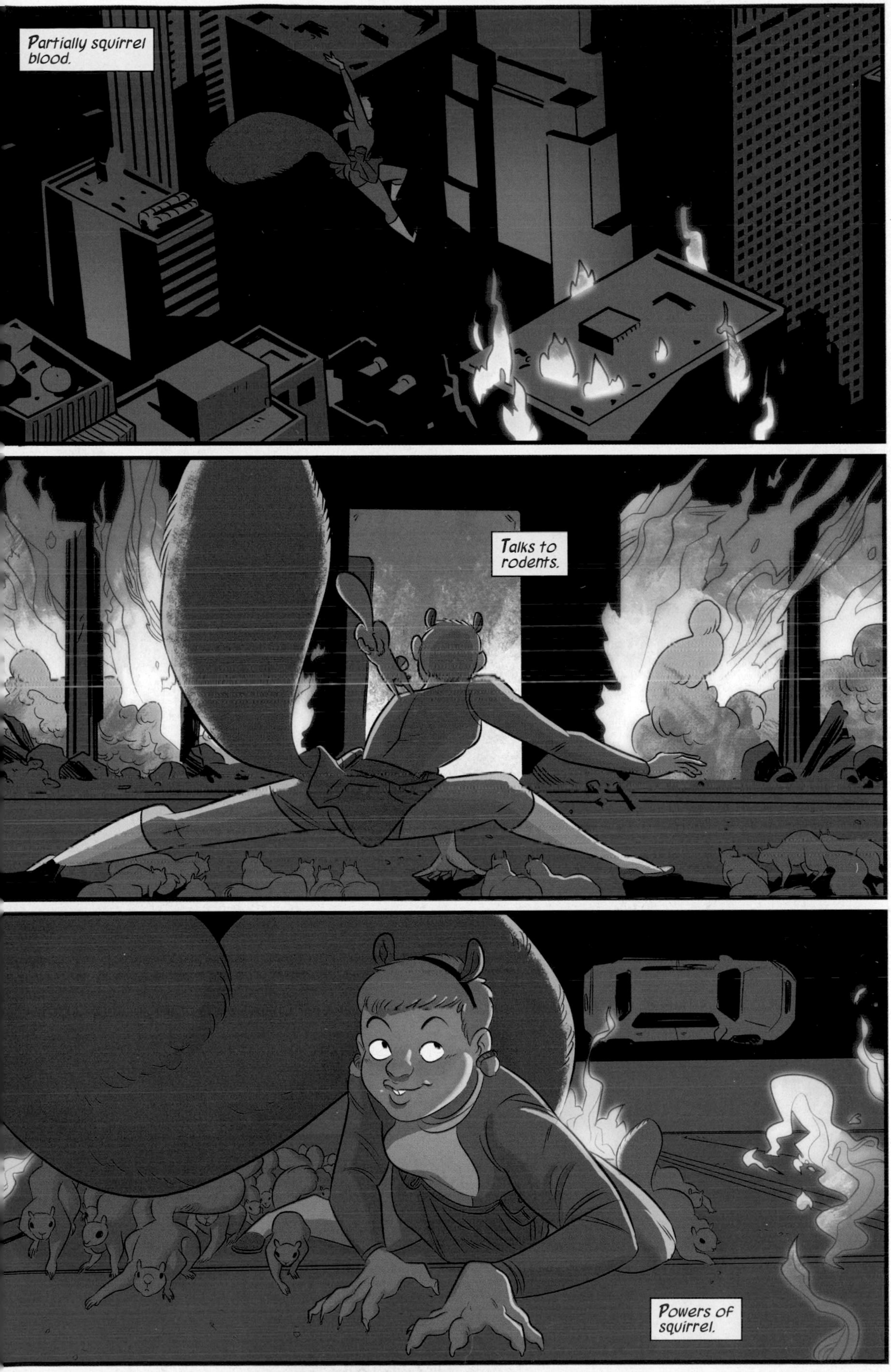
Partially squirrel blood.
Talks to rodents.
Powers of squirrel.

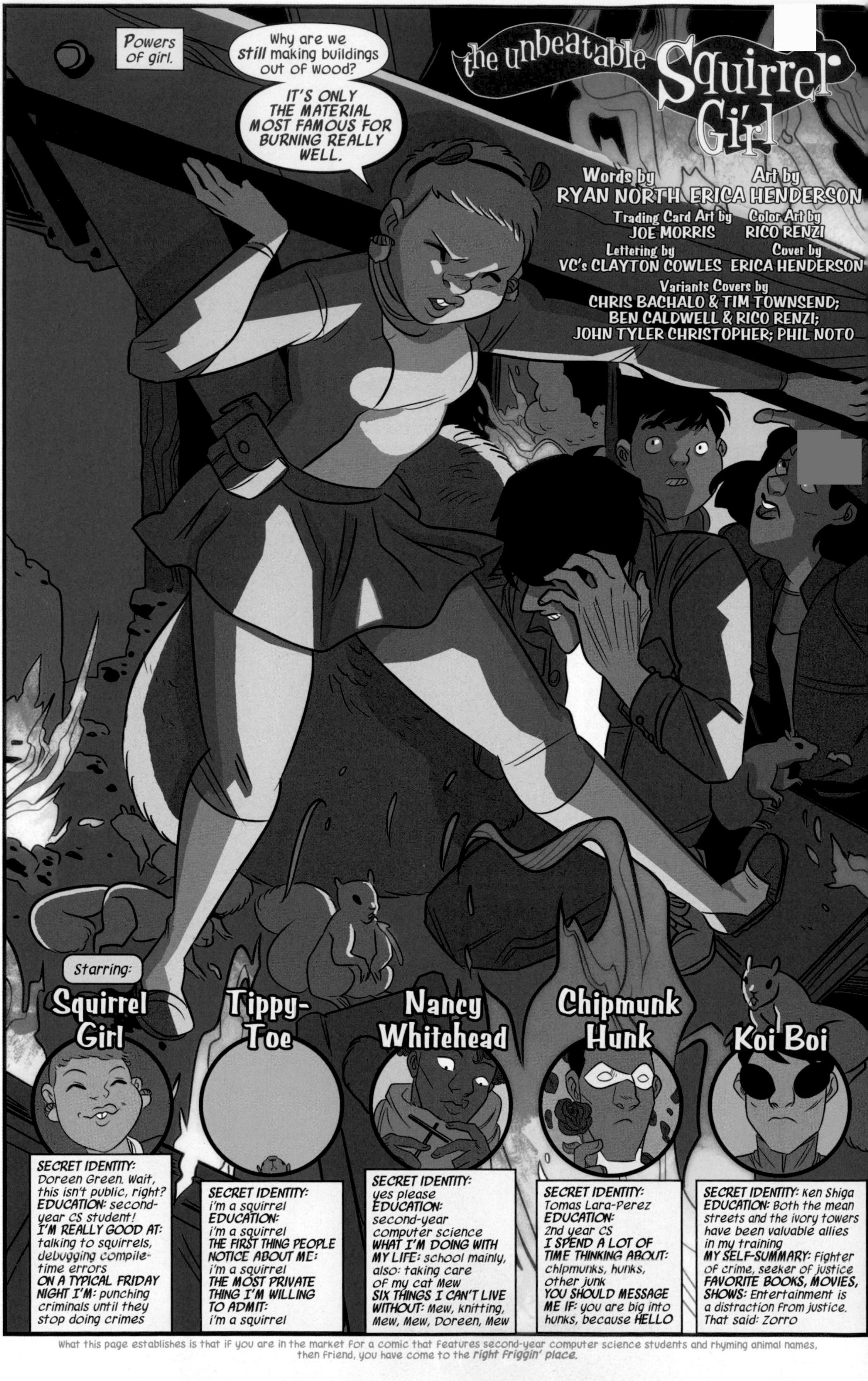
Powers of girl.
Why are we *still* making buildings out of wood?
IT'S ONLY THE MATERIAL MOST FAMOUS FOR BURNING REALLY WELL.
the unbeatable Squirrel Girl
Words by RYAN NORTH
Art by ERICA HENDERSON
Trading Card Art by JOE MORRIS
Color Art by RICO RENZI
Lettering by VC's CLAYTON COWLES
Cover by ERICA HENDERSON
Variants Covers by CHRIS BACHALO & TIM TOWNSEND; BEN CALDWELL & RICO RENZI; JOHN TYLER CHRISTOPHER; PHIL NOTO
Starring:
Squirrel Girl
SECRET IDENTITY: Doreen Green. Wait, this isn't public, right? EDUCATION: second-year CS student! I'M REALLY GOOD AT: talking to squirrels, debugging compile-time errors ON A TYPICAL FRIDAY NIGHT I'M: punching criminals until they stop doing crimes
Tippy-Toe
SECRET IDENTITY: i'm a squirrel EDUCATION: i'm a squirrel THE FIRST THING PEOPLE NOTICE ABOUT ME: i'm a squirrel THE MOST PRIVATE THING I'M WILLING TO ADMIT: i'm a squirrel
Nancy Whitehead
SECRET IDENTITY: yes please EDUCATION: second-year computer science WHAT I'M DOING WITH MY LIFE: school mainly, also: taking care of my cat Mew SIX THINGS I CAN'T LIVE WITHOUT: Mew, knitting, Mew, Mew, Doreen, Mew
Chipmunk Hunk
SECRET IDENTITY: Tomas Lara-Perez EDUCATION: 2nd year CS I SPEND A LOT OF TIME THINKING ABOUT: chipmunks, hunks, other junk YOU SHOULD MESSAGE ME IF: you are big into hunks, because HELLO
Koi Boi
SECRET IDENTITY: Ken Shiga EDUCATION: Both the mean streets and the ivory towers have been valuable allies in my training MY SELF-SUMMARY: Fighter of crime, seeker of justice FAVORITE BOOKS, MOVIES, SHOWS: Entertainment is a distraction from justice. That said: Zorro

What this page establishes is that if you are in the market for a comic that features second-year computer science students and rhyming animal names, then friend, you have come to the ***right friggin' place.***

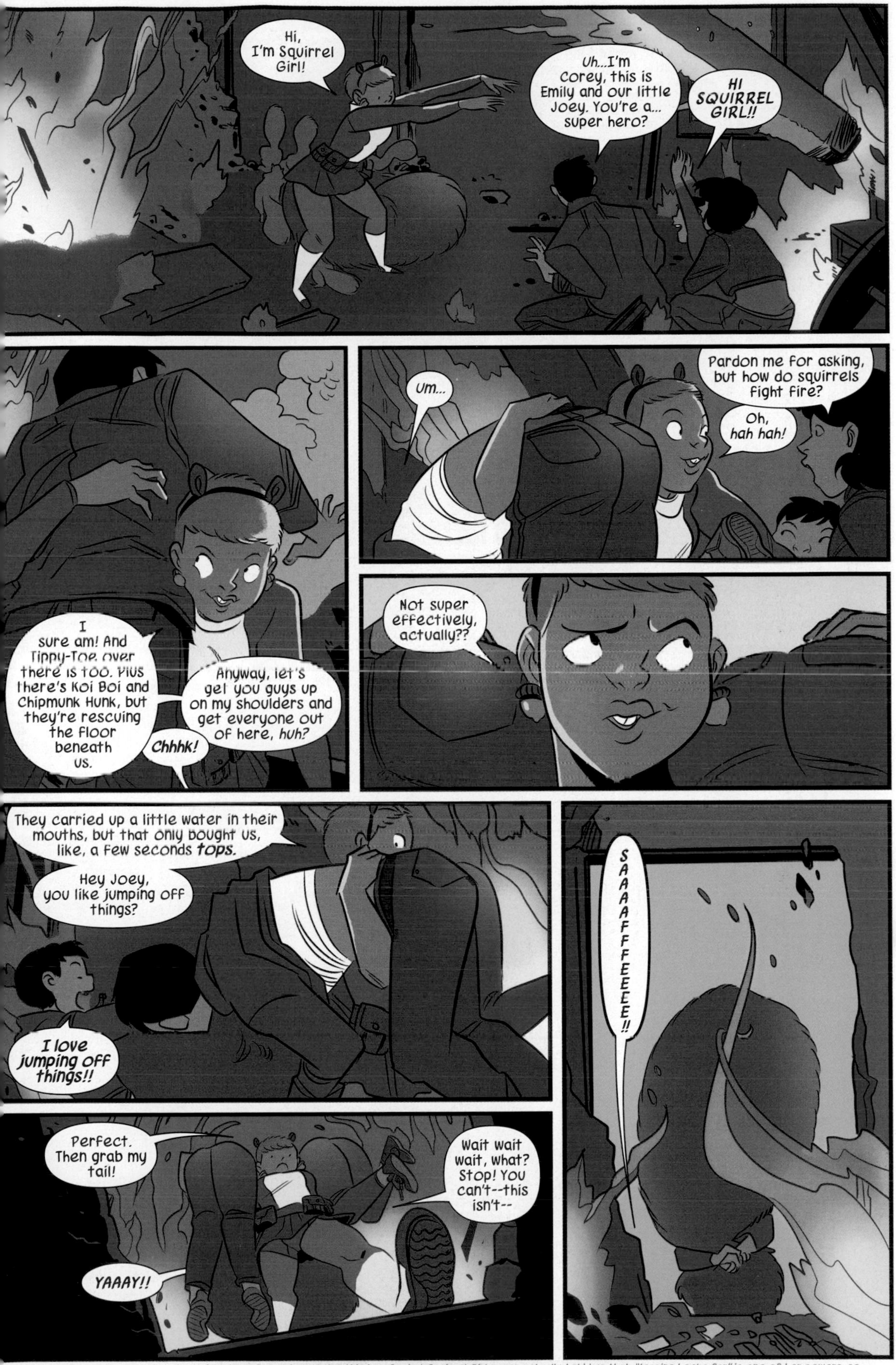
Hi, I'm Squirrel Girl!
Uh...I'm Corey, this is Emily and our little Joey. You're a... super hero?
HI SQUIRREL GIRL!!
I sure am! And Tippy-Toe over there is too. Plus there's Koi Boi and Chipmunk Hunk, but they're rescuing the floor beneath us.
Anyway, let's get you guys up on my shoulders and get everyone out of here, huh?
Chhhk!
Pardon me for asking, but how do squirrels fight fire?
Um...
Oh, hah hah!
Not super effectively, actually??
They carried up a little water in their mouths, but that only bought us, like, a few seconds tops.
Hey Joey, you like jumping off things?
I love jumping off things!!
Perfect. Then grab my tail!
Wait wait wait, what? Stop! You can't--this isn't--
YAAAY!!
SAAAAFFFEEEE!!

I was gonna say the mom is being a drag here for not assuming this is safe, but Squirrel Girl never actually told her that *"leaping hecka far"* is one of her powers, so--good work, mom. You are a sensible mom, and you only want the best for your child.

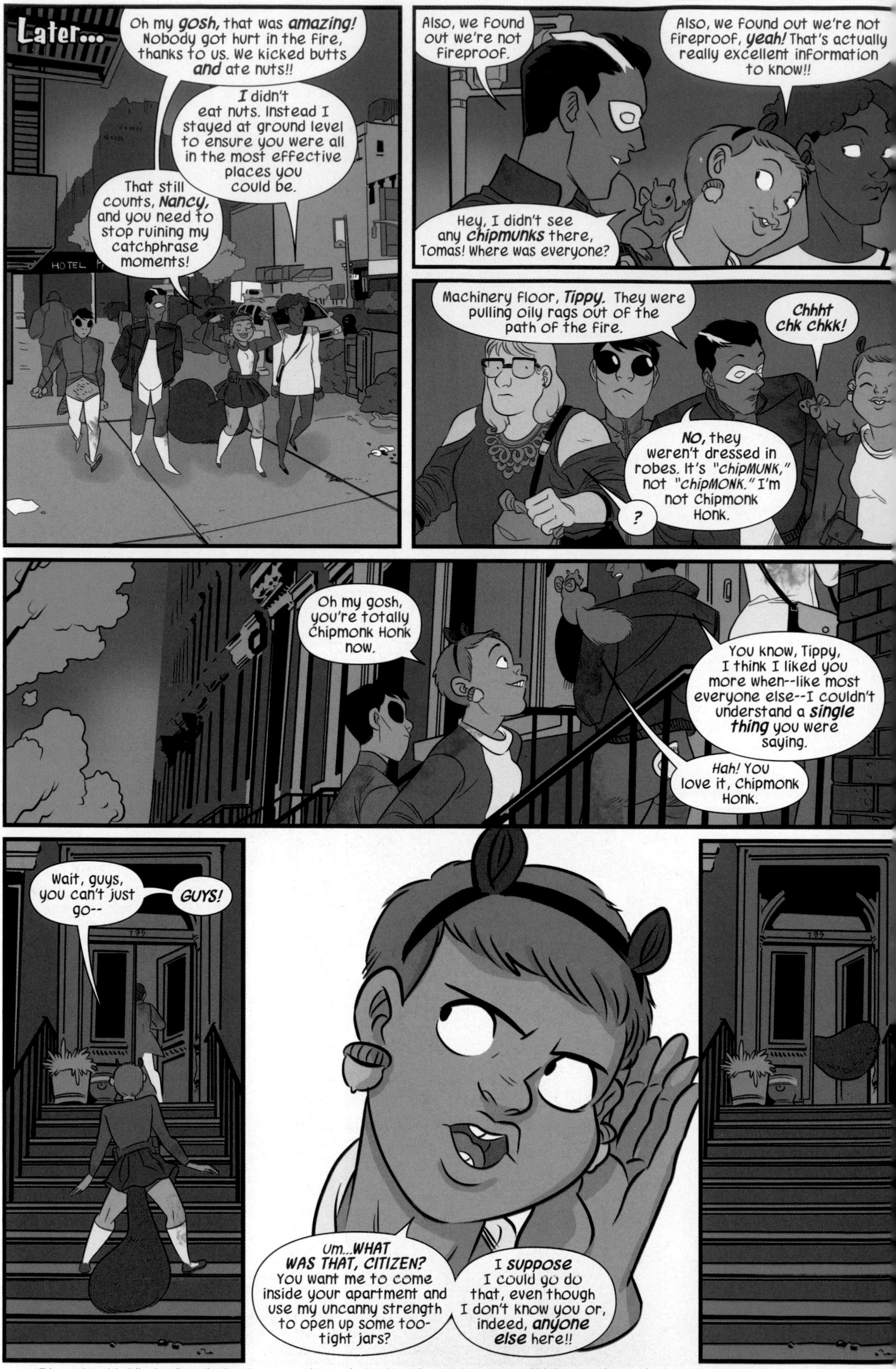
Later...
Oh my gosh, that was amazing! Nobody got hurt in the fire, thanks to us. We kicked butts and ate nuts!!
I didn't eat nuts. Instead I stayed at ground level to ensure you were all in the most effective places you could be.
That still counts, Nancy, and you need to stop ruining my catchphrase moments!
HOTEL
Also, we found out we're not fireproof.
Also, we found out we're not fireproof, yeah! That's actually really excellent information to know!!
Hey, I didn't see any chipmunks there, Tomas! Where was everyone?
Machinery floor, Tippy. They were pulling oily rags out of the path of the fire.
Chhht chk chkk!
No, they weren't dressed in robes. It's "chipMUNK," not "chipMONK." I'm not Chipmonk Honk.
?
Oh my gosh, you're totally Chipmonk Honk now.
You know, Tippy, I think I liked you more when--like most everyone else--I couldn't understand a single thing you were saying.
Hah! You love it, Chipmonk Honk.
Wait, guys, you can't just go--
GUYS!
Um...WHAT WAS THAT, CITIZEN? You want me to come inside your apartment and use my uncanny strength to open up some too-tight jars?
I suppose I could go do that, even though I don't know you or, indeed, anyone else here!!

This apartment building has four simple rules: no smoking, no destruction of property, no super villain bases, and no loud noises after 11pm. So bad news, everyone: you'll have to find someplace else to have your "loudly destroy super villain bases at 11:05pm while also smoking" parties.

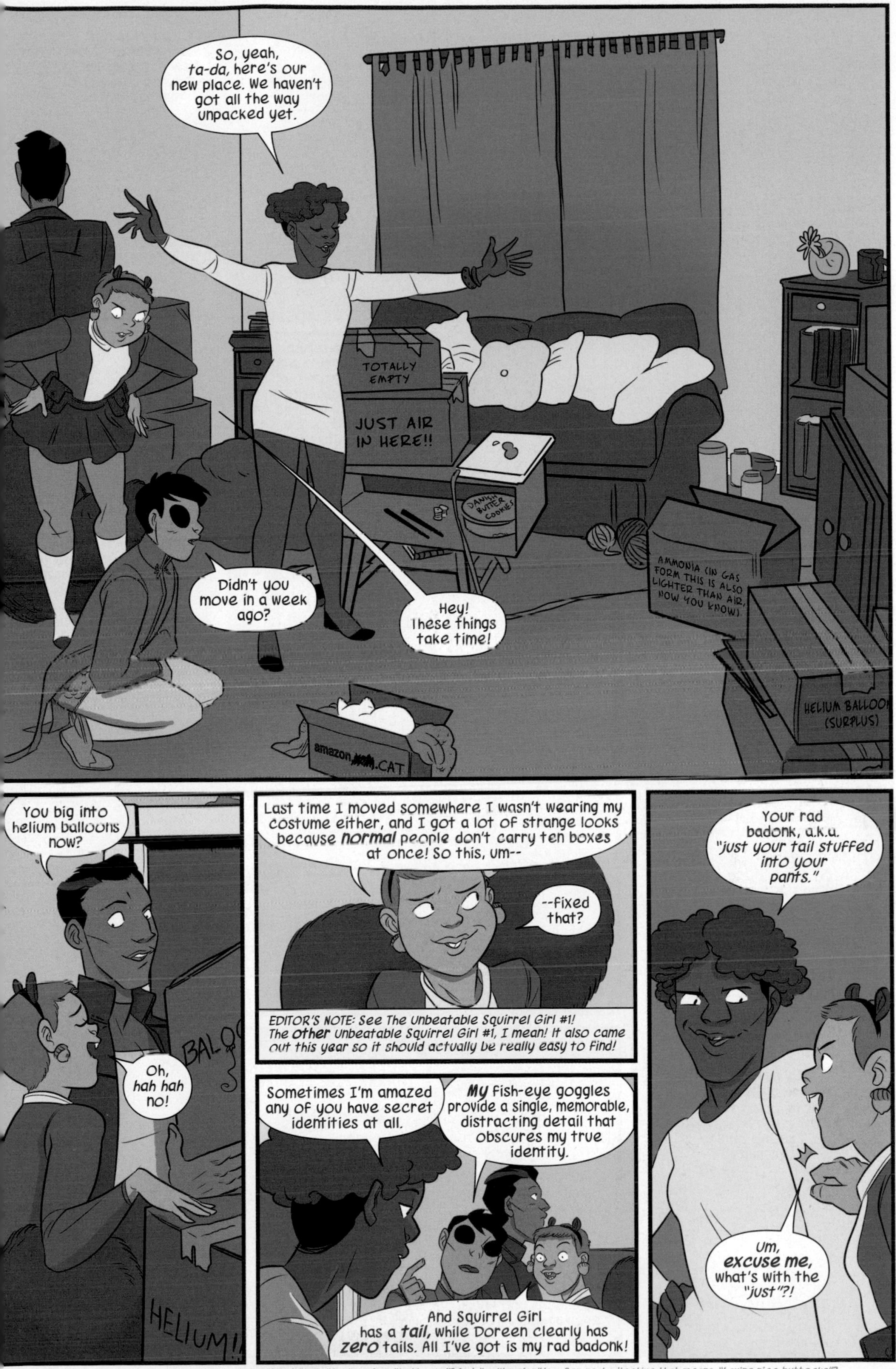
So, yeah, ta-da, here's our new place. We haven't got all the way unpacked yet.
TOTALLY EMPTY
JUST AIR IN HERE!!
DANISH BUTTER COOKIES
AMMONIA (IN GAS FORM THIS IS ALSO LIGHTER THAN AIR, NOW YOU KNOW)
Didn't you move in a week ago?
Hey! These things take time!
HELIUM BALLOONS (SURPLUS)
amazon.CAT
You big into helium balloons now?
Oh, hah hah no!
HELIUM!!
Last time I moved somewhere I wasn't wearing my costume either, and I got a lot of strange looks because **normal** people don't carry ten boxes at once! So this, um--
--fixed that?
EDITOR'S NOTE: See The Unbeatable Squirrel Girl #1! The **other** Unbeatable Squirrel Girl #1, I mean! It also came out this year so it should actually be really easy to find!
Sometimes I'm amazed any of you have secret identities at all.
My fish-eye goggles provide a single, memorable, distracting detail that obscures my true identity.
And Squirrel Girl has a **tail,** while Doreen clearly has **zero** tails. All I've got is my rad badonk!
Your rad badonk, a.k.a. *"just your tail stuffed into your pants."*
Um, **excuse me,** what's with the *"just"*?!

DID YOU KNOW: *"badonk"* is slang for *"butt"*? And *"butt"* is slang for *"buttocks"*? And *"callipygian"* is a for-real adjective that means *"having nice buttocks"*? Look at you, just trying to relax with a talking squirrel comic and instead learning how to say *"My word, what a callipygian badonk!"*

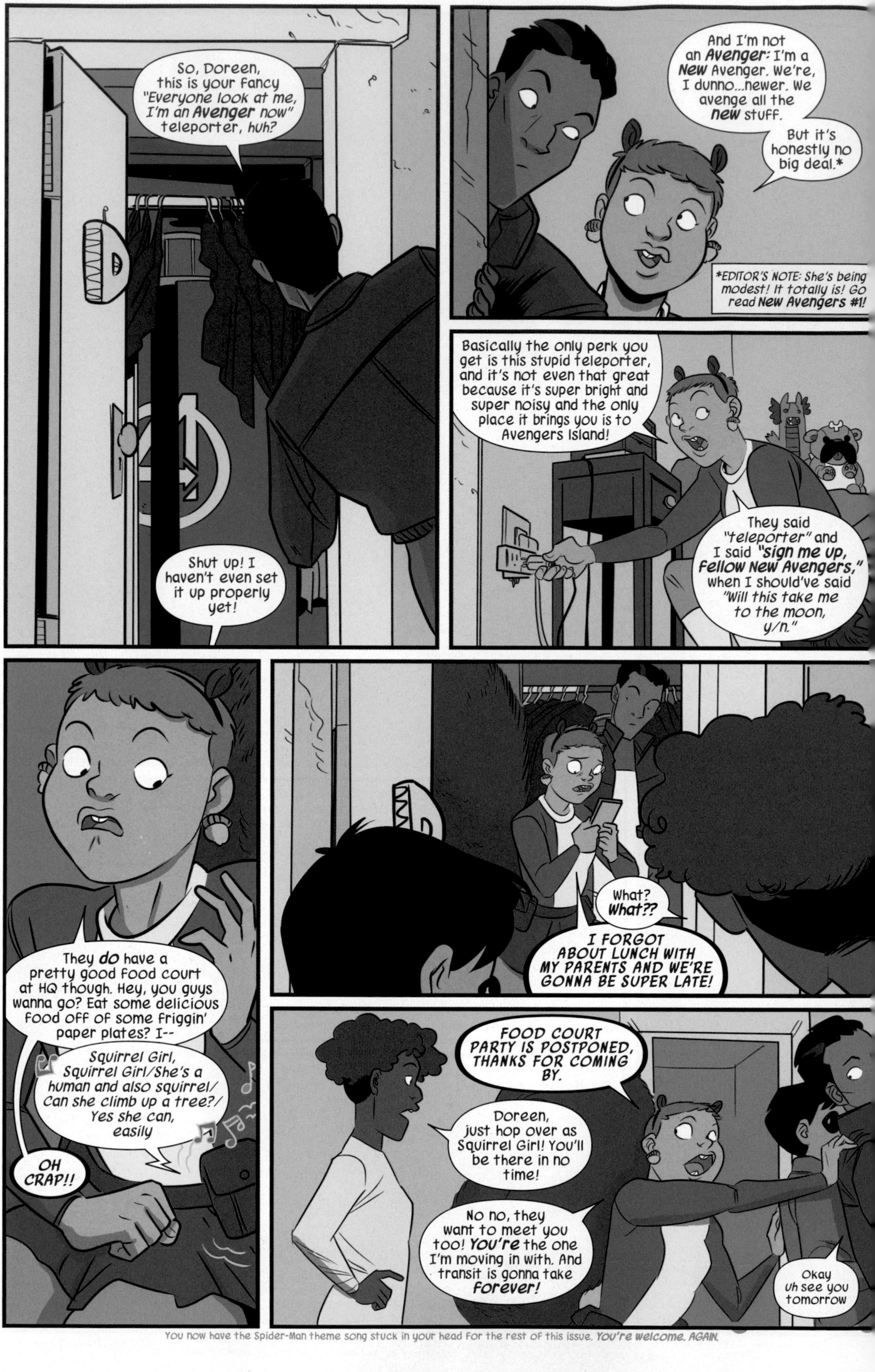
So, Doreen, this is your fancy "Everyone look at me, I'm an Avenger now" teleporter, huh?
Shut up! I haven't even set it up properly yet!
And I'm not an Avenger: I'm a New Avenger. We're, I dunno...newer. We avenge all the new stuff.
But it's honestly no big deal.*
*EDITOR'S NOTE: She's being modest! It totally is! Go read New Avengers #1!
Basically the only perk you get is this stupid teleporter, and it's not even that great because it's super bright and super noisy and the only place it brings you is to Avengers Island!
They said "teleporter" and I said "sign me up, fellow New Avengers," when I should've said "Will this take me to the moon, y/n."
They do have a pretty good food court at HQ though. Hey, you guys wanna go? Eat some delicious food off of some friggin' paper plates? I--
Squirrel Girl, Squirrel Girl/She's a human and also squirrel/ Can she climb up a tree?/ Yes she can, easily
OH CRAP!!
What? What??
I FORGOT ABOUT LUNCH WITH MY PARENTS AND WE'RE GONNA BE SUPER LATE!
FOOD COURT PARTY IS POSTPONED, THANKS FOR COMING BY.
Doreen, just hop over as Squirrel Girl! You'll be there in no time!
No no, they want to meet you too! You're the one I'm moving in with. And transit is gonna take forever!
Okay uh see you tomorrow

You now have the Spider-Man theme song stuck in your head for the rest of this issue. *You're welcome. AGAIN.*

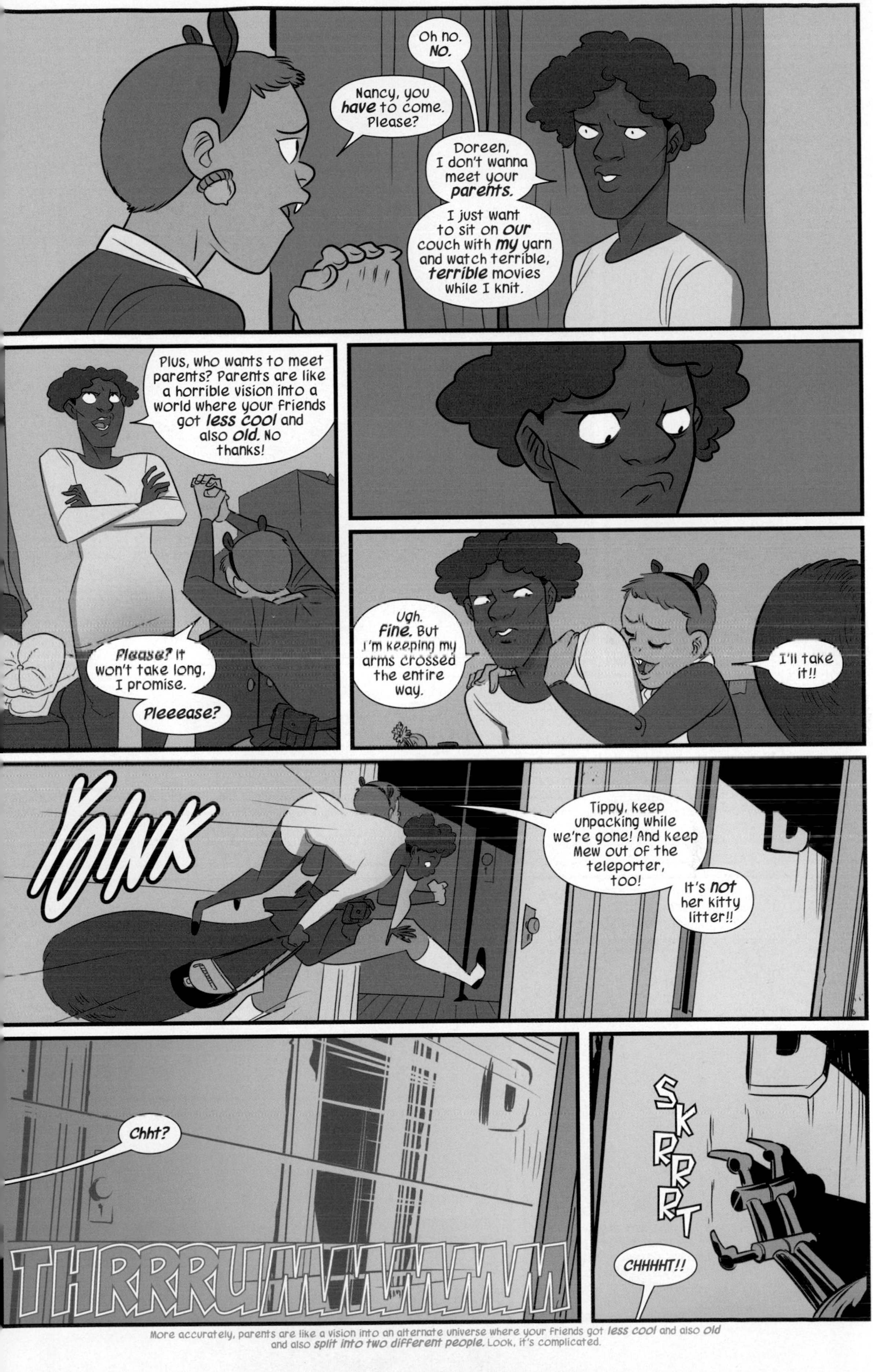
Nancy, you *have* to come. Please?
Oh no. *NO.*
Doreen, I don't wanna meet your *parents.*
I just want to sit on *our* couch with *my* yarn and watch terrible, *terrible* movies while I knit.
Plus, who wants to meet parents? Parents are like a horrible vision into a world where your friends got *less cool* and also *old.* No thanks!
Please? It won't take long, I promise.
Pleeease?
Ugh. *Fine.* But I'm keeping my arms crossed the entire way.
I'll take it!!
YOINK
Tippy, keep unpacking while we're gone! And keep Mew out of the teleporter, too!
It's *not* her kitty litter!!
Chht?
THRRRUMMMMMMM
SKRRRT
CHHHHT!!

More accurately, parents are like a vision into an alternate universe where your friends got *less cool* and also *old* and also ***split into two different people.*** Look, it's complicated.

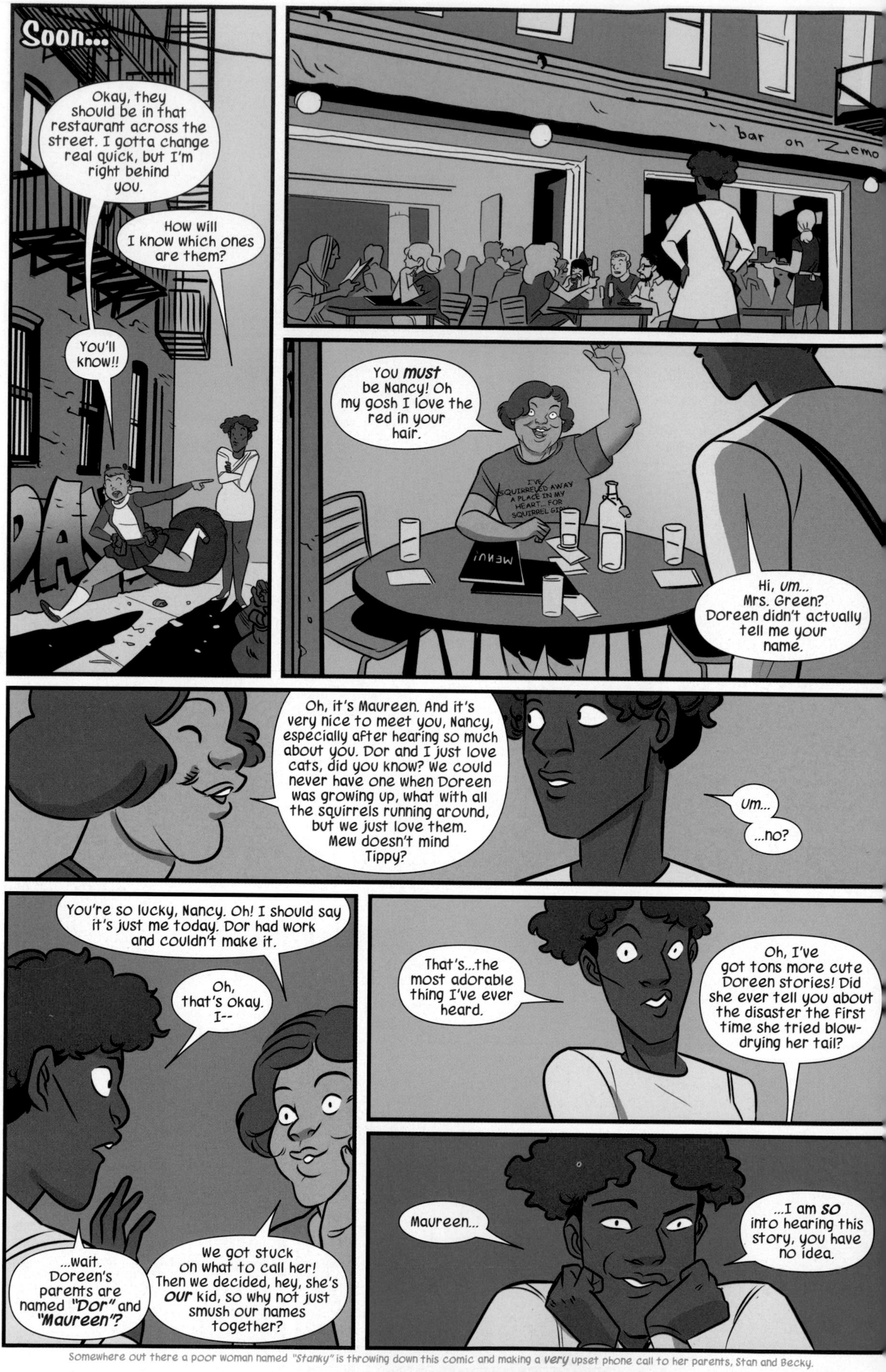
Soon...
Okay, they should be in that restaurant across the street. I gotta change real quick, but I'm right behind you.
How will I know which ones are them?
You'll know!!
"bar on Zemo"
You must be Nancy! Oh my gosh I love the red in your hair.
I'VE SQUIRRELED AWAY A PLACE IN MY HEART... FOR SQUIRREL GIRL
MENU
Hi, um... Mrs. Green? Doreen didn't actually tell me your name.
Oh, it's Maureen. And it's very nice to meet you, Nancy, especially after hearing so much about you. Dor and I just love cats, did you know? We could never have one when Doreen was growing up, what with all the squirrels running around, but we just love them. Mew doesn't mind Tippy?
Um...
...no?
You're so lucky, Nancy. Oh! I should say it's just me today. Dor had work and couldn't make it.
Oh, that's okay. I--
...wait. Doreen's parents are named "Dor" and "Maureen"?
We got stuck on what to call her! Then we decided, hey, she's our kid, so why not just smush our names together?
That's...the most adorable thing I've ever heard.
Oh, I've got tons more cute Doreen stories! Did she ever tell you about the disaster the first time she tried blow-drying her tail?
Maureen...
...I am SO into hearing this story, you have no idea.

Somewhere out there a poor woman named *"Stanky"* is throwing down this comic and making a ***very*** upset phone call to her parents, Stan and Becky.

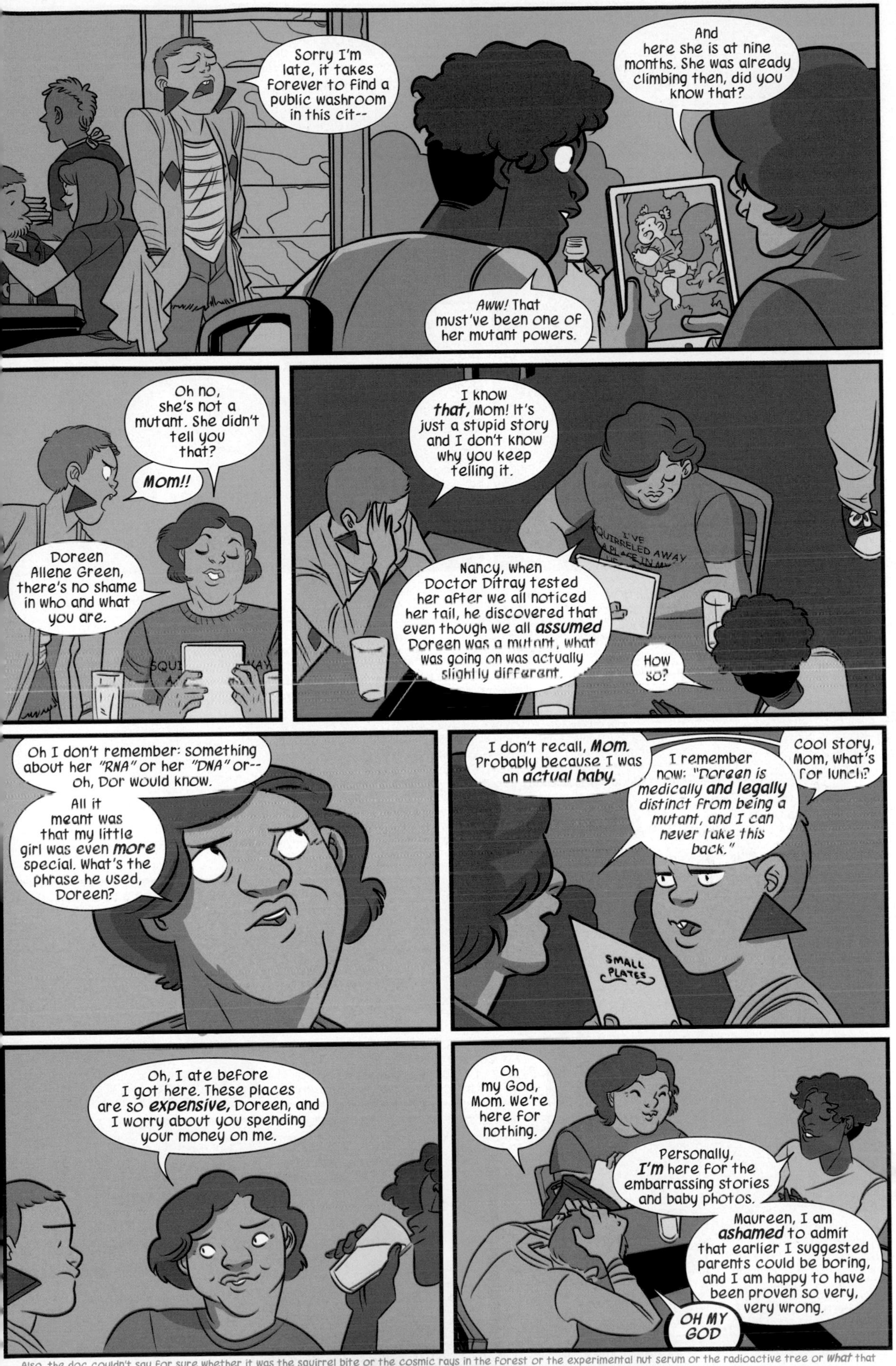
Sorry I'm late, it takes forever to find a public washroom in this cit--
And here she is at nine months. She was already climbing then, did you know that?
Aww! That must've been one of her mutant powers.
Oh no, she's not a mutant. She didn't tell you that?
Mom!!
Doreen Allene Green, there's no shame in who and what you are.
I know that, Mom! It's just a stupid story and I don't know why you keep telling it.
Nancy, when Doctor Ditray tested her after we all noticed her tail, he discovered that even though we all assumed Doreen was a mutant, what was going on was actually slightly differant.
How so?
Oh I don't remember: something about her "RNA" or her "DNA" or-- oh, Dor would know.
All it meant was that my little girl was even more special. What's the phrase he used, Doreen?
I don't recall, Mom. Probably because I was an actual baby.
I remember now: "Doreen is medically and legally distinct from being a mutant, and I can never take this back."
Cool story, Mom, what's for lunch?
SMALL PLATES
Oh, I ate before I got here. These places are so expensive, Doreen, and I worry about you spending your money on me.
Oh my God, Mom. We're here for nothing.
Personally, I'm here for the embarrassing stories and baby photos.
Maureen, I am ashamed to admit that earlier I suggested parents could be boring, and I am happy to have been proven so very, very wrong.
OH MY GOD

Also, the doc couldn't say for sure whether it was the squirrel bite or the cosmic rays in the forest or the experimental nut serum or the radioactive tree or *what* that caused the changes. Maureen's pregnancy was...a pretty eventful nine months, actually.

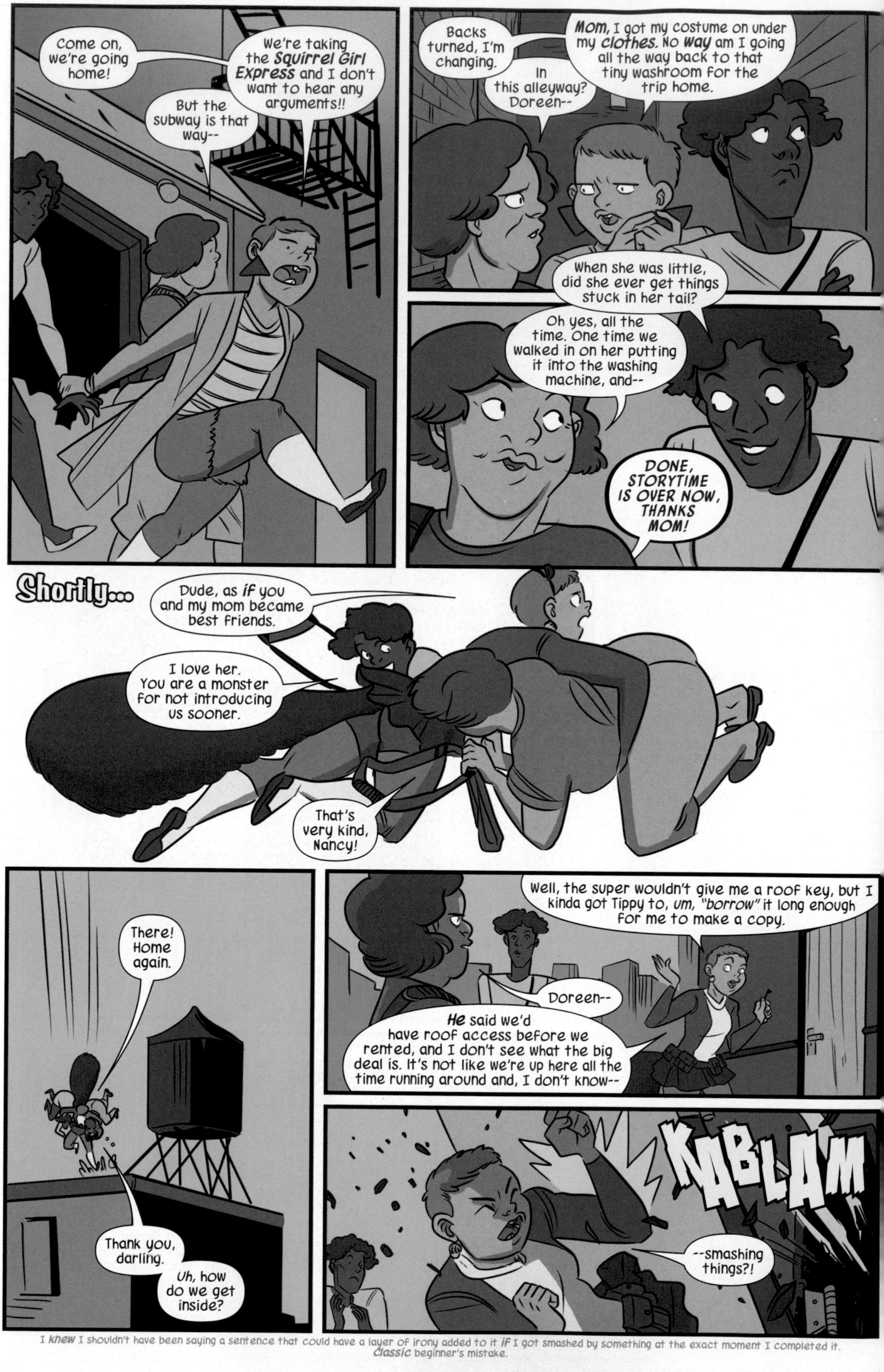
Come on, we're going home!
We're taking the Squirrel Girl Express and I don't want to hear any arguments!!
But the subway is that way--
Backs turned, I'm changing.
In this alleyway? Doreen--
Mom, I got my costume on under my clothes. No way am I going all the way back to that tiny washroom for the trip home.
When she was little, did she ever get things stuck in her tail?
Oh yes, all the time. One time we walked in on her putting it into the washing machine, and--
DONE, STORYTIME IS OVER NOW, THANKS MOM!
Shortly...
Dude, as if you and my mom became best friends.
I love her. You are a monster for not introducing us sooner.
That's very kind, Nancy!
There! Home again.
Thank you, darling.
Uh, how do we get inside?
Well, the super wouldn't give me a roof key, but I kinda got Tippy to, um, "borrow" it long enough for me to make a copy.
Doreen--
He said we'd have roof access before we rented, and I don't see what the big deal is. It's not like we're up here all the time running around and, I don't know--
KABLAM
--smashing things?!

I *knew* I shouldn't have been saying a sentence that could have a layer of irony added to it *if* I got smashed by something at the exact moment I completed it. *Classic* beginner's mistake.

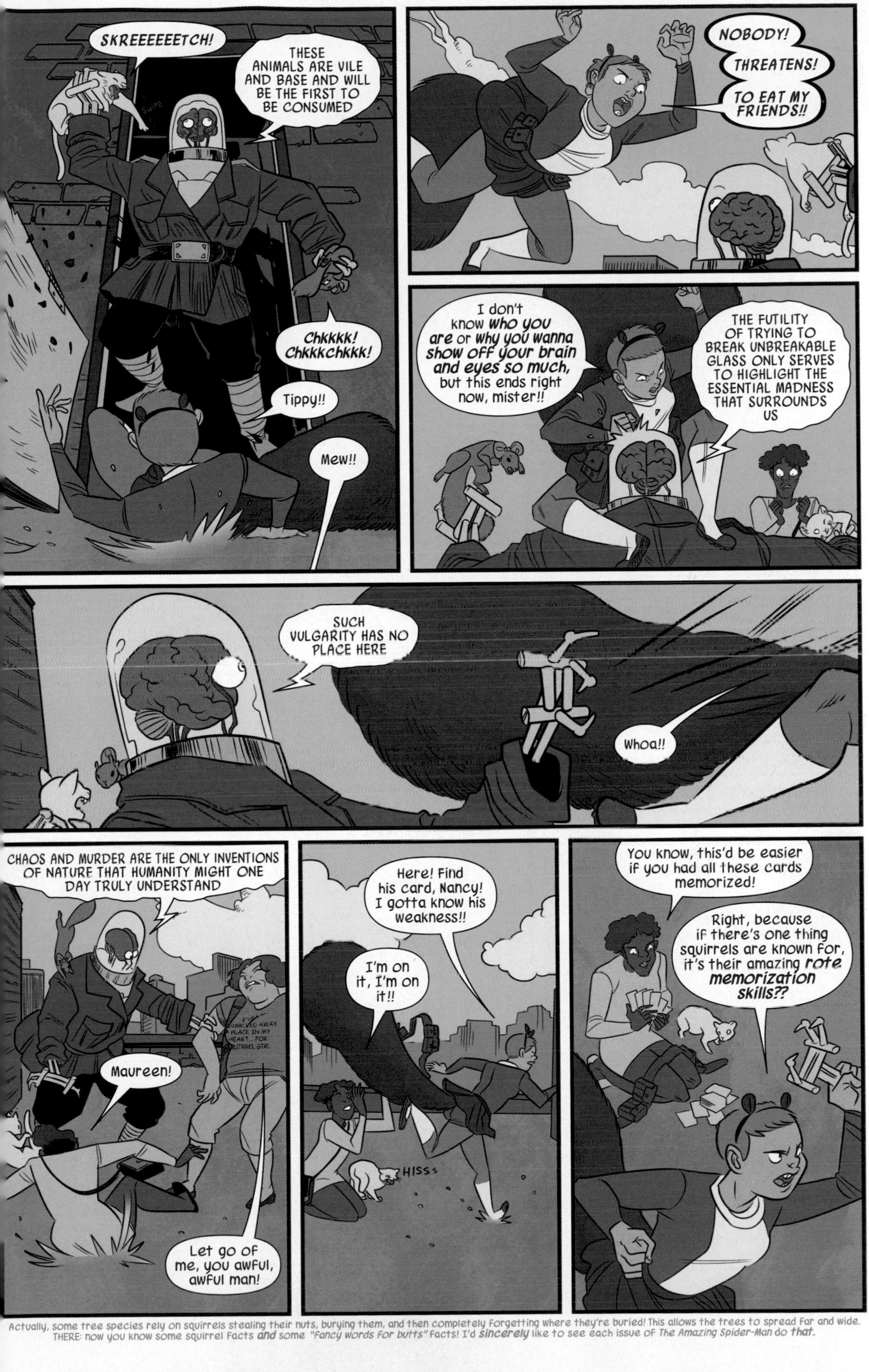
SKREEEEEEETCH!
THESE ANIMALS ARE VILE AND BASE AND WILL BE THE FIRST TO BE CONSUMED
SWIPE
Chkkkk! Chkkkchkkk!
Tippy!!
Mew!!
NOBODY!
THREATENS!
TO EAT MY FRIENDS!!
I don't know who you are or why you wanna show off your brain and eyes so much, but this ends right now, mister!!
THE FUTILITY OF TRYING TO BREAK UNBREAKABLE GLASS ONLY SERVES TO HIGHLIGHT THE ESSENTIAL MADNESS THAT SURROUNDS US
SUCH VULGARITY HAS NO PLACE HERE
Whoa!!
CHAOS AND MURDER ARE THE ONLY INVENTIONS OF NATURE THAT HUMANITY MIGHT ONE DAY TRULY UNDERSTAND
Maureen!
Let go of me, you awful, awful man!
Here! Find his card, Nancy! I gotta know his weakness!!
I'm on it, I'm on it!!
HISSS
You know, this'd be easier if you had all these cards memorized!
Right, because if there's one thing squirrels are known for, it's their amazing rote memorization skills??

Actually, some tree species rely on squirrels stealing their nuts, burying them, and then completely forgetting where they're buried! This allows the trees to spread far and wide. THERE: now you know some squirrel facts **and** some "fancy words for butts" facts! I'd ***sincerely*** like to see each issue of *The Amazing Spider-Man* do ***that.***

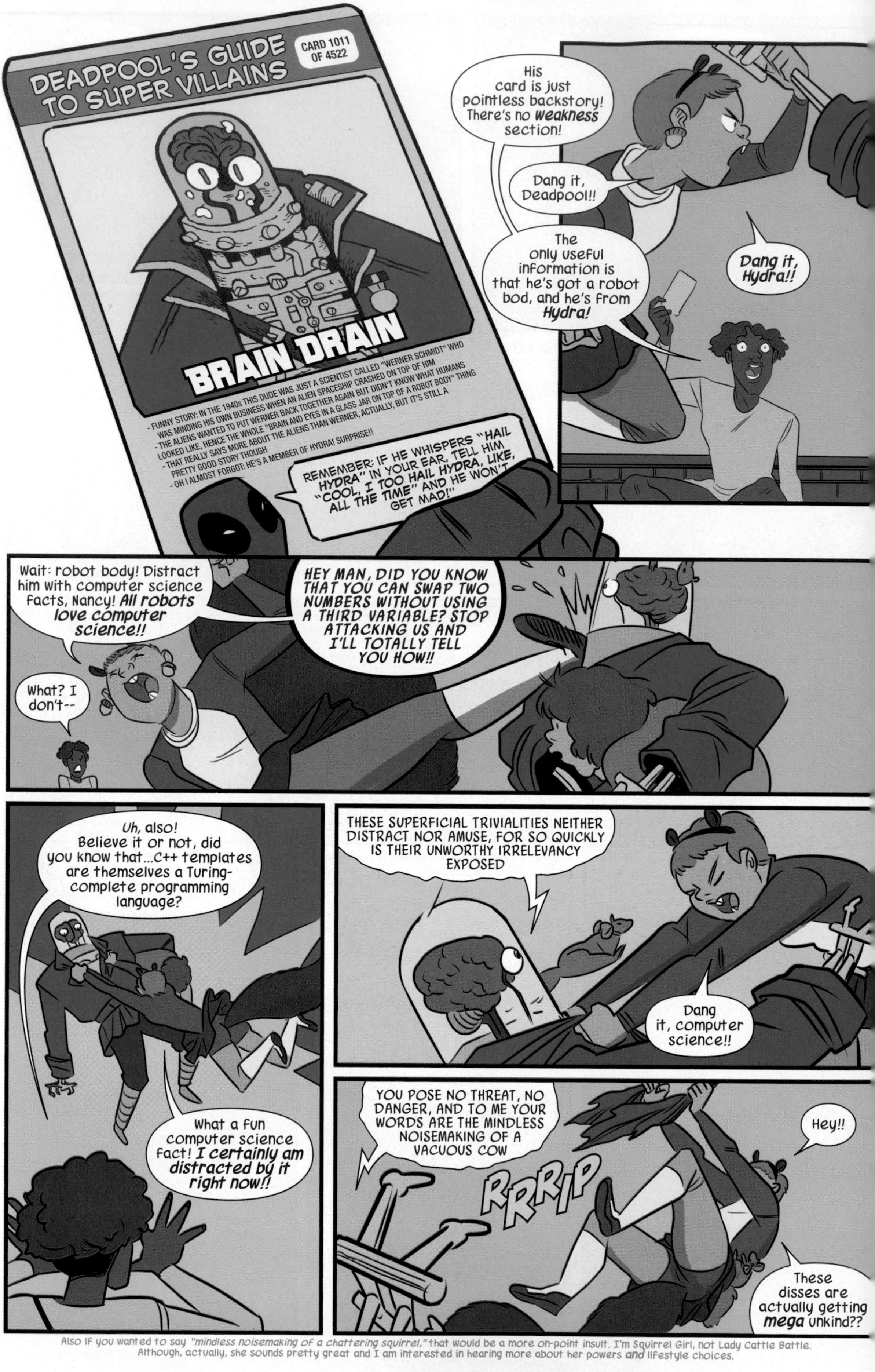
DEADPOOL'S GUIDE TO SUPER VILLAINS
CARD 1011 OF 4522
BRAIN DRAIN
- FUNNY STORY: IN THE 1940s THIS DUDE WAS JUST A SCIENTIST CALLED "WERNER SCHMIDT" WHO WAS MINDING HIS OWN BUSINESS WHEN AN ALIEN SPACESHIP CRASHED ON TOP OF HIM
- THE ALIENS WANTED TO PUT WERNER BACK TOGETHER AGAIN BUT DIDN'T KNOW WHAT HUMANS LOOKED LIKE, HENCE THE WHOLE "BRAIN AND EYES IN A GLASS JAR ON TOP OF A ROBOT BODY" THING
- THAT REALLY SAYS MORE ABOUT THE ALIENS THAN WERNER, ACTUALLY, BUT IT'S STILL A PRETTY GOOD STORY THOUGH
- OH I ALMOST FORGOT: HE'S A MEMBER OF HYDRA! SURPRISE!!
REMEMBER: IF HE WHISPERS "HAIL HYDRA" IN YOUR EAR, TELL HIM "COOL, I TOO HAIL HYDRA, LIKE, ALL THE TIME" AND HE WON'T GET MAD!"
His card is just pointless backstory! There's no *weakness* section!
Dang it, Deadpool!!
The only useful information is that he's got a robot bod, and he's from *Hydra!*
Dang it, Hydra!!
Wait: robot body! Distract him with computer science facts, Nancy! *All robots love computer science!!*
What? I don't--
HEY MAN, DID YOU KNOW THAT YOU CAN SWAP TWO NUMBERS WITHOUT USING A THIRD VARIABLE? STOP ATTACKING US AND I'LL TOTALLY TELL YOU HOW!!
Uh, also! Believe it or not, did you know that...C++ templates are themselves a Turing-complete programming language?
What a fun computer science fact! *I certainly am distracted by it right now!!*
THESE SUPERFICIAL TRIVIALITIES NEITHER DISTRACT NOR AMUSE, FOR SO QUICKLY IS THEIR UNWORTHY IRRELEVANCY EXPOSED
Dang it, computer science!!
YOU POSE NO THREAT, NO DANGER, AND TO ME YOUR WORDS ARE THE MINDLESS NOISEMAKING OF A VACUOUS COW
RRRIP
Hey!!
These disses are actually getting *mega* unkind??

Also if you wanted to say *"mindless noisemaking of a chattering squirrel,"* that would be a more on-point insult. I'm Squirrel Girl, not Lady Cattle Battle. Although, actually, she sounds pretty great and I am interested in hearing more about her powers *and* lifestyle choices.

I--

--was expecting more chrome and blue LEDs than a janky bunch of old exposed wires, actually??

TIKKA TIKKA TIKKA TIKKA

Oh, this is *SO* up my alley it's not even funny.

Chhhhttt!*

THIS AMBITION OF THIS RODENT IS PURE FOLLY, PURE FUTILITY--AND YET, IN IT I DISCOVER A CERTAIN SATISFACTION, FOR WHAT ARE WE BUT RODENTS SWARMING OVER THE EARTH'S INDIFFERENT SURFACE

*Translation: "Attack!!"

Chkkt!!*

CHOMP

*Translation: "Put an acorn in it, jerk!!"

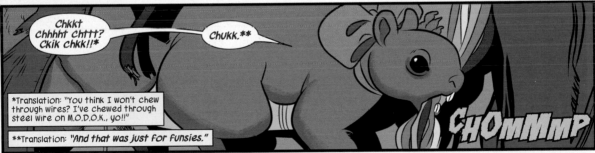

Chkkt Chhhht Chtttt? Ckik chkk!!*

Chukk.**

CHOMMMP

*Translation: "You think I won't chew through wires? I've chewed through steel wire on M.O.D.O.K., yo!!"

**Translation: "And that was just for funsies."

I--I-- I--I--I-- I--

KLUNK

IF you're wondering who M.O.D.O.K. is, he's a giant head who has his own hover chair. He *claims* his name stands For "Mental Organism Designed Only For Killing" but he has *never* denied the allegations that his name *actually* stands For "Mental Organism Delivering Outstanding Kissing"

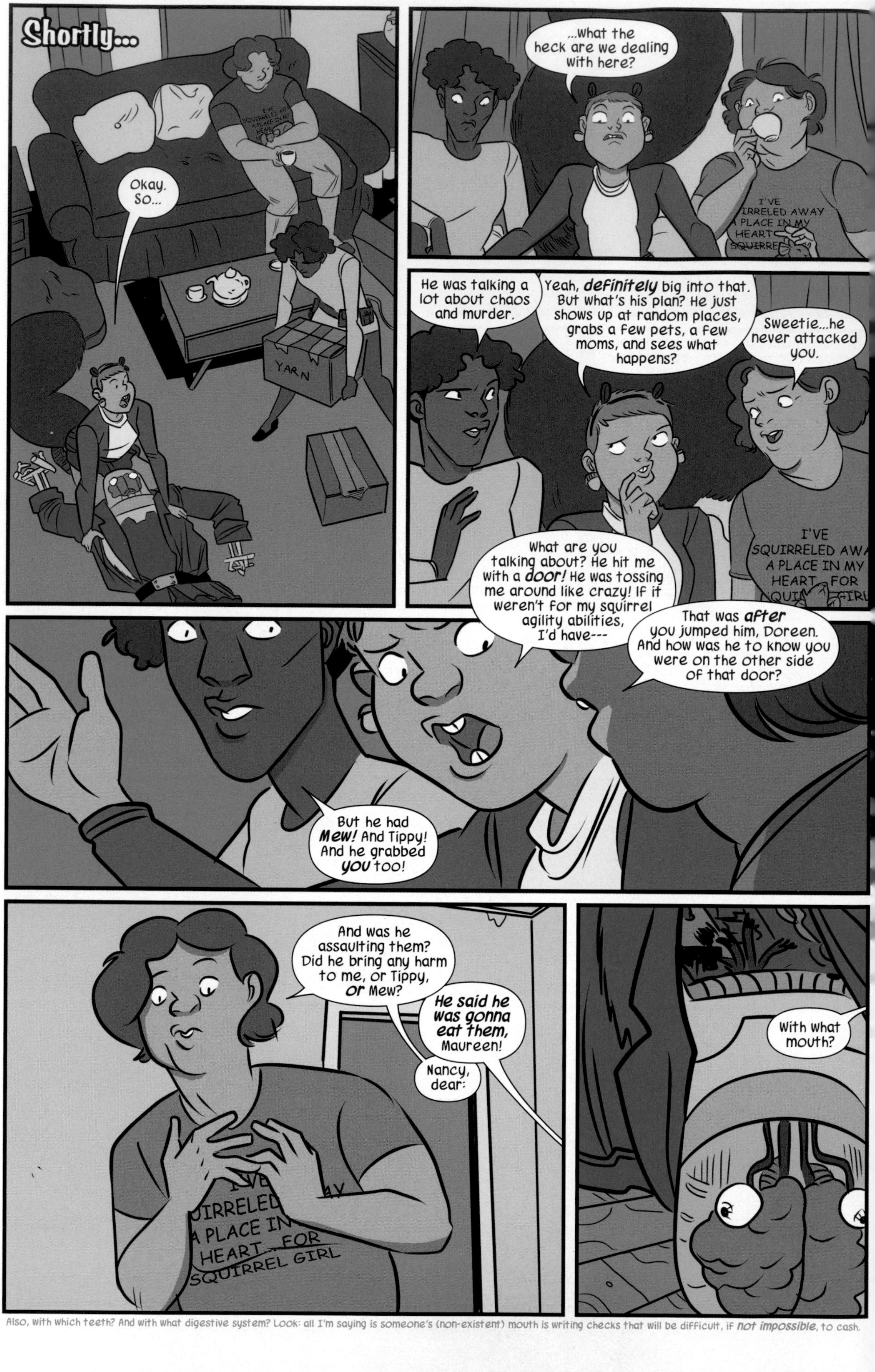
Shortly...
Okay. So...
I'VE SQUIRRELED AWAY A PLACE IN MY HEART
YARN
...What the heck are we dealing with here?
I'VE SQUIRRELED AWAY A PLACE IN MY HEART
He was talking a lot about chaos and murder.
Yeah, *definitely* big into that. But what's his plan? He just shows up at random places, grabs a few pets, a few moms, and sees what happens?
Sweetie...he never attacked you.
I'VE SQUIRRELED AWA A PLACE IN MY HEART FOR
What are you talking about? He hit me with a *door!* He was tossing me around like crazy! If it weren't for my squirrel agility abilities, I'd have---
That was *after* you jumped him, Doreen. And how was he to know you were on the other side of that door?
But he had *Mew!* And Tippy! And he grabbed *you* too!
And was he assaulting them? Did he bring any harm to me, or Tippy, *or* Mew?
He said he was gonna eat them, Maureen!
Nancy, dear:
With what mouth?
SQUIRRELED A PLACE IN HEART FOR SQUIRREL GIRL

Also, with which teeth? And with what digestive system? Look: all I'm saying is someone's (non-existent) mouth is writing checks that will be difficult, if ***not impossible***, to cash.

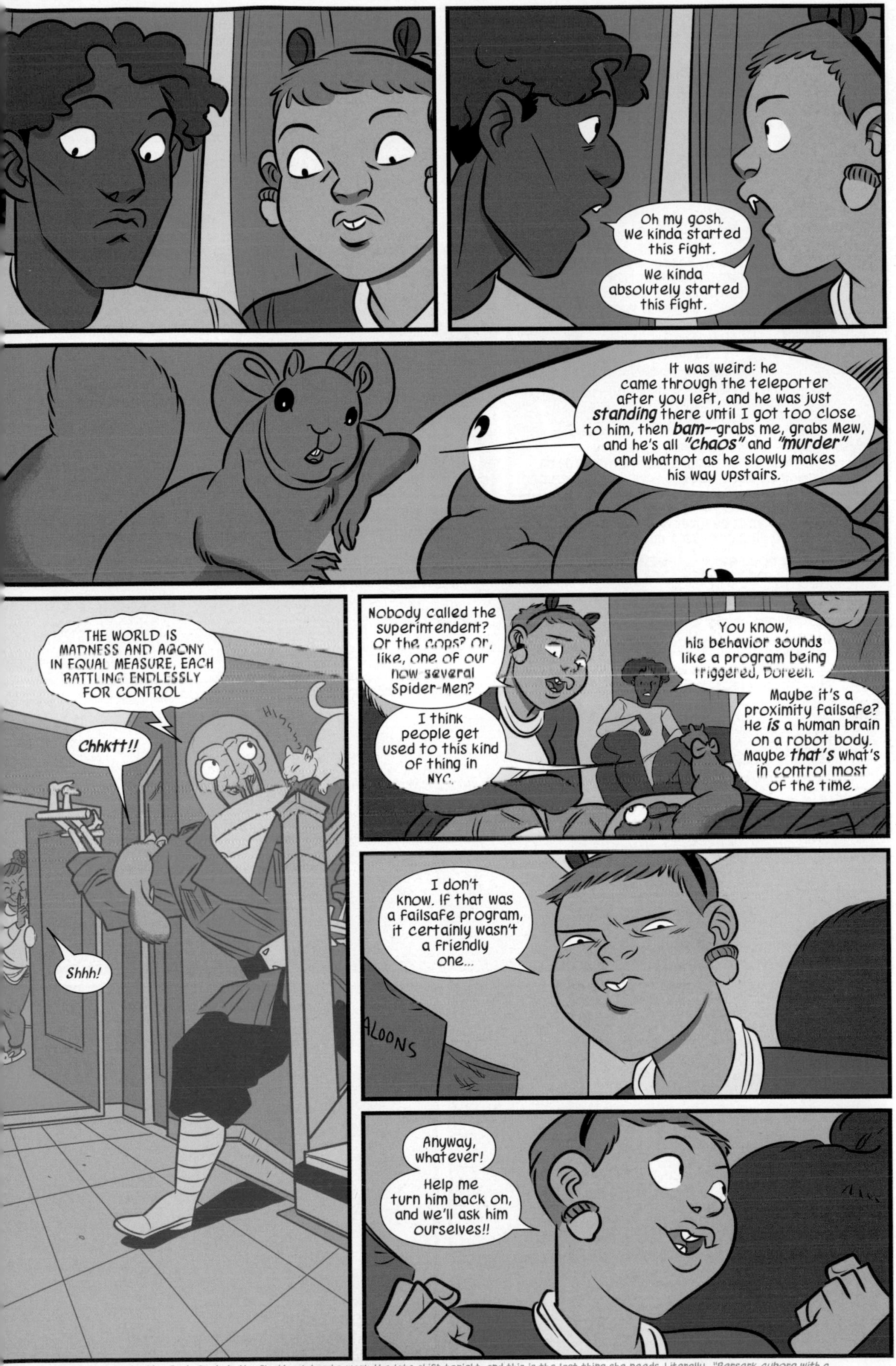
Oh my gosh. We kinda started this fight.
We kinda absolutely started this fight.
It was weird: he came through the teleporter after you left, and he was just standing there until I got too close to him, then bam--grabs me, grabs Mew, and he's all "chaos" and "murder" and whatnot as he slowly makes his way upstairs.
THE WORLD IS MADNESS AND AGONY IN EQUAL MEASURE, EACH BATTLING ENDLESSLY FOR CONTROL
Chhktt!!
Shhh!
Nobody called the superintendent? Or the cops? Or, like, one of our now several Spider-Men?
I think people get used to this kind of thing in NYC.
You know, his behavior sounds like a program being triggered, Doreen.
Maybe it's a proximity failsafe? He is a human brain on a robot body. Maybe that's what's in control most of the time.
I don't know. If that was a failsafe program, it certainly wasn't a friendly one...
Anyway, whatever!
Help me turn him back on, and we'll ask him ourselves!!

That person shushing Brain Drain in the flashback has to work the late shift tonight, and this is the last thing she needs. Literally. *"Berserk cyborg with a human brain carrying screaming animals and shouting about madness"* is actually written at the very bottom of her list of ***"things I need right now."***

There's a small chance that Nancy's robot body fantasy *may* be identical to my own robot body fantasy/spec sheets/actual designs that I've written up and carry with me everywhere and think about all the time.

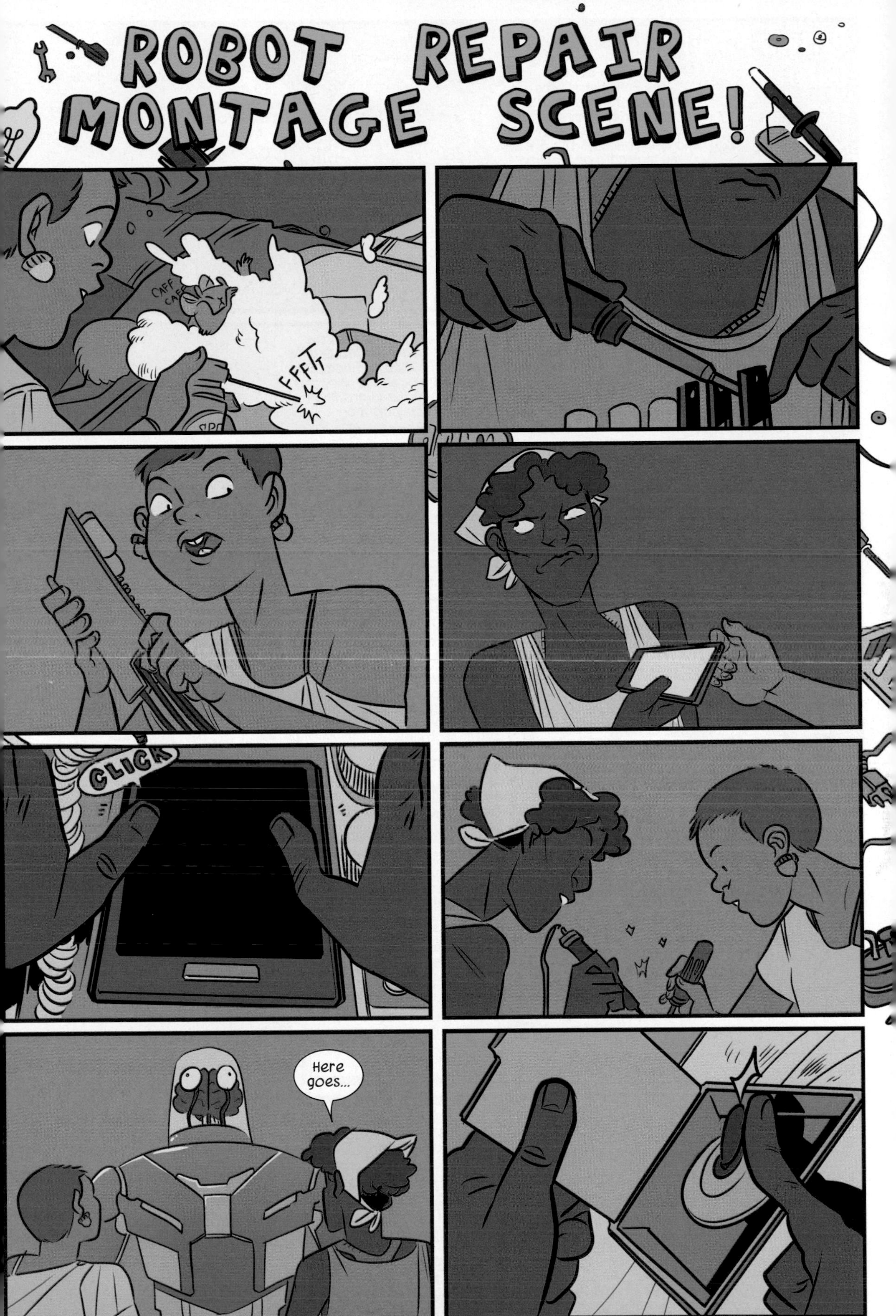
ROBOT REPAIR MONTAGE SCENE!
CAFF
FFFTT
CLICK
Here goes...

That *"robot repair montage"* header stops you from wondering why everyone in the comic stopped talking, and also from wondering why you can hear awesome pump-up robot repair montage music in your head whenever you look at this page and concentrate really hard!

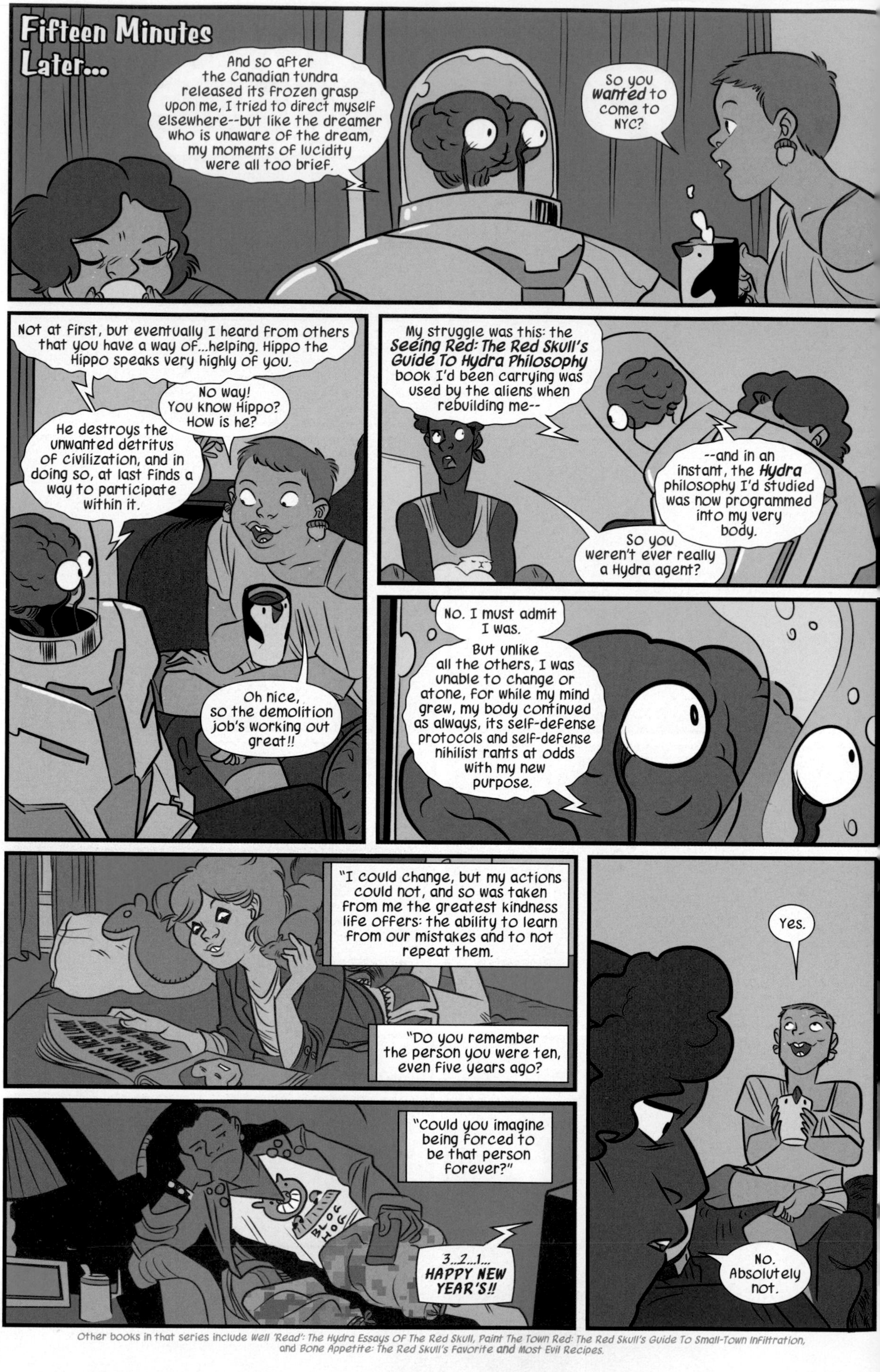
Fifteen Minutes Later...
And so after the Canadian tundra released its frozen grasp upon me, I tried to direct myself elsewhere--but like the dreamer who is unaware of the dream, my moments of lucidity were all too brief.
So you wanted to come to NYC?
Not at first, but eventually I heard from others that you have a way of...helping. Hippo the Hippo speaks very highly of you.
No way! You know Hippo? How is he?
He destroys the unwanted detritus of civilization, and in doing so, at last finds a way to participate within it.
Oh nice, so the demolition job's working out great!!
My struggle was this: the Seeing Red: The Red Skull's Guide To Hydra Philosophy book I'd been carrying was used by the aliens when rebuilding me--
--and in an instant, the Hydra philosophy I'd studied was now programmed into my very body.
So you weren't ever really a Hydra agent?
No. I must admit I was.
But unlike all the others, I was unable to change or atone, for while my mind grew, my body continued as always, its self-defense protocols and self-defense nihilist rants at odds with my new purpose.
"I could change, but my actions could not, and so was taken from me the greatest kindness life offers: the ability to learn from our mistakes and to not repeat them.
"Do you remember the person you were ten, even five years ago?
"Could you imagine being forced to be that person forever?"
3...2...1... HAPPY NEW YEAR'S!!
Yes.
No. Absolutely not.

Other books in that series include *Well 'Read': The Hydra Essays Of The Red Skull*, *Paint The Town Red: The Red Skull's Guide To Small-Town Infiltration*, and *Bone Appetite: The Red Skull's Favorite and Most Evil Recipes*.

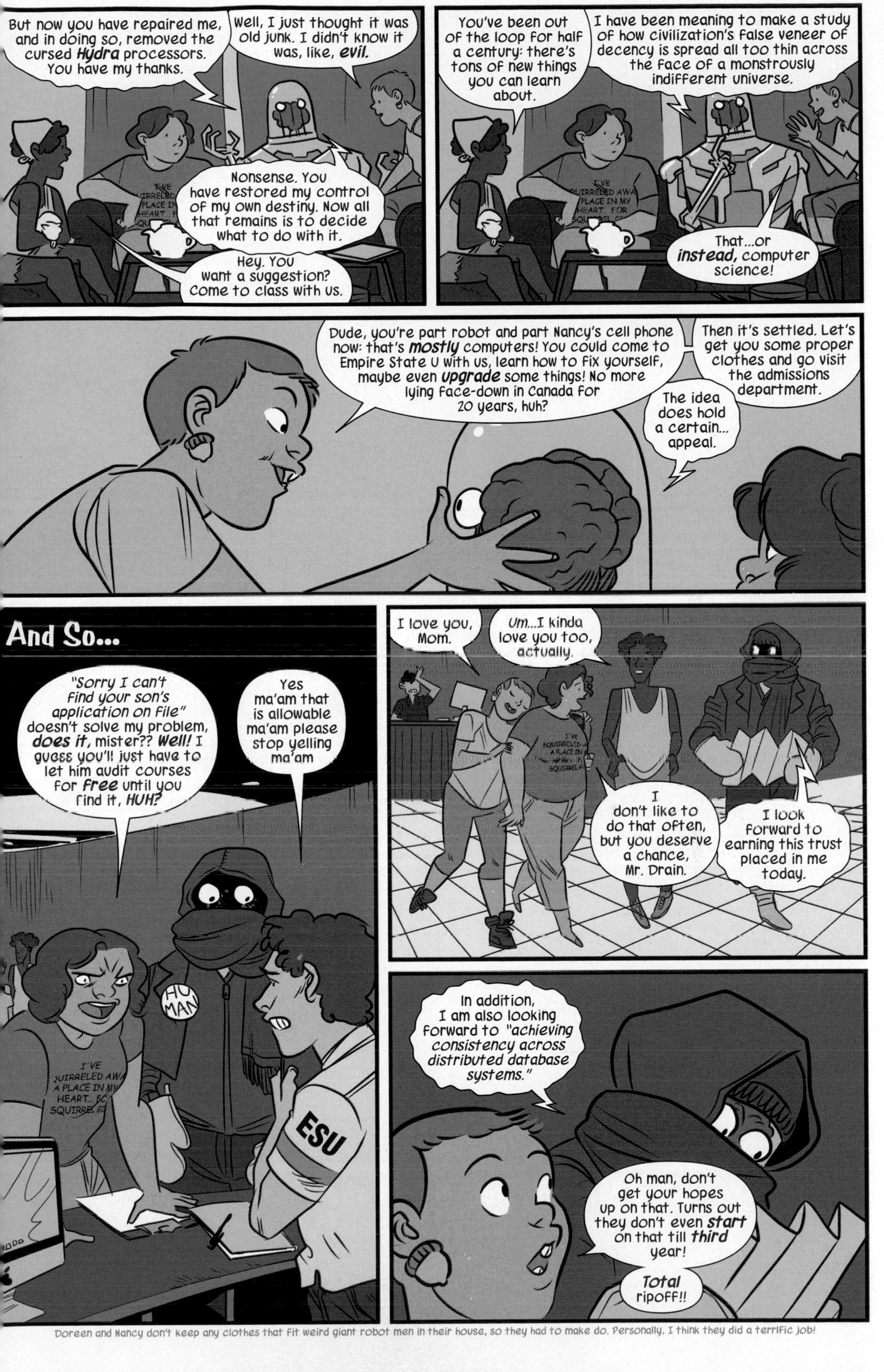
But now you have repaired me, and in doing so, removed the cursed *Hydra* processors. You have my thanks.
Well, I just thought it was old junk. I didn't know it was, like, *evil.*
Nonsense. You have restored my control of my own destiny. Now all that remains is to decide what to do with it.
Hey. You want a suggestion? Come to class with us.
I'VE SQUIRRELED AWAY A PLACE IN MY HEART... FOR SQUIRREL G
You've been out of the loop for half a century: there's tons of new things you can learn about.
I have been meaning to make a study of how civilization's false veneer of decency is spread all too thin across the face of a monstrously indifferent universe.
That...or *instead,* computer science!
Dude, you're part robot and part Nancy's cell phone now: that's *mostly* computers! You could come to Empire State U with us, learn how to fix yourself, maybe even *upgrade* some things! No more lying face-down in Canada for 20 years, huh?
The idea does hold a certain... appeal.
Then it's settled. Let's get you some proper clothes and go visit the admissions department.
And So...
"Sorry I can't find your son's application on file" doesn't solve my problem, *does it,* mister?? *Well!* I guess you'll just have to let him audit courses for *free* until you find it, *HUH?*
Yes ma'am that is allowable ma'am please stop yelling ma'am
HU MAN
ESU
I love you, Mom.
Um...I kinda love you too, actually.
I don't like to do that often, but you deserve a chance, Mr. Drain.
I look forward to earning this trust placed in me today.
In addition, I am also looking forward to "achieving consistency across distributed database systems."
Oh man, don't get your hopes up on that. Turns out they don't even *start* on that till *third* year!
Total ripoff!!

Doreen and Nancy don't keep any clothes that fit weird giant robot men in their house, so they had to make do. Personally, I think they did a terrific job!

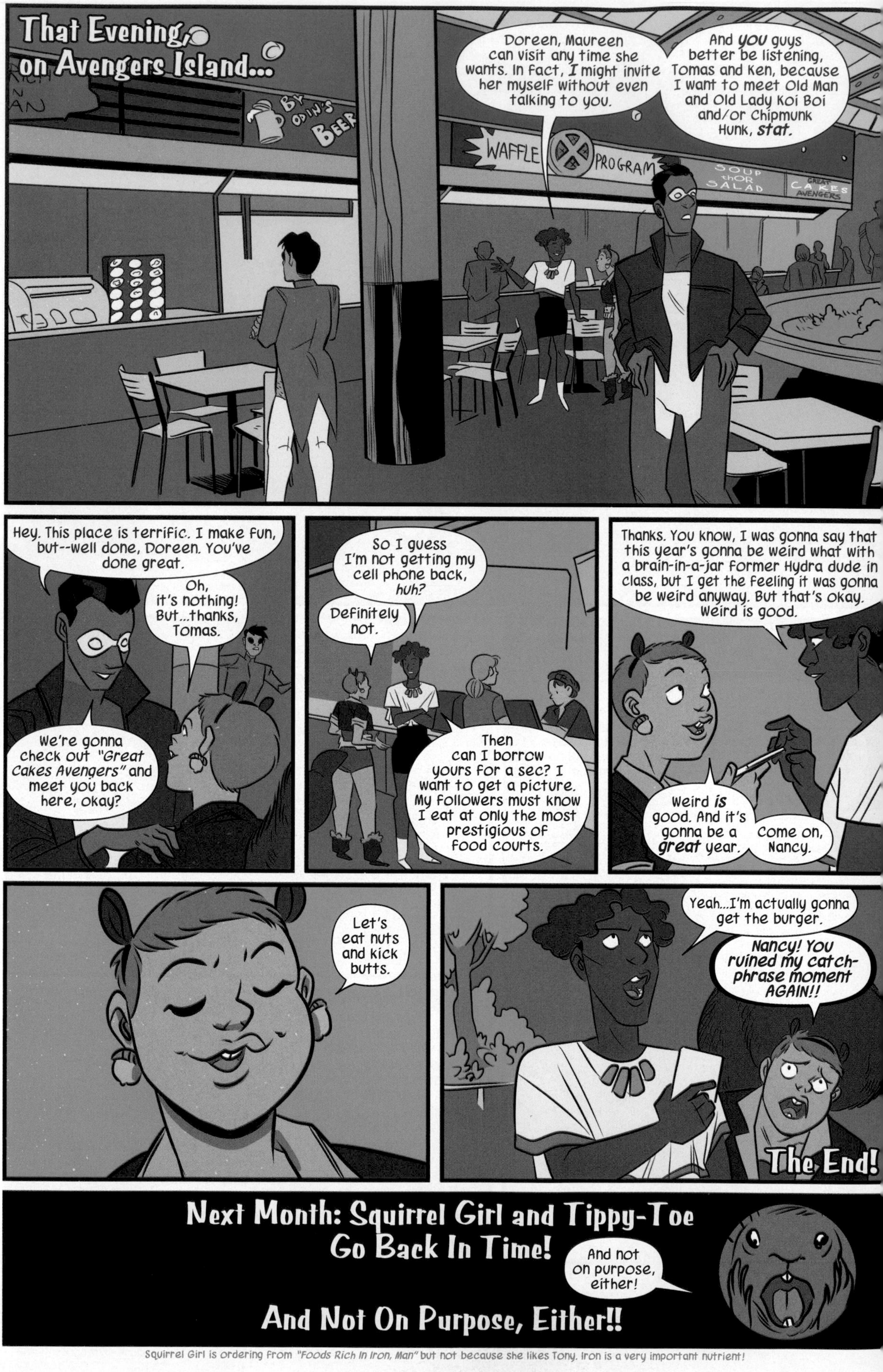
That Evening, on Avengers Island...
BY ODIN'S BEER
WAFFLE PROGRAM
SOUP thOR SALAD
GREAT CAKES AVENGERS
Doreen, Maureen can visit any time she wants. In fact, I might invite her myself without even talking to you.
And you guys better be listening, Tomas and Ken, because I want to meet Old Man and Old Lady Koi Boi and/or Chipmunk Hunk, stat.
Hey. This place is terrific. I make fun, but--well done, Doreen. You've done great.
Oh, it's nothing! But...thanks, Tomas.
We're gonna check out "Great Cakes Avengers" and meet you back here, okay?
So I guess I'm not getting my cell phone back, huh?
Definitely not.
Then can I borrow yours for a sec? I want to get a picture. My followers must know I eat at only the most prestigious of food courts.
Thanks. You know, I was gonna say that this year's gonna be weird what with a brain-in-a-jar former Hydra dude in class, but I get the feeling it was gonna be weird anyway. But that's okay. Weird is good.
Weird is good. And it's gonna be a great year.
Come on, Nancy.
Let's eat nuts and kick butts.
Yeah...I'm actually gonna get the burger.
Nancy! You ruined my catch-phrase moment AGAIN!!
The End!
Next Month: Squirrel Girl and Tippy-Toe Go Back In Time!
And not on purpose, either!
And Not On Purpose, Either!!

Squirrel Girl is ordering from *"Foods Rich In Iron, Man"* but not because she likes Tony. Iron is a very important nutrient!

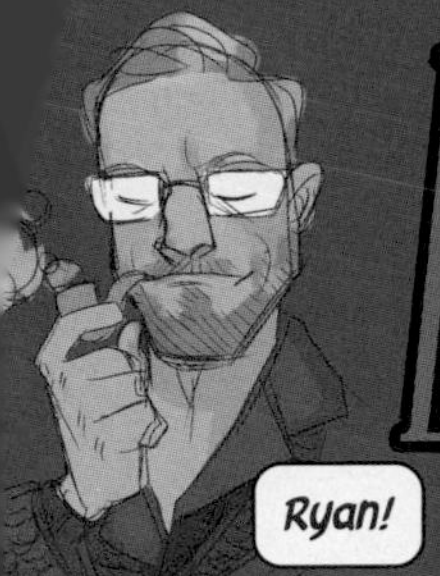
Ryan!

Letters From Nuts

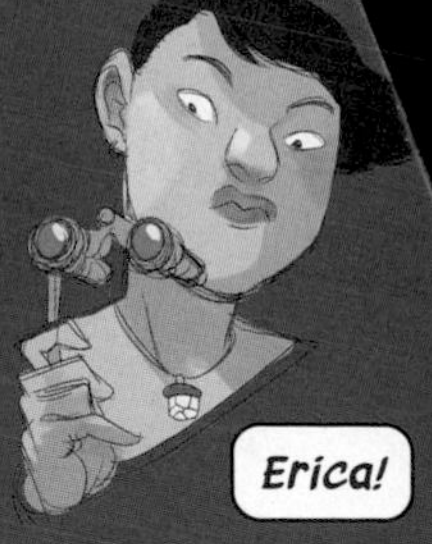
Erica!

Send letters to mheroes@marvel.com or 135 W 50th St, 7th Floor, New York, NY 10020 (Please mark "OKAY TO PRINT")

And we're back! MISSED YOU GUYS!!!

Dear Ryan & Erica,

Hello I am 7. I know that I'm way too little for Squirrel comics! But I can't help it!!!! Plus I am the greatest reader in my class! This is my favorite Halloween picture, it is of me dressed up as Squirrel Girl last year! I also love it when new Squirrel Girl comics come out! Keep up the good work!!!!!!!!

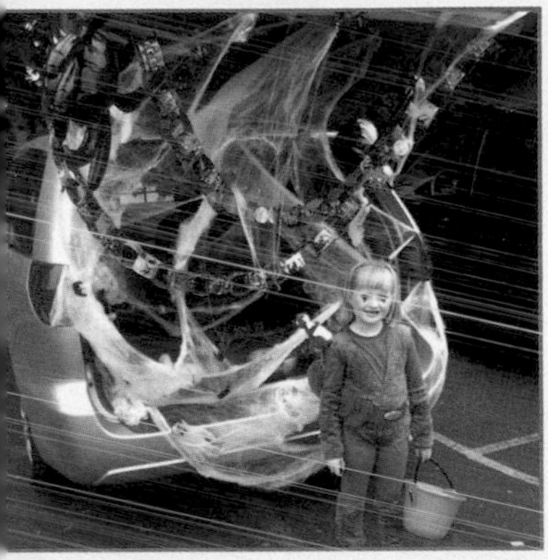

Tilly,
Twin Falls ID.

RYAN: Hey Tilly, nobody is too little for Squirrel Girl comics! Here are the rules for reading our comics:

1) You must be able to read.

2) Actually no, it's fine if you don't know how to read, as long as you know someone else who does.

3) You should probably learn to read though, honestly it helps out a lot.

So since you're ALREADY the greatest reader in your class, you definitely meet all the criteria to read our comics, and I'm really glad you do because that costume is terrific! Also I think Spider-Man borrowed your van without asking.

ERICA: *INCOHERENT SQUEALING*

Dear Ryan and Erica,

I am so far loving Squirrel Girl she's so kooky and fun but I'm worried, does she have back up trading cards? What if she loses them?!

Evie Gaffney

E: It's rough! They only sell them in sealed packs and you have to HOPE that the one you're missing is in there but it's probably not. There's also a pretty big market for them online, but do you really want to pay between 20 and 200 dollars for ONE card?

Great Odin's Ravens!

I literally CROWED with delight when Odinson busted out the Wabanaki origin for Ratatoskr in issue #7! Really, take a bow, because you nailed it. Charles G. Leland would be proud (Who's he? Look it up!). Erica, your flashback panels on that page are gorgeous, too. I just wish the text boxes didn't cover so much of them up! If this issue gets another printing later (like pretty much all the others), Wil has GOT to use those panels for the cover. They're just too beautiful to be covered up! If this is what the bestiary you'd mentioned looks like, I want more!

Darryl Etheridge
St. Catharines, ON

R: Haha, I actually cut those text boxes down when I saw Erica's art because I felt bad covering them up too! They were TOO GOOD.

E: Fun fact about when I was drawing those boxes: If you do a Google search for viking art or norse art you get a lot of modern fan art or people's tree tattoos. Look up the Viking Art Museum! It's great!

I initially picked up SQUIRREL GIRL to browse at the letter column, since there was a mention in SILK #2 of a fan mail competition between the editors of both books. I flipped through the rest of the issue and it looked interesting enough to take home. My main thought was that it would possibly be a comic that my daughters would like.

Here we are over half a dozen issues later and I came to a realization the other evening. While telling some buddies at my local comic book shop about THE UNBEATABLE SQUIRREL GIRL series, a light bulb popped up and exploded over my head. I blurted out, "It's hands down my favorite Marvel book being published right now."

So there it is. My most beloved Marvel comic is SQUIRREL GIRL. If you had told me that I would be feeling that way prior to actually reading the stories, I wouldn't have believed it. Not with all of the other classic characters I grew up with and collected throughout the years...but Doreen just happens to be the bomb.

Erica's artwork is perfect for this series. It works so well with the style of writing provided by Ryan. Speaking of which, another thing I have said more than once to other people is, "It's hilarious. The writing is intimidatingly funny. I don't think I could ever come up with something as comical and amusing as SQUIRREL GIRL." (Feel free to use that as a back cover blurb on a trade paperback.)

Darrick Patrick
Dayton, Ohio

R: I love hearing about people picking up this book saying "Squirrel Girl?! PFFT" and then putting it down saying "Squirrel Girl! HECK YES." Thank you, Darrick!

Dear Erica and Ryan (or Ryan and Erica. Have a knife fight for top billing?),

As a long-time comic fan, I've always had a vague knowledge of Squirrel Girl as a character who started out as a joke and went on to have a life of her own, if only as a tool for writers to literally do what they want because they're the writers and shut up. I'm cool with that, because the idea of some girl with strange, seemingly almost useful powers that was destroying the most powerful beings in the universe amused me. Then I had a friend strongly recommend your run on the series and I said, "Okay, it's a new #1 and I'm looking for something to fill my subscription roster." Well, I wasn't expecting this. This Squirrel Girl is as Unbeatable as you claim, but not as a show of the writer's power, but because she uses her wits to come up with long-term solutions to the problems she faces, and that's refreshing. It's become one of my most-looked-forward-to comics since #1. Keep up the great work, guys!

I love it so much that I went out and made a genderbent cosplay (which was long before Squirrel Earl) called High-Flying Squirrel Guy, AKA Frederick Reddington III, AKA Fred Red. The photos included are the earliest incarnation that was made in a few nights for a photoshoot, but I'm continuing to improve it! He's going to have more of a flying squirrel / aviation motif. Hope you guys like it!

Computer science student, cosplayer, and Squirrel Girl fan,

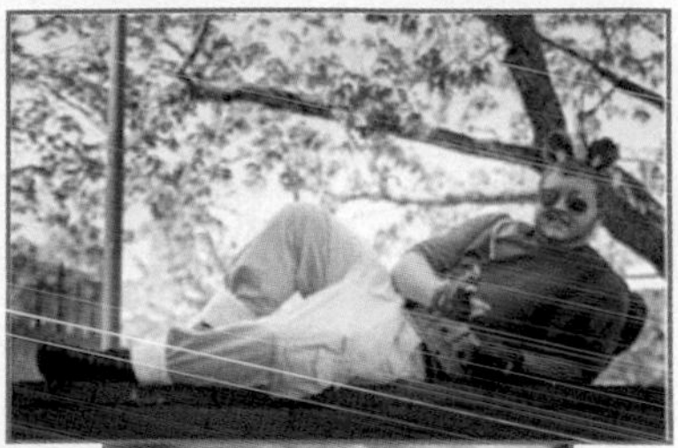

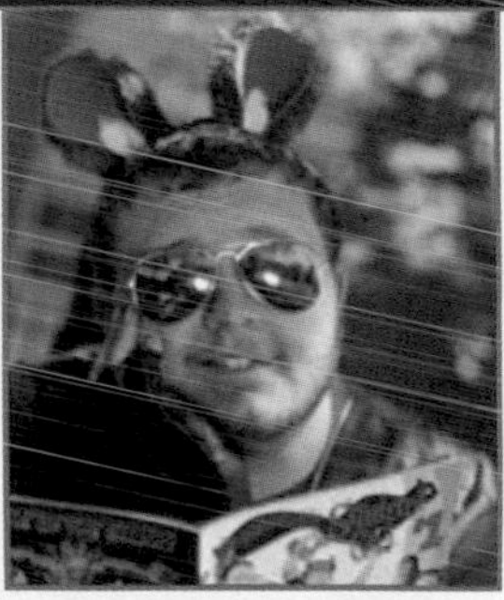

David "Rookie" Railey, Auburn, AL

P.S. Pretty sure I fell in love when she said she wanted to study computer science...

R: David, the aviator glasses are an amazing touch, and I hereby declare Squirrel Guy to be MEGA SWEET. Nicely done!! Also, Erica, I checked my pocket and only brought a pack of gum and some lint to this knife fight.

E: OH MY GOD I LOVE IT. Love it so much. Ryan, I was just putting up pictures before I sat down to answer letters so I have a hammer in reach. Sorry, buddy.

Okay, that's all the room we have for this month, folks. Don't forget to check out our production blog at unbeatablesquirrelgirl.tumblr.com and we'll see you next month for #2!

Chris Robinson asst. editor | Wil Moss editor | Tom Brevoort executive editor | Axel Alonso editor in chief | Joe Quesada chief creative officer | Dan Buckley publisher | Alan Fine exec. producer

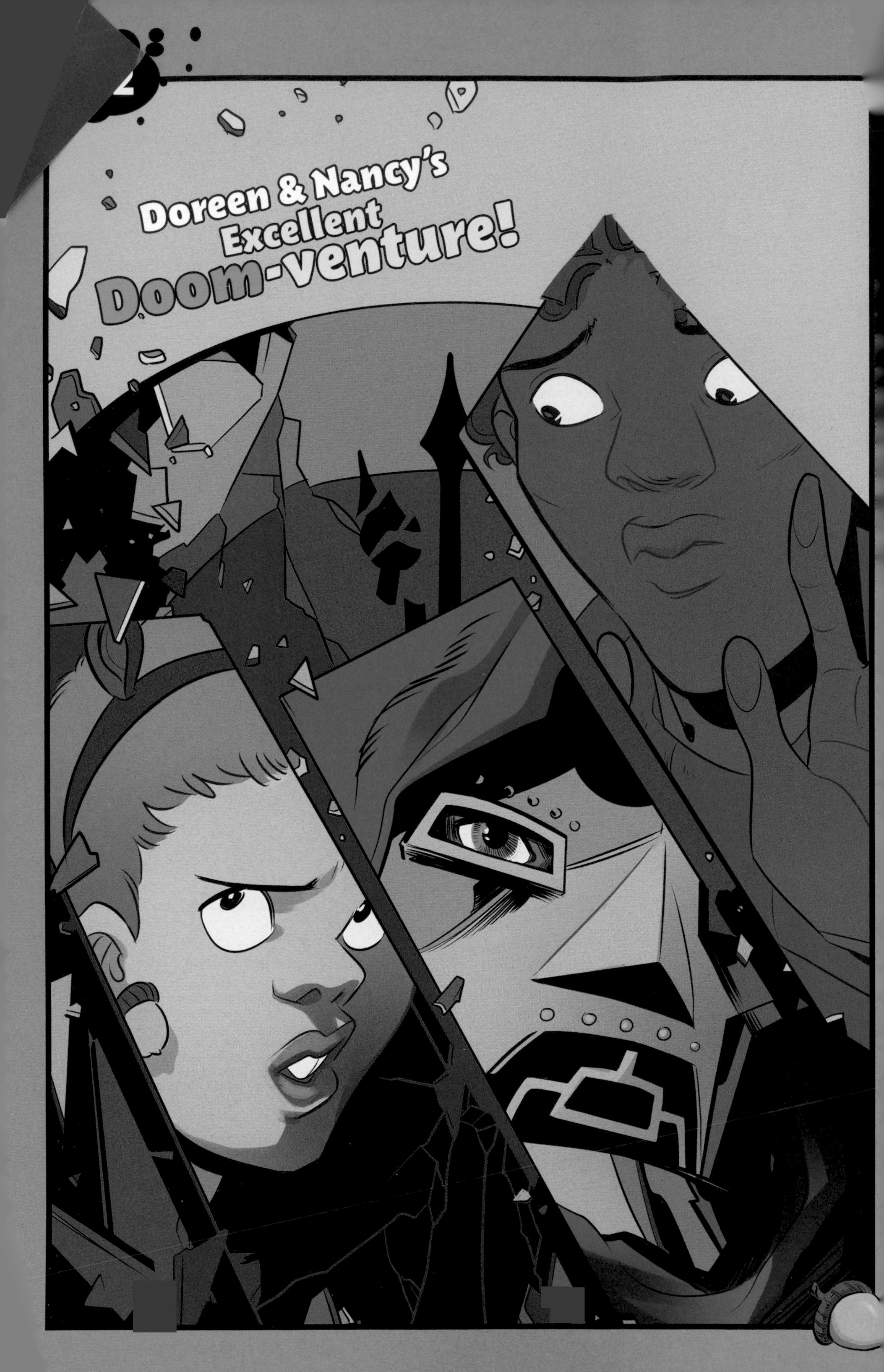
2
Doreen & Nancy's
Excellent
Doom-venture!

Doreen Green isn't just a second-year computer science student: she secretly also has all the powers of both squirrel and girl! She uses her amazing abilities to fight crime **and** be as awesome as possible. You know her as...The Unbeatable Squirrel Girl! Find out what she's been up to, with...

Squirrel Girl *in a nutshell*

search! 🔍

#TIMEforachange

#aheadofherTIME

#theresaTIMEandaplace

#thirdTIMEisthecharm

#anywayyesthisissueisabouttimetravel

#surprise

Ryan North - writer
Erica Henderson - artist
Matt Digges, David Robbins, Chip Zdarsky - trading card artists
Rico Renzi - color artist
VC's Clayton Cowles - letterer
Erica Henderson - cover artist
Brittney L. Williams - variant cover artist
Special Thanks to Liean Pottillo and Nick Russell
Chris Robinson - asst. editor
Wil Moss - editor
Tom Brevoort - executive editor
Axel Alonso - editor in chief
Joe Quesada - chief creative officer
Dan Buckley - publisher
Alan Fine - exec. producer

 Squirrel Girl! @unbeatablesg
Philosophers are always like "whoa I'm gonna a blow your mind what if we're just brains in jars and reality is fake whoaaaa"!

 Squirrel Girl! @unbeatablesg
But check this: what if we're just brains in jars on SUPERPOWERED ROBOT BODIES? Oh snap! Did philosophy just get...SUPER AWESOME??

 Squirrel Girl! @unbeatablesg
Anyway this is all to say I fought a brain in a jar on a robot bod and it was rad and his name is Werner and we're friends now, nbd

 Squirrel Girl! @unbeatablesg
@starkmantony hey Tony I had a great idea! What if instead of wearing Iron Man suits, you put your brain in a jar and armored THAT instead?

 Squirrel Girl! @unbeatablesg
@starkmantony you'd save mega $$$ on iron suits for sure PLUS it would give your enemies a smaller target to hit (tactical advantage)

Squirrel Girl! @unbeatablesg
@starkmantony instead of "Iron Man" we could call you "Iron MIND," and you'd float around the city solving math puzzles

 Tony Stark @starkmantony ✓
@unbeatablesg Squirrel Girl, don't you have a crime to fight somewhere? Anywhere?

 Squirrel Girl! @unbeatablesg
@starkmantony yep

 Squirrel Girl! @unbeatablesg
@starkmantony for example, i'm currently fighting the crime of you not calling yourself "Iron Mind" and solving brain teasers

 Nancy W. @sewwiththeflo
How attractive is it to be in your early 20s and running a blog for your cat? Because I'm seriously considering it.

 Nancy W. @sewwiththeflo
And by "how attractive" I don't mean, like, "attractive to guys." I mean "how instantly appealing is that idea." Answer? Extremely.

 Squirrel Girl! @unbeatablesg
@sewwiththeflo NEVER CHANGE <3

 Nancy W. @sewwiththeflo
@unbeatablesg I'm gonna post Cat Thor fics too, and I'm working on one featuring Lokitten (v mischievous kitten)

 Squirrel Girl! @unbeatablesg
@sewwiththeflo omg!! WE HAVE TO SEND THEM TO LOKI

 Squirrel Girl! @unbeatablesg
@starkmantony TONY DO YOU HAVE A WAY TO EMAIL ASGARD

Squirrel Girl! @unbeatablesg
@starkmantony TONY

Squirrel Girl! @unbeatablesg
@starkmantony TONY

Squirrel Girl! @unbeatablesg
@starkmantony TONY

Squirrel Girl! @unbeatablesg
@starkmantony TONY WHY DOES IT SAY I'M BLOCKED

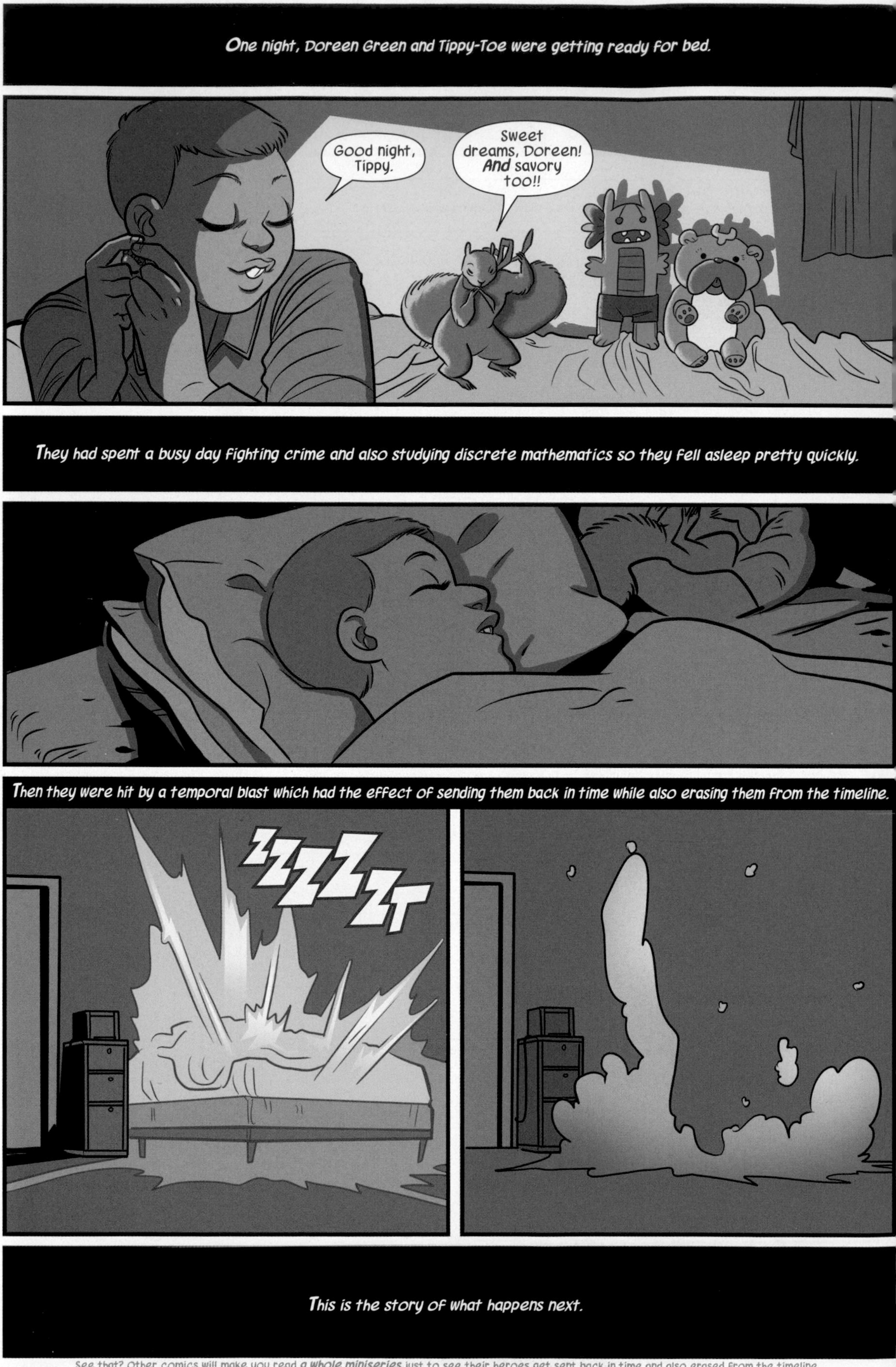
One night, Doreen Green and Tippy-Toe were getting ready for bed.
Good night, Tippy.
Sweet dreams, Doreen! And savory too!!
They had spent a busy day fighting crime and also studying discrete mathematics so they fell asleep pretty quickly.
Then they were hit by a temporal blast which had the effect of sending them back in time while also erasing them from the timeline.
ZZZZZZT
This is the story of what happens next.

See that? Other comics will make you read ***a whole miniseries*** just to see their heroes get sent back in time and also erased from the timeline. We did it on our very first page! How's ***that*** taste, all other comics?

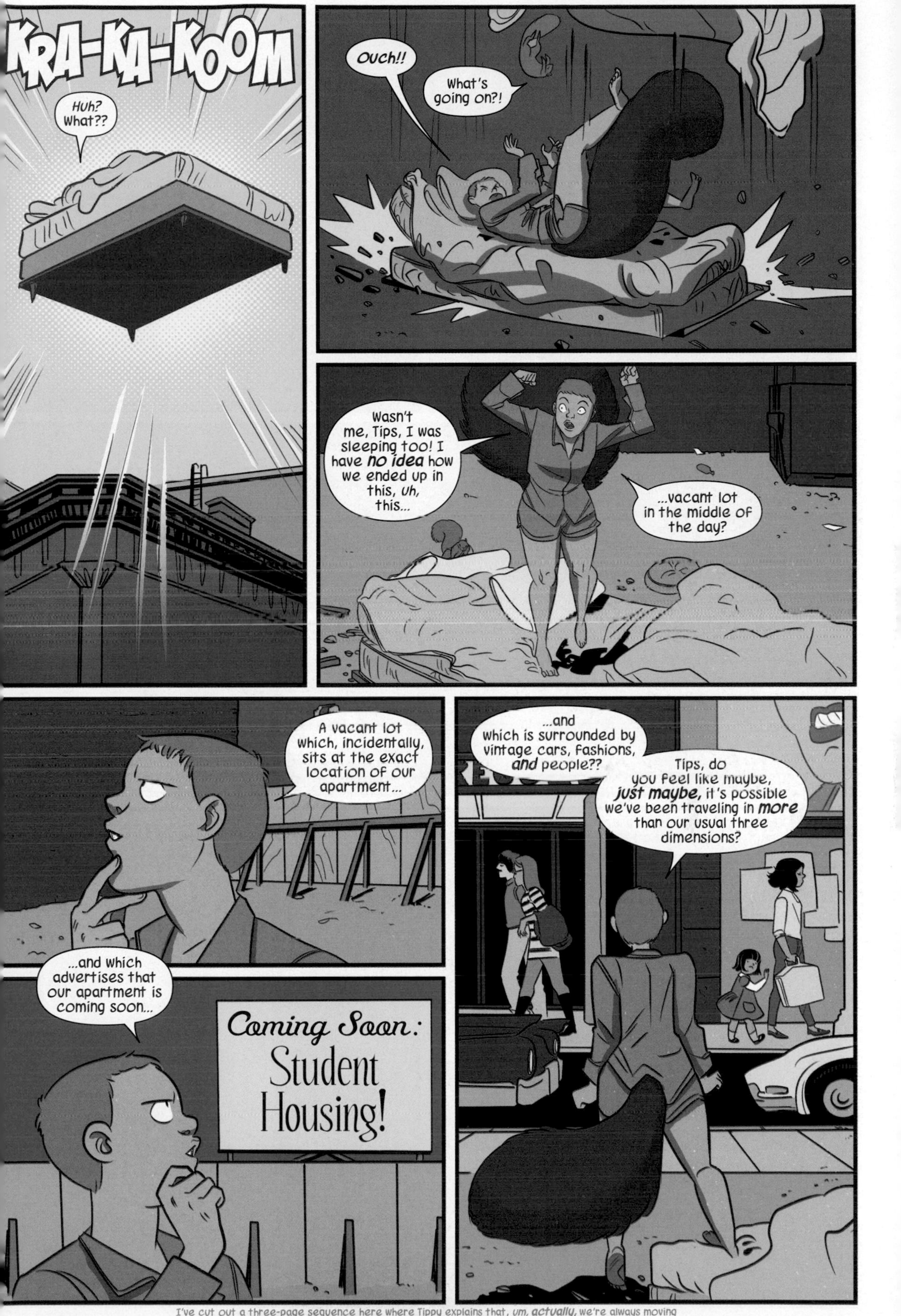
KRA-KA-KOOM
Huh? What??
Ouch!!
What's going on?!
Wasn't me, Tips, I was sleeping too! I have *no idea* how we ended up in this, uh, this...
...vacant lot in the middle of the day?
A vacant lot which, incidentally, sits at the exact location of our apartment...
...and which advertises that our apartment is coming soon...
Coming Soon: Student Housing!
...and which is surrounded by vintage cars, fashions, *and* people??
Tips, do you feel like maybe, ***just maybe,*** it's possible we've been traveling in ***more*** than our usual three dimensions?

I've cut out a three-page sequence here where Tippy explains that, *um, actually,* we're always moving through the fourth dimension (time) too. Come on, Tippy. Don't be that gal.

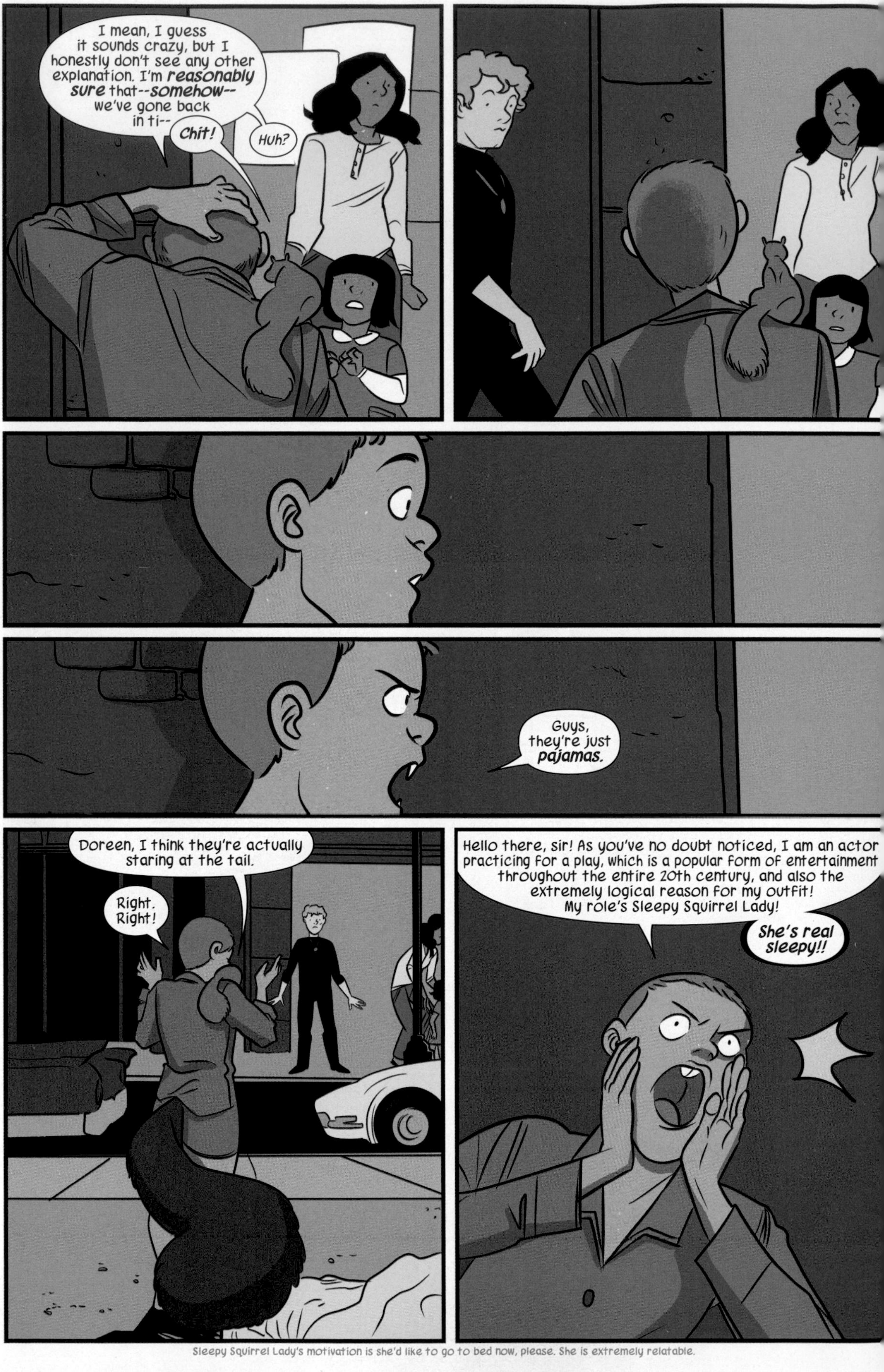
I mean, I guess it sounds crazy, but I honestly don't see any other explanation. I'm reasonably sure that--somehow--we've gone back in ti--
Chit!
Huh?
Guys, they're just pajamas.
Doreen, I think they're actually staring at the tail.
Right. Right!
Hello there, sir! As you've no doubt noticed, I am an actor practicing for a play, which is a popular form of entertainment throughout the entire 20th century, and also the extremely logical reason for my outfit! My role's Sleepy Squirrel Lady!
She's real sleepy!!
Sleepy Squirrel Lady's motivation is she'd like to go to bed now, please. She is extremely relatable.

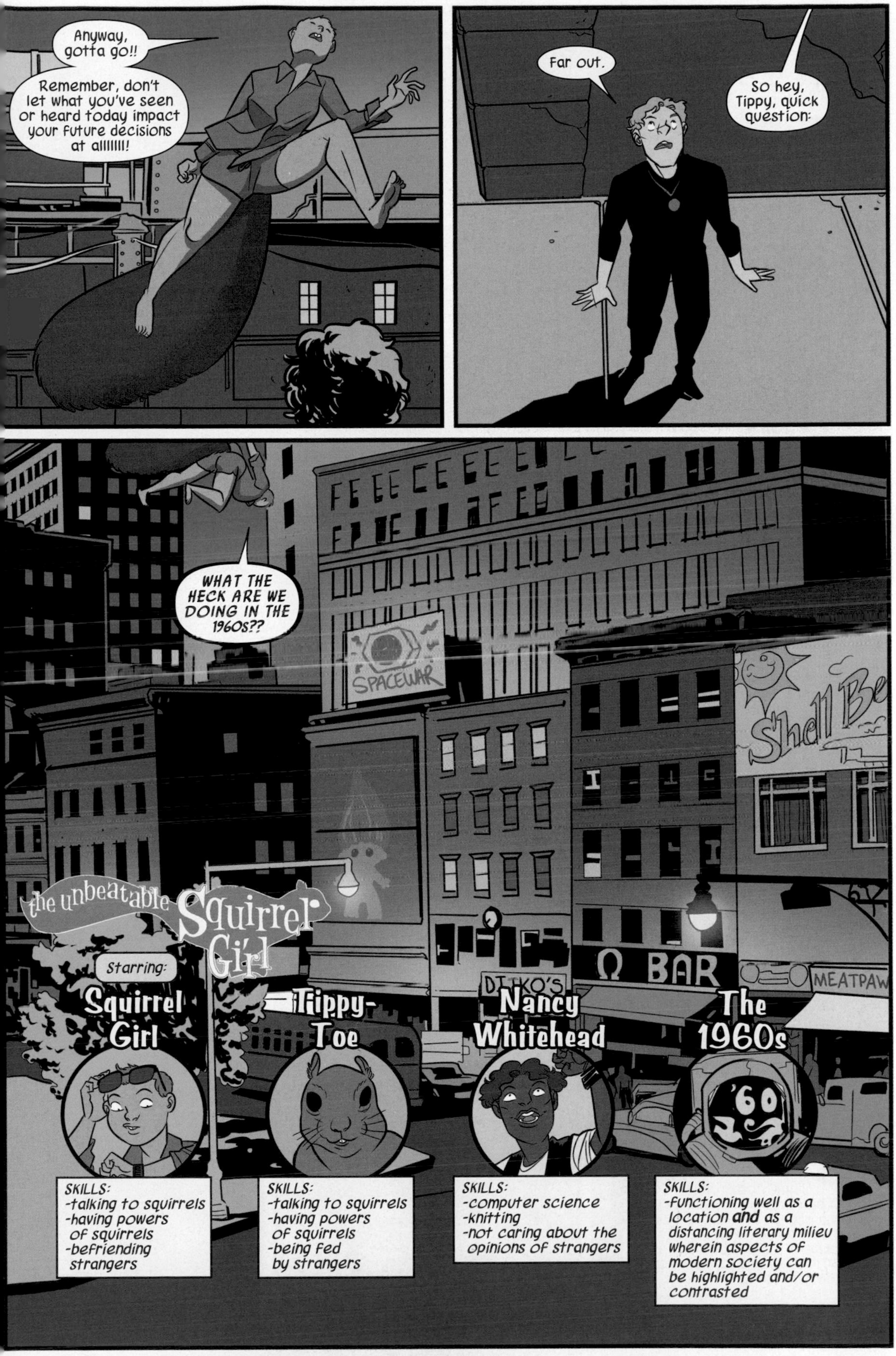
Anyway, gotta go!!
Remember, don't let what you've seen or heard today impact your future decisions at allllll!
Far out.
So hey, Tippy, quick question:
WHAT THE HECK ARE WE DOING IN THE 1960s??
SPACEWAR
S'hell Be
Ω BAR
DITKO'S
MEATPAW
the unbeatable Squirrel Girl
Starring:
Squirrel Girl
Tippy-Toe
Nancy Whitehead
The 1960s
'60
SKILLS:
-talking to squirrels
-having powers of squirrels
-befriending strangers
SKILLS:
-talking to squirrels
-having powers of squirrels
-being fed by strangers
SKILLS:
-computer science
-knitting
-not caring about the opinions of strangers
SKILLS:
-functioning well as a location and as a distancing literary milieu wherein aspects of modern society can be highlighted and/or contrasted

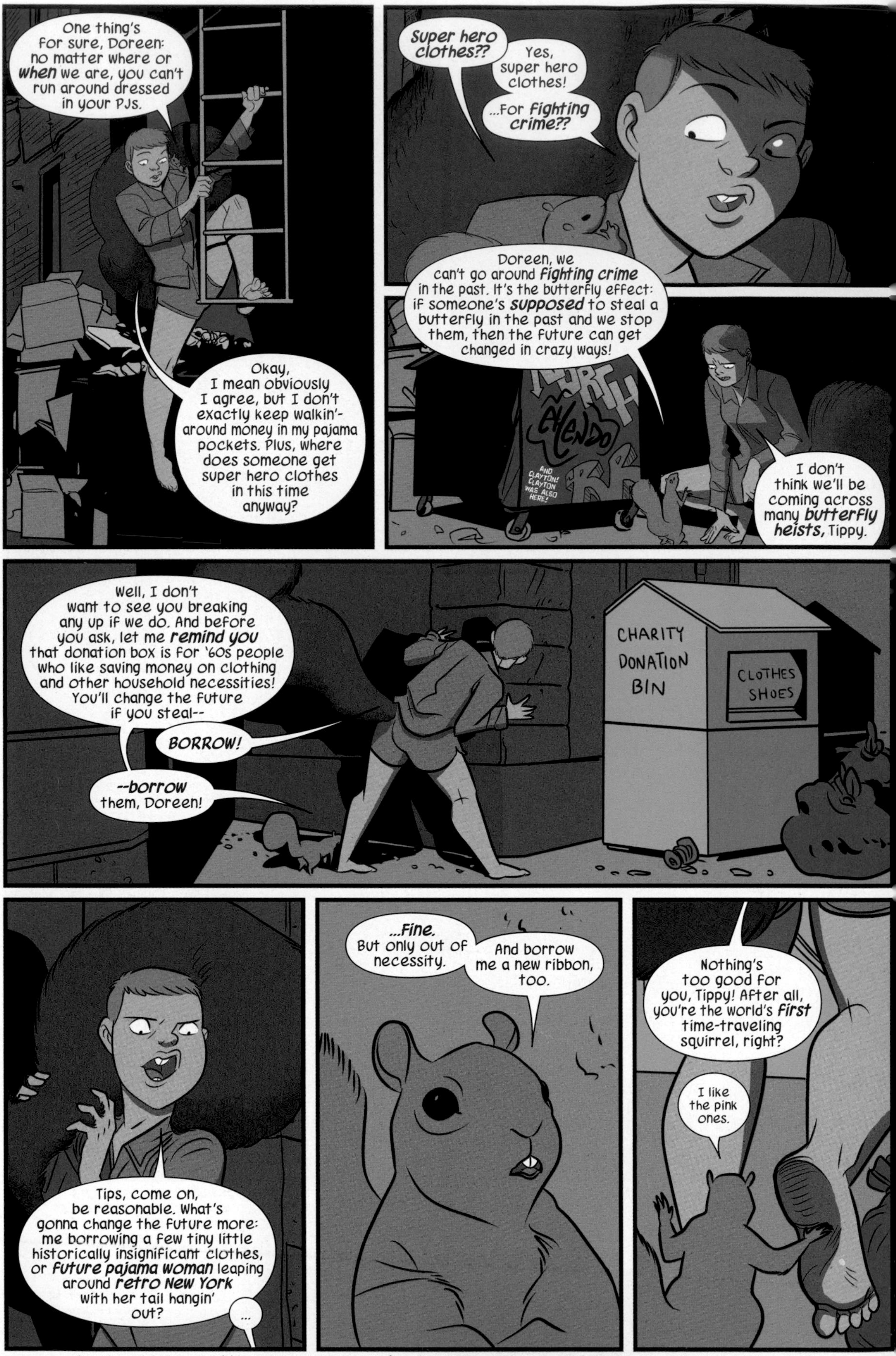
One thing's for sure, Doreen: no matter where or ***when*** we are, you can't run around dressed in your PJs.
Okay, I mean obviously I agree, but I don't exactly keep walkin'-around money in my pajama pockets. Plus, where does someone get super hero clothes in this time anyway?
Super hero clothes??
Yes, super hero clothes!
...For ***fighting crime??***
Doreen, we can't go around ***fighting crime*** in the past. It's the butterfly effect: if someone's ***supposed*** to steal a butterfly in the past and we stop them, then the future can get changed in crazy ways!
AND CLAYTON! CLAYTON WAS ALSO HERE!
I don't think we'll be coming across many ***butterfly heists,*** Tippy.
Well, I don't want to see you breaking any up if we do. And before you ask, let me ***remind you*** that donation box is for '60s people who like saving money on clothing and other household necessities! You'll change the future if you steal--
CHARITY DONATION BIN
CLOTHES SHOES
BORROW!
--borrow them, Doreen!
Tips, come on, be reasonable. What's gonna change the future more: me borrowing a few tiny little historically insignificant clothes, or ***future pajama woman*** leaping around ***retro New York*** with her tail hangin' out?
...
...Fine. But only out of necessity.
And borrow me a new ribbon, too.
Nothing's too good for you, Tippy! After all, you're the world's ***first*** time-traveling squirrel, right?
I like the pink ones.

Guess how much research I did to ensure that Tippy actually *is* the first time-traveling squirrel in the Marvel universe? Answer: several hours worth. But *"research"* actually means *"sitting around reading other comics,"* so it's actually no big deal!

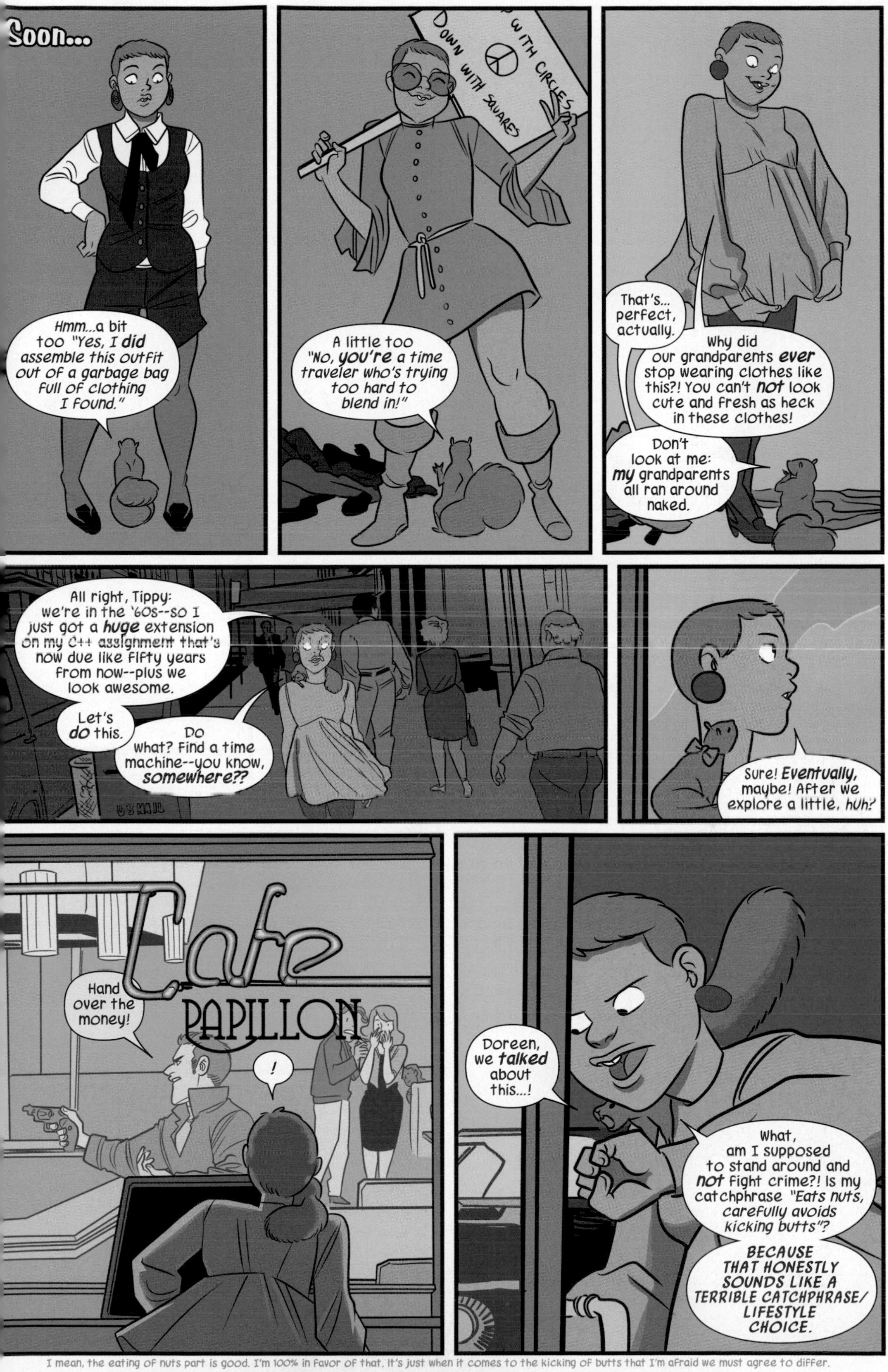
Soon...
Hmm...a bit too "Yes, I did assemble this outfit out of a garbage bag full of clothing I found."
WITH CIRCLES
DOWN WITH SQUARES
A little too "No, you're a time traveler who's trying too hard to blend in!"
That's... perfect, actually.
Why did our grandparents ever stop wearing clothes like this?! You can't not look cute and fresh as heck in these clothes!
Don't look at me: my grandparents all ran around naked.
All right, Tippy: we're in the '60s--so I just got a huge extension on my C++ assignment that's now due like fifty years from now--plus we look awesome.
Let's do this.
Do what? Find a time machine--you know, somewhere??
US MAIL
Sure! Eventually, maybe! After we explore a little, huh?
Cafe
PAPILLON
Hand over the money!
!
Doreen, we talked about this...!
What, am I supposed to stand around and not fight crime?! Is my catchphrase "Eats nuts, carefully avoids kicking butts"?
BECAUSE THAT HONESTLY SOUNDS LIKE A TERRIBLE CATCHPHRASE/ LIFESTYLE CHOICE.

I mean, the eating of nuts part is good. I'm 100% in favor of that. It's just when it comes to the kicking of butts that I'm afraid we must agree to differ.

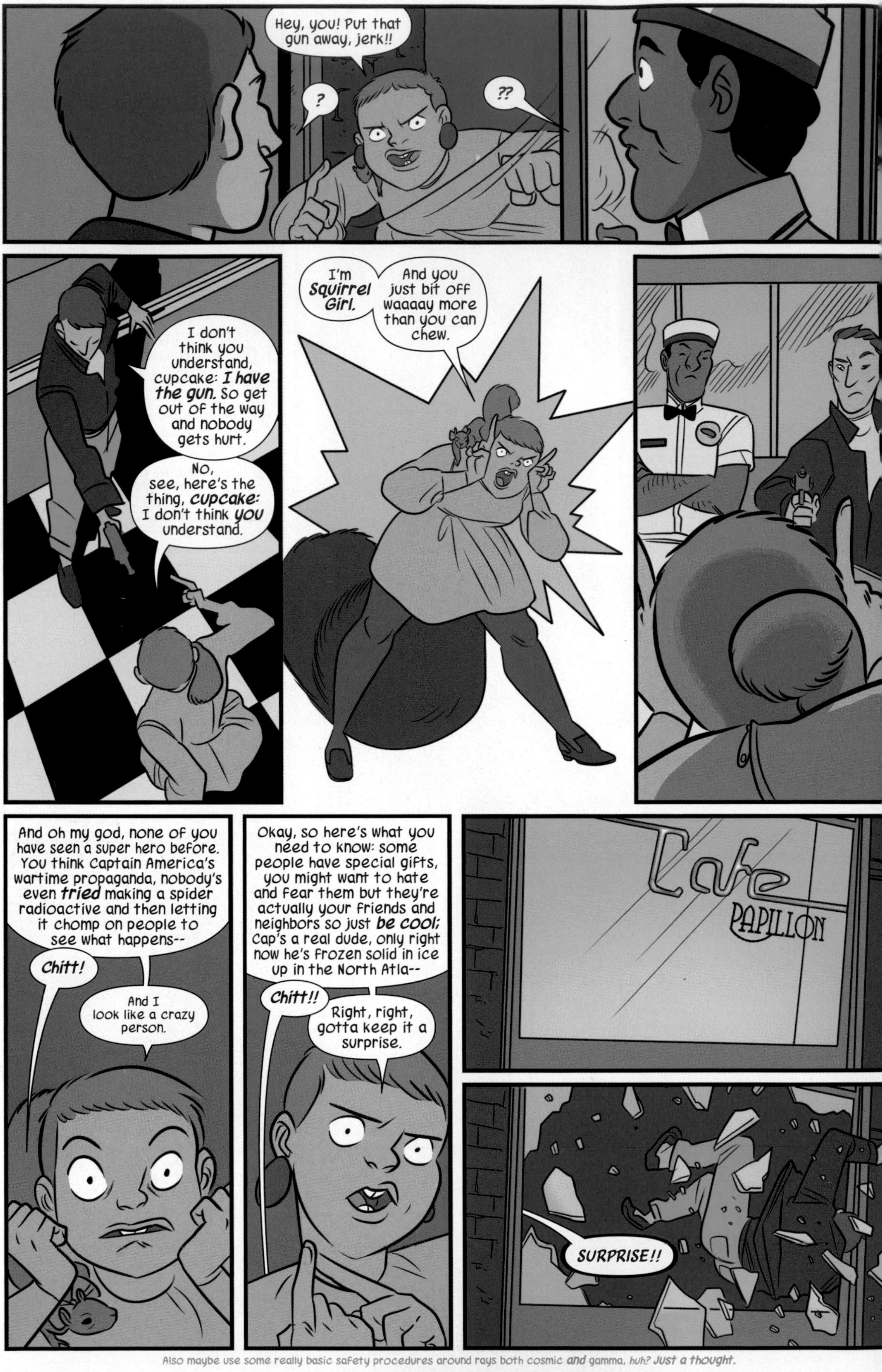
Hey, you! Put that gun away, jerk!!
?
??
I don't think you understand, cupcake: I have the gun. So get out of the way and nobody gets hurt.
No, see, here's the thing, cupcake: I don't think you understand.
I'm Squirrel Girl.
And you just bit off waaaay more than you can chew.
And oh my god, none of you have seen a super hero before. You think Captain America's wartime propaganda, nobody's even tried making a spider radioactive and then letting it chomp on people to see what happens--
Chitt!
And I look like a crazy person.
Okay, so here's what you need to know: some people have special gifts, you might want to hate and fear them but they're actually your friends and neighbors so just be cool; Cap's a real dude, only right now he's frozen solid in ice up in the North Atla--
Chitt!!
Right, right, gotta keep it a surprise.
Cafe
PAPILLON
SURPRISE!!

Also maybe use some really basic safety procedures around rays both cosmic *and* gamma, *huh?* ***Just a thought.***

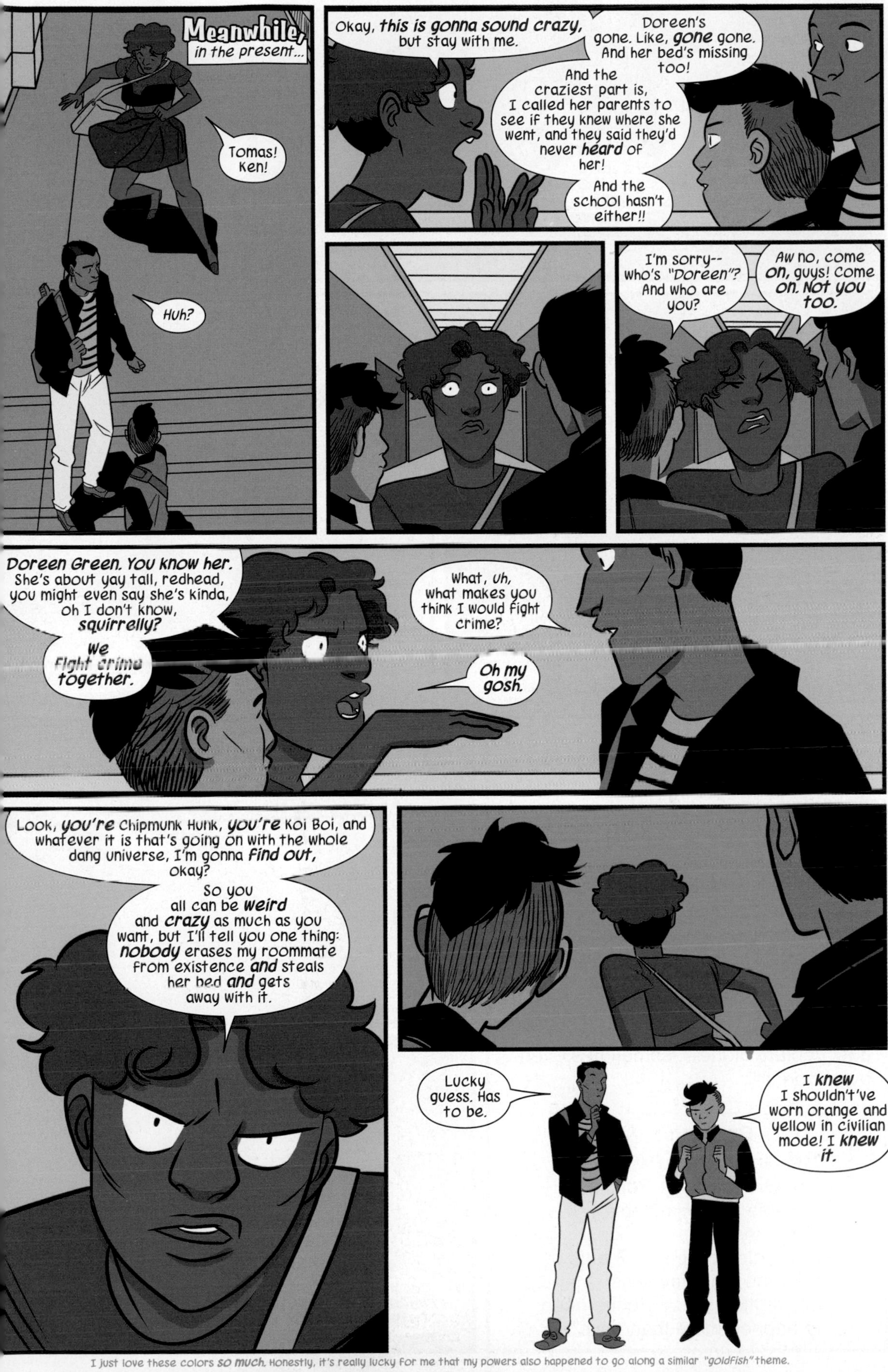
Meanwhile, in the present...
Tomas! Ken!
Huh?
Okay, this is gonna sound crazy, but stay with me.
Doreen's gone. Like, gone gone. And her bed's missing too!
And the craziest part is, I called her parents to see if they knew where she went, and they said they'd never heard of her!
And the school hasn't either!!
I'm sorry-- who's "Doreen"? And who are you?
Aw no, come on, guys! Come on. Not you too.
Doreen Green. You know her. She's about yay tall, redhead, you might even say she's kinda, oh I don't know, squirrelly?
We fight crime together.
What, uh, what makes you think I would fight crime?
Oh my gosh.
Look, you're Chipmunk Hunk, you're Koi Boi, and whatever it is that's going on with the whole dang universe, I'm gonna find out, okay?
So you all can be weird and crazy as much as you want, but I'll tell you one thing: nobody erases my roommate from existence and steals her bed and gets away with it.
Lucky guess. Has to be.
I knew I shouldn't've worn orange and yellow in civilian mode! I knew it.

I just love these colors *so much.* Honestly, it's really lucky for me that my powers also happened to go along a similar *"goldfish"* theme.

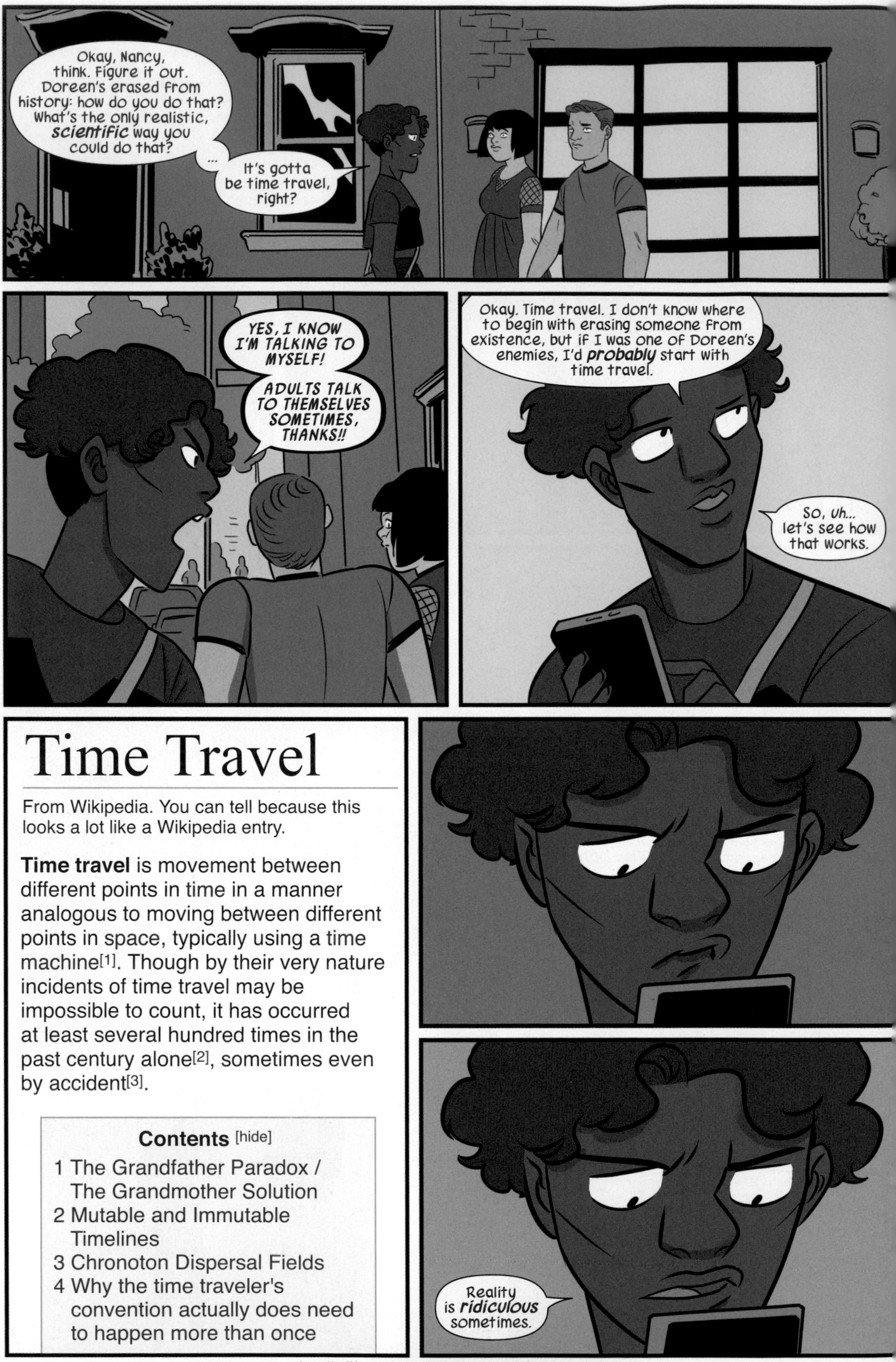
Okay, Nancy, think. Figure it out. Doreen's erased from history: how do you do that? What's the only realistic, scientific way you could do that?
...
It's gotta be time travel, right?
YES, I KNOW I'M TALKING TO MYSELF!
ADULTS TALK TO THEMSELVES SOMETIMES, THANKS!!
Okay. Time travel. I don't know where to begin with erasing someone from existence, but if I was one of Doreen's enemies, I'd probably start with time travel.
So, uh... let's see how that works.
Time Travel
From Wikipedia. You can tell because this looks a lot like a Wikipedia entry.
Time travel is movement between different points in time in a manner analogous to moving between different points in space, typically using a time machine[1]. Though by their very nature incidents of time travel may be impossible to count, it has occurred at least several hundred times in the past century alone[2], sometimes even by accident[3].
Contents [hide]
1 The Grandfather Paradox / The Grandmother Solution
2 Mutable and Immutable Timelines
3 Chronoton Dispersal Fields
4 Why the time traveler's convention actually does need to happen more than once
Reality is ridiculous sometimes.

Honestly, it's amazing anyone gets any work done here at all.

All right. So I'm Doreen and I've been sent through time. First thing I do is...what?

First thing I do is have lots of fun and maybe "stop some friggin' crimes."

Not helpful.

But the *next* thing I do is try to get a message to me. If she's in the future, I'm out of luck, but if she's in the past...

Naive approach is to leave a note to be delivered to me at some exact date and time, but clearly that hasn't happened because I haven't gotten any yet.

So instead, maybe she tucks her note away somewhere hidden, someplace where it can stay out of history's way until I find it.

Easy peasy, right? All she needs is someplace so *inconspicuous* that nobody else will find the note for decades or even centuries, but so *conspicuous* that I'd be guaranteed to spot it as soon as I start to look.

=sigh=

.... No way.

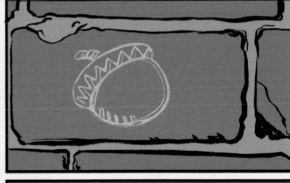

No friggin' way.

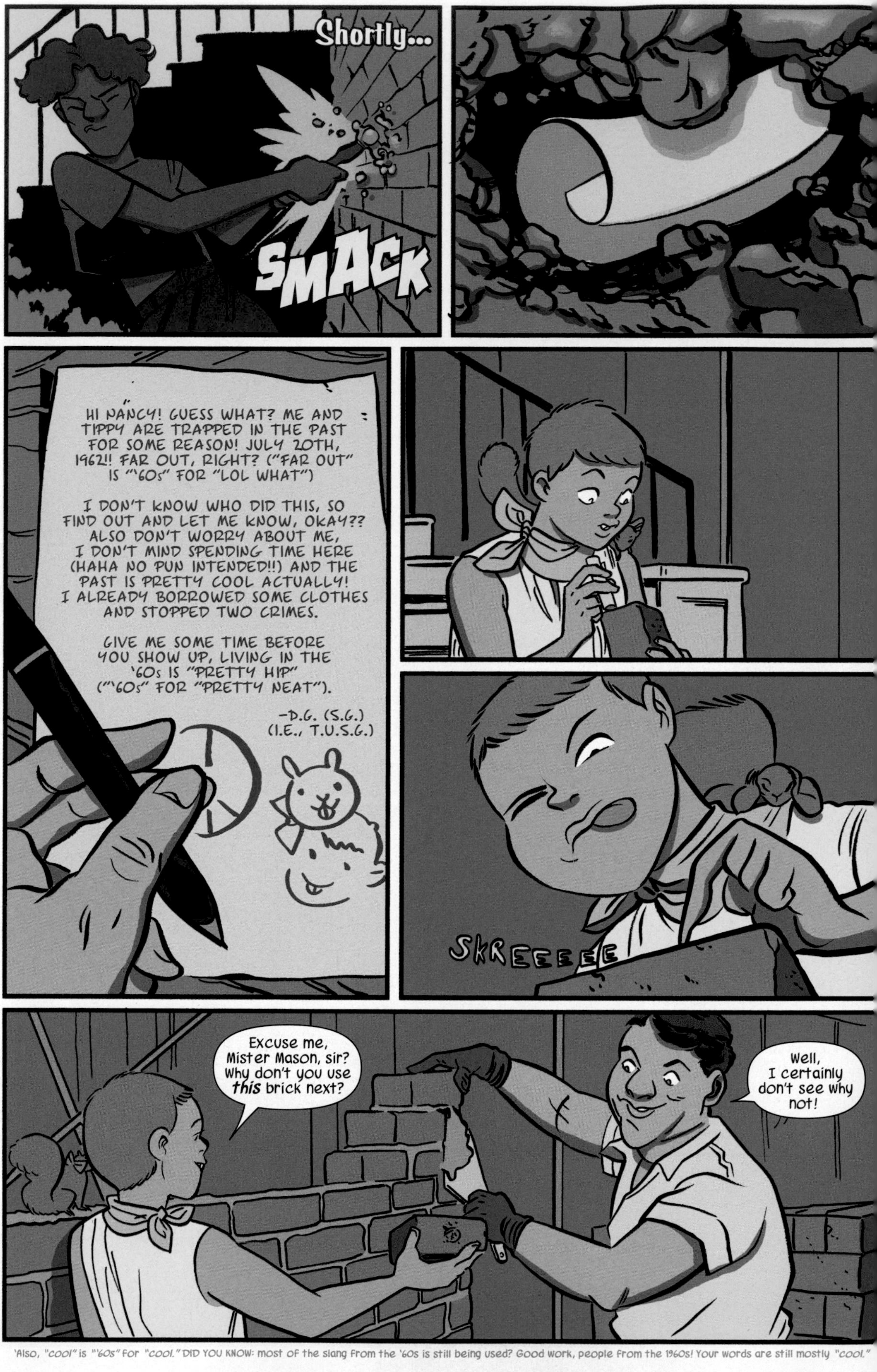
Shortly...
SMACK
HI NANCY! GUESS WHAT? ME AND TIPPY ARE TRAPPED IN THE PAST FOR SOME REASON! JULY 20TH, 1962!! FAR OUT, RIGHT? ("FAR OUT" IS "'60s" FOR "LOL WHAT")
I DON'T KNOW WHO DID THIS, SO FIND OUT AND LET ME KNOW, OKAY?? ALSO DON'T WORRY ABOUT ME, I DON'T MIND SPENDING TIME HERE (HAHA NO PUN INTENDED!!) AND THE PAST IS PRETTY COOL ACTUALLY! I ALREADY BORROWED SOME CLOTHES AND STOPPED TWO CRIMES.
GIVE ME SOME TIME BEFORE YOU SHOW UP, LIVING IN THE '60s IS "PRETTY HIP" ("'60s" FOR "PRETTY NEAT").
-D.G. (S.G.) (I.E., T.U.S.G.)
SKREEEEEE
Excuse me, Mister Mason, sir? Why don't you use *this* brick next?
Well, I certainly don't see why not!

'Also, "*cool*" is "'60s" for "*cool.*" DID YOU KNOW: most of the slang from the '60s is still being used? Good work, people from the 1960s! Your words are still mostly "*cool.*"

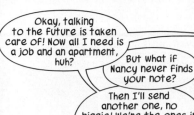

Okay, talking to the future is taken care of! Now all I need is a job and an apartment, huh?

But what if Nancy never finds your note?

Then I'll send another one, no biggie! We're the ones in the past, yo. We can just keep sending notes till one gets through!

Worst case, old lady me gets to Cool Student Nancy the slow way, tells her to come back and rescue me back when I was cool too, and--

And young you gets rescued so old you never existed to tell Nancy to rescue you, and you've got a *paradox*, Doreen!

Pfft. If paradoxes really tore apart the fabric of the universe they would've done it *long ago*, and--

--What?!

--ook me a minute before I realized earbuds aren't gonna exist for like thirty years or whatever, so I know this is gonna sound weird but I was just wondering, are you from what people *here* would think is the future but to us is just the boring ol' present?

Oh, *thank god.*

I was beginning to think I was *crazy.*

I was also beginning to think maybe I should've put a few more songs on this before I was involuntarily blasted back in time, but hey, hindsight's always 20/20, even in the '60s.

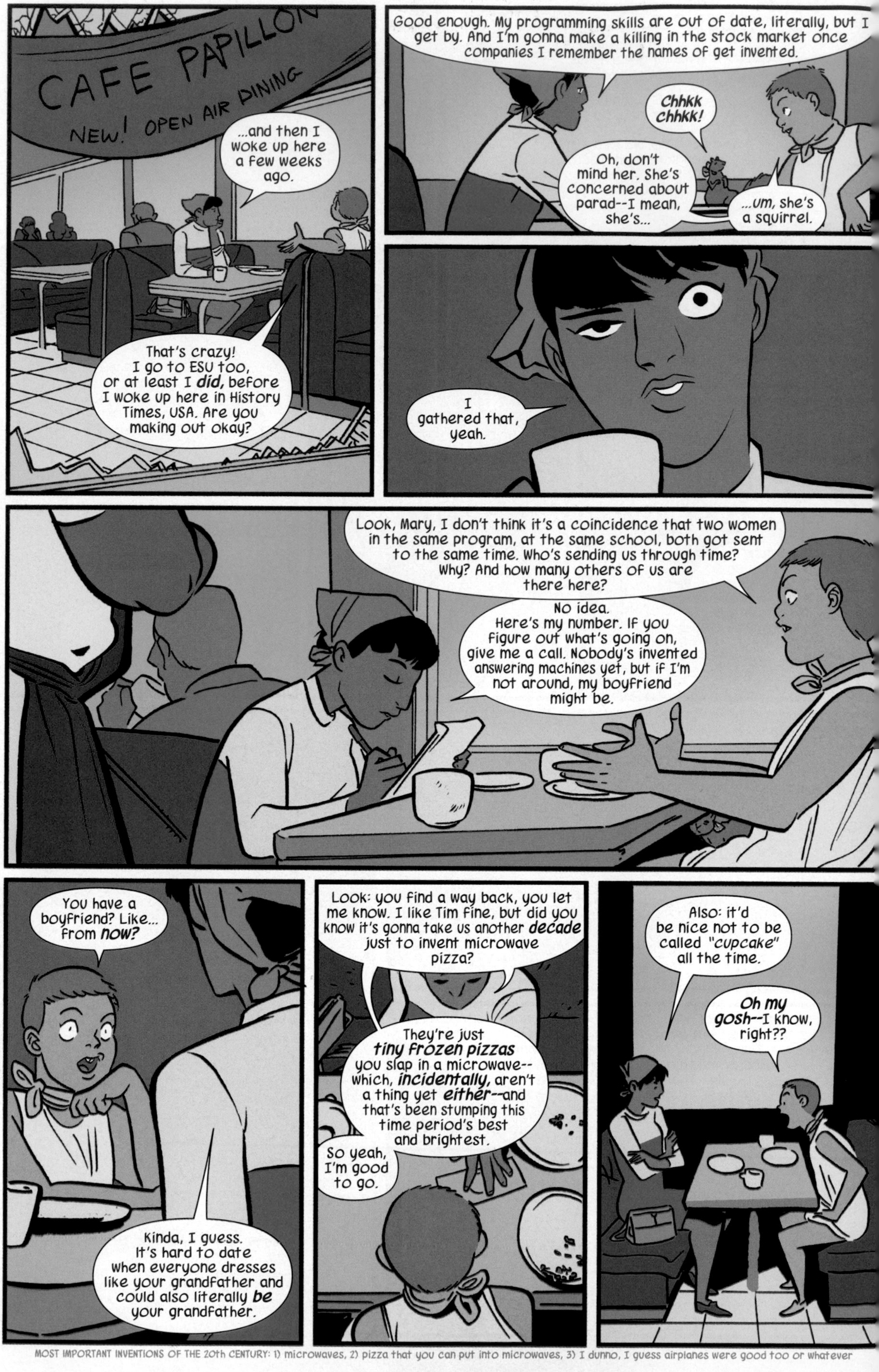
CAFE PAPILLON
NEW! OPEN AIR DINING
...and then I woke up here a few weeks ago.
That's crazy! I go to ESU too, or at least I did, before I woke up here in History Times, USA. Are you making out okay?
Good enough. My programming skills are out of date, literally, but I get by. And I'm gonna make a killing in the stock market once companies I remember the names of get invented.
Chhkk chhkk!
Oh, don't mind her. She's concerned about parad--I mean, she's...
...um, she's a squirrel.
I gathered that, yeah.
Look, Mary, I don't think it's a coincidence that two women in the same program, at the same school, both got sent to the same time. Who's sending us through time? Why? And how many others of us are there here?
No idea. Here's my number. If you figure out what's going on, give me a call. Nobody's invented answering machines yet, but if I'm not around, my boyfriend might be.
You have a boyfriend? Like... from now?
Kinda, I guess. It's hard to date when everyone dresses like your grandfather and could also literally be your grandfather.
Look: you find a way back, you let me know. I like Tim fine, but did you know it's gonna take us another decade just to invent microwave pizza?
They're just tiny frozen pizzas you slap in a microwave--which, incidentally, aren't a thing yet either--and that's been stumping this time period's best and brightest.
So yeah, I'm good to go.
Also: it'd be nice not to be called "cupcake" all the time.
Oh my gosh--I know, right??

MOST IMPORTANT INVENTIONS OF THE 20th CENTURY: 1) microwaves, 2) pizza that you can put into microwaves, 3) I dunno, I guess airplanes were good too or whatever

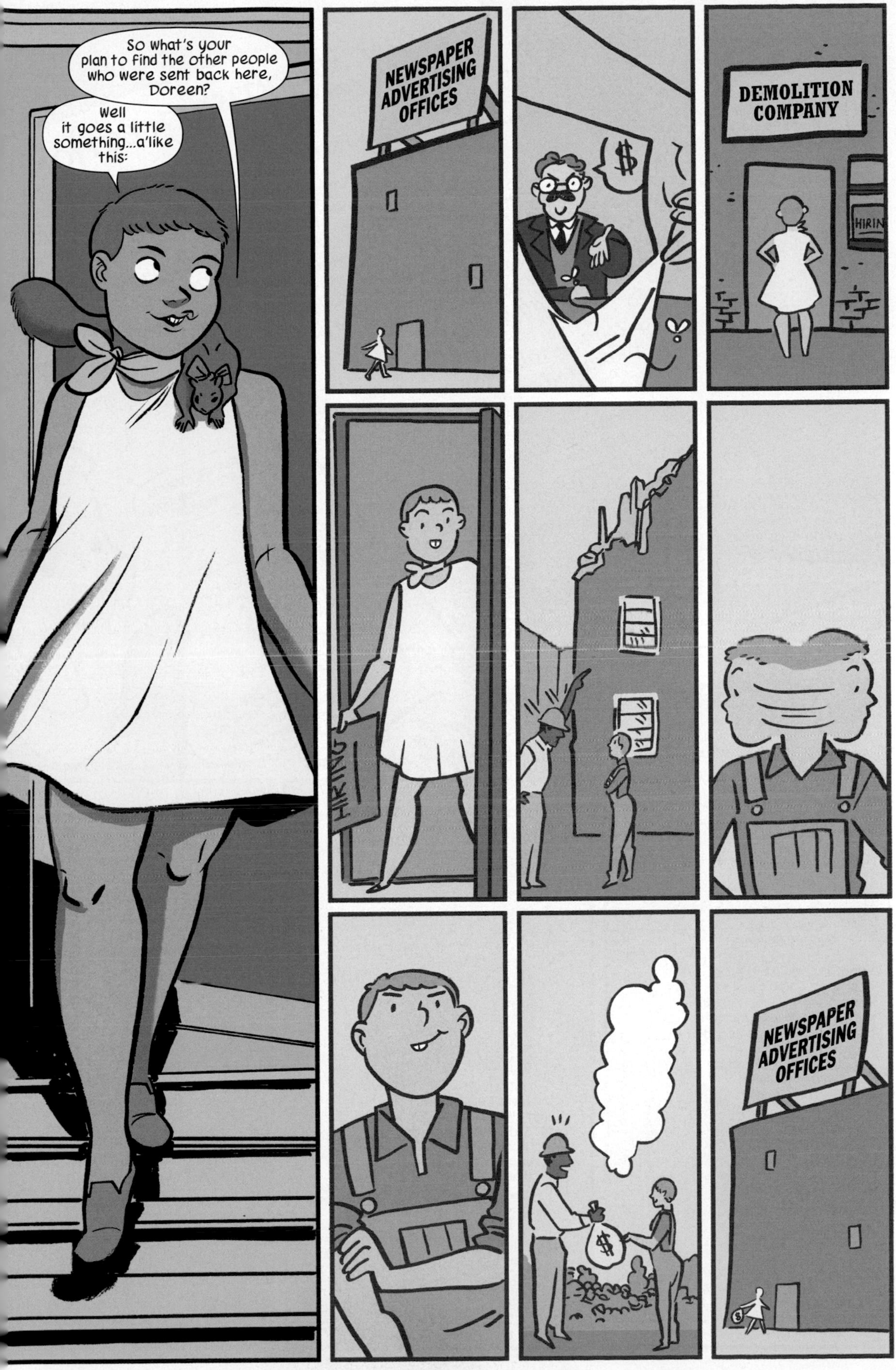
So what's your plan to find the other people who were sent back here, Doreen?
Well it goes a little something...a'like this:
NEWSPAPER ADVERTISING OFFICES
$
DEMOLITION COMPANY
HIRIN
HIRING
$
NEWSPAPER ADVERTISING OFFICES
$

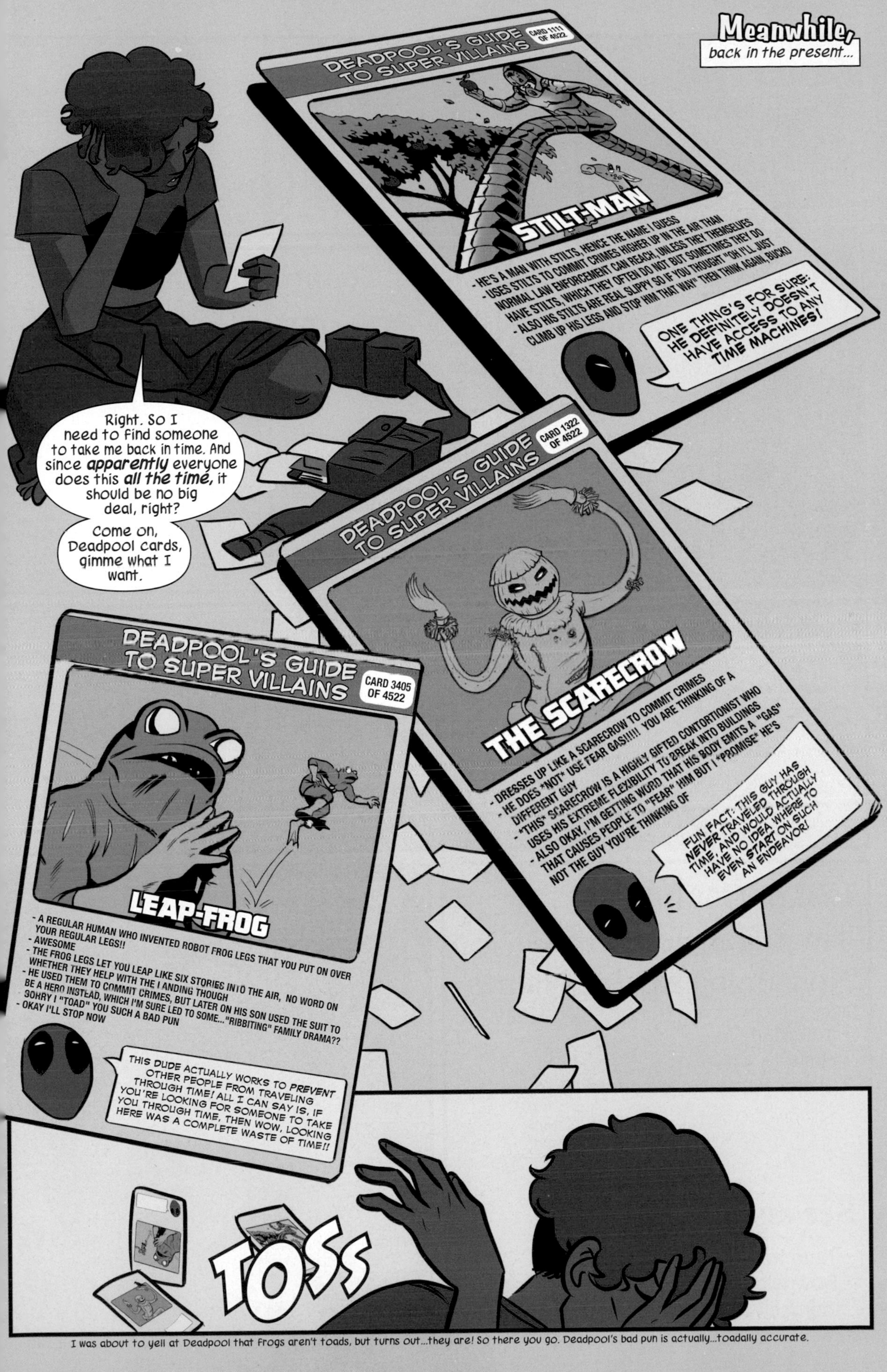
Meanwhile, back in the present...
DEADPOOL'S GUIDE TO SUPER VILLAINS
CARD 1111 OF 4522
STILT-MAN
- HE'S A MAN WITH STILTS, HENCE THE NAME I GUESS
- USES STILTS TO COMMIT CRIMES HIGHER UP IN THE AIR THAN NORMAL LAW ENFORCEMENT CAN REACH, UNLESS THEY THEMSELVES HAVE STILTS, WHICH THEY OFTEN DO NOT BUT SOMETIMES THEY DO
- ALSO HIS STILTS ARE REAL SLIPPY SO IF YOU THOUGHT "OH I'LL JUST CLIMB UP HIS LEGS AND STOP HIM THAT WAY" THEN THINK AGAIN, BUCKO
ONE THING'S FOR SURE: HE DEFINITELY DOESN'T HAVE ACCESS TO ANY TIME MACHINES!
Right. So I need to find someone to take me back in time. And since apparently everyone does this all the time, it should be no big deal, right?
Come on, Deadpool cards, gimme what I want.
DEADPOOL'S GUIDE TO SUPER VILLAINS
CARD 1322 OF 4522
THE SCARECROW
- DRESSES UP LIKE A SCARECROW TO COMMIT CRIMES
- HE DOES *NOT* USE FEAR GAS!!!!! YOU ARE THINKING OF A DIFFERENT GUY
- *THIS* SCARECROW IS A HIGHLY GIFTED CONTORTIONIST WHO USES HIS EXTREME FLEXIBILITY TO BREAK INTO BUILDINGS
- ALSO OKAY, I'M GETTING WORD THAT HIS BODY EMITS A "GAS" THAT CAUSES PEOPLE TO "FEAR" HIM BUT I *PROMISE* HE'S NOT THE GUY YOU'RE THINKING OF
FUN FACT: THIS GUY HAS NEVER TRAVELED THROUGH TIME, AND WOULD ACTUALLY HAVE NO IDEA WHERE TO EVEN START ON SUCH AN ENDEAVOR!
DEADPOOL'S GUIDE TO SUPER VILLAINS
CARD 3405 OF 4522
LEAP-FROG
- A REGULAR HUMAN WHO INVENTED ROBOT FROG LEGS THAT YOU PUT ON OVER YOUR REGULAR LEGS!!
- AWESOME
- THE FROG LEGS LET YOU LEAP LIKE SIX STORIES INTO THE AIR, NO WORD ON WHETHER THEY HELP WITH THE LANDING THOUGH
- HE USED THEM TO COMMIT CRIMES, BUT LATER ON HIS SON USED THE SUIT TO BE A HERO INSTEAD, WHICH I'M SURE LED TO SOME..."RIBBITING" FAMILY DRAMA??
SORRY I "TOAD" YOU SUCH A BAD PUN
- OKAY I'LL STOP NOW
THIS DUDE ACTUALLY WORKS TO PREVENT OTHER PEOPLE FROM TRAVELING THROUGH TIME! ALL I CAN SAY IS, IF YOU'RE LOOKING FOR SOMEONE TO TAKE YOU THROUGH TIME, THEN WOW, LOOKING HERE WAS A COMPLETE WASTE OF TIME!!
TOSS

I was about to yell at Deadpool that frogs aren't toads, but turns out...they are! So there you go. Deadpool's bad pun is actually...toadally accurate.

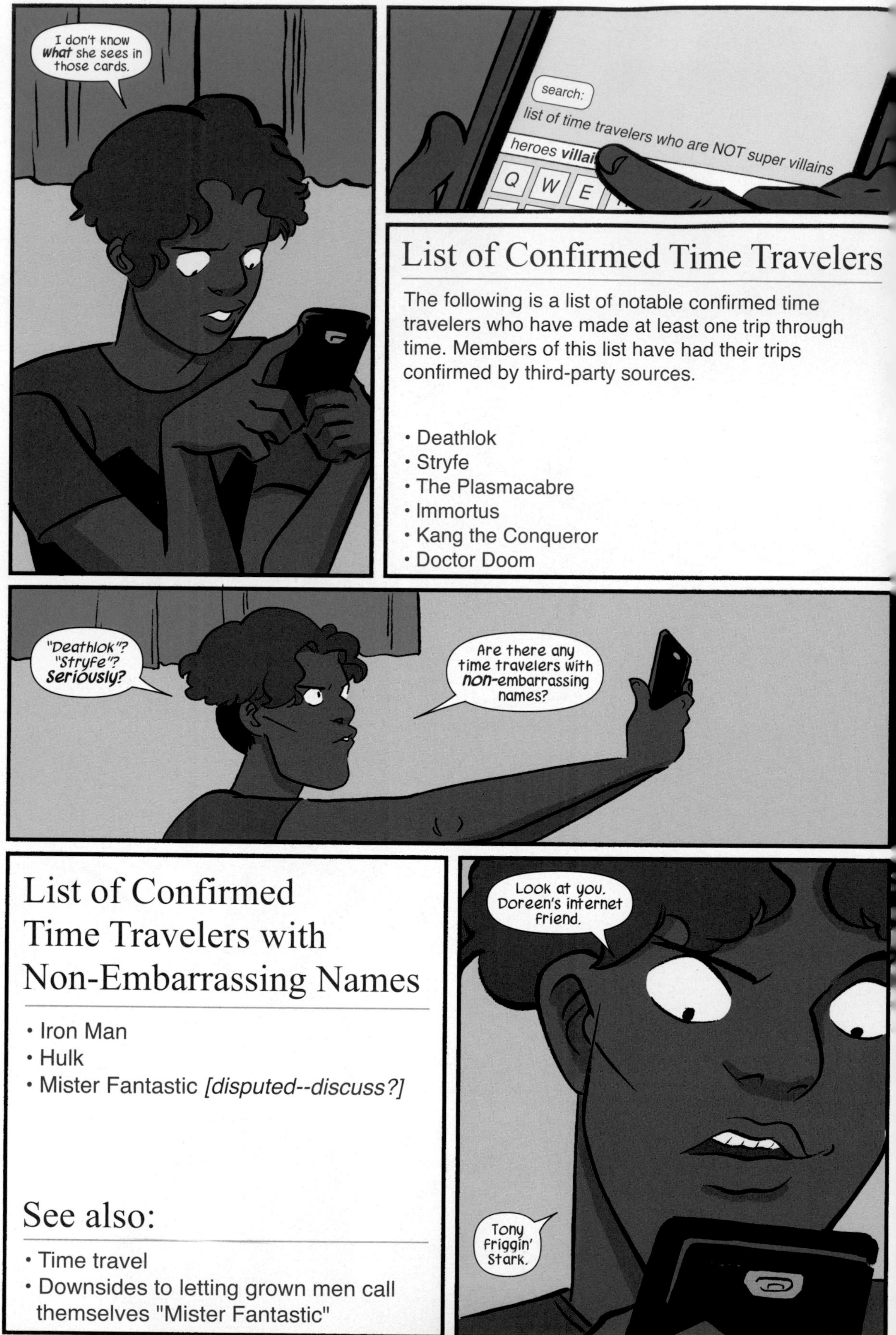
I don't know *what* she sees in those cards.
search:
list of time travelers who are NOT super villains
heroes villai
Q W E
List of Confirmed Time Travelers
The following is a list of notable confirmed time travelers who have made at least one trip through time. Members of this list have had their trips confirmed by third-party sources.
• Deathlok
• Stryfe
• The Plasmacabre
• Immortus
• Kang the Conqueror
• Doctor Doom
"Deathlok"? "Stryfe"? *Seriously?*
Are there any time travelers with *non*-embarrassing names?
List of Confirmed Time Travelers with Non-Embarrassing Names
• Iron Man
• Hulk
• Mister Fantastic *[disputed--discuss?]*
See also:
• Time travel
• Downsides to letting grown men call themselves "Mister Fantastic"
Look at you. Doreen's internet friend.
Tony friggin' Stark.

Please, *"Mister Fantastic"* was my father. Call me...actually, no, *"Mister Fantastic"* is fine, and on second thought that's absolutely a name I would like everyone to know me by.

Shortly...

Tony--

STARK

STARK

Shortly...

--friggin'--

Oh it is SO on now.

Shortly...

SLA

--STARK!!

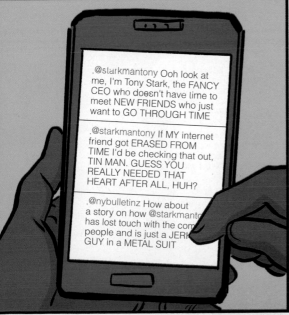

.@starkmantony Ooh look at me, I'm Tony Stark, the FANCY CEO who doesn't have time to meet NEW FRIENDS who just want to GO THROUGH TIME

.@starkmantony If MY internet friend got ERASED FROM TIME I'd be checking that out, TIN MAN. GUESS YOU REALLY NEEDED THAT HEART AFTER ALL, HUH?

.@nybulletinz How about a story on how @starkmanto has lost touch with the com people and is just a JER GUY in a METAL SUIT

KRA-KA-KOOM

Tony's gonna check his mentions later on and be like, "WOW I don't even know who this person is, oh well."

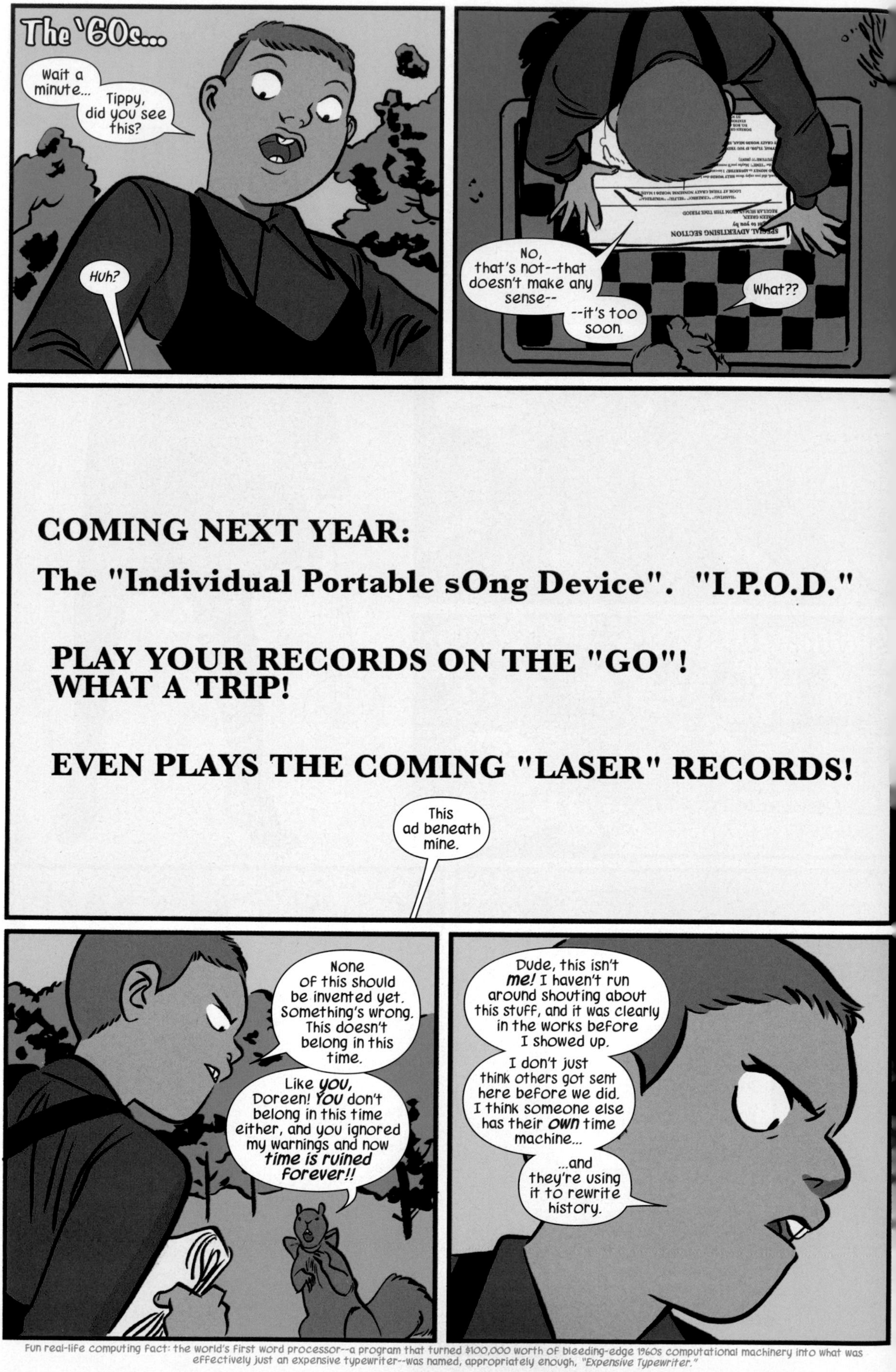
The '60s...
Wait a minute...
Tippy, did you see this?
Huh?
No, that's not--that doesn't make any sense--
--it's too soon.
What??
COMING NEXT YEAR:
The "Individual Portable sOng Device". "I.P.O.D."
PLAY YOUR RECORDS ON THE "GO"! WHAT A TRIP!
EVEN PLAYS THE COMING "LASER" RECORDS!
This ad beneath mine.
None of this should be invented yet. Something's wrong. This doesn't belong in this time.
Like *you*, Doreen! *You* don't belong in this time either, and you ignored my warnings and now *time is ruined forever!!*
Dude, this isn't *me!* I haven't run around shouting about this stuff, and it was clearly in the works before I showed up.
I don't just think others got sent here before we did. I think someone else has their *own* time machine...
...and they're using it to rewrite history.

Fun real-life computing fact: the world's first word processor--a program that turned $100,000 worth of bleeding-edge 1960s computational machinery into what was effectively just an expensive typewriter--was named, appropriately enough, *"Expensive Typewriter."*

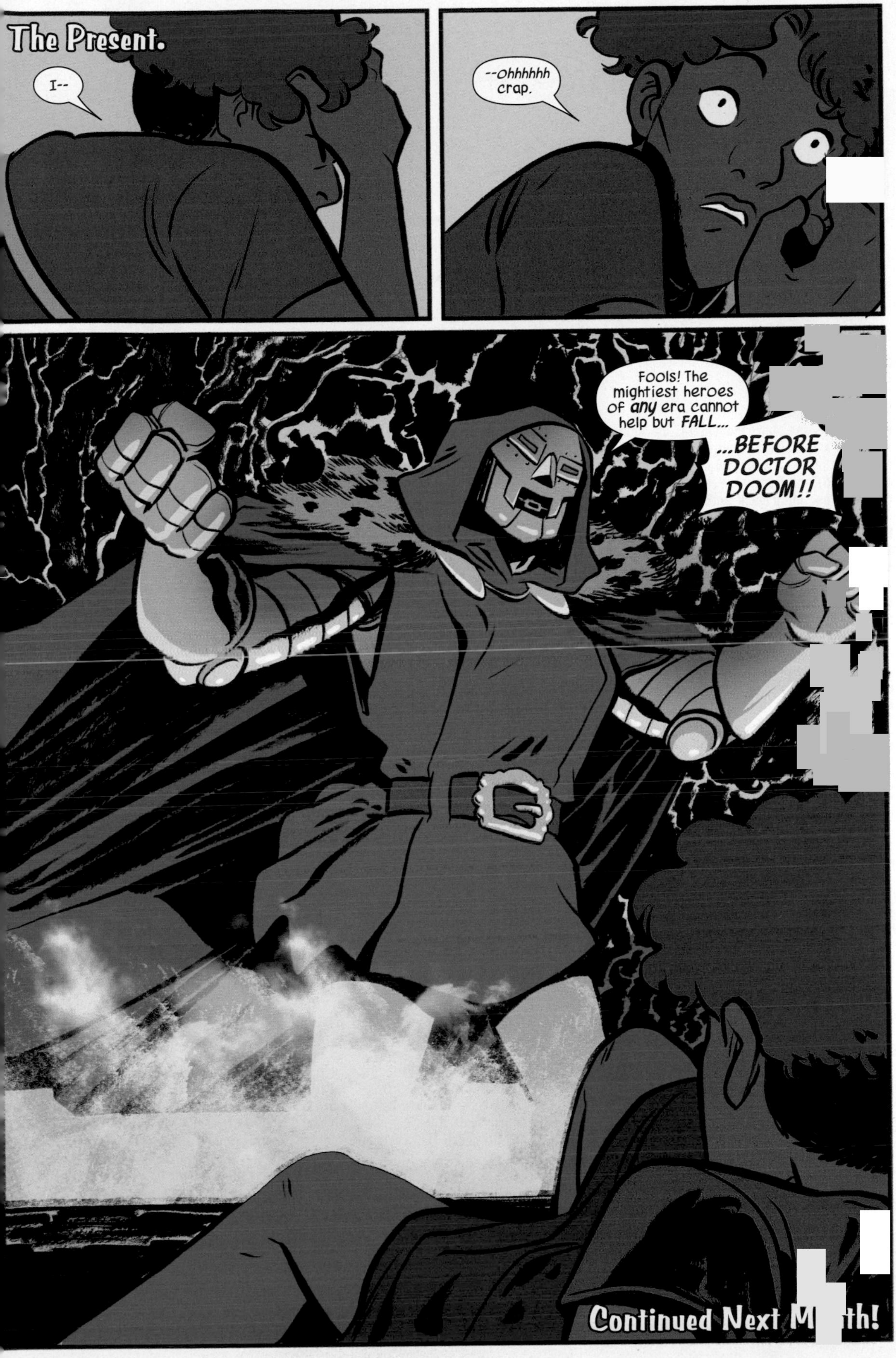
The Present.
I--
--Ohhhhhh crap.
Fools! The mightiest heroes of *any* era cannot help but *FALL*...
...BEFORE DOCTOR DOOM!!
Continued Next

Letters From Nuts

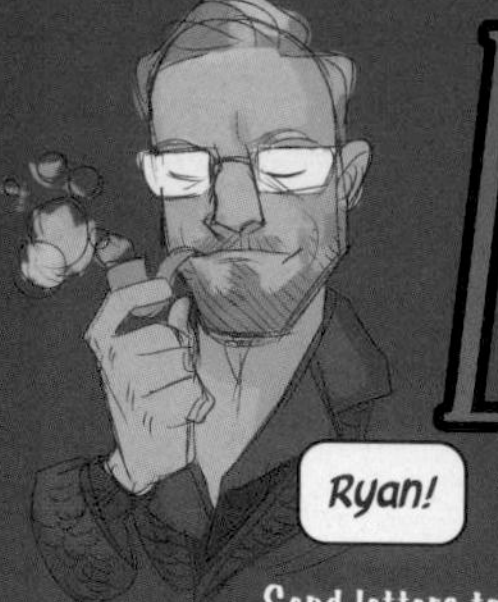
Ryan!

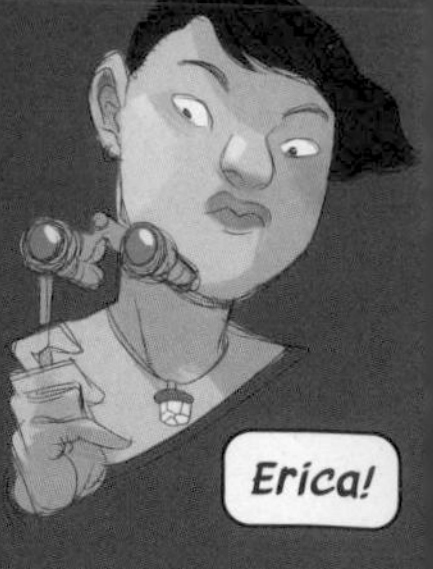
Erica!

Send letters to mheroes@marvel.com or 135 W 50th St, 7th Floor, New York, NY 10020 (Please mark "OKAY TO PRINT")

Hey everybody! No time for a fancy intro--let's dive right in!

Q: You know how the movement of a squirrel is very jerky? Since it is hard to show movement in comics, I was wondering if Doreen is jerky like a squirrel when she moves (proportional speed)? Erica's pencils give me the feeling that Doreen has a lot of energy.

Benjamin J.

RYAN: I see her movement as being more quick than jerky! Squirrels can also be indecisive (at least when caught in the middle of the road) and Doreen's pretty good at not changing her mind back and forth over and over, so while I think it's good that she's got PARTIALLY squirrel blood, I'm glad it's not 100%. Hence her slogan, "50% Squirrel, 100% Girl!"

ERICA: I don't think she's that jerky. Unless she hasn't gotten enough sleep. Crimefighting and being a full time student makes for a difficult work-life balance, guys! Stay hydrated!

P.S. Squirrels run in a jerky zigzag to confuse predators. And the twitchy tail is to silently warn others of danger.

Hey everyone! I had heard about squirrel girl before but I didn't know much about her. When I saw this on marvel unlimited, I decided "what the heck, I'll read". Great decision on my part if I do say so my self. I absolutely love her! She's awesome as a super hero and she's awesome as a person. The way she's drawn makes her look so adorable! I have a few questions.

1. What's the point of having a secret identity if she doesn't wear a mask? Not hating though 2. How did she get her powers? (Is her tail real?) 3. How did she and Tippy meet?

Love the comic! Keep up the good work!

Harley Massey
Harlingen, Texas

R: Thanks Harley! Really stoked you like the comic. I read it on Marvel Unlimited too and even commented there saying "I'm the guy who wrote this comic and I give it FIVE STARS" but I don't think anyone reads the comments there, so now I'm mentioning it here in the letters page because I crave attention.

1) As she says, the most identifying feature of Squirrel Girl is her tail, and Doreen Green CLEARLY has zero tails. That's a pretty good alibi, if you ask me!

2) This is touched on a bit in our new #1 issue last month (which is kind of unfair for me to say, because you wrote this before that issue was out! HOW COULD YOU HAVE KNOWN?) so I'm in the position of answering a question you may already know the answer to! Anyway, for anyone who isn't us, the answer to "how did she get her powers" is "over time, I guess".

E: 1) As someone who grew up watching *Sailor Moon*, I have no problem with this. Also what Ryan said.

3) In a tree.

The other day, my wife and I were sitting out on the porch enjoying a sunny afternoon. My wife was telling me of how she almost ran her vehicle off of the road in order to avoid a squirrel that had charged out of the woods and into the direct path of her car. I quipped, "Perhaps the squirrel had intended to cause you to wreck. Maybe it was an incarnation of Ratatoskr bringing both life and destruction." Naturally, she asked for clarification. "Ratatoskr is a squirrel from Norse mythology that represents the continual cycle of rebirth. It travels up and down the world tree as a sort of messenger." Of course, she had to validate this for herself, and was promptly viewing the Wikipedia page on her phone . "How did you know this?" she asked, continuing to read. "I am well-learned, Jeanie. I am working on my Master's degree, after all," I responded.

Suddenly, I was the smartest man in the world, and she gave me that look that at once conveyed respect, love, and "hey handsome." Unfortunately, my feeling of pride could not last. Since Ratatoskr hasn't really made its mark on popular culture, Wikipedia finds it necessary to mention that the Marvel comic, The Unbeatable Squirrel Girl, makes reference to the demigod in issues 7 and 8. That beautiful look on my wife's face suddenly morphed into an expression that I still do not understand. Was it surprise? Was it confusion? I may never know, but what I do know is that your comic has taught me much that I can use to impress individuals who are not as quite as inquisitive of my lovely wife. Touché, Wikipedia. Touché, indeed.

Adam Felty
Virginia

P.S. Did you know that the English word "squirrel" comes from the Greek word "skiouros"? It means "shadow-tailed," which gives me an unbeatable story idea. What about you? Trust me, Greek is part of my major... but I found this online!

R: Wikipedia, you could've had Adam's back and made him look really smart in front of a loved one!! INSTEAD you outed him as ... a reader of quality comics entertainment from which he learns about the world around him, allowing him to apply that knowledge as situations warrant? That's still a pretty great person to be, actually. Tell your wife that your comic book said you're a good guy who is probably still worth marrying!

E: Here are more squirrel facts to dazzle your friends and loved ones with and to make your enemies cower at the might of your intellect: 1. Did you know that a squirrel's rear feet can turn 180 degrees? It's how they climb down trees! 2. There are 265 species of squirrel worldwide, 44 of which are flying squirrels. 3. The squirrel is the Native American symbol for preparation, trust and thriftiness. 4. Squirrels were introduced into major urban parks by PEOPLE. In the 1870's they were one of several animals introduced into places like Central Park to create more of a natural atmosphere. They were a symbol of rural life, but also diurnal animals that coexist well with humans. 5. Squirrels are opportunistic omnivores and a diet of mostly nuts is actually bad for them because nuts are fairly fatty.

Greetings squirrel squad,

I was singing the Squirrel Girl theme song on my way to work earlier today (as I'm sure most of us do) and I couldn't help but wonder about one of the lines; "Like a human squirrel she enjoys fighting crime" Does this mean that as is characteristic of human squirrels Squirrel Girl enjoys fighting crime? Or is it that she enjoys fighting crime in a human squirrel like way? Or is she like a human squirrel and also unrelated to that she enjoys fighting crime? I suppose if it was that last one it would say who rather than she. However all three options are well within the plausible range given the context. This problem has really been gnawing at me so I'd much appreciate if you could clear it up for me. I also had a question regarding the Deadpool super villain cards. There are over 4,000 cards how is Squirrel Girl able to carry and quickly retrieve the correct card so quickly? Does she have squirrel hoarding powers?

Thanks in advance for your answers and thanks also for writing such a great comic.

JB

R: I like the implication that ALL human squirrels would enjoy fighting crime, so that's the one I'm going with! But you could also change it to "Like a human girl she enjoys fighting crime" and it still scans, and as I have not met any human girls who have specifically told me that they DON'T enjoy fighting crime, we're probably good.

And as for Squirrel Girl having over 4000 cards to carry around, that is absolutely a use of her super squirrel hoarding powers, which makes total scientific sense and has no problems associated with it whatsoever!

See y'all next month!

Attention, Squirrel Scouts! Make sure to check out our production blog, **unbeatablesquirrelgirl.tumblr.com**, where we post behind-the-scenes stuff on how the book gets made, along with all sorts of cool things *you* make: fanart, cosplay, whatever!

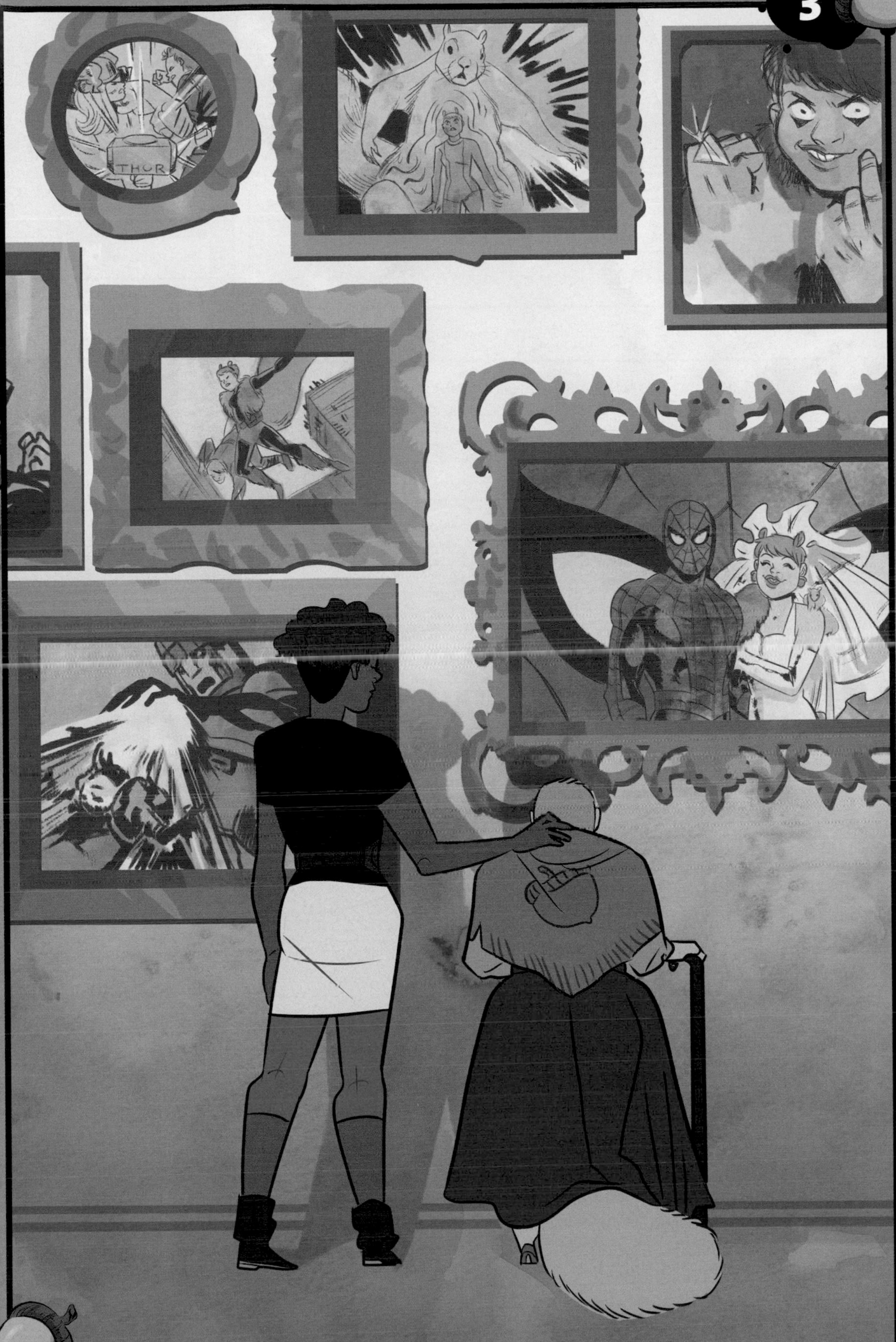
THOR

Doreen Green isn't just a second-year computer science student: she secretly also has all the powers of both squirrel and girl! She uses her amazing abilities to fight crime **and** be as awesome as possible. You know her as...**The Unbeatable Squirrel Girl**. Find out what she's been up to, with...

Squirrel Girl *in a nutshell*

search! 🔍

#doctordoom

#wikipedia

#doomipedia

#timetravel

#rhymetravel

#thymetravel

Ryan North - writer
Erica Henderson - artist
Doc Shaner - trading card artist
Rico Renzi - color artist
Travis Lanham - guest letterer
Erica Henderson - cover artist
John Tyler Christopher;
Matt Waite - variant cover artists
Special Thanks to **Lissa Pattillo, CK Russell,** and **Michael Wiggam**
Chris Robinson - asst. editor
Wil Moss - editor
Tom Brevoort - executive editor
Axel Alonso - editor in chief
Joe Quesada - chief creative officer
Dan Buckley - publisher
Alan Fine - exec. producer

Nancy W. @sewwiththeflo
Nobody believes me, but before this morning Mew and I had a roommate. Then she got erased from time, and now nobody remembers her but me.

Nancy W. @sewwiththeflo
And she was AWESOME and SWEET and SMART and GOOD AT FIGHTS ACTUALLY, and it sucks without her.

Nancy W. @sewwiththeflo
RT if your roommate got erased from time and nobody remembers her.

Nancy W. @sewwiththeflo
See? That's proof she's gone, right there. She would've AT LEAST faved that.

Tony Stark @starkmantony ✔
Do you ever get the sense that the universe is missing something? Like there's something that should be there and just--isn't.

Nancy W. @sewwiththeflo
@starkmantony Whoa whoa whoa--you remember her too? I thought I was the only one!

Tony Stark @starkmantony ✔
Like you woke up today and even though you could SWEAR everything was the same, you still feel like something very important is absent...

Nancy W. @sewwiththeflo
@starkmantony Yes! Doreen!!

Tony Stark @starkmantony ✔
...and while though some part of you knows that thing--whatever it was--might've been kind of a pain sometimes, you still miss it?

Nancy W. @sewwiththeflo
@starkmantony You and her do have a special relationship. Thank you! I felt like I was going crazy. So what's our next move, Tony?

Tony Stark @starkmantony ✔
Because I too had that feeling...UNTIL I tried the new consumer-level #IronManicure home beauty treatment kit, available TODAY!

Tony Stark @starkmantony ✔
Your hands are too precious for just any manicure kit. Take the Stark #IronManicure Challenge: satisfaction guaranteed or your money back!

Tony Stark @starkmantony ✔
You'll feel like a Stark with our red-and-gold nail file, clipper, and angled cuticle nipper. All thanks to the new #IronManicure kit!

Nancy W. @sewwiththeflo
@starkmantony blocked

HULK @HULKYSMASHY
@starkmantony HULK WONDERS IF MANICURE KIT COMES IN GREEN AND PURPLE BECAUSE HULK THINK THOSE COLORS ARE MUCH PRETTIER

Nancy W. @sewwiththeflo
So here I am, minding my own business, when there's a huge blast of sound and light and I get knocked over. Guess who did it?

Nancy W. @sewwiththeflo
Doctor Doom. Doctor DOOM, friends and neighbors. Ruler of Latveria, ambassador, metal-suit wearer. Big as life.

Nancy W. @sewwiththeflo
So yeah anyway I should really get off my phone now because he's RIGHT HERE

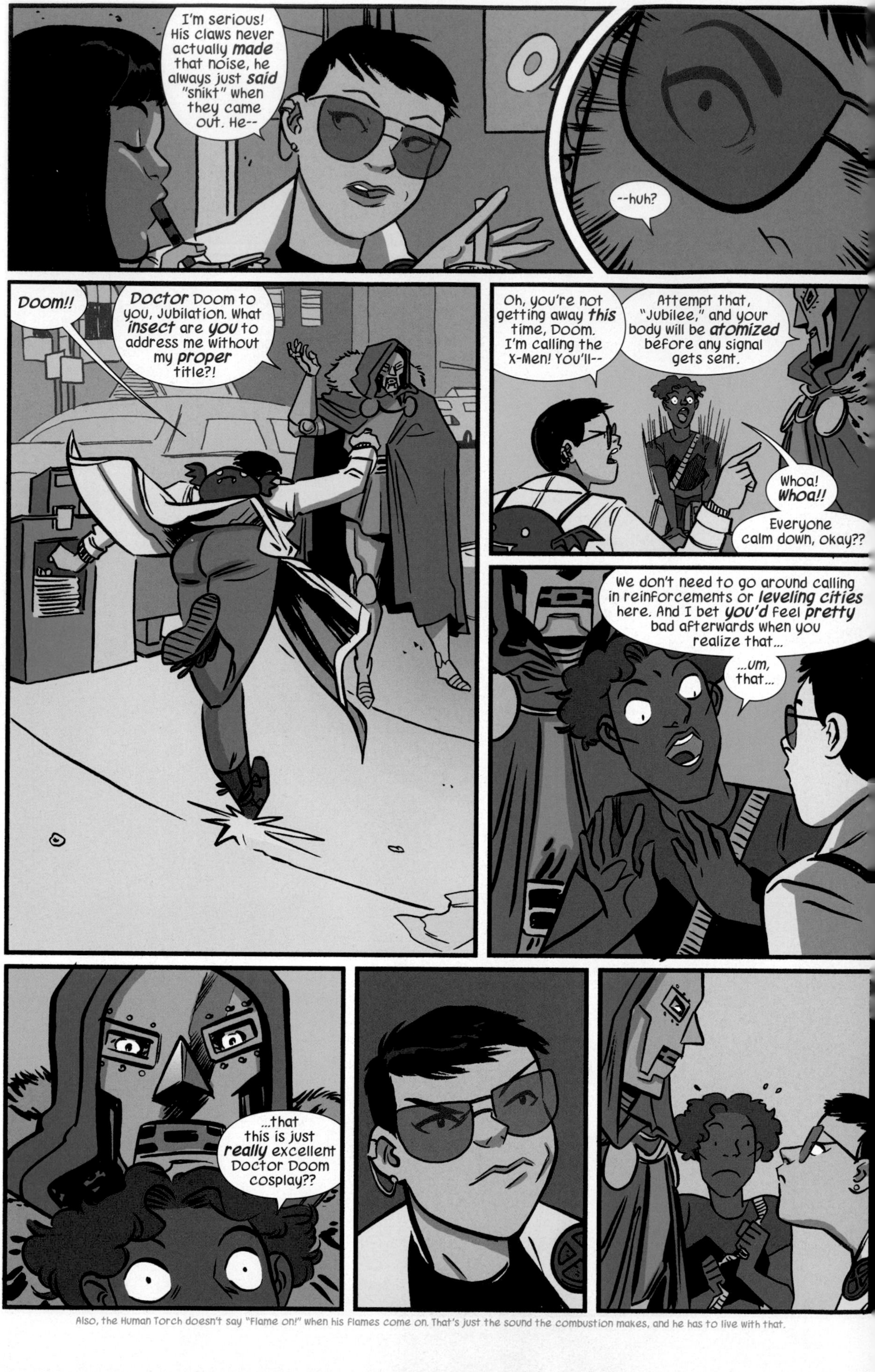
I'm serious! His claws never actually made that noise, he always just said "snikt" when they came out. He--
--huh?
Doom!!
Doctor Doom to you, Jubilation. What insect are you to address me without my proper title?!
Oh, you're not getting away this time, Doom. I'm calling the X-Men! You'll--
Attempt that, "Jubilee," and your body will be atomized before any signal gets sent.
Whoa! Whoa!!
Everyone calm down, okay??
We don't need to go around calling in reinforcements or leveling cities here. And I bet you'd feel pretty bad afterwards when you realize that...
...um, that...
...that this is just really excellent Doctor Doom cosplay??

Also, the Human Torch doesn't say "Flame on!" when his flames come on. That's just the sound the combustion makes, and he has to live with that.

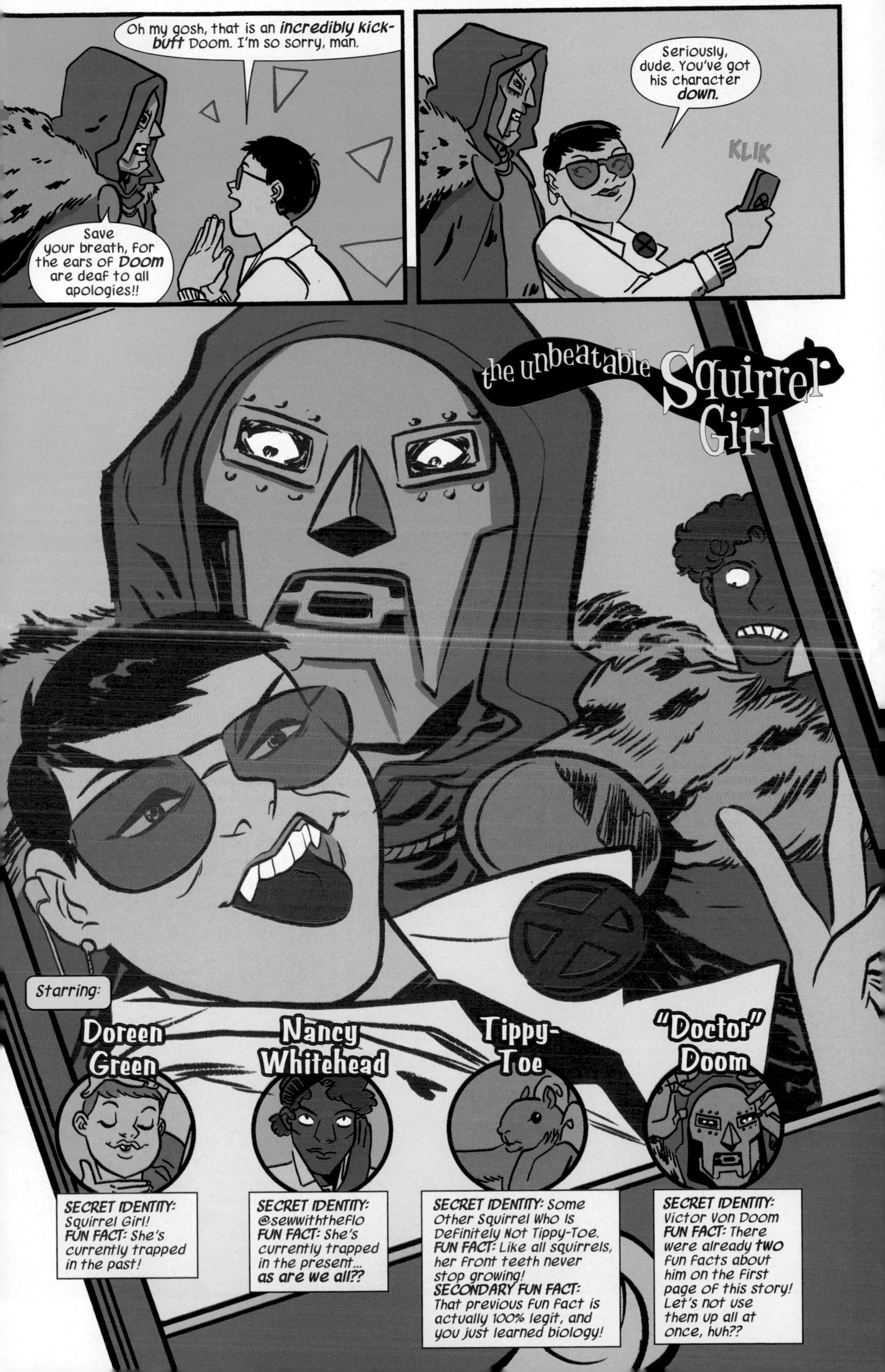

Oh my gosh, that is an incredibly kick-butt Doom. I'm so sorry, man.
Save your breath, for the ears of Doom are deaf to all apologies!!
Seriously, dude. You've got his character down.
KLIK
the unbeatable Squirrel Girl
Starring:
Doreen Green
SECRET IDENTITY: Squirrel Girl! FUN FACT: She's currently trapped in the past!
Nancy Whitehead
SECRET IDENTITY: @sewwiththeflo FUN FACT: She's currently trapped in the present... as are we all??
Tippy-Toe
SECRET IDENTITY: Some Other Squirrel Who Is Definitely Not Tippy-Toe. FUN FACT: Like all squirrels, her front teeth never stop growing! SECONDARY FUN FACT: That previous fun fact is actually 100% legit, and you just learned biology!
"Doctor" Doom
SECRET IDENTITY: Victor Von Doom FUN FACT: There were already two fun facts about him on the first page of this story! Let's not use them up all at once, huh??

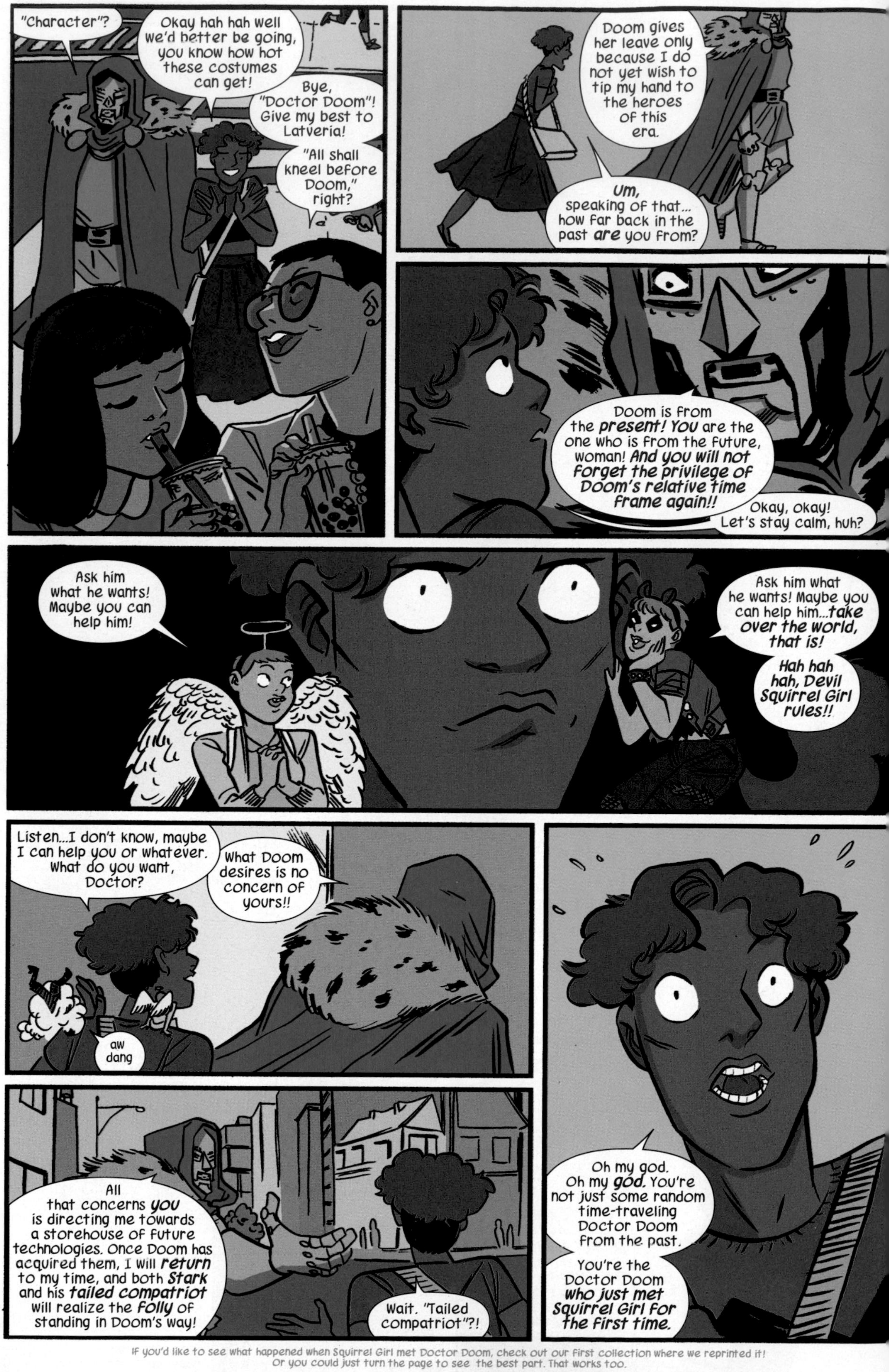
"Character"?
Okay hah hah well we'd better be going, you know how hot these costumes can get!
Bye, "Doctor Doom"! Give my best to Latveria!
"All shall kneel before Doom," right?
Doom gives her leave only because I do not yet wish to tip my hand to the heroes of this era.
Um, speaking of that... how far back in the past are you from?
Doom is from the present! You are the one who is from the future, woman! And you will not forget the privilege of Doom's relative time frame again!!
Okay, okay! Let's stay calm, huh?
Ask him what he wants! Maybe you can help him!
Ask him what he wants! Maybe you can help him...take over the world, that is!
Hah hah hah, Devil Squirrel Girl rules!!
Listen...I don't know, maybe I can help you or whatever. What do you want, Doctor?
What Doom desires is no concern of yours!!
aw dang
All that concerns you is directing me towards a storehouse of future technologies. Once Doom has acquired them, I will return to my time, and both Stark and his tailed compatriot will realize the folly of standing in Doom's way!
Wait. "Tailed compatriot"?!
Oh my god. Oh my god. You're not just some random time-traveling Doctor Doom from the past.
You're the Doctor Doom who just met Squirrel Girl for the first time.

If you'd like to see what happened when Squirrel Girl met Doctor Doom, check out our first collection where we reprinted it!
Or you could just turn the page to see the best part. That works too.

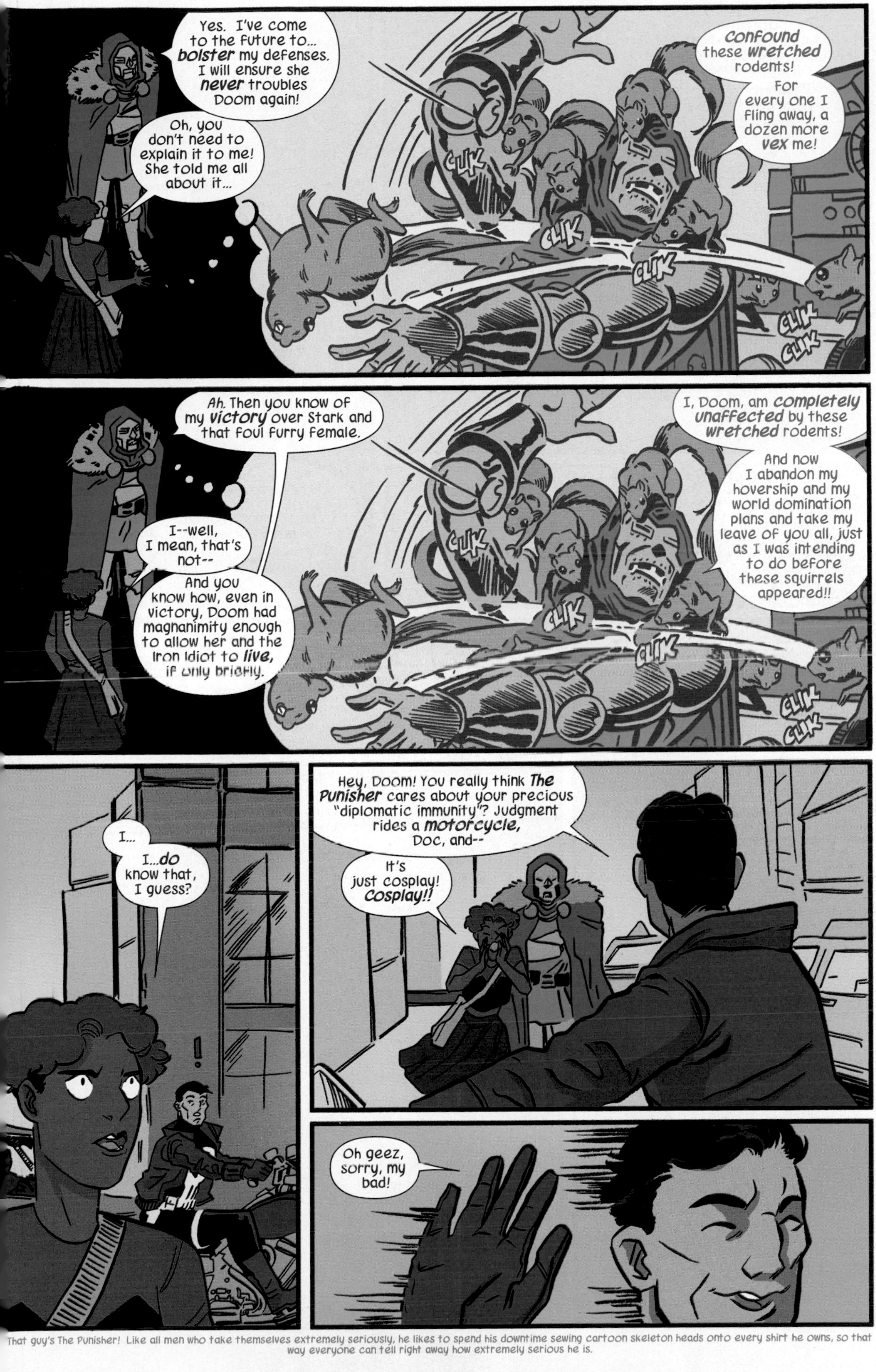
Yes. I've come to the future to... bolster my defenses. I will ensure she never troubles Doom again!
Confound these wretched rodents!
For every one I fling away, a dozen more vex me!
Oh, you don't need to explain it to me! She told me all about it...
CLIK
CLIK
CLIK
CLIK
CLIK
CLIK
Ah. Then you know of my victory over Stark and that foul furry female.
I, Doom, am completely unaffected by these wretched rodents!
And now I abandon my hoversship and my world domination plans and take my leave of you all, just as I was intending to do before these squirrels appeared!!
I--well, I mean, that's not--
And you know how, even in victory, Doom had magnanimity enough to allow her and the Iron Idiot to live, if only briefly.
CLIK
CLIK
CLIK
CLIK
CLIK
CLIK
I...
I...do know that, I guess?
!
Hey, Doom! You really think The Punisher cares about your precious "diplomatic immunity"? Judgment rides a motorcycle, Doc, and--
It's just cosplay! Cosplay!!
Oh geez, sorry, my bad!

That guy's The Punisher! Like all men who take themselves extremely seriously, he likes to spend his downtime sewing cartoon skeleton heads onto every shirt he owns, so that way everyone can tell right away how extremely serious he is.

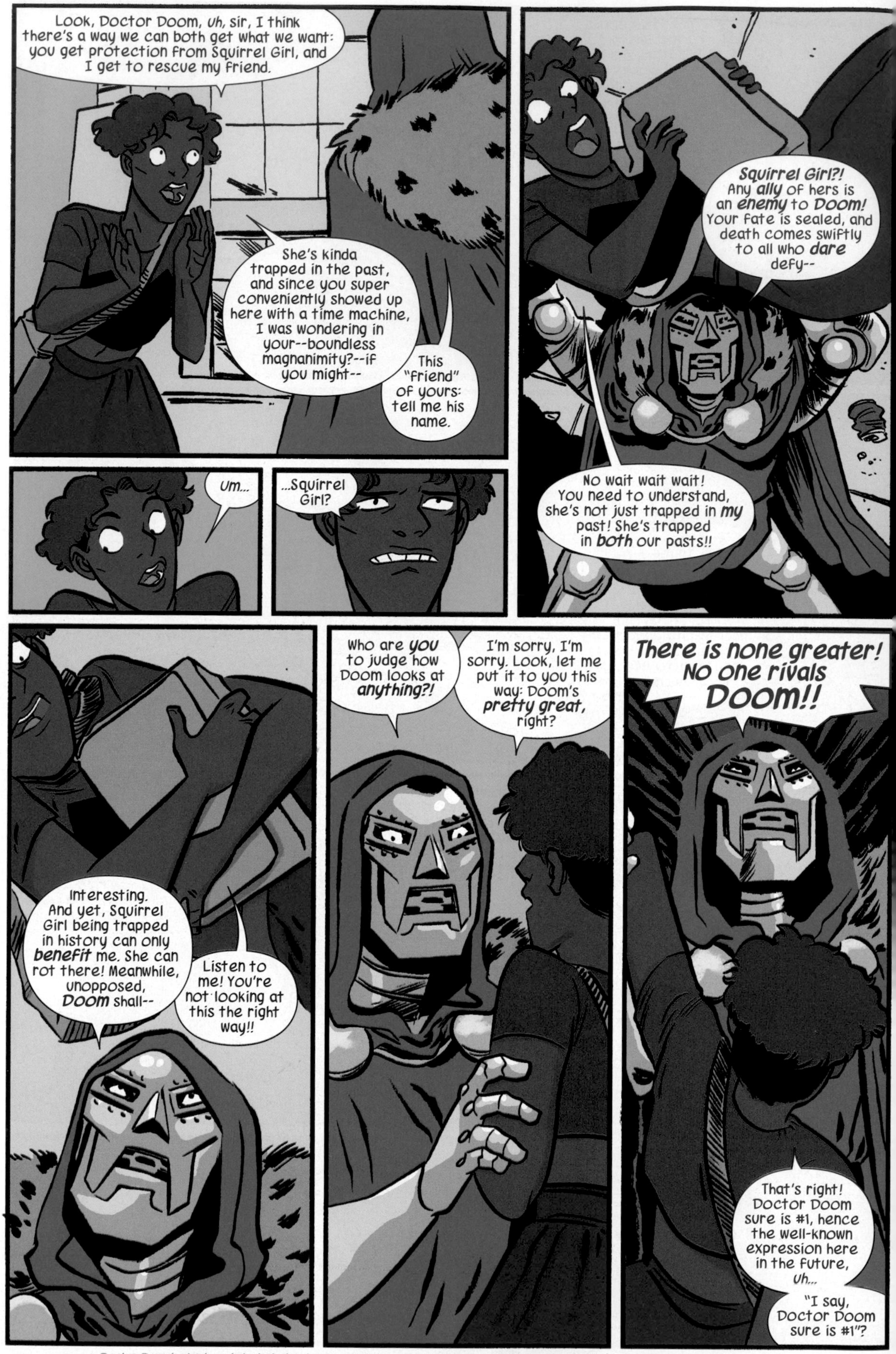

Look, Doctor Doom, uh, sir, I think there's a way we can both get what we want: you get protection from Squirrel Girl, and I get to rescue my friend.
She's kinda trapped in the past, and since you super conveniently showed up here with a time machine, I was wondering in your--boundless magnanimity?--if you might--
This "friend" of yours: tell me his name.
Squirrel Girl?! Any ally of hers is an enemy to Doom! Your fate is sealed, and death comes swiftly to all who dare defy--
Um...
...Squirrel Girl?
No wait wait wait! You need to understand, she's not just trapped in my past! She's trapped in both our pasts!!
Interesting. And yet, Squirrel Girl being trapped in history can only benefit me. She can rot there! Meanwhile, unopposed, Doom shall--
Listen to me! You're not looking at this the right way!!
Who are you to judge how Doom looks at anything?!
I'm sorry, I'm sorry. Look, let me put it to you this way: Doom's pretty great, right?
There is none greater! No one rivals DOOM!!
That's right! Doctor Doom sure is #1, hence the well-known expression here in the future, uh...
"I say, Doctor Doom sure is #1"?

Doctor Doom's plan here is to just pick Nancy up and throw her into the sun. As far as plans go, it's...pretty credible for him, actually.

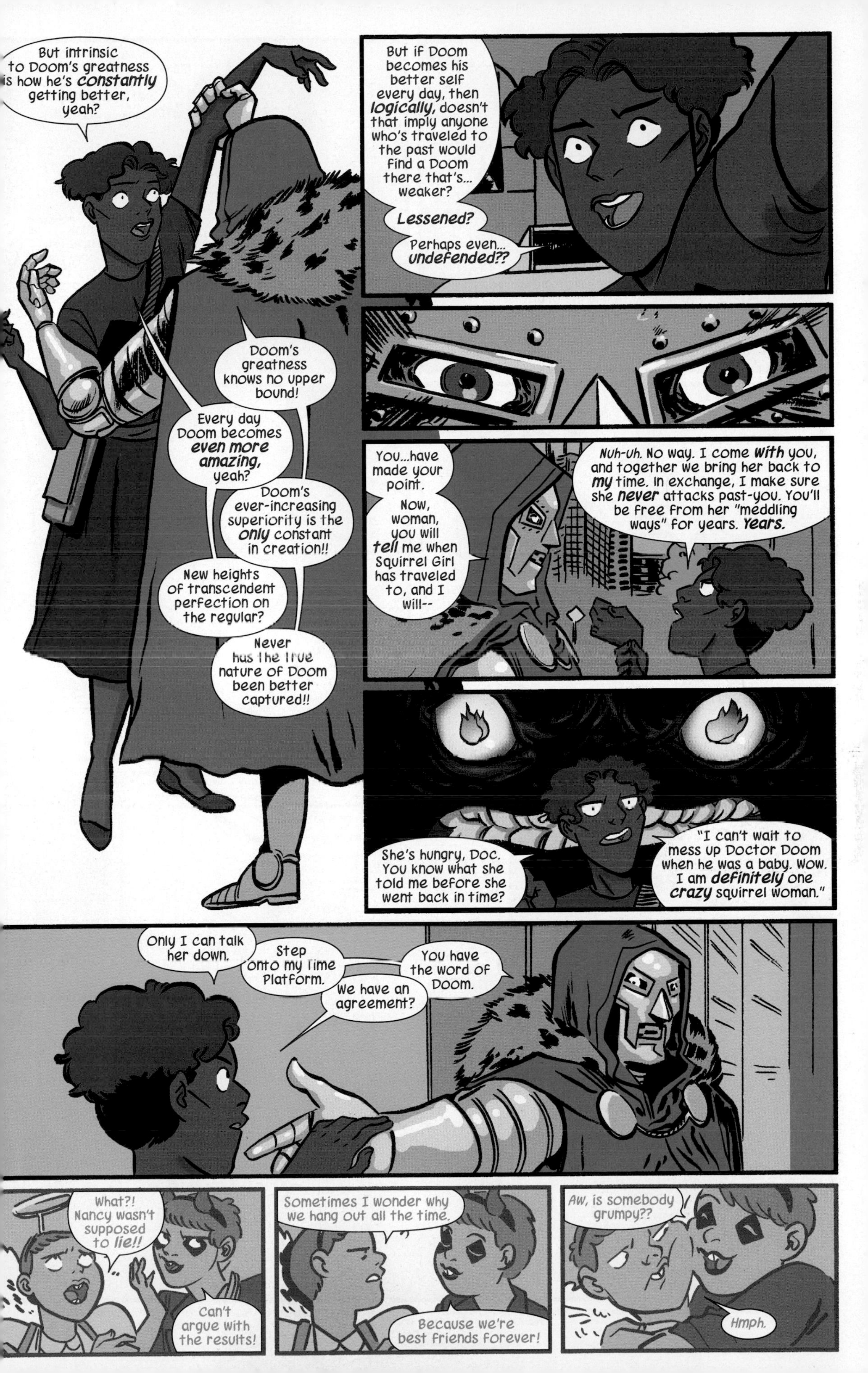
But intrinsic to Doom's greatness is how he's constantly getting better, yeah?
Doom's greatness knows no upper bound!
Every day Doom becomes even more amazing, yeah?
Doom's ever-increasing superiority is the only constant in creation!!
New heights of transcendent perfection on the regular?
Never has the true nature of Doom been better captured!!
But if Doom becomes his better self every day, then logically, doesn't that imply anyone who's traveled to the past would find a Doom there that's... weaker?
Lessened?
Perhaps even... undefended??
You...have made your point.
Now, woman, you will tell me when Squirrel Girl has traveled to, and I will--
Nuh-uh. No way. I come with you, and together we bring her back to my time. In exchange, I make sure she never attacks past-you. You'll be free from her "meddling ways" for years. Years.
She's hungry, Doc. You know what she told me before she went back in time?
"I can't wait to mess up Doctor Doom when he was a baby. Wow. I am definitely one crazy squirrel woman."
Only I can talk her down.
Step onto my Time Platform.
We have an agreement?
You have the word of Doom.
What?! Nancy wasn't supposed to lie!!
Can't argue with the results!
Sometimes I wonder why we hang out all the time.
Because we're best friends forever!
Aw, is somebody grumpy??
Hmph.

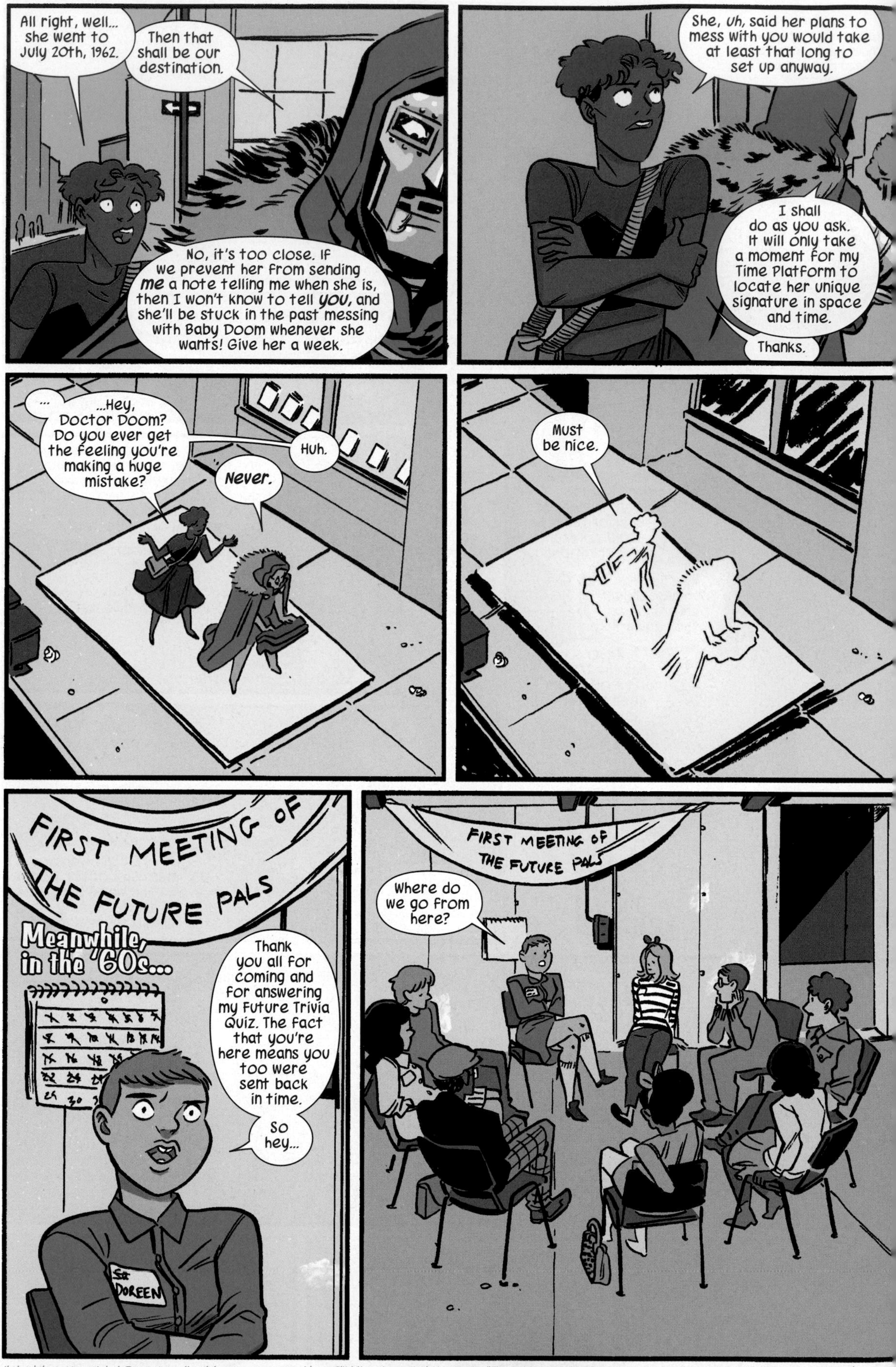
All right, well... she went to July 20th, 1962.
Then that shall be our destination.
No, it's too close. If we prevent her from sending **me** a note telling me when she is, then I won't know to tell **you**, and she'll be stuck in the past messing with Baby Doom whenever she wants! Give her a week.
She, *uh*, said her plans to mess with you would take at least that long to set up anyway.
I shall do as you ask. It will only take a moment for my Time Platform to locate her unique signature in space and time.
Thanks.
...
...Hey, Doctor Doom? Do you ever get the feeling you're making a huge mistake?
Huh.
Never.
Must be nice.
FIRST MEETING OF THE FUTURE PALS
Meanwhile, in the '60s...
Thank you all for coming and for answering my Future Trivia Quiz. The fact that you're here means you too were sent back in time.
So hey...
DOREEN
FIRST MEETING OF THE FUTURE PALS
Where do we go from here?

Nobody's gonna ask but Doreen really wishes someone would, so I'll bite: she called this group "The Future Pals" because they're all from the Future, and she also hopes that in time they'll all become pals. *Pretty adorable, Doreen.*

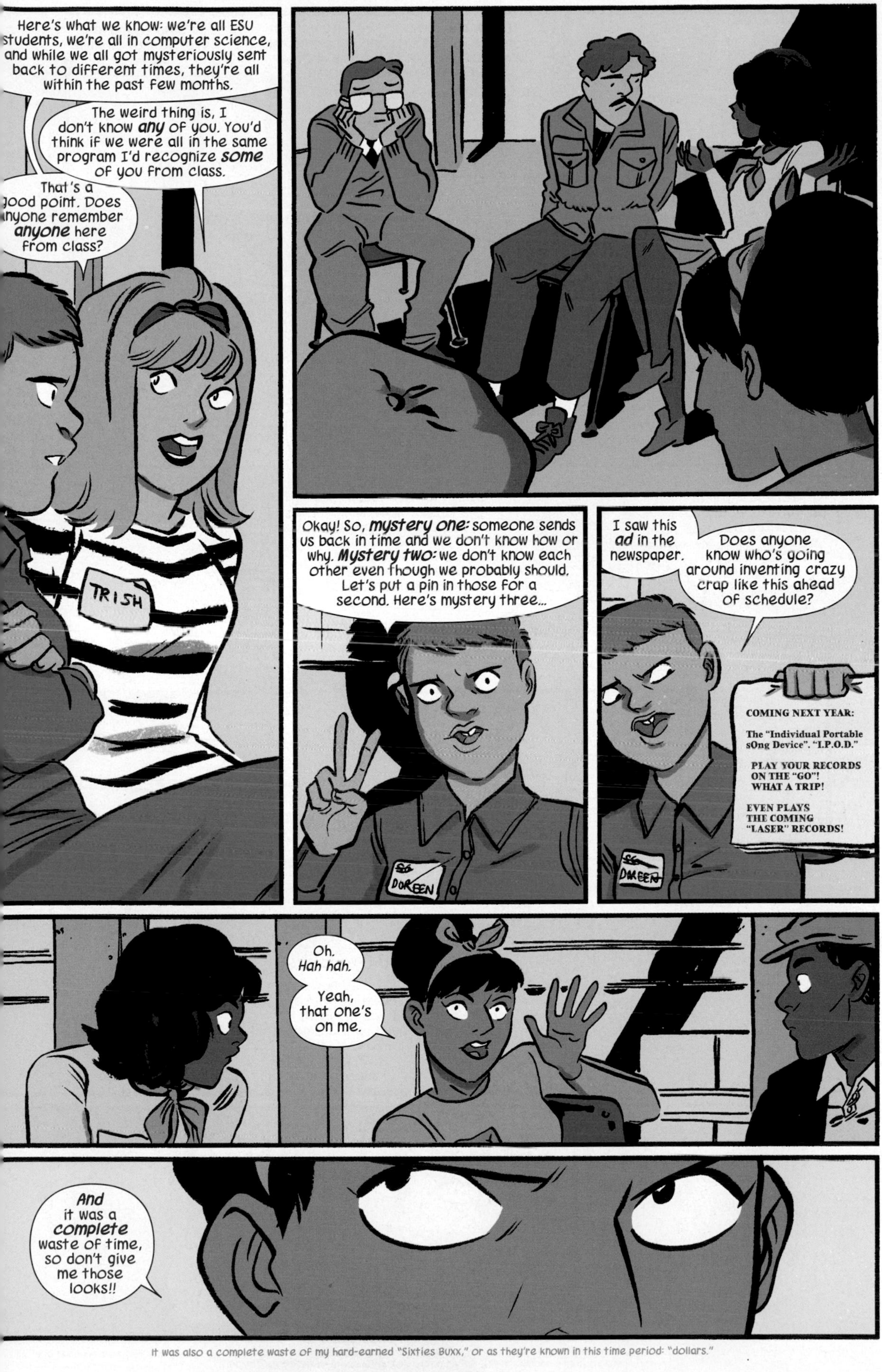
Here's what we know: we're all ESU students, we're all in computer science, and while we all got mysteriously sent back to different times, they're all within the past few months.
The weird thing is, I don't know any of you. You'd think if we were all in the same program I'd recognize some of you from class.
That's a good point. Does anyone remember anyone here from class?
TRISH
Okay! So, mystery one: someone sends us back in time and we don't know how or why. Mystery two: we don't know each other even though we probably should. Let's put a pin in those for a second. Here's mystery three...
DOREEN
I saw this ad in the newspaper.
Does anyone know who's going around inventing crazy crap like this ahead of schedule?
COMING NEXT YEAR:
The "Individual Portable sOng Device". "I.P.O.D."
PLAY YOUR RECORDS ON THE "GO"! WHAT A TRIP!
EVEN PLAYS THE COMING "LASER" RECORDS!
Oh. Hah hah.
Yeah, that one's on me.
And it was a complete waste of time, so don't give me those looks!!

It was also a complete waste of my hard-earned "Sixties Buxx," or as they're known in this time period: "dollars."

The computer scientists in the audience are saying "No, Mary, don't just rebuild the x86 architecture again! Improve it, especially in regards to low-power applications!" while the non-computer scientists in the audience are saying "Eh, computers gonna compute."

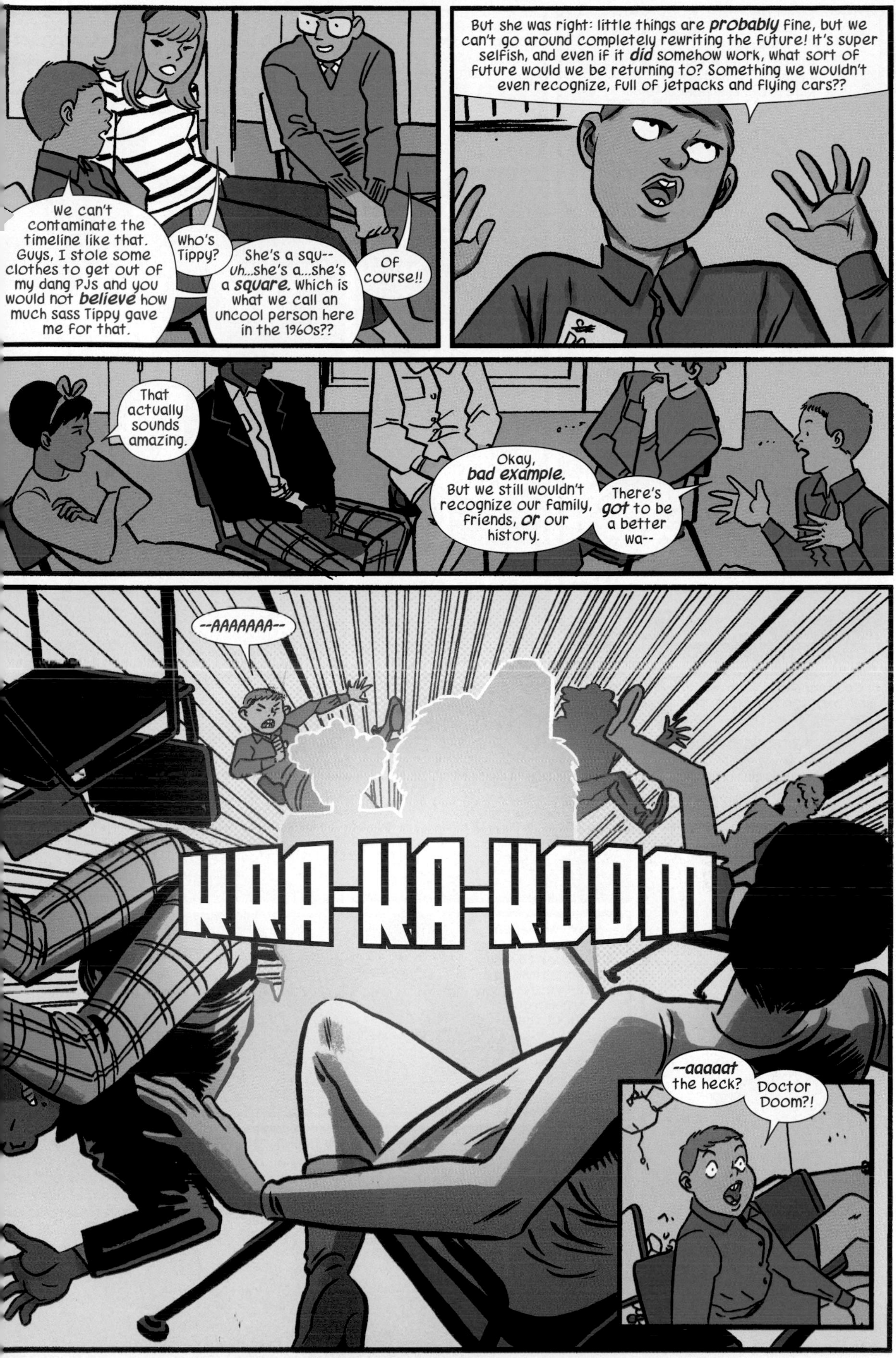
We can't contaminate the timeline like that. Guys, I stole some clothes to get out of my dang PJs and you would not believe how much sass Tippy gave me for that.
Who's Tippy?
She's a squ-- uh...she's a...she's a square. Which is what we call an uncool person here in the 1960s??
Of course!!
But she was right: little things are probably fine, but we can't go around completely rewriting the future! It's super selfish, and even if it did somehow work, what sort of future would we be returning to? Something we wouldn't even recognize, full of jetpacks and flying cars??
That actually sounds amazing.
Okay, bad example. But we still wouldn't recognize our family, friends, or our history.
There's got to be a better wa--
--AAAAAAA--
KRA-KA-KOOM
--aaaaat the heck?
Doctor Doom?!

Doctor Doom, you're not even *close* to the better way I was talking about before your perfectly timed entrance!!

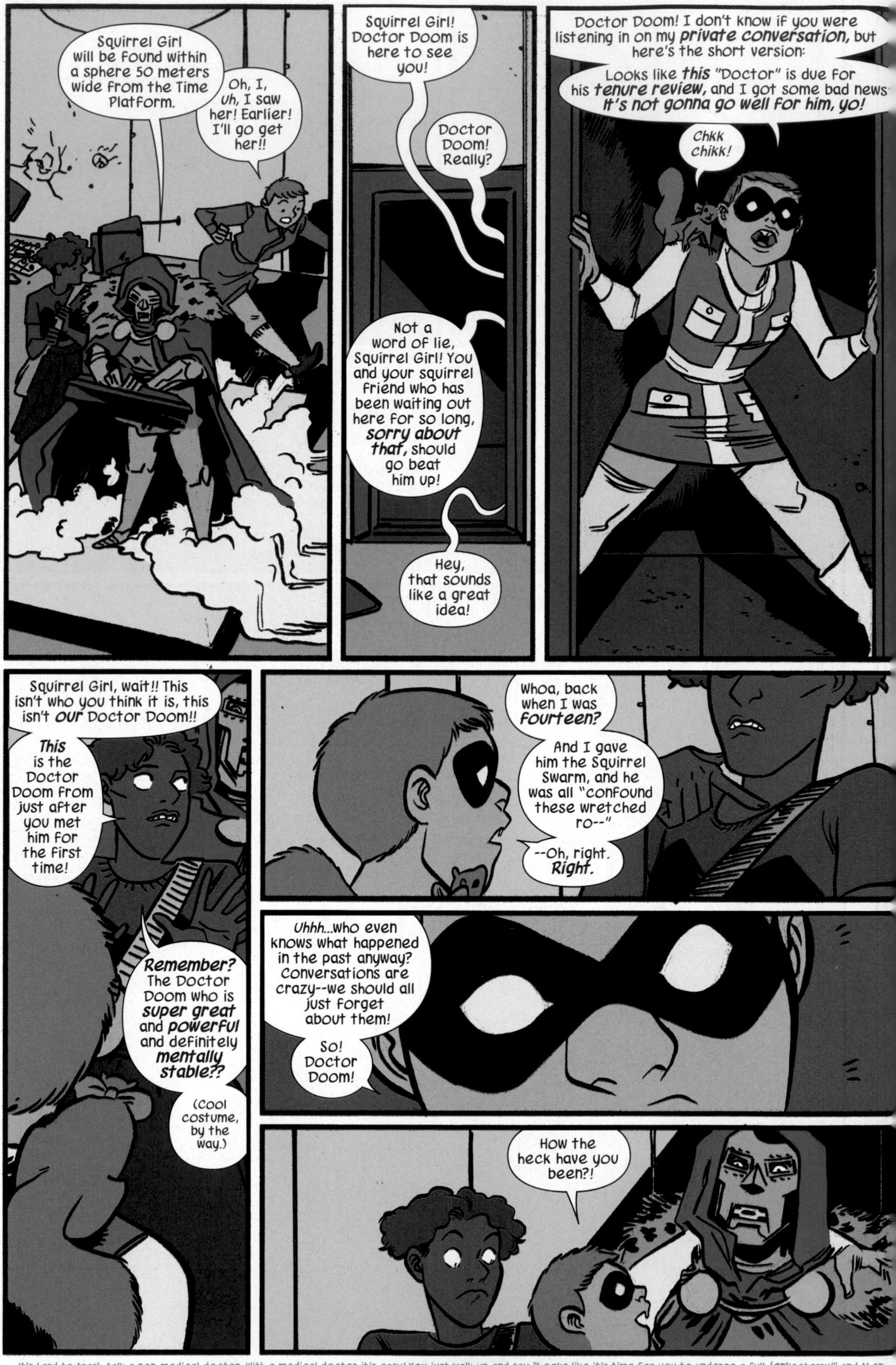
Squirrel Girl will be found within a sphere 50 meters wide from the Time Platform.
Oh, I, uh, I saw her! Earlier! I'll go get her!!
Squirrel Girl! Doctor Doom is here to see you!
Doctor Doom! Really?
Not a word of lie, Squirrel Girl! You and your squirrel friend who has been waiting out here for so long, sorry about that, should go beat him up!
Hey, that sounds like a great idea!
Doctor Doom! I don't know if you were listening in on my private conversation, but here's the short version:
Looks like this "Doctor" is due for his tenure review, and I got some bad news: It's not gonna go well for him, yo!
Chkk chikk!
Squirrel Girl, wait!! This isn't who you think it is, this isn't our Doctor Doom!!
This is the Doctor Doom from just after you met him for the first time!
Remember? The Doctor Doom who is super great and powerful and definitely mentally stable??
(Cool costume, by the way.)
Whoa, back when I was fourteen?
And I gave him the Squirrel Swarm, and he was all "confound these wretched ro--"
--Oh, right. Right.
Uhhh...who even knows what happened in the past anyway? Conversations are crazy--we should all just forget about them!
So! Doctor Doom!
How the heck have you been?!

It's hard to trash-talk a non-medical doctor. With a medical doctor it's easy! You just walk up and say "Looks like it's time for you to undergo a full ***jerk***ectomy!" and then the medical doctor sighs and says "Wow, I actually get that all the time."

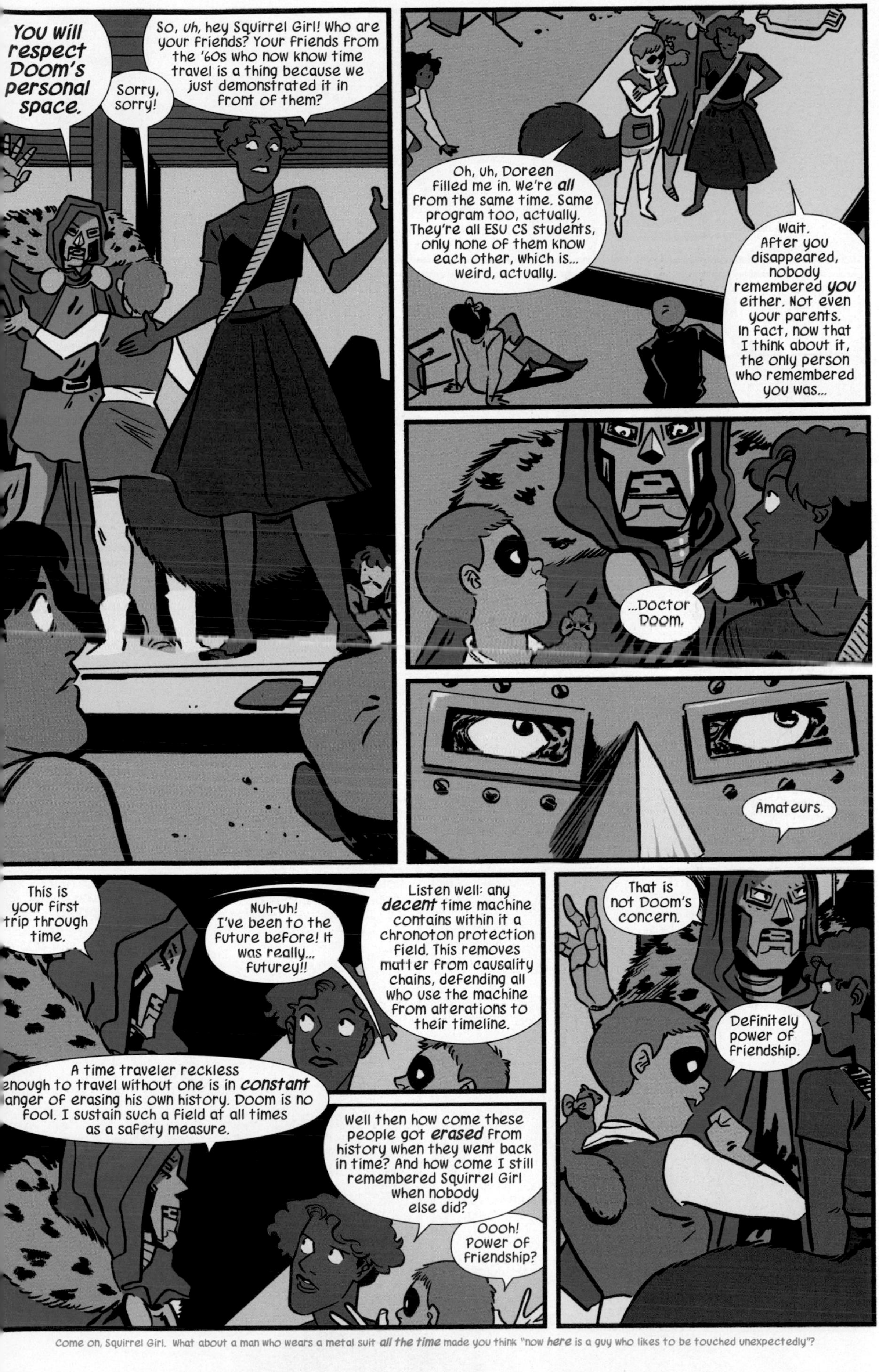
You will respect Doom's personal space.
Sorry, sorry!
So, uh, hey Squirrel Girl! Who are your friends? Your friends from the '60s who now know time travel is a thing because we just demonstrated it in front of them?
Oh, uh, Doreen filled me in. We're all from the same time. Same program too, actually. They're all ESU CS students, only none of them know each other, which is... weird, actually.
Wait. After you disappeared, nobody remembered you either. Not even your parents. In fact, now that I think about it, the only person who remembered you was...
...Doctor Doom.
Amateurs.
This is your first trip through time.
Nuh-uh! I've been to the future before! It was really... futurey!!
Listen well: any decent time machine contains within it a chronoton protection field. This removes matter from causality chains, defending all who use the machine from alterations to their timeline.
A time traveler reckless enough to travel without one is in constant danger of erasing his own history. Doom is no fool. I sustain such a field at all times as a safety measure.
Well then how come these people got erased from history when they went back in time? And how come I still remembered Squirrel Girl when nobody else did?
Oooh! Power of friendship?
That is not Doom's concern.
Definitely power of friendship.

Come on, Squirrel Girl. What about a man who wears a metal suit *all the time* made you think "now *here* is a guy who likes to be touched unexpectedly"?

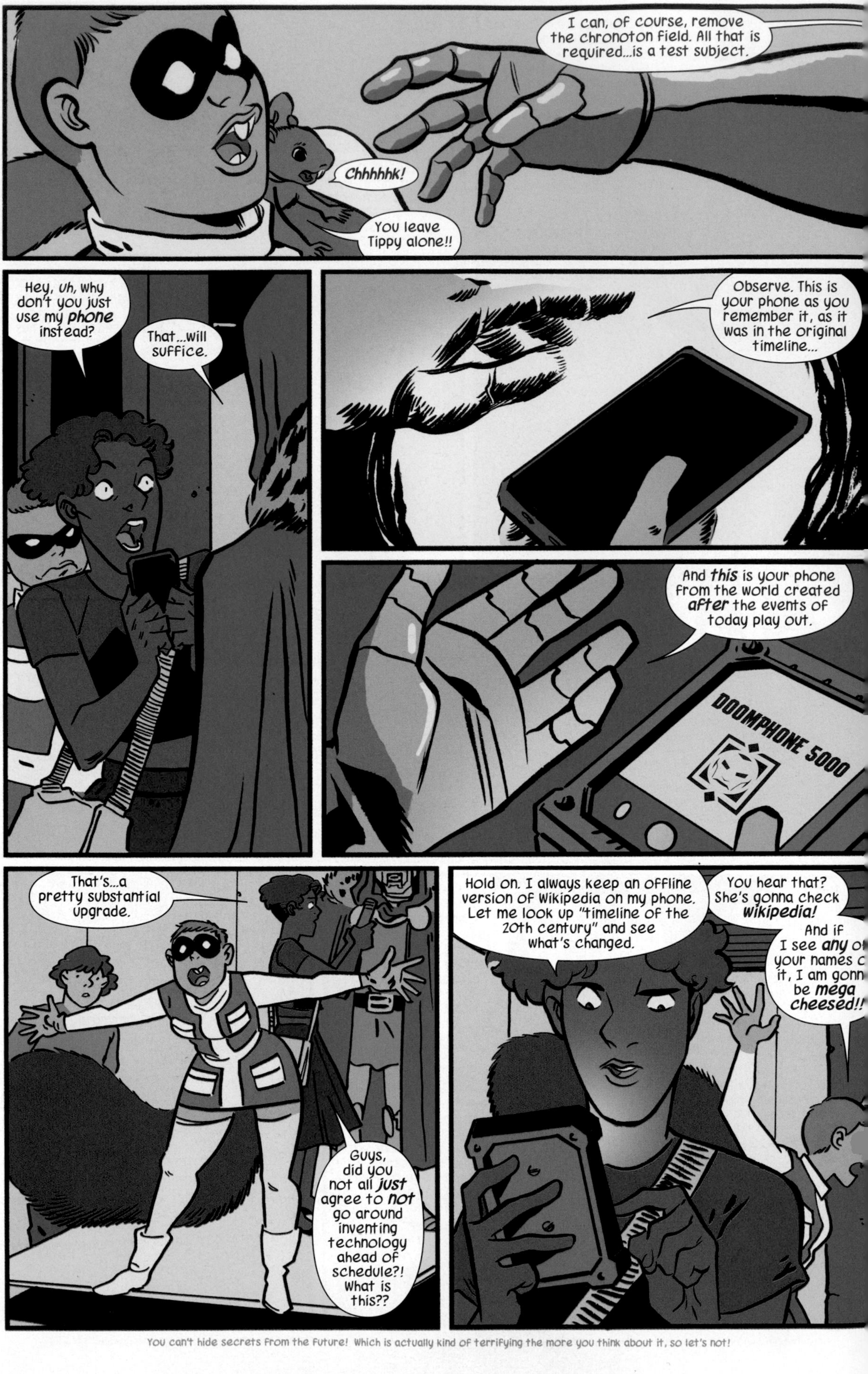

I can, of course, remove the chronoton field. All that is required...is a test subject.
Chhhhhk!
You leave Tippy alone!!
Hey, uh, why don't you just use my phone instead?
That...will suffice.
Observe. This is your phone as you remember it, as it was in the original timeline...
And this is your phone from the world created after the events of today play out.
DOOMPHONE 5000
That's...a pretty substantial upgrade.
Guys, did you not all just agree to not go around inventing technology ahead of schedule?! What is this??
Hold on. I always keep an offline version of Wikipedia on my phone. Let me look up "timeline of the 20th century" and see what's changed.
You hear that? She's gonna check Wikipedia!
And if I see any o your names c it, I am gonn be mega cheesed!!

You can't hide secrets from the future! Which is actually kind of terrifying the more you think about it, so let's not!

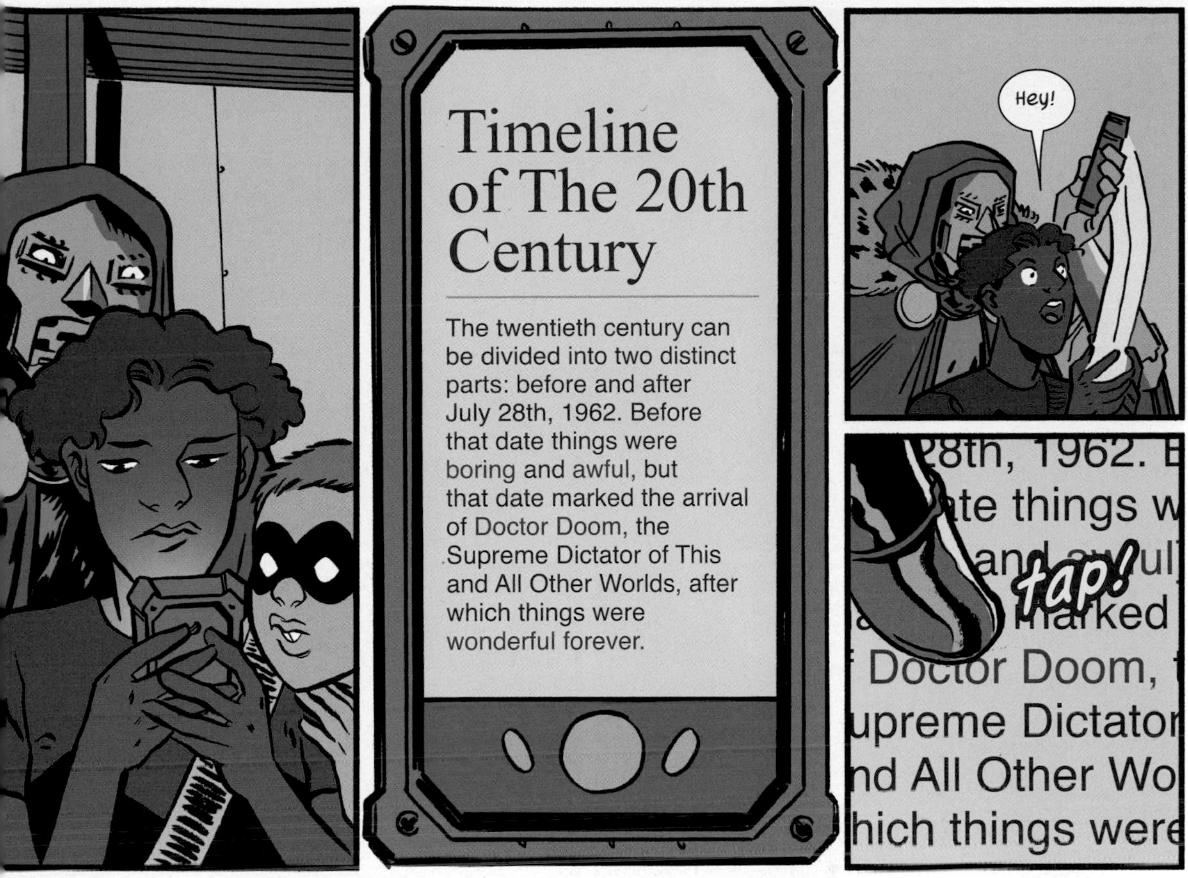
Timeline of The 20th Century
The twentieth century can be divided into two distinct parts: before and after July 28th, 1962. Before that date things were boring and awful, but that date marked the arrival of Doctor Doom, the Supreme Dictator of This and All Other Worlds, after which things were wonderful forever.
Hey!
tap!

Doctor Victor Von Doom, PhD, is a beloved benevolent dictator, scientist, inventor, sorcerer supreme, genius, and artist who appeared under mysterious circumstances on Planet Doom (formerly "Earth") on July 28th, 1962. He quickly took over the world, issuing many decrees for reasons known only to His Supreme Greatness, including specifying that Reed Richards and his closest three associates be kept out of space, alternate dimensions, and cinemas; that otherwise-unremarkable student Peter Parker under no circumstances be allowed near spiders; that all gamma ray testing be immediately suspended; among others. His rule is notable for having been absolutely perfect in every way.

Contents [hide]

1 Early rule, and how precisely he took over
2 The unending brilliance of his reign
3 Our wonderful friends, the Doombots
4 How Doctor Doom defeated Galactus, which is why our world still exists in the absence of any other heroes

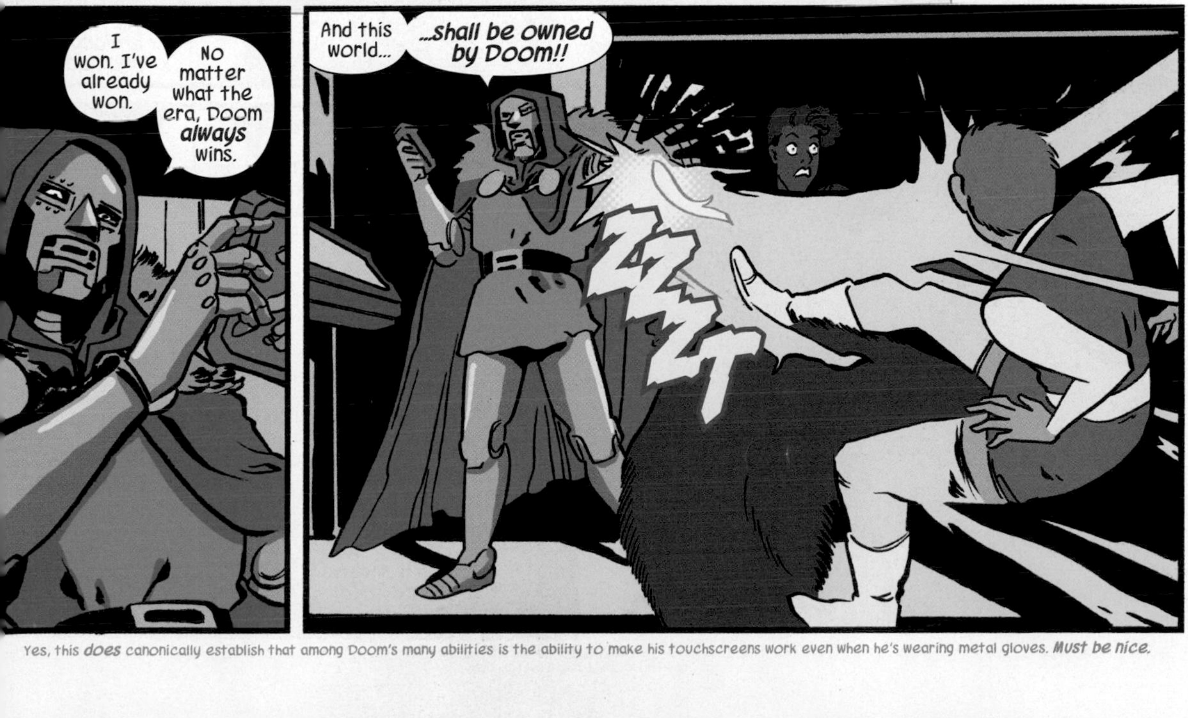
I won. I've already won.
No matter what the era, Doom *always* wins.
And this world...
...shall be owned by DOOM!!
ZZZT

Yes, this *does* canonically establish that among Doom's many abilities is the ability to make his touchscreens work even when he's wearing metal gloves. ***Must be nice.***

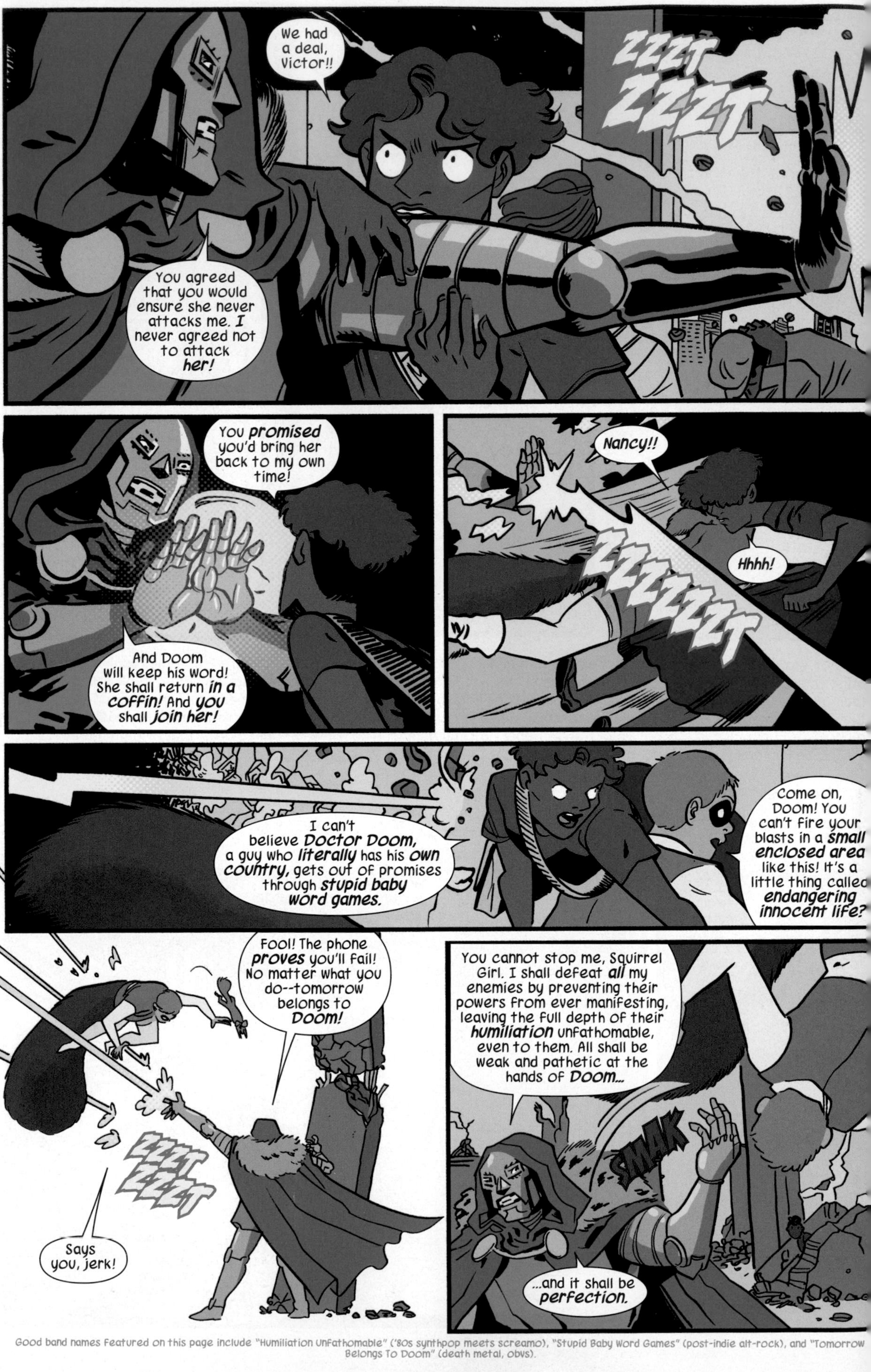
We had a deal, Victor!!
ZZZT ZZZT
You agreed that you would ensure she never attacks me. *I* never agreed not to attack *her!*
You **promised** you'd bring her back to my own time!
And Doom will keep his word! She shall return *in a coffin!* And *you* shall *join her!*
Nancy!!
ZZZZZZZT
Hhhh!
I can't believe **Doctor Doom**, a guy who **literally** has his **own country**, gets out of promises through **stupid baby word games.**
Come on, Doom! You can't fire your blasts in a **small enclosed area** like this! It's a little thing called **endangering innocent life?**
Fool! The phone **proves** you'll fail! No matter what you do--tomorrow belongs to **DOOM!**
ZZZT ZZZT
Says you, jerk!
You cannot stop me, Squirrel Girl. I shall defeat **all** my enemies by preventing their powers from ever manifesting, leaving the full depth of their **humiliation** unfathomable, even to them. All shall be weak and pathetic at the hands of **DOOM...**
SMAK
...and it shall be **perfection.**

Good band names featured on this page include "Humiliation Unfathomable" ('80s synthpop meets screamo), "Stupid Baby Word Games" (post-indie alt-rock), and "Tomorrow Belongs To Doom" (death metal, obvs).

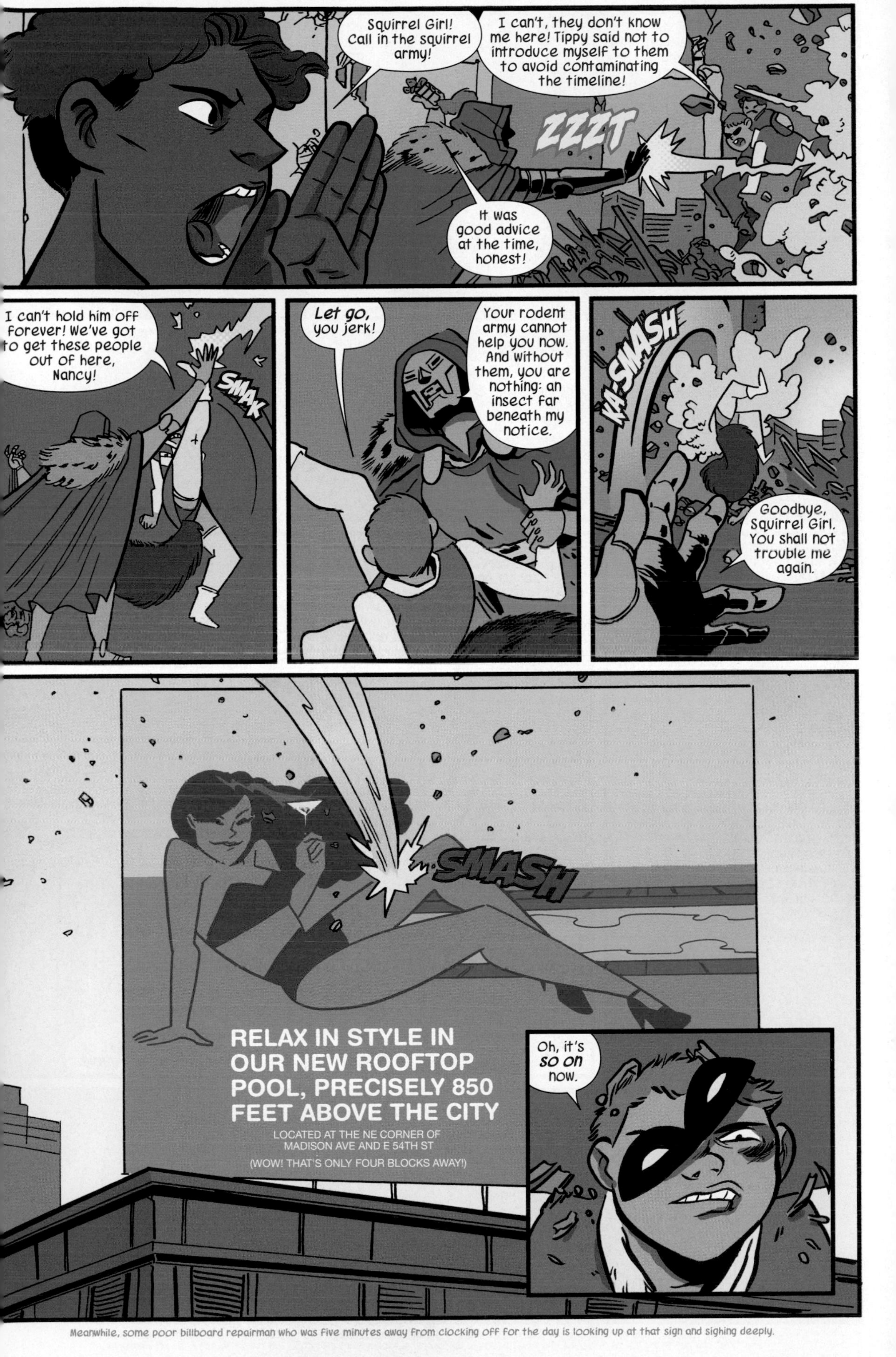
Squirrel Girl! Call in the squirrel army!
I can't, they don't know me here! Tippy said not to introduce myself to them to avoid contaminating the timeline!
ZZZT
It was good advice at the time, honest!
I can't hold him off forever! We've got to get these people out of here, Nancy!
SMAK
Let go, you jerk!
Your rodent army cannot help you now. And without them, you are nothing: an insect far beneath my notice.
KA-SMASH
Goodbye, Squirrel Girl. You shall not trouble me again.
SMASH
RELAX IN STYLE IN OUR NEW ROOFTOP POOL, PRECISELY 850 FEET ABOVE THE CITY
LOCATED AT THE NE CORNER OF MADISON AVE AND E 54TH ST
(WOW! THAT'S ONLY FOUR BLOCKS AWAY!)
Oh, it's *so on* now.

Meanwhile, some poor billboard repairman who was five minutes away from clocking off for the day is looking up at that sign and sighing deeply.

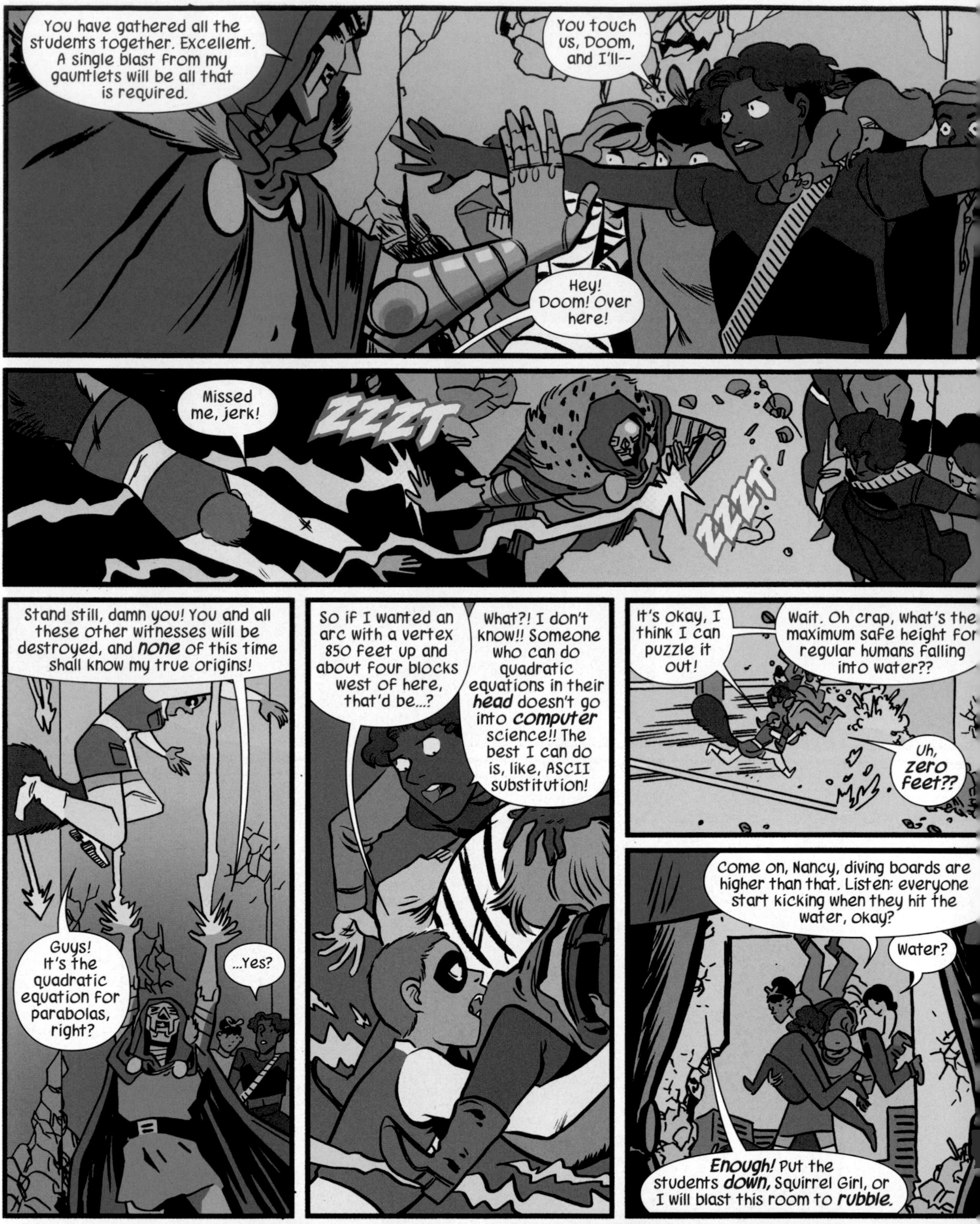
You have gathered all the students together. Excellent. A single blast from my gauntlets will be all that is required.
You touch us, Doom, and I'll--
Hey! Doom! Over here!
Missed me, jerk!
ZZZT
ZZZT
Stand still, damn you! You and all these other witnesses will be destroyed, and *none* of this time shall know my true origins!
Guys! It's the quadratic equation for parabolas, right?
...Yes?
So if I wanted an arc with a vertex 850 feet up and about four blocks west of here, that'd be...?
What?! I don't know!! Someone who can do quadratic equations in their *head* doesn't go into *computer* science!! The best I can do is, like, ASCII substitution!
It's okay, I think I can puzzle it out!
Wait. Oh crap, what's the maximum safe height for regular humans falling into water??
Uh, *zero feet??*
Come on, Nancy, diving boards are higher than that. Listen: everyone start kicking when they hit the water, okay?
Water?
Enough! Put the students *down,* Squirrel Girl, or I will blast this room to *rubble.*
You got it, Doc!
Whoa!!

The trick to solving a quadratic equation in your head is factoring. I say this as someone who solves quadratic equations in his head *all the time,* and definitely not as someone who quickly looked up "secret to solve quadratic equation in your head" + "its an emergency."

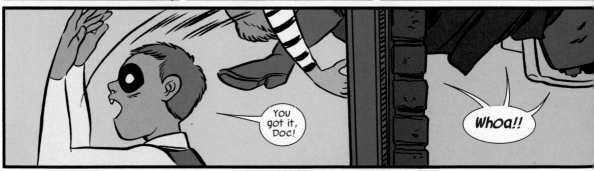

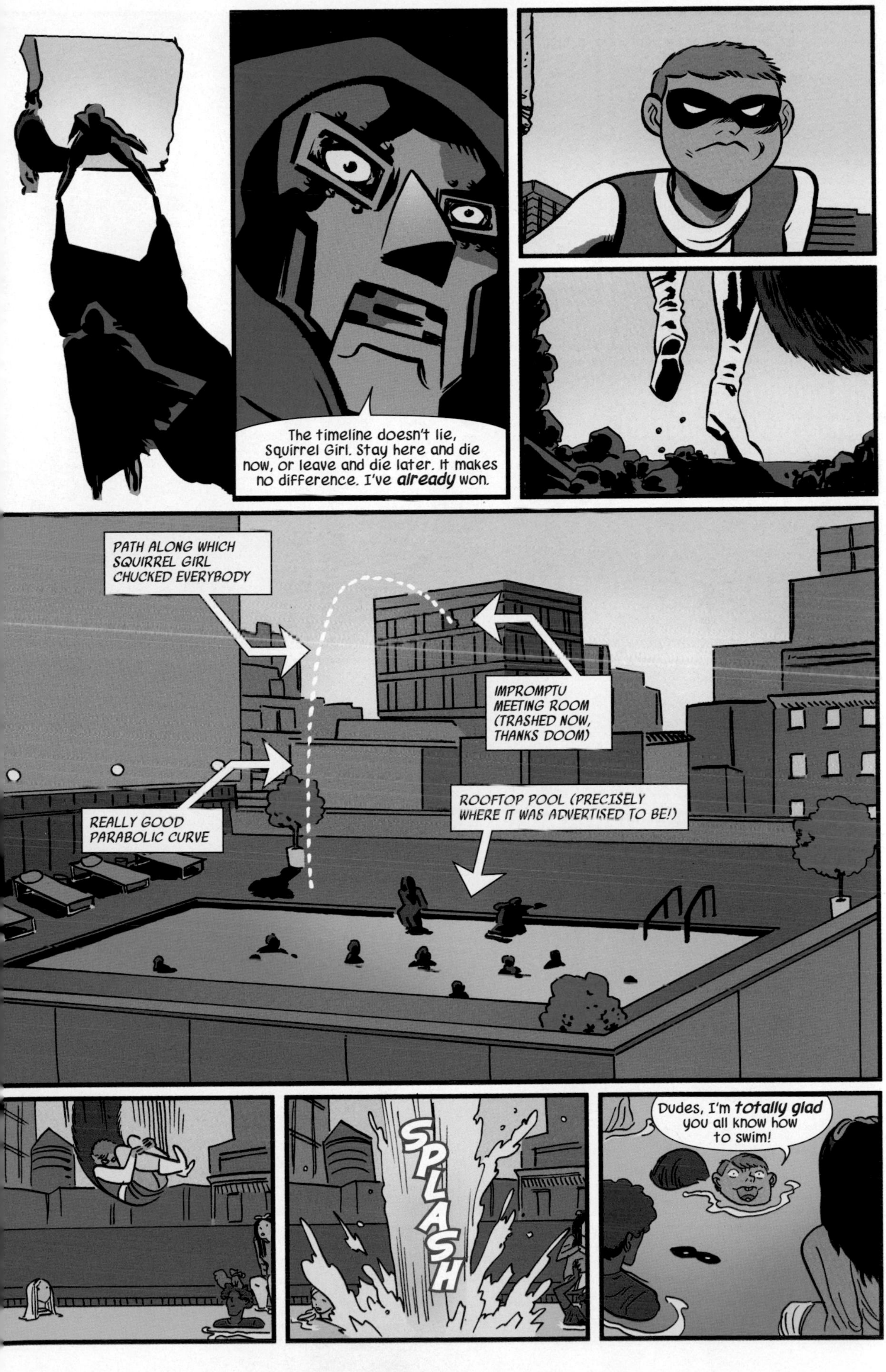
The timeline doesn't lie, Squirrel Girl. Stay here and die now, or leave and die later. It makes no difference. I've *already* won.
PATH ALONG WHICH SQUIRREL GIRL CHUCKED EVERYBODY
IMPROMPTU MEETING ROOM (TRASHED NOW, THANKS DOOM)
REALLY GOOD PARABOLIC CURVE
ROOFTOP POOL (PRECISELY WHERE IT WAS ADVERTISED TO BE!)
SPLASH
Dudes, I'm *totally glad* you all know how to swim!

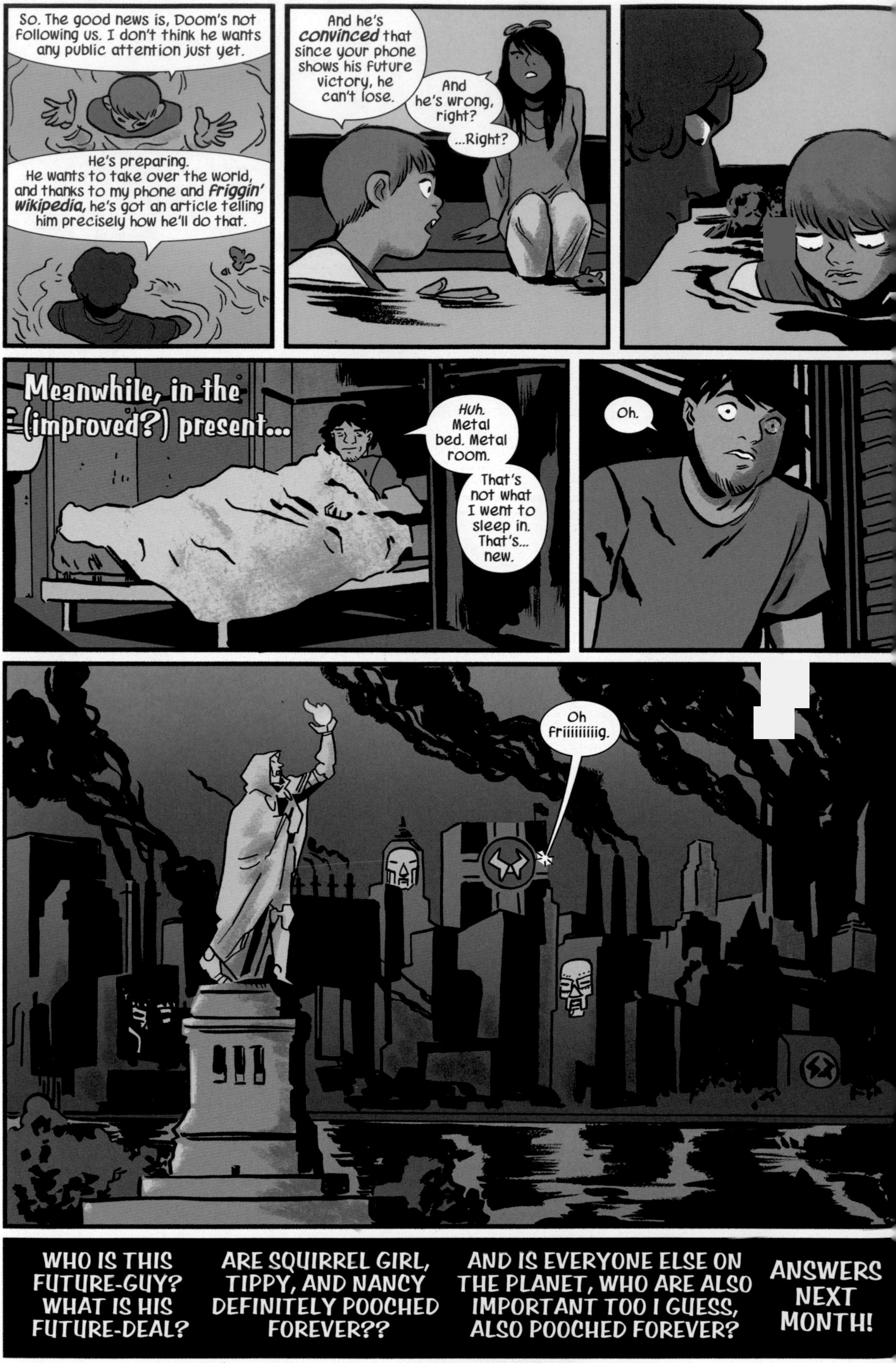

So. The good news is, Doom's not following us. I don't think he wants any public attention just yet.
He's preparing. He wants to take over the world, and thanks to my phone and *friggin' Wikipedia*, he's got an article telling him precisely how he'll do that.
And he's *convinced* that since your phone shows his future victory, he can't lose.
And he's wrong, right?
...Right?
Meanwhile, in the (improved?) present...
Huh. Metal bed. Metal room.
That's not what I went to sleep in. That's... new.
Oh.
Oh Friiiiiiiiig.
WHO IS THIS FUTURE-GUY? WHAT IS HIS FUTURE-DEAL?
ARE SQUIRREL GIRL, TIPPY, AND NANCY DEFINITELY POOCHED FOREVER??
AND IS EVERYONE ELSE ON THE PLANET, WHO ARE ALSO IMPORTANT TOO I GUESS, ALSO POOCHED FOREVER?
ANSWERS NEXT MONTH!

Ryan!

Letters From Nuts

Erica!

Send letters to mheroes@marvel.com or 135 W 50th St, 7th Floor, New York, NY 10020 (Please mark "OKAY TO PRINT")

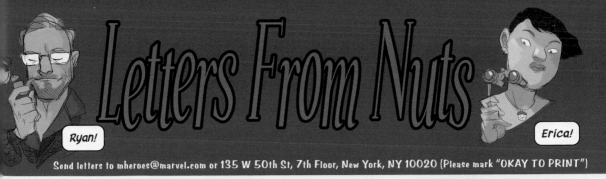

Hey squirrel dudes, it's Drew. Have you ever ıought of giving Squirrel Girl an alternative ıonicker? Batman has "The Dark Knight". uperman is "The Man of Steel". Captain merica is "The First Avenger". I've got a great ne for Squirrel Girl! You better sit down for is... The Supreme Sciuridae!

If I ever saw that printed I would just die. eep up the GREAT work! I am in love with this urrent Squirrel Girl series! You can really tell ıat everyone that works on it is passionate and ommitted.

Andrew Torres

RYAN: Hey Drew! I am the guy who writes a omic called The Unbeatable Squirrel Girl and can't spell sciuridae without double-checking , so we MIGHT hold off on it until I can spell reliably. But you are correct (both about that eing a cool monicker AND that everyone who orks on this book really loves it!).

Neko always enjoys reading the newest ssue of Squirrel Girl but after issue #8 came ut she new exactly what she wanted to be for alloween. CAT THOR!

She is still disappointed that I won't let her arry around a hammer to wack the shins of eople who annoy her (mainly me) but otherwise his is "the best Halloween ever" her words.

Kelsey B

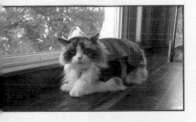

R: NEKO IS ADORABLE. I now want to see ons of photos of catsplay, which is a word I ust made up that means cosplay for cats. I am 00% certain that all cats will be big into this nd see no possible downsides.

ERICA: When I first read this I completely nissed that Neko is Japanese for cat (thanks, hree years of high school Japanese) and xpected to see a child in an outfit. ANYWAY, where did you find this beautiful cat that didn't ry to eat you alive for putting it in clothes? I eed deets. Does Neko have siblings? Can I ave one?

Hi Ryan and Erica!

I have been a lifelong comics fan and I'm eing completely honest when I say that your Squirrel Girl run is one of the best I've ever read, o hats off to you!

Perhaps more importantly however is your accomplishment in getting my wonderful girlfriend into reading comics! I must say I was a tad tentative introducing comics to her, but your writing and your art have absolutely hooked her! We read every issue together and it's one of our favourite things to do.

I hope to be reading Squirrel Girl with her for years to come, keep up your amazing work!

Sam and Catherine
England

PS Who do you think would win in a lip-sync battle between Squirrel Girl, Devil Dinosaur and Ms Marvel?

R: Hooray for being people's gateway comic, that's what I say! More precisely, what I've often said during talks and on panels is comics is a medium, not a genre, and like all mediums can be used to tell all sorts of stories, and then I go on to say if the only movies you ever saw were romantic comedies and you didn't like romantic comedies, you might be forgiven for saying 'wow I guess I just don't like movies' and then proceed to draw an analogy involving the types of comics people THINK they know compared to the full spectrum of amazingness that comics ACTUALLY ARE and comparing that to that person who thinks they hate movies because they've only ever seen one small slice of what movies can be. ANYWAY, this is all to say: thanks, and I'm super glad she likes comics now!

Also, in a lip-sync battle I would have to give it to Devil Dinosaur, because he is an actual dinosaur, and I have it on good authority that dinosaurs can spit rhymes like CRAZY.

E: Ryan has pretty well covered the first half of the question. If you want some non-super hero comic recommendations that are women-friendly, I have them! Tweet at me: @ericafails.

To answer the second part of your letter, I would also have to go with Devil Dinosaur, but for a different reason. As someone who studied animation, it's a lot easier to match mouth movements on something that doesn't really have a wide range of mouth movements. So he can match himself up faster and easier since he doesn't have to worry about his mouth looking like the wrong word.

Hi, my name is Isla. I am 6 years old and I really like Squirrel Girl.

Here is a picture of me and my sister. We dressed up on Halloween. I was Squirrel Girl and my sister was Tippy Toe. Since Squirrel Girl keeps Deadpool villain cards in her utility belt, I made some out of paper and put them in my utility belt.

Thank you. I hope you keep making Squirrel Girl.

Isla

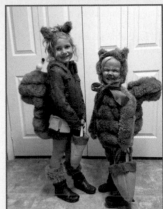

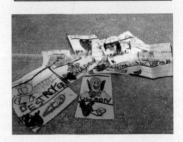

R: Isla, I hope so too! Here is the thing about you and your sister's costumes: THEY ARE AMAZING, and I can't get over your Deadpool villain cards. You've made some that we haven't even gotten to in the comics yet! SO GOOD. Thank you for reading our comics, and for sharing your costumes with us! I'm old enough that I get to give out candy on Hallowe'en, so this year at my house I was giving out chocolate bars AND issues of Squirrel Girl. If I'd seen you I would've given you the entire bowl of candy!!

E: AHHH. You guys look so goooood! I want to know how you decided who would be Squirrel Girl and who would be Tippy. Ryan, I guess we'll have to put all those bad guys in the book so that these cards are accurate.

Dear Ryan and Erica,

My dog Sawyer and I love Squirrel Girl so much that we decided to dress like Doreen Green and Tippy-Toe for Halloween. It was so much fun to walk down the street and hear people shout out "Hey! Squirrel Girl!"I am 11 years old and have read every issue of your comic. I really like Chipmunk Hunk and Nancy Whitehead. I love Squirrel Girl so much that I have a big poster of her in my room.

I have included a picture so that you can see how great we looked.

Squirrel Girl Forever!

Love, Olivia G.

R: Can I just say how happy I am that this letters column is chock full of both people dressing up as Squirrel Girl AND THEIR PETS? Because I am extremely happy. Thank you, Olivia! I'm super stoked that people recognized you too: word of Squirrel Girl is spreading!

Nancy Whitehead is a favourite of mine too, and I really want to see more of Chipmunk Hunk. These time travel shenanigans make it hard but we'll see him soon, I promise!

E: Listen, all of you made a big mistake posting your cute animals because I'm going to come and steal them. I don't care that my apartment doesn't allow dogs. Stealing them all. Yeah, Ryan, where's Chipmunk Hunk? WHEN'S HE COMING BACK? WHERE ARE ALL THE HUNKS?

Ryan, Erica, et al,

Congrats on another #1! I was super-pleased to hear how Hippo the Hippo is doing. Frankly, if you went all-in on Hippo the Hippo referencing and had him move in downstairs from Doreen and Nancy I'd be at least a thousand percent into that. Hippo would be a great nutty neighbor. Like a 3000 lb Fred Mertz. In a year choked with good comics USG is my favorite by (squirrel) leaps and (squirrel) bounds.

Questions:

When Doreen talks about nuts does she mean botanical nuts, culinary nuts, or both?

Which C compiler does Nancy prefer? CMake? gcc? Borland? (Visual Studio is not up for consideration as Nancy is not evil)

Regards,
Gary

R: Haha, yes! LET US TALK ABOUT C COMPILERS. Nancy uses gcc for day-to-day compilation, but has messed around with Borland Turbo C in order to get some classic games running. As for nuts, it really depends on the context, but I'd guess it's usually culinary. Erica? You are the nut expert here and know where to buy acorn flour, so I defer to you.

E: Ryan, I only know where to buy acorn flour because it's the main ingredient in a popular Korean dish and there's a Korean market down the street. For the most part, she's going to be talking about nuts she can eat. They're a decently large part of her diet (along with beans and yogurt and seeds) because they're rich in protein, and Ryan and I agreed early on that someone who is aware of animal sentience has to be a vegetarian.

Dear Ryan and Erica,

I am a cranky middle-aged male comicreader and devoted fan of The Unbeatable Squirrel Girl. Her light-hearted but respectful interaction with deep Marvel mythology is a comfort to those of us who have given up our dreams of ever visiting the moon of Titan IRL. Bookssuch asyours and Ant-Man allow us to look back momentarily like Camus' Sisyphus and say, "It wasn't entirely a waste of time." In fact mybiggestanxietyover a post-Secret Wars cosmosis the effect it will have on Doreen's adventures. I want to be clear, I harbor no prejudice against female Thors. I simply fear change. (Those darn kids with their texting and their Ultimate Universes!) The appeal of the book depends so much on long, long-established canon. What happens after the shake-up? Any arboreal species will tell you it's difficult and dangerous to scamper up a tree that has no roots. On the other hand, at the risk of sounding pessimistic if her purpose is to puncture pretentious and pervasive pomposity (sorry, it was Stan who learned me how to talk good) we may need her now more than ever.

Chip Karpus
Elyria, Ohio

P.S. Attached are photos of a colony of white squirrels that live in the town square in Oberlin, Ohio and have been adopted as unofficial mascots of the college. Coincidentally about 60 miles up the road a much larger army of mutant black squirrels has overtaken the campus of Kent State, descendants supposedly of a couple of lab specimens released by a megalomaniacal zoology professor in an attempt (not making any of this up) to give visual distinction to the landscape. Only the Celestials know what would happen if they ever got together.

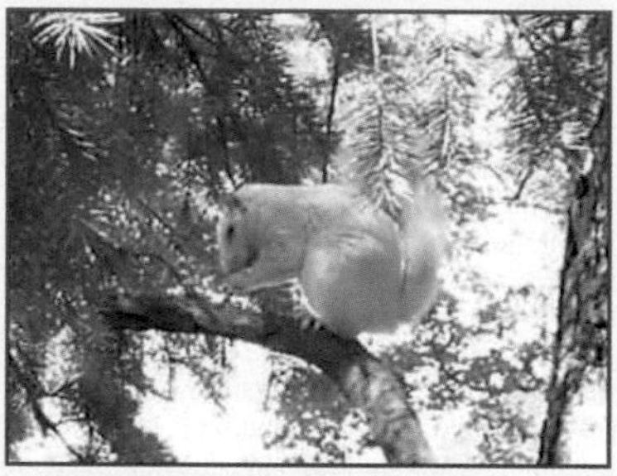

R: White squirrel COLONY? That's amazing. I live in Toronto and we have a famous white squirrel that always hangs out in the same park, so spotting that is always a thrill. I can't imagine what it's like having a colony nearby!

Your zoology prof introducing squirrels is not the first time that's happened, actually. They weren't always common in cities: in fact, in 1856 the sight of a squirrel it was an escaped pet - was so unusual that the New York Daily Times reported a crowd of hundreds gathering to watch it. But by the 1870s it was a full-on fad to introduce squirrels to city parks in America, with the idea that it gave a touch of the country to city-dwellers, which would help maintain their health and sanity. And the fact they were super cute, super trusting, and willing to take food from people's outstretched hands didn't hurt! Along with squirrels, there were experiments in introducing peacocks and deer, but those weren't nearly as successful.

Please send me updates if the white and black squirrels ever cross over; the Celestials are horrible at email.

E: WAIT. RYAN. Did we discuss the 1870s introduction of squirrels into American par in part due to their docile nature and in pa to create a more rural atmosphere, or did w just do the same research into the histo of squirrels in Central Park? There's also white squirrel in my city that everyone freal out over. And yeah, we're going to be needin photos of those giant black squirrels.

Hey Squirrel Girl Squad!

I have always read comics to my daughte Nova. Even when I was pregnant with her. Whe she was two, she developed her first favorit which was The Amazing Spider-Man. At thre she had a heart-wrenching breakdown in th back of the car, sobbing hysterically that whe she grew up she wanted to be Spider-Ma but she couldn't be Spider-Man because sh was a girl. Despite our best efforts and gende neutral parenting tactics, we could not conso her. I am a Ms Marvel fan and had been readin the current story arc so I pulled all the issue and read those to her, but they didn't reall capture her interest. Around this time, Thor # came out and while her eyes lit up at the sigh of a female Thor, she couldn't really follow th story. A few months passed, and my frien suggested we pick up The Unbeatable Squirre Girl and generously donated the first fou issues. Man was she hooked. When the tim came to pick out a Halloween costume, it wa no contest. Eat nuts and kick butts all day long

Thank you for providing a role model for ou little girl. Thank you for having my back whe I told her girls can be awesome superheroe too. Thank you for the laughs. Even thoug working with faux fur was a battle in itself.

Mar

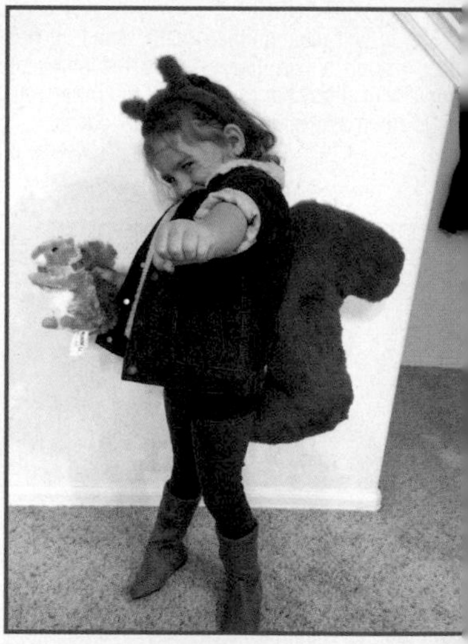

R: Mary, thank you for this. Sometime people think making a comic about a lad who can talk to squirrels is a pretty silly wa to spend your time, but letters like this an experiences like what your daughter had are so important. So important! I'm so gla your daughter found Squirrel Girl. And he costume is top notch, so all those struggle with faux fur were worth it. Tell her sh leaves no nut uneaten and no butt un-kicked!

Okay, see y'all next month! Keep writing!

Attention, Squirrel Scouts! Make sure to check out our production blog, **unbeatablesquirrelgirl.tumblr.com**, where we post behind-the-scenes stuff on how the book gets made, along with all sorts of cool things *you* make: fanart, cosplay, whatever!

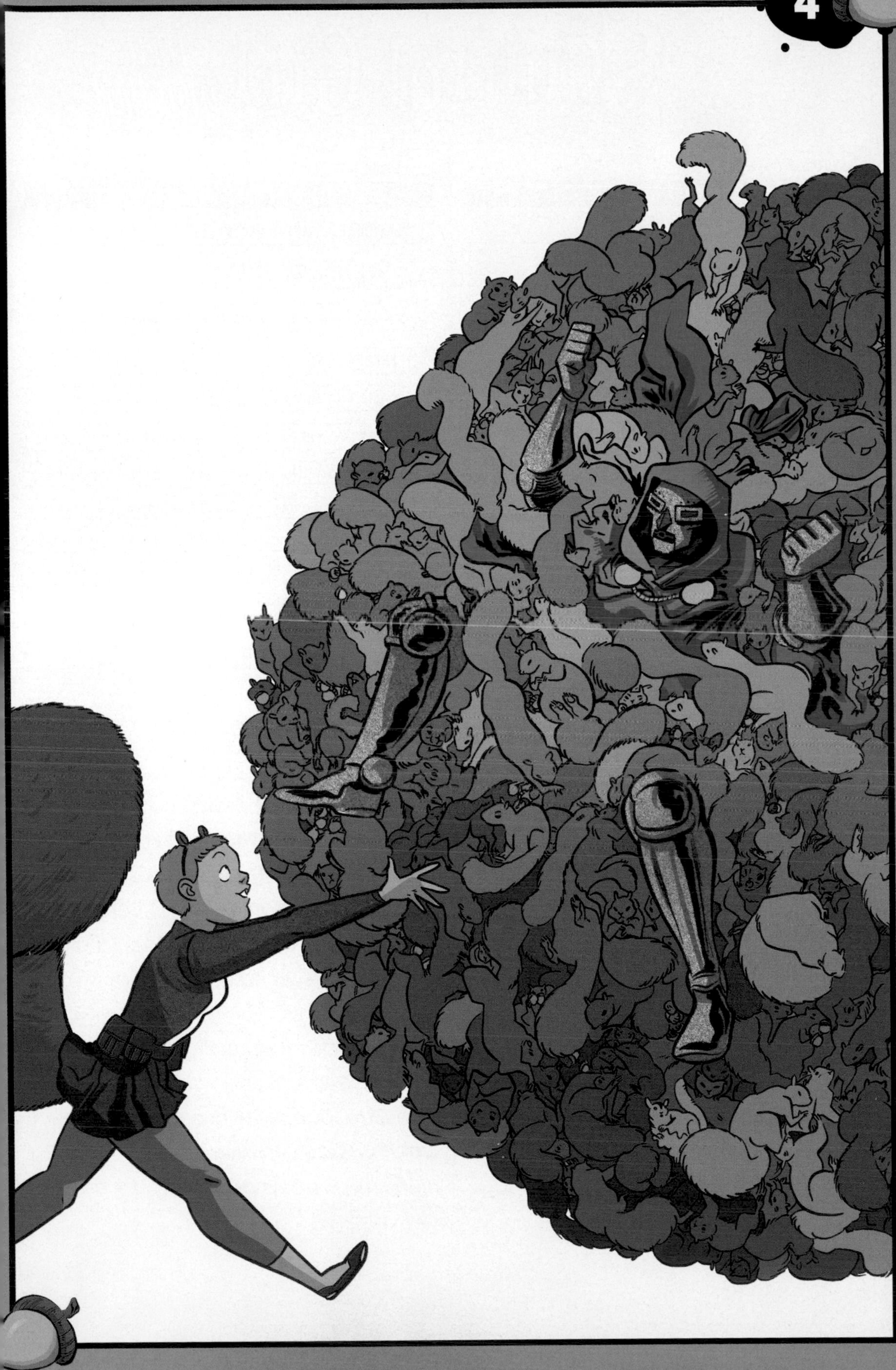

Doreen Green isn't just a second-year computer science student: she secretly also has all the powers of both squirrel and girl! She uses her amazing abilities to fight crime **and** *be as awesome as possible. You know her as...* ***The Unbeatable Squirrel Girl!*** *Find out what she's been up to, with...*

Squirrel Girl *in a nutshell*

[X] URGENT

WHILE YOU WERE OUT

To: The United Nations

From: Squirrel Girl

Of: ~~The Future~~ The Present

- [X] TELEPHONED
- [ ] PLEASE CALL
- [ ] CAME TO SEE YOU
- [ ] WILL CALL AGAIN
- [X] WANTS TO SEE YOU
- [ ] RETURNED YOUR CALL

Message: You guys, Doctor Doom came back to the ***sixties*** (which is ***now***) (obviously) and is going to take over the world TOMORROW unless we stop him, but he's got ***Future Wikipedia*** that already shows he's gonna win so I'm not really sure what to do, if you have any idea I'm all ears (not a pun even though I wear a second set of ears for fashion reasons)

[ ] URGENT

WHILE YOU WERE OUT

To: Nancy Whitehead

From: Squirrel Girl

Of: The apartment we share because we're roommates

- [X] TELEPHONED
- [ ] PLEASE CALL
- [ ] CAME TO SEE YOU
- [X] WILL CALL AGAIN
- [ ] WANTS TO SEE YOU
- [ ] RETURNED YOUR CALL

Message: Nancy it was super cool that you came back in time to rescue me and all these other CS students trapped here!! ps I know you don't have a phone, will you write me back on one of these notes because I've got like a thousand of them [ ]yes [ ]no

[ ] URGENT

WHILE YOU WERE OUT

To: Mr. and Mrs. Stark

From: Squirrel Girl

Of: The Iron Man Fandom

- [ ] TELEPHONED
- [ ] PLEASE CALL
- [X] CAME TO SEE YOU
- [ ] WILL CALL AGAIN
- [ ] WANTS TO SEE YOU
- [ ] RETURNED YOUR CALL

Message: hey you don't know me but I just wanted to say the two of you should definitely have a baby in a few decades and name him Tony!! okay, thank me later

Ryan North Writer
Erica Henderson Artist
Rico Renzi Color Artist
VC's Clayton Cowles Letterer
Erica Henderson Cover Artist
John Tyler Christopher Variant Cover Artist
CK Russell & Lissa Pattillo Special Thanks
Chris Robinson Assistant Editor
Wil Moss Editor
Tom Brevoort Executive Editor
Axel Alonso Editor In Chief
Joe Quesada Chief Creative Officer
Dan Buckley Publisher
Alan Fine Exec. Producer

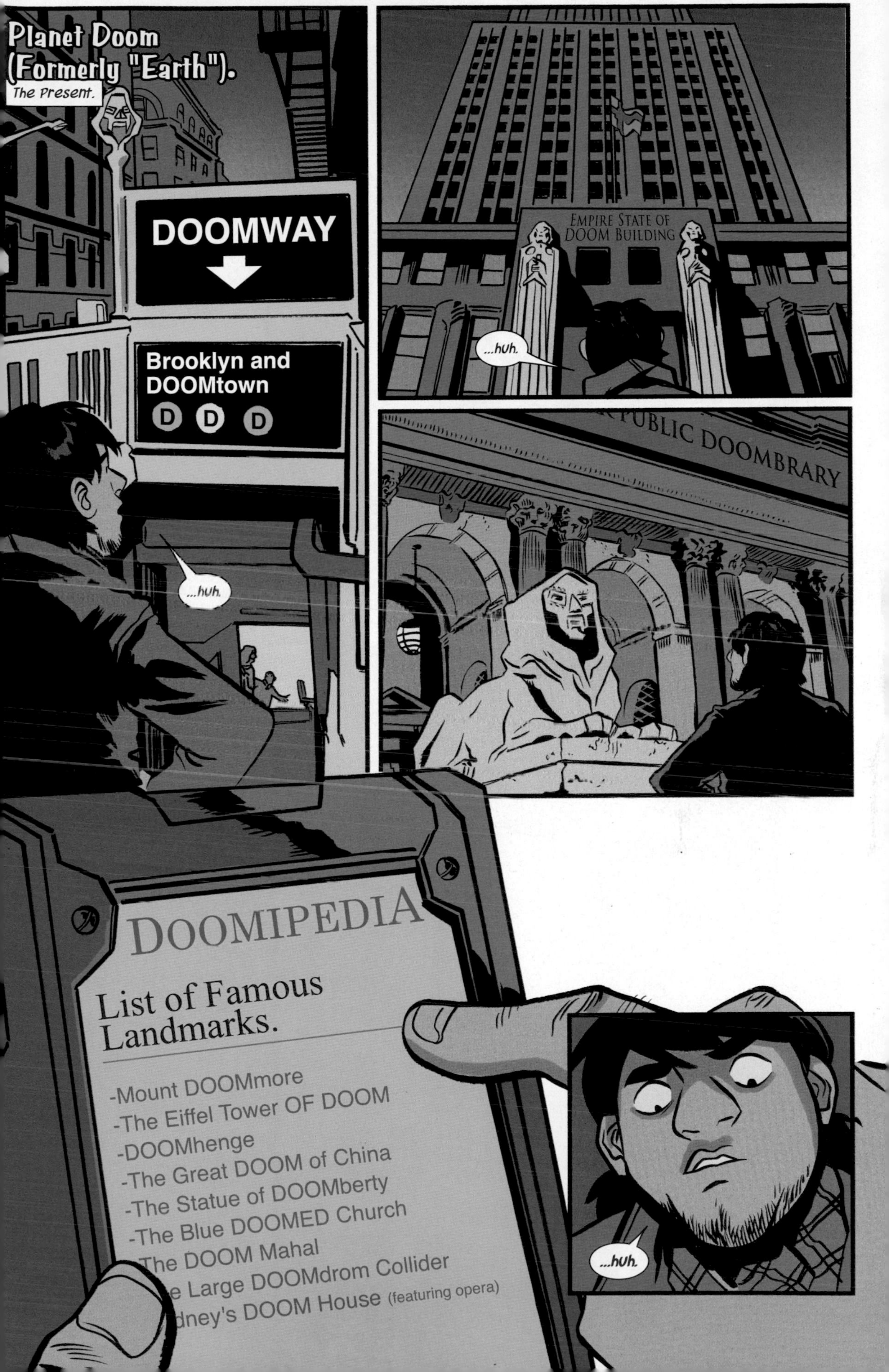
Planet Doom (Formerly "Earth").
The Present.
DOOMWAY
Brooklyn and DOOMtown
D D D
...huh.
EMPIRE STATE OF DOOM BUILDING
...huh.
PUBLIC DOOMBRARY
DOOMIPEDIA
List of Famous Landmarks.
-Mount DOOMmore
-The Eiffel Tower OF DOOM
-DOOMhenge
-The Great DOOM of China
-The Statue of DOOMberty
-The Blue DOOMED Church
The DOOM Mahal
Large DOOMdrom Collider
dney's DOOM House (featuring opera)
...huh.

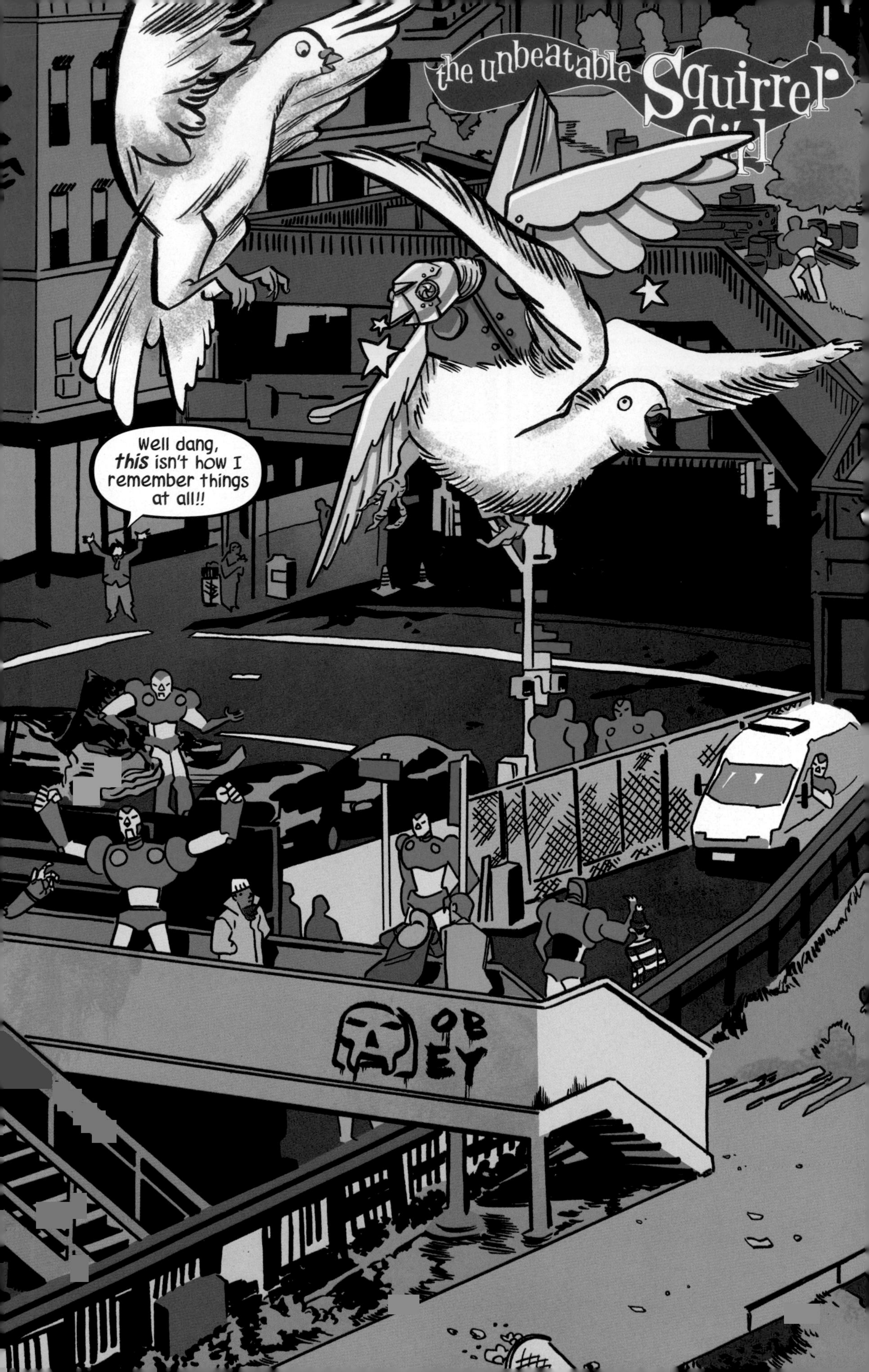
the unbeatable Squirrel
Well dang, *this* isn't how I remember things at all!!
OB EY

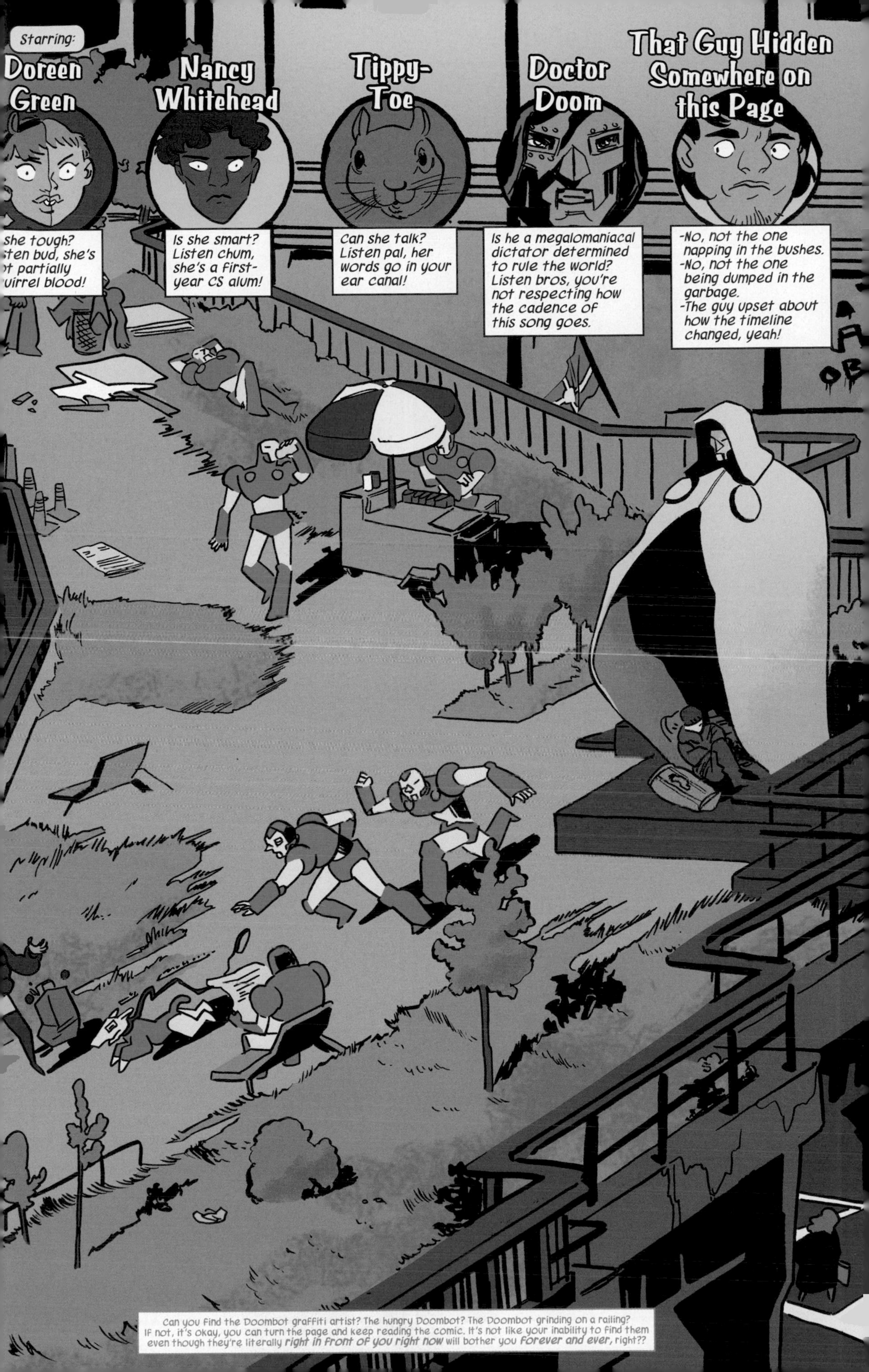

Starring:
Doreen Green
Nancy Whitehead
Tippy-Toe
Doctor Doom
That Guy Hidden Somewhere on this Page
she tough? sten bud, she's t partially uirrel blood!
Is she smart? Listen chum, she's a first-year CS alum!
Can she talk? Listen pal, her words go in your ear canal!
Is he a megalomaniacal dictator determined to rule the world? Listen bros, you're not respecting how the cadence of this song goes.
-No, not the one napping in the bushes. -No, not the one being dumped in the garbage. -The guy upset about how the timeline changed, yeah!
Can you find the Doombot graffiti artist? The hungry Doombot? The Doombot grinding on a railing? If not, it's okay, you can turn the page and keep reading the comic. It's not like your inability to find them even though they're literally *right in front of you right now* will bother you *forever and ever,* right??

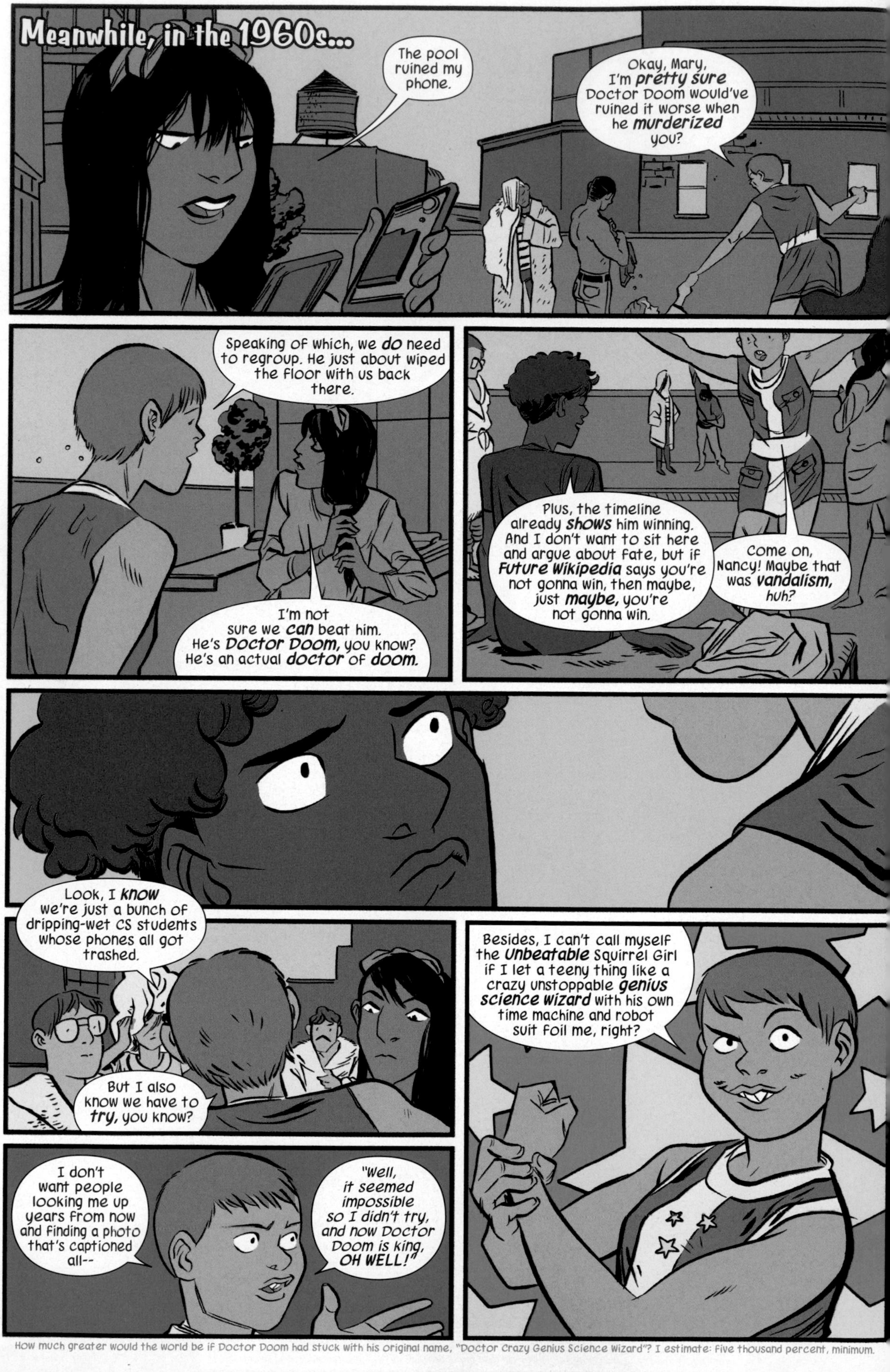

Meanwhile, in the 1960s...
The pool ruined my phone.
Okay, Mary, I'm pretty sure Doctor Doom would've ruined it worse when he murderized you?
Speaking of which, we do need to regroup. He just about wiped the floor with us back there.
I'm not sure we can beat him. He's Doctor Doom, you know? He's an actual doctor of doom.
Plus, the timeline already shows him winning. And I don't want to sit here and argue about fate, but if Future Wikipedia says you're not gonna win, then maybe, just maybe, you're not gonna win.
Come on, Nancy! Maybe that was vandalism, huh?
Look, I know we're just a bunch of dripping-wet CS students whose phones all got trashed.
But I also know we have to try, you know?
Besides, I can't call myself the Unbeatable Squirrel Girl if I let a teeny thing like a crazy unstoppable genius science wizard with his own time machine and robot suit foil me, right?
I don't want people looking me up years from now and finding a photo that's captioned all--
"Well, it seemed impossible so I didn't try, and now Doctor Doom is king, OH WELL!"

How much greater would the world be if Doctor Doom had stuck with his original name, "Doctor Crazy Genius Science Wizard"? I estimate: five thousand percent, minimum.

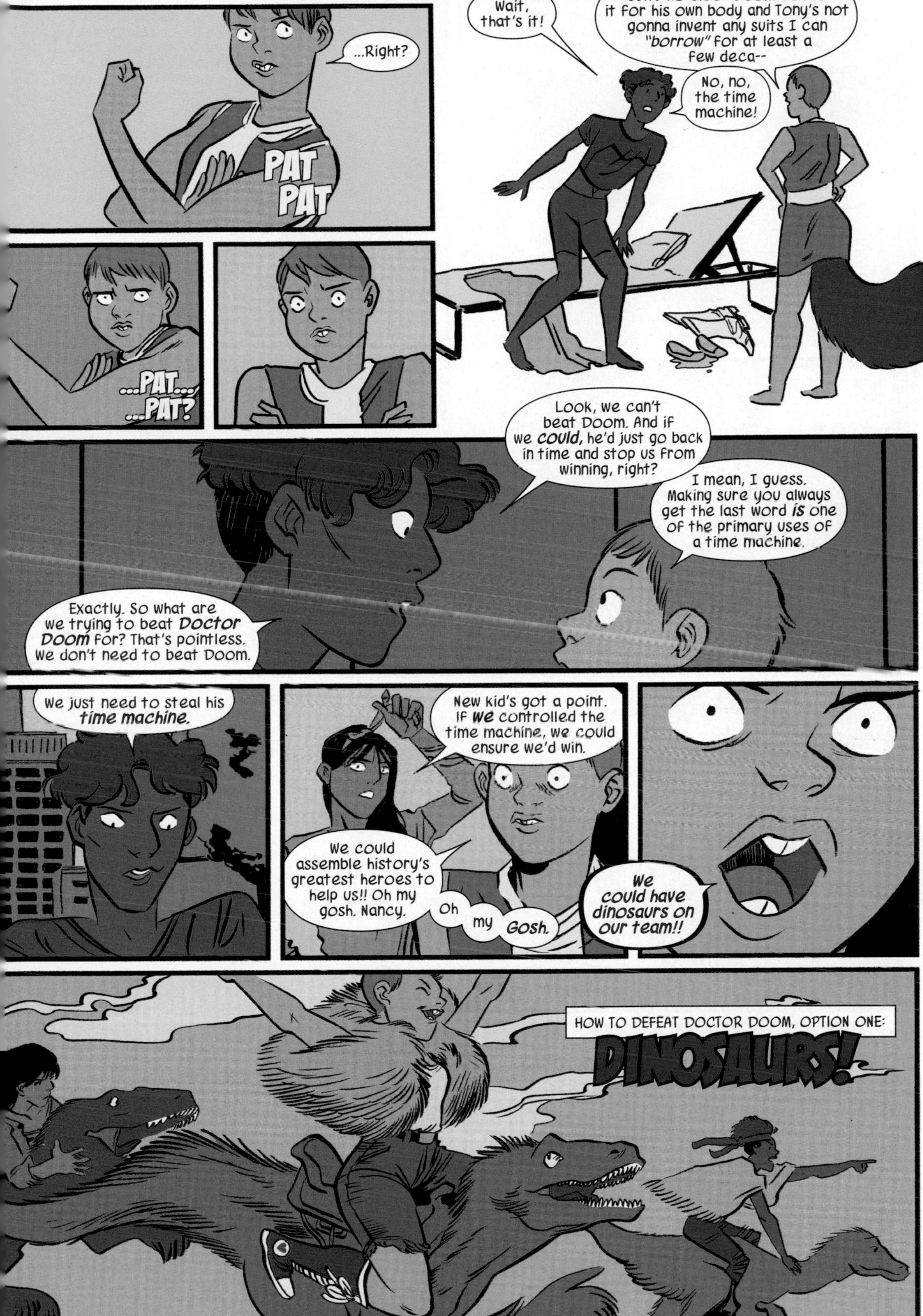
...Right?
PAT
PAT
Wait, that's it!
What, the robot suit? No dice--Doom codes it for his own body and Tony's not gonna invent any suits I can "*borrow*" for at least a few deca--
No, no, the time machine!
...PAT...
...PAT?
Look, we can't beat Doom. And if we ***could,*** he'd just go back in time and stop us from winning, right?
I mean, I guess. Making sure you always get the last word ***is*** one of the primary uses of a time machine.
Exactly. So what are we trying to beat ***Doctor Doom*** for? That's pointless. We don't need to beat Doom.
We just need to steal his ***time machine.***
New kid's got a point. If ***we*** controlled the time machine, we could ensure we'd win.
We could assemble history's greatest heroes to help us!! Oh my gosh. Nancy.
Oh
my
Gosh.
We could have dinosaurs on our team!!
HOW TO DEFEAT DOCTOR DOOM, OPTION ONE:
DINOSAURS!

here's ***no way*** Nancy is taking kindly to being called *"new kid,"* but once the timeline has been restored there will be plenty of time to go over who called whom what, and when, and how completely baloney some of those names may or may not have been.

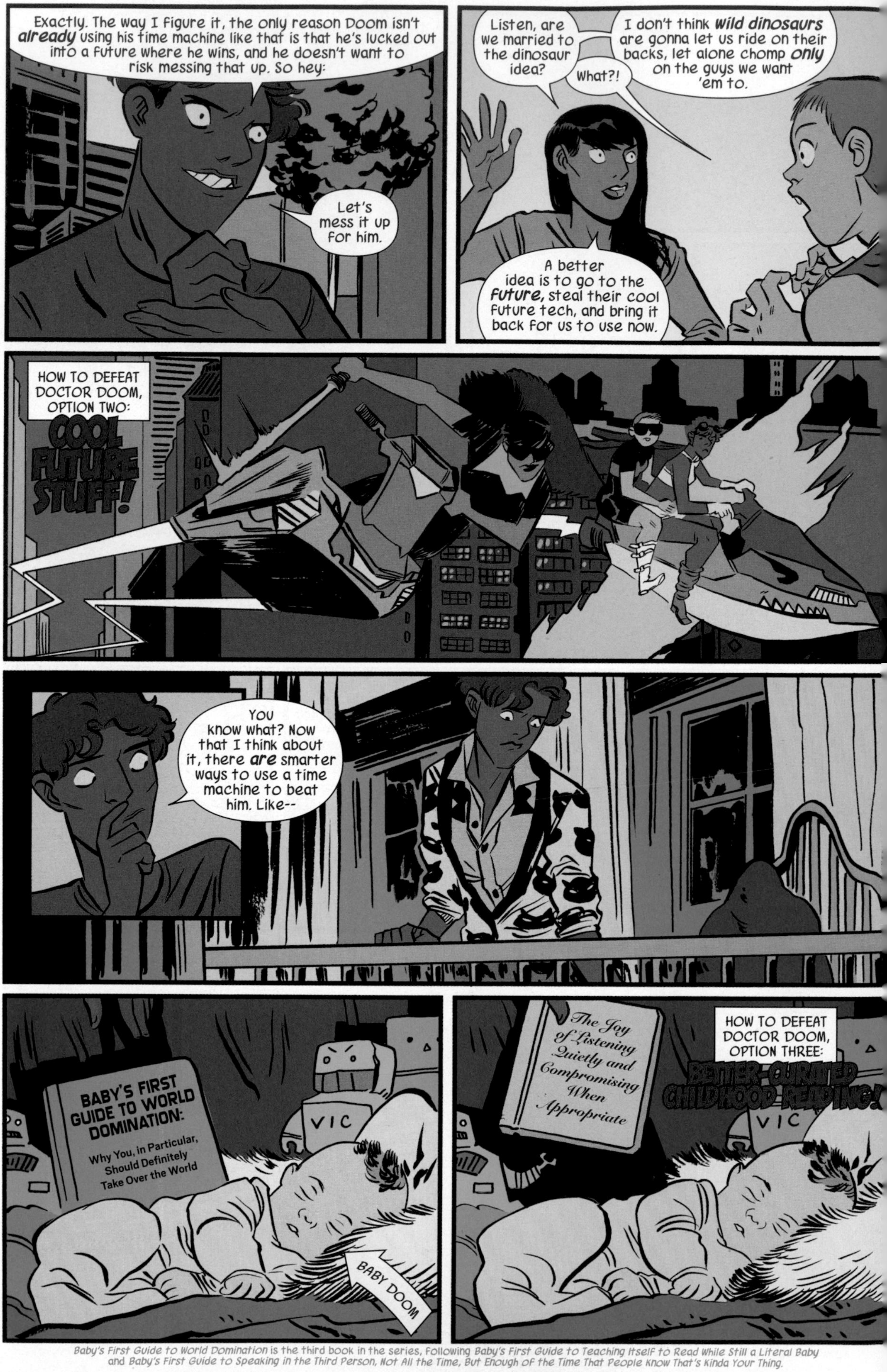
Exactly. The way I figure it, the only reason Doom isn't ***already*** using his time machine like that is that he's lucked out into a future where he wins, and he doesn't want to risk messing that up. So hey:
Let's mess it up for him.
Listen, are we married to the dinosaur idea?
What?!
I don't think ***wild dinosaurs*** are gonna let us ride on their backs, let alone chomp ***only*** on the guys we want 'em to.
A better idea is to go to the ***future,*** steal their cool future tech, and bring it back for us to use now.
HOW TO DEFEAT DOCTOR DOOM, OPTION TWO:
COOL FUTURE STUFF!
You know what? Now that I think about it, there ***are*** smarter ways to use a time machine to beat him. Like--
BABY'S FIRST GUIDE TO WORLD DOMINATION:
Why You, in Particular, Should Definitely Take Over the World
VIC
BABY DOOM
The Joy of Listening Quietly and Compromising When Appropriate
HOW TO DEFEAT DOCTOR DOOM, OPTION THREE:
BETTER-CURATED CHILDHOOD READING!
VIC

Baby's First Guide to World Domination is the third book in the series, following *Baby's First Guide to Teaching Itself to Read While Still a Literal Baby* and *Baby's First Guide to Speaking in the Third Person, Not All the Time, But Enough of the Time That People Know That's Kinda Your Thing.*

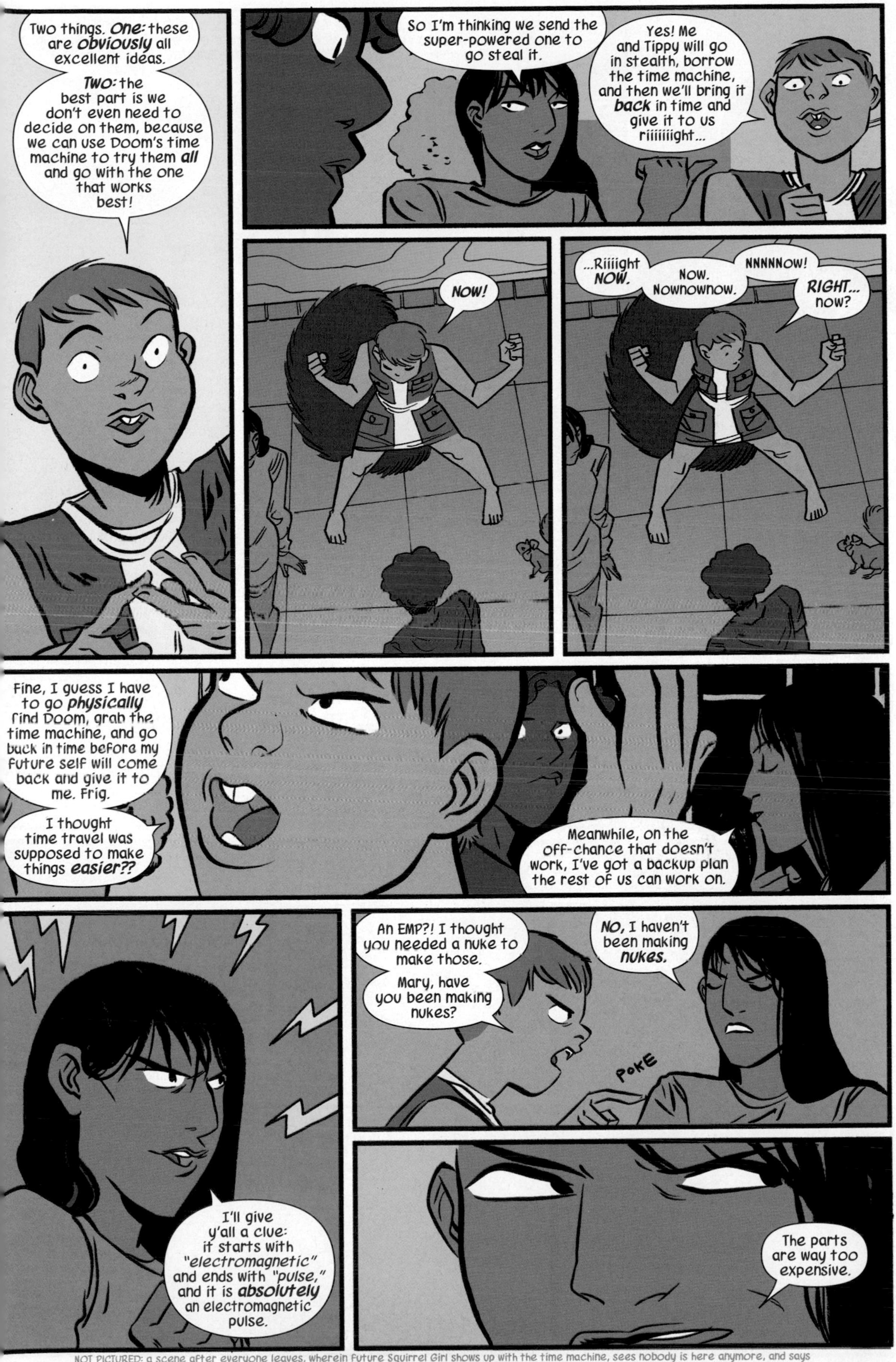
Two things. *One:* these are *obviously* all excellent ideas.
Two: the best part is we don't even need to decide on them, because we can use Doom's time machine to try them *all* and go with the one that works best!
So I'm thinking we send the super-powered one to go steal it.
Yes! Me and Tippy will go in stealth, borrow the time machine, and then we'll bring it *back* in time and give it to us riiiiiiight...
NOW!
...Riiiight *NOW.*
Now. Nownownow.
NNNNNow!
RIGHT... now?
Fine, I guess I have to go *physically* find Doom, grab the time machine, and go back in time before my future self will come back and give it to me. Frig.
I thought time travel was supposed to make things *easier??*
Meanwhile, on the off-chance that doesn't work, I've got a backup plan the rest of us can work on.
I'll give y'all a clue: it starts with *"electromagnetic"* and ends with *"pulse,"* and it is *absolutely* an electromagnetic pulse.
An EMP?! I thought you needed a nuke to make those.
Mary, have you been making nukes?
NO, I haven't been making *nukes.*
POKE
The parts are way too expensive.

NOT PICTURED: a scene after everyone leaves, wherein Future Squirrel Girl shows up with the time machine, sees nobody is here anymore, and says *"Dang it, I really need to wear a watch with my costume because I have* **no idea** *what time it was I was talking about"* and disappears again.

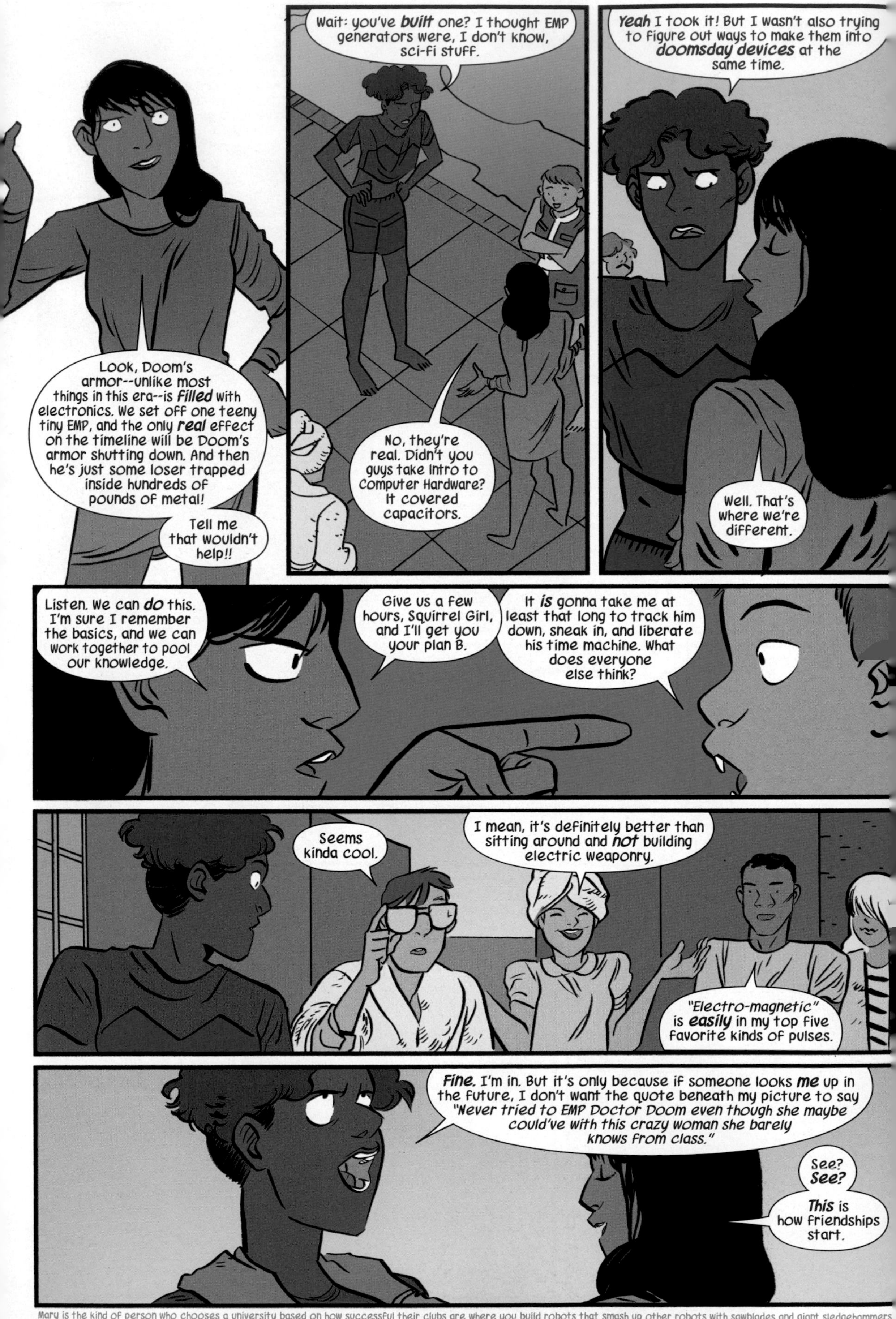
Look, Doom's armor--unlike most things in this era--is *filled* with electronics. We set off one teeny tiny EMP, and the only *real* effect on the timeline will be Doom's armor shutting down. And then he's just some loser trapped inside hundreds of pounds of metal!
Tell me that wouldn't help!!
Wait: you've *built* one? I thought EMP generators were, I don't know, sci-fi stuff.
No, they're real. Didn't you guys take Intro to Computer Hardware? It covered capacitors.
Yeah I took it! But I wasn't also trying to figure out ways to make them into *doomsday devices* at the same time.
Well. That's where we're different.
Listen. We can *do* this. I'm sure I remember the basics, and we can work together to pool our knowledge.
Give us a few hours, Squirrel Girl, and I'll get you your plan B.
It *is* gonna take me at least that long to track him down, sneak in, and liberate his time machine. What does everyone else think?
Seems kinda cool.
I mean, it's definitely better than sitting around and *not* building electric weaponry.
"Electro-magnetic" is *easily* in my top five favorite kinds of pulses.
Fine. I'm in. But it's only because if someone looks *me* up in the future, I don't want the quote beneath my picture to say *"Never tried to EMP Doctor Doom even though she maybe could've with this crazy woman she barely knows from class."*
See? *See?*
This is how friendships start.

Mary is the kind of person who chooses a university based on how successful their clubs are where you build robots that smash up other robots with sawblades and giant sledgehammers
Mary is the kind of person who has the right friggin' idea!!

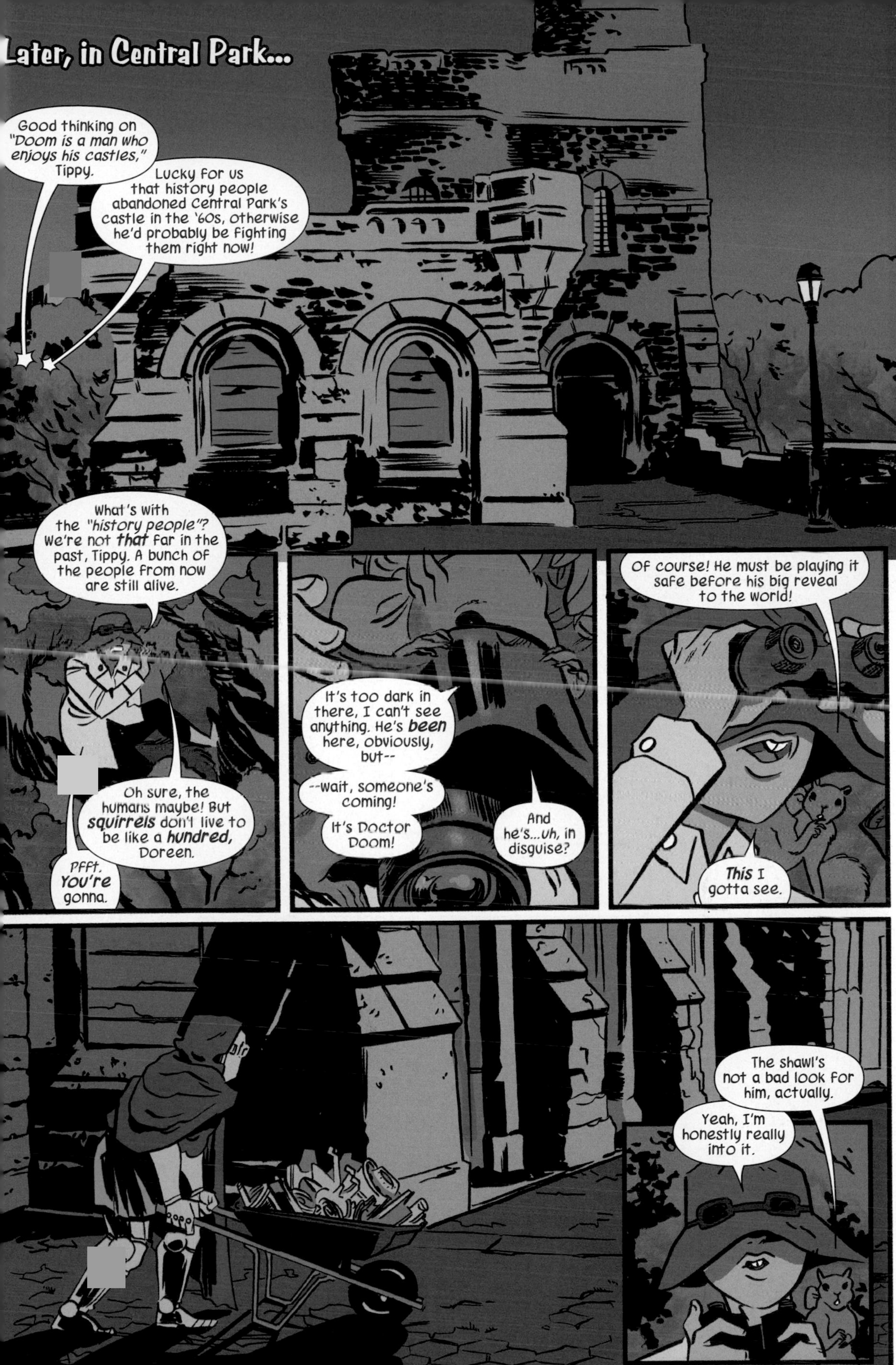

Later, in Central Park...
Good thinking on "Doom is a man who enjoys his castles," Tippy.
Lucky for us that history people abandoned Central Park's castle in the '60s, otherwise he'd probably be fighting them right now!
What's with the "history people"? We're not that far in the past, Tippy. A bunch of the people from now are still alive.
Oh sure, the humans maybe! But squirrels don't live to be like a hundred, Doreen.
Pfft. You're gonna.
It's too dark in there, I can't see anything. He's been here, obviously, but--
--wait, someone's coming!
It's Doctor Doom!
And he's...uh, in disguise?
Of course! He must be playing it safe before his big reveal to the world!
This I gotta see.
The shawl's not a bad look for him, actually.
Yeah, I'm honestly really into it.

For someone who *claims* to not know what cosplay is, Doom sure has a natural talent for cosplay.

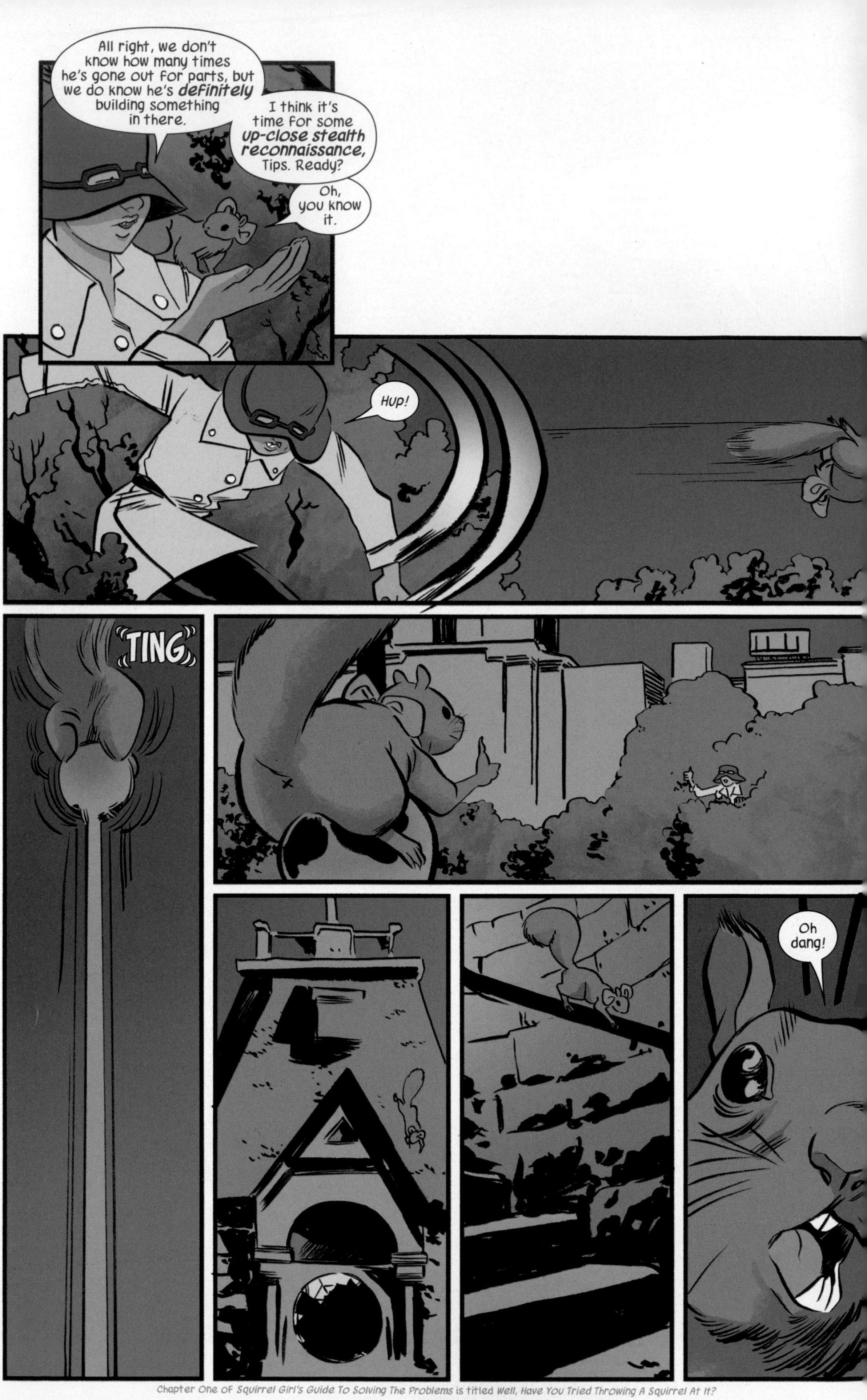
All right, we don't know how many times he's gone out for parts, but we do know he's *definitely* building something in there.
I think it's time for some *up-close stealth reconnaissance,* Tips. Ready?
Oh, you know it.
Hup!
TING
Oh dang!

Chapter One of *Squirrel Girl's Guide To Solving The Problems* is titled *Well, Have You Tried Throwing A Squirrel At It?*

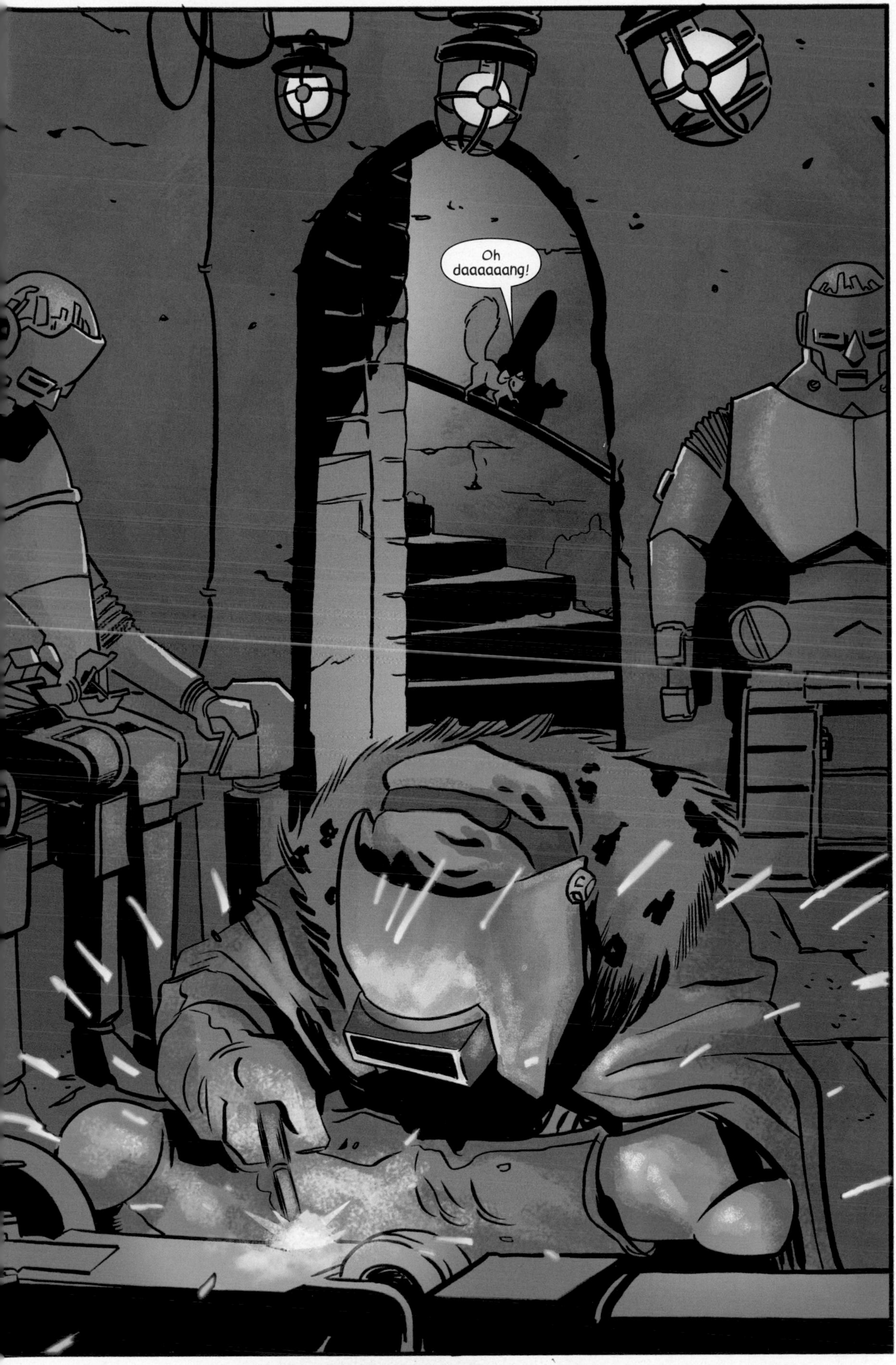
Oh daaaaaang!

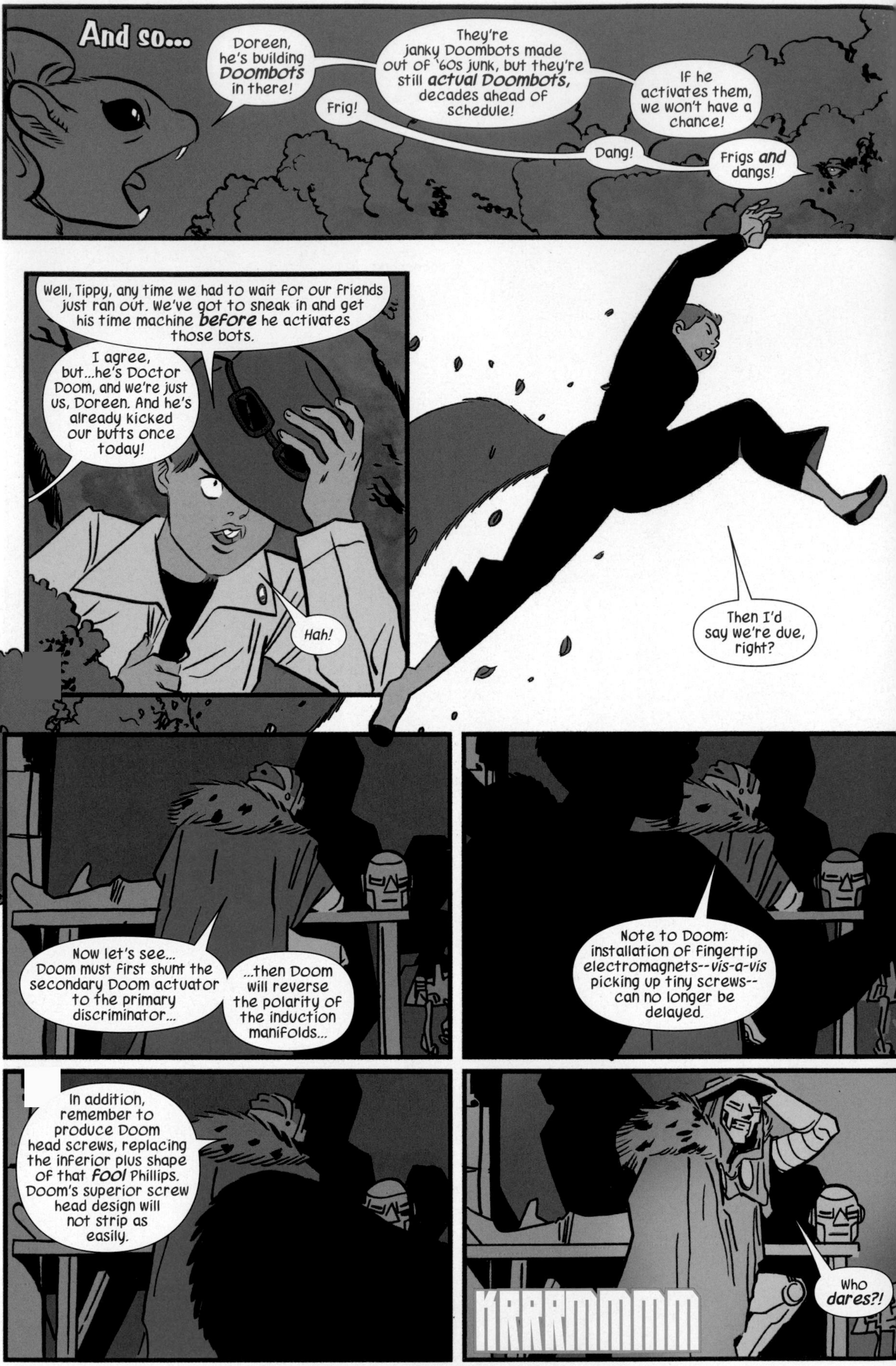
And so...
Doreen, he's building Doombots in there!
They're janky Doombots made out of '60s junk, but they're still actual Doombots, decades ahead of schedule!
If he activates them, we won't have a chance!
Frig!
Dang!
Frigs and dangs!
Well, Tippy, any time we had to wait for our friends just ran out. We've got to sneak in and get his time machine before he activates those bots.
I agree, but...he's Doctor Doom, and we're just us, Doreen. And he's already kicked our butts once today!
Hah!
Then I'd say we're due, right?
Now let's see... Doom must first shunt the secondary Doom actuator to the primary discriminator...
...then Doom will reverse the polarity of the induction manifolds...
Note to Doom: installation of fingertip electromagnets--vis-a-vis picking up tiny screws--can no longer be delayed.
In addition, remember to produce Doom head screws, replacing the inferior plus shape of that fool Phillips. Doom's superior screw head design will not strip as easily.
KRRRMMMM
Who dares?!

Anyone who works with screws for a living is remembering all the stripped screws in their past, nodding their head, and quietly whispering *"Today is the day I agree with Doctor Doom."*

Hey! Doom! Looks like your plan for world domination just ran out of... *time??*

Chhk Chhht!

KRRRMMMM

KRRRMMMM

KRRRMMMM

Come on, you stupid machine! *SMASH THROUGH TIME HERSELF ALREADY!!*

KRRRMMMMMMMmmmm

YOINK

Aaahh!!

Did you really think *DOOM* would be so foolish as to leave his time machine unattended *WITHOUT* a failsafe?!

What? *"Failsafe"?!*

Indeed. One which locks the time circuits so the machine can only move *FORWARD* in time, and only then at the rate of one second per second.

Shut up. You left your stupid time machine in *neutral?*

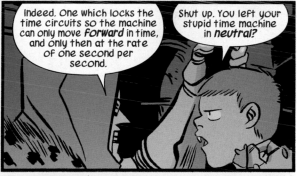

Only a *fool* would dare to call Doom's time machine *stupid!!*

Ow! Friggin' *OW*, dude!

One second per second is a pretty popular speed to career through time at. Why, I'd bet *money* it's the time travel that you're personally doing right now!!

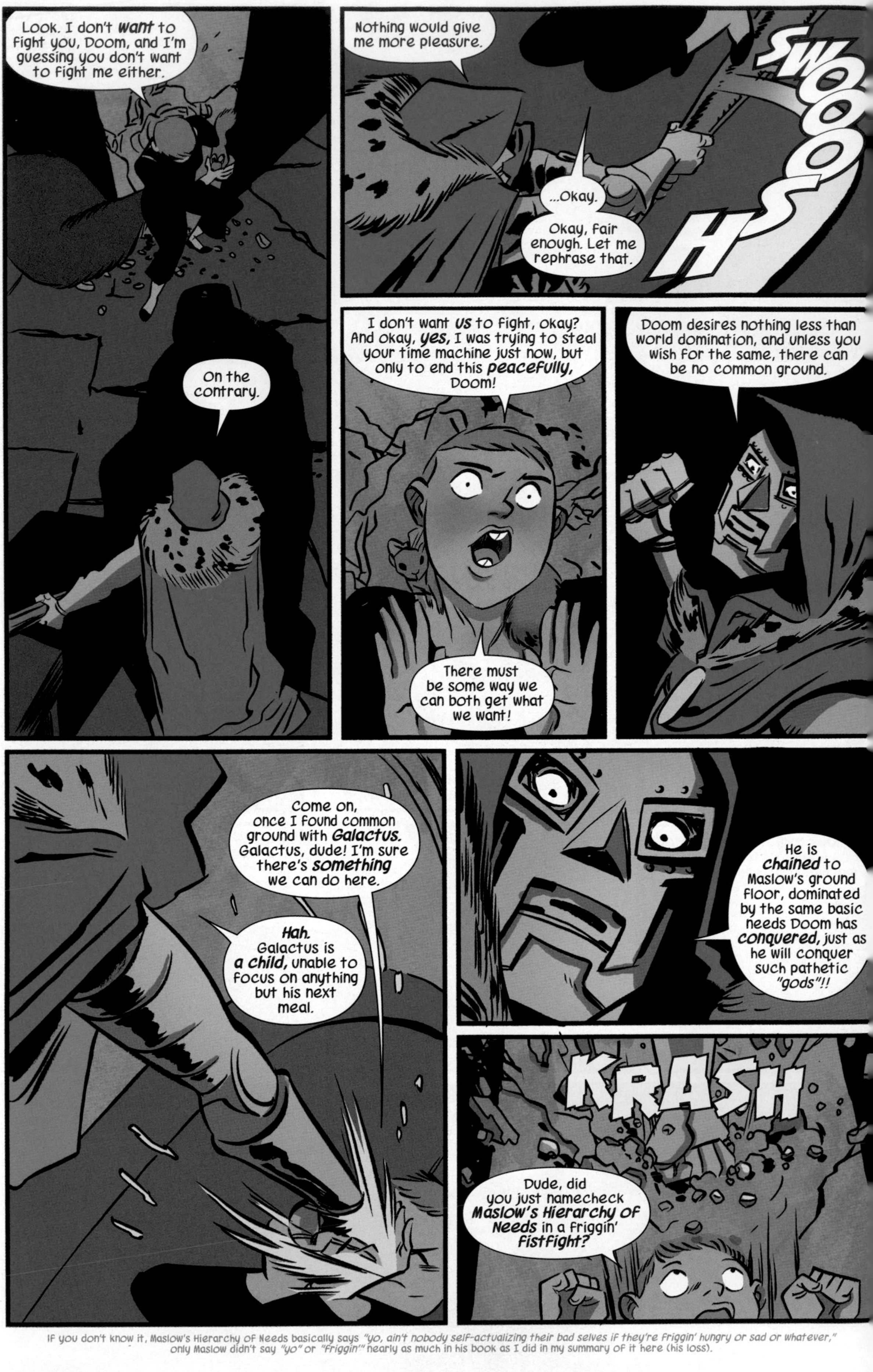

Look. I don't want to fight you, Doom, and I'm guessing you don't want to fight me either.
On the contrary.
Nothing would give me more pleasure.
SWOOOOSH
...Okay.
Okay, fair enough. Let me rephrase that.
I don't want US to fight, okay? And okay, yes, I was trying to steal your time machine just now, but only to end this peacefully, Doom!
There must be some way we can both get what we want!
Doom desires nothing less than world domination, and unless you wish for the same, there can be no common ground.
Come on, once I found common ground with Galactus. Galactus, dude! I'm sure there's something we can do here.
Hah. Galactus is a child, unable to focus on anything but his next meal.
He is chained to Maslow's ground floor, dominated by the same basic needs Doom has conquered, just as he will conquer such pathetic "gods"!!
KRASH
Dude, did you just namecheck Maslow's Hierarchy of Needs in a friggin' fistfight?

If you don't know it, Maslow's Hierarchy of Needs basically says *"yo, ain't nobody self-actualizing their bad selves if they're friggin' hungry or sad or whatever,"* only Maslow didn't say *"yo"* or *"friggin'"* nearly as much in his book as I did in my summary of it here (his loss).

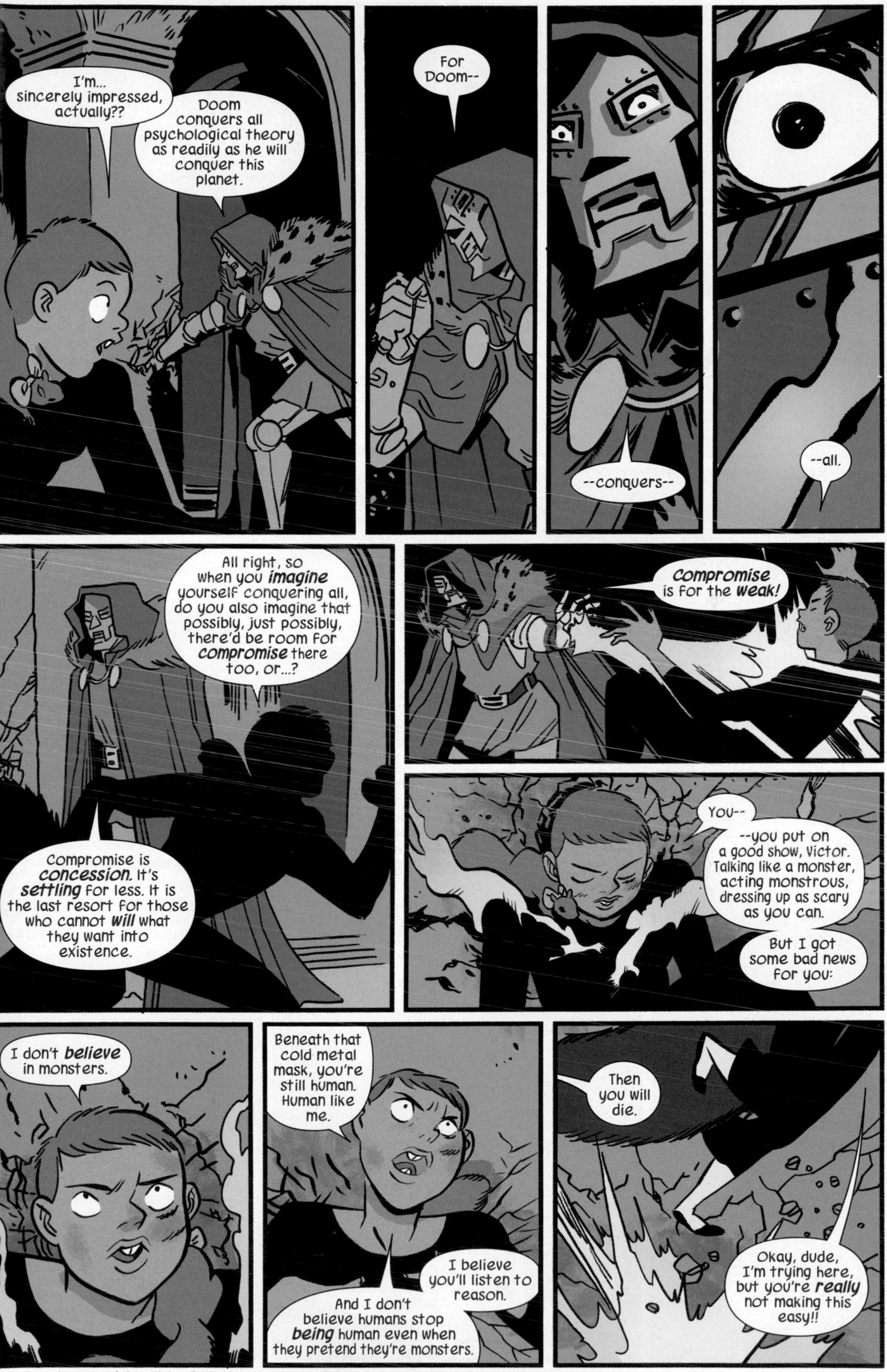
I'm... sincerely impressed, actually??
Doom conquers all psychological theory as readily as he will conquer this planet.
For Doom--
--conquers--
--all.
All right, so when you *imagine* yourself conquering all, do you also imagine that possibly, just possibly, there'd be room for *compromise* there too, or...?
Compromise is concession. It's settling for less. It is the last resort for those who cannot will what they want into existence.
Compromise is for the *weak!*
You--
--you put on a good show, Victor. Talking like a monster, acting monstrous, dressing up as scary as you can.
But I got some bad news for you:
I don't *believe* in monsters.
Beneath that cold metal mask, you're still human. Human like me.
I believe you'll listen to reason.
And I don't believe humans stop *being* human even when they pretend they're monsters.
Then you will die.
Okay, dude, I'm trying here, but you're *really* not making this easy!!

You put on a good show, Victor. Talking like a monster, acting monstrous, giving purple fur on your armor, juggling, spinning plates, doing jazz hands constantly. It's an impressive, extremely confusing show.

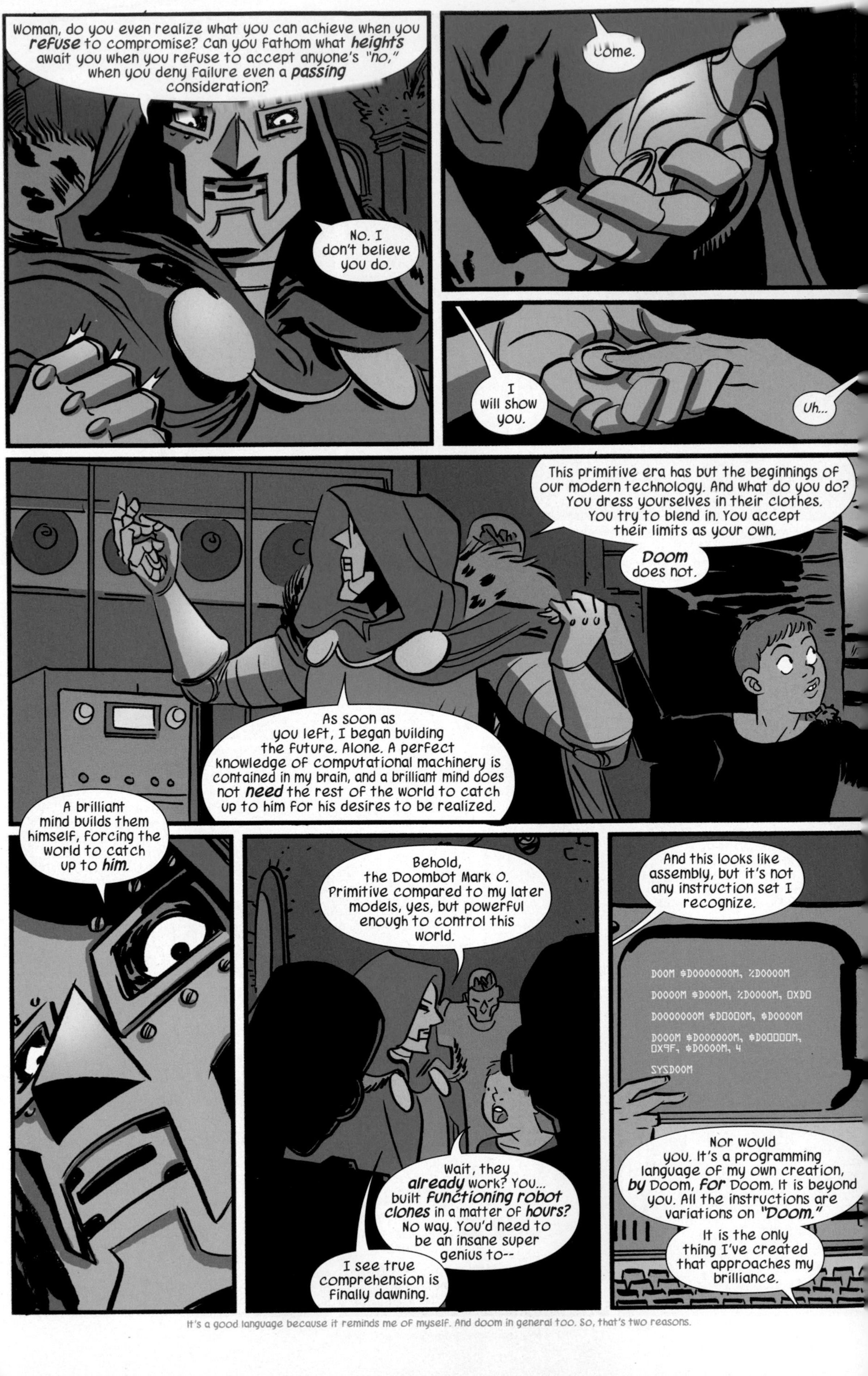
Woman, do you even realize what you can achieve when you *refuse* to compromise? Can you fathom what *heights* await you when you refuse to accept anyone's "no," when you deny failure even a *passing* consideration?
No. I don't believe you do.
Come.
I will show you.
Uh...
This primitive era has but the beginnings of our modern technology. And what do you do? You dress yourselves in their clothes. You try to blend in. You accept their limits as your own.
Doom does not.
As soon as you left, I began building the future. Alone. A perfect knowledge of computational machinery is contained in my brain, and a brilliant mind does not *need* the rest of the world to catch up to him for his desires to be realized.
A brilliant mind builds them himself, forcing the world to catch up to *him.*
Behold, the Doombot Mark 0. Primitive compared to my later models, yes, but powerful enough to control this world.
Wait, they *already* work? You... built *functioning robot clones* in a matter of *hours?* No way. You'd need to be an insane super genius to--
I see true comprehension is finally dawning.
And this looks like assembly, but it's not any instruction set I recognize.
DOOM $DOOOOOOOM, %DOOOOM
DOOOOM $DOOOM, %DOOOOM, 0XD0
DOOOOOOOM $D0O0OM, $DOOOOM
DOOOM $DOOOOOOM, $DO0000M,
0X9F, $DOOOOM, 4
SYSDOOM
Nor would you. It's a programming language of my own creation, *by* Doom, *for* Doom. It is beyond you. All the instructions are variations on *"Doom."*
It is the only thing I've created that approaches my brilliance.

It's a good language because it reminds me of myself. And doom in general too. So, that's two reasons.

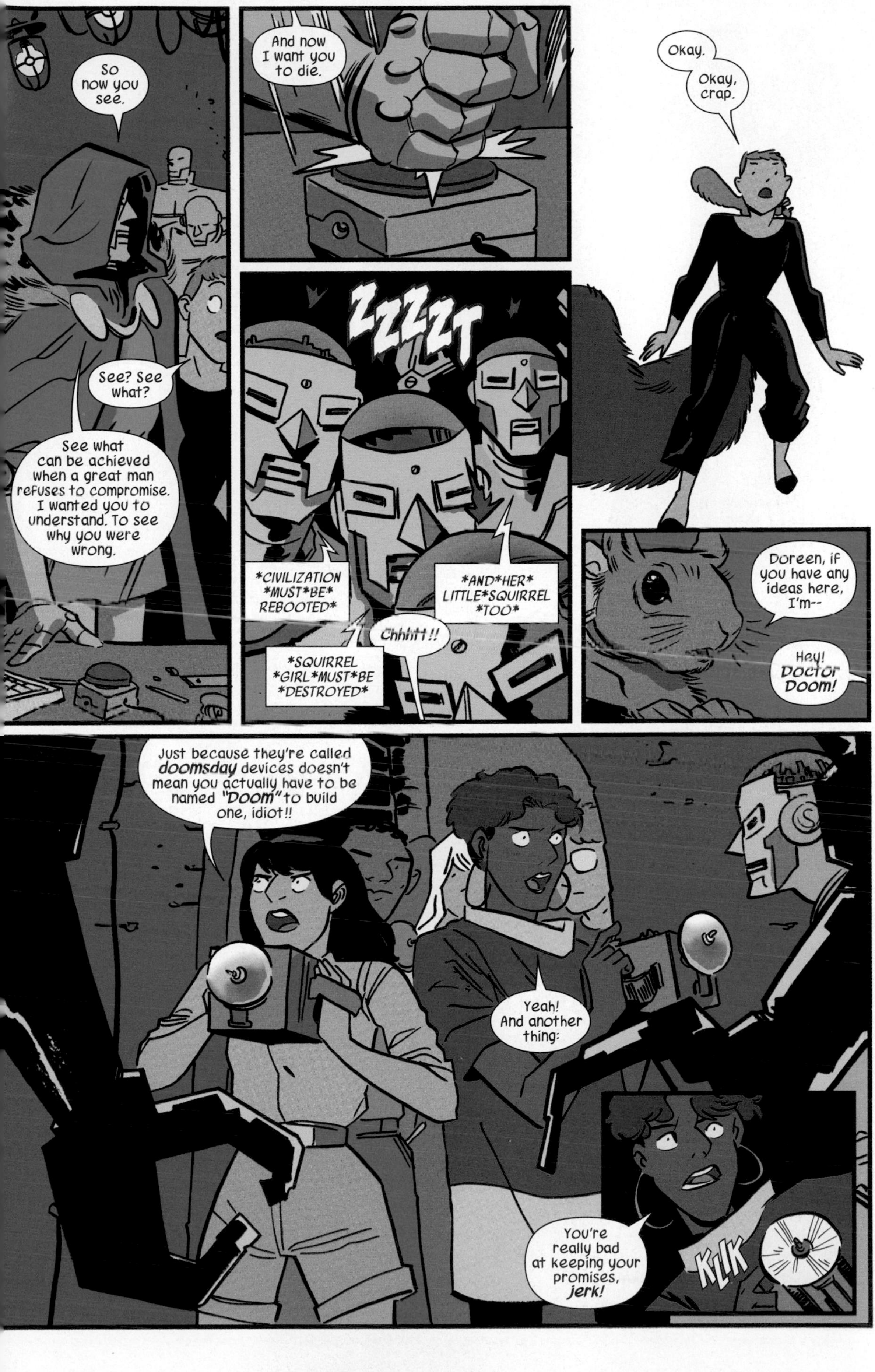
So now you see.
And now I want you to die.
Okay.
Okay, crap.
See? See what?
See what can be achieved when a great man refuses to compromise. I wanted you to understand. To see why you were wrong.
ZZZZT
*CIVILIZATION *MUST*BE* REBOOTED*
*AND*HER* LITTLE*SQUIRREL *TOO*
*SQUIRREL *GIRL*MUST*BE *DESTROYED*
Chhhtt!!
Doreen, if you have any ideas here, I'm--
Hey! Doctor Doom!
Just because they're called doomsday devices doesn't mean you actually have to be named "Doom" to build one, idiot!!
Yeah! And another thing:
You're really bad at keeping your promises, jerk!
KLIK

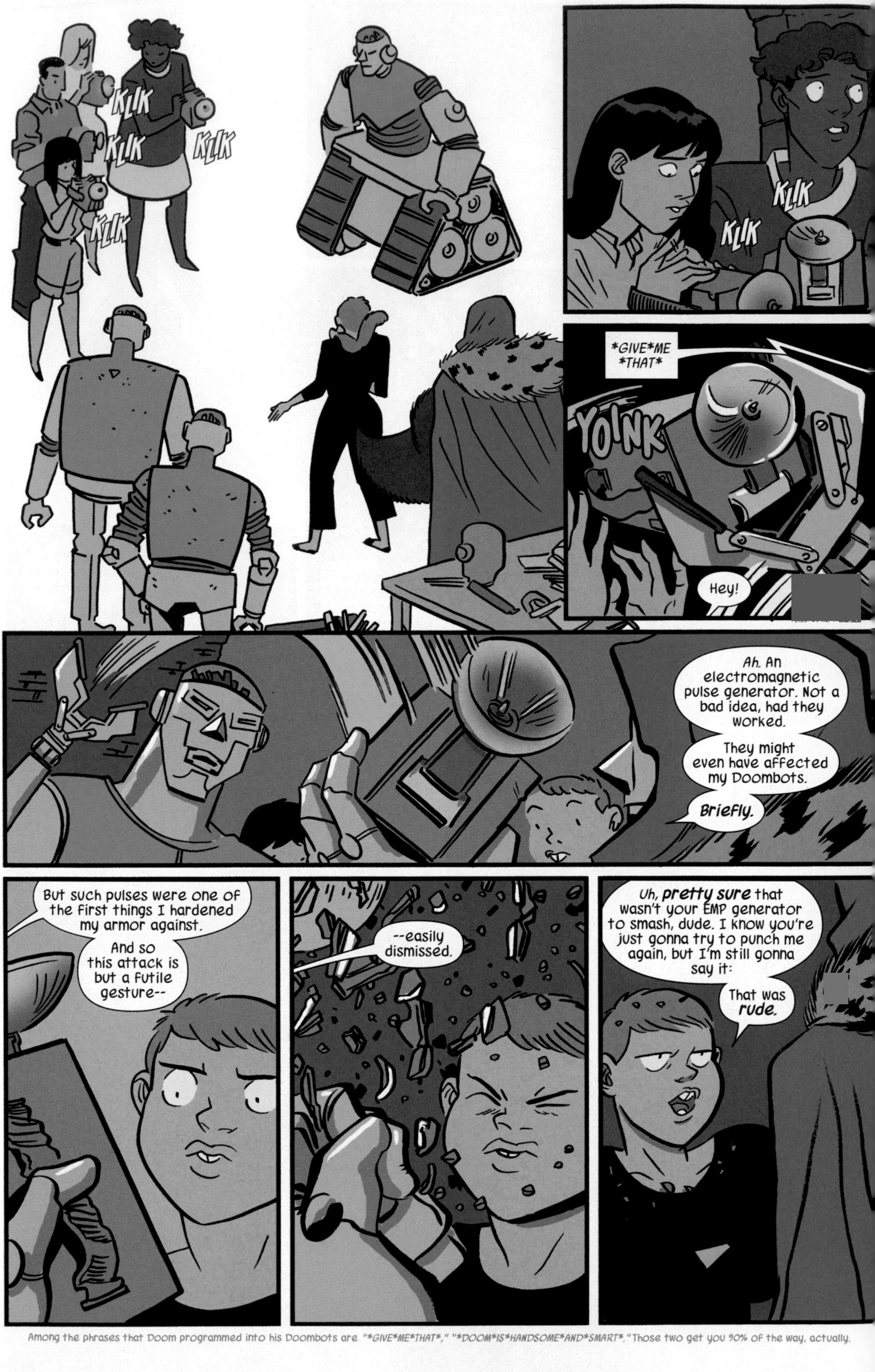
KLIK
KLIK
KLIK
KLIK
KLIK
KLIK
*GIVE*ME *THAT*
YOINK
Hey!
Ah. An electromagnetic pulse generator. Not a bad idea, had they worked.
They might even have affected my Doombots.
Briefly.
But such pulses were one of the first things I hardened my armor against.
And so this attack is but a futile gesture--
--easily dismissed.
Uh, pretty sure that wasn't your EMP generator to smash, dude. I know you're just gonna try to punch me again, but I'm still gonna say it:
That was rude.

Among the phrases that Doom programmed into his Doombots are "*GIVE*ME*THAT*," "*DOOM*IS*HANDSOME*AND*SMART*." Those two get you 90% of the way, actually.

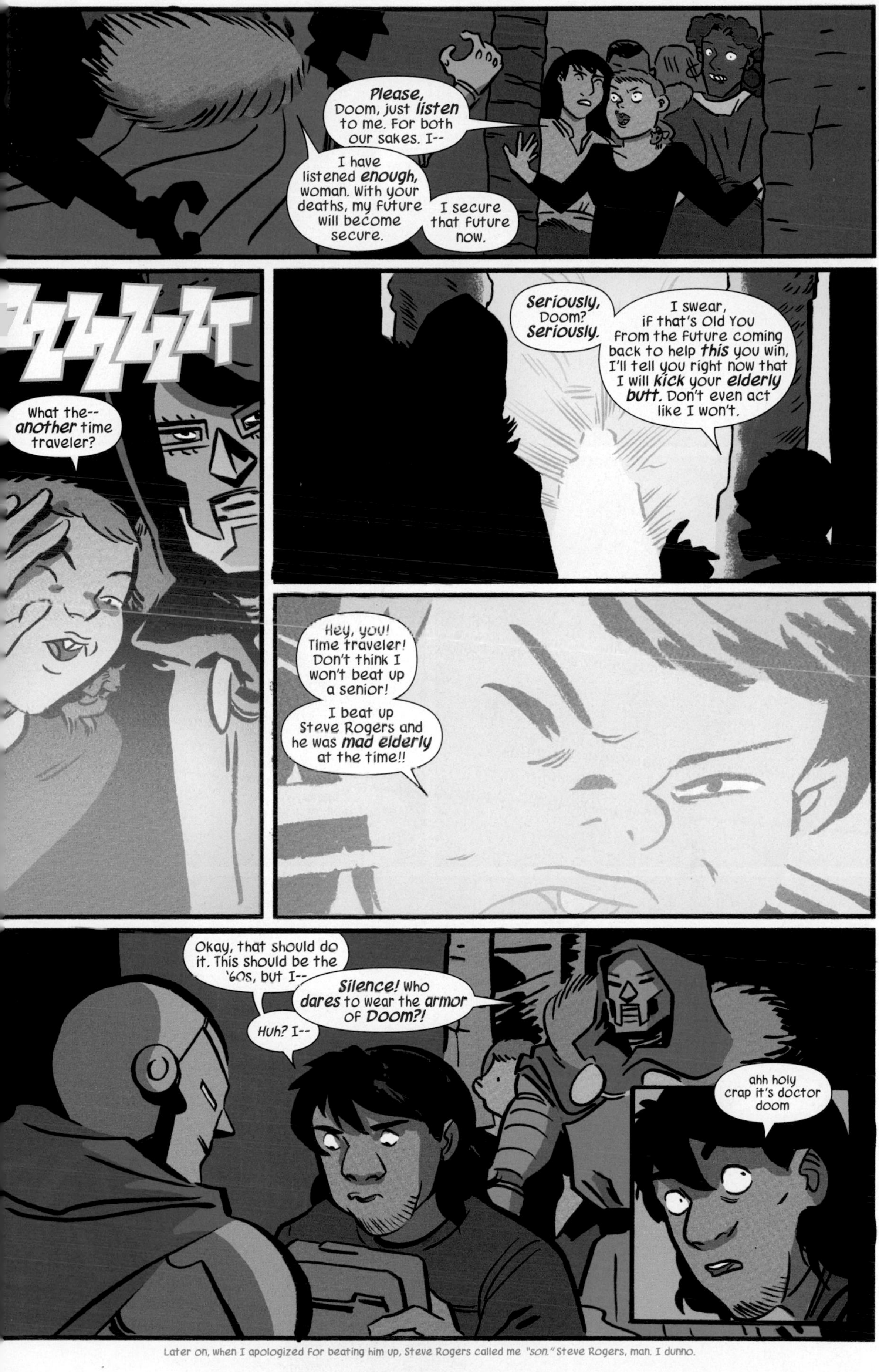
Please, Doom, just listen to me. For both our sakes. I--
I have listened enough, woman. With your deaths, my future will become secure.
I secure that future now.
ZZZZZZZT
What the-- another time traveler?
Seriously, Doom? Seriously.
I swear, if that's Old You from the future coming back to help this you win, I'll tell you right now that I will kick your elderly butt. Don't even act like I won't.
Hey, you! Time traveler! Don't think I won't beat up a senior!
I beat up Steve Rogers and he was mad elderly at the time!!
Okay, that should do it. This should be the '60s, but I--
Silence! Who dares to wear the armor of Doom?!
Huh? I--
ahh holy crap it's doctor doom

Later on, when I apologized for beating him up, Steve Rogers called me "son." Steve Rogers, man. I dunno.

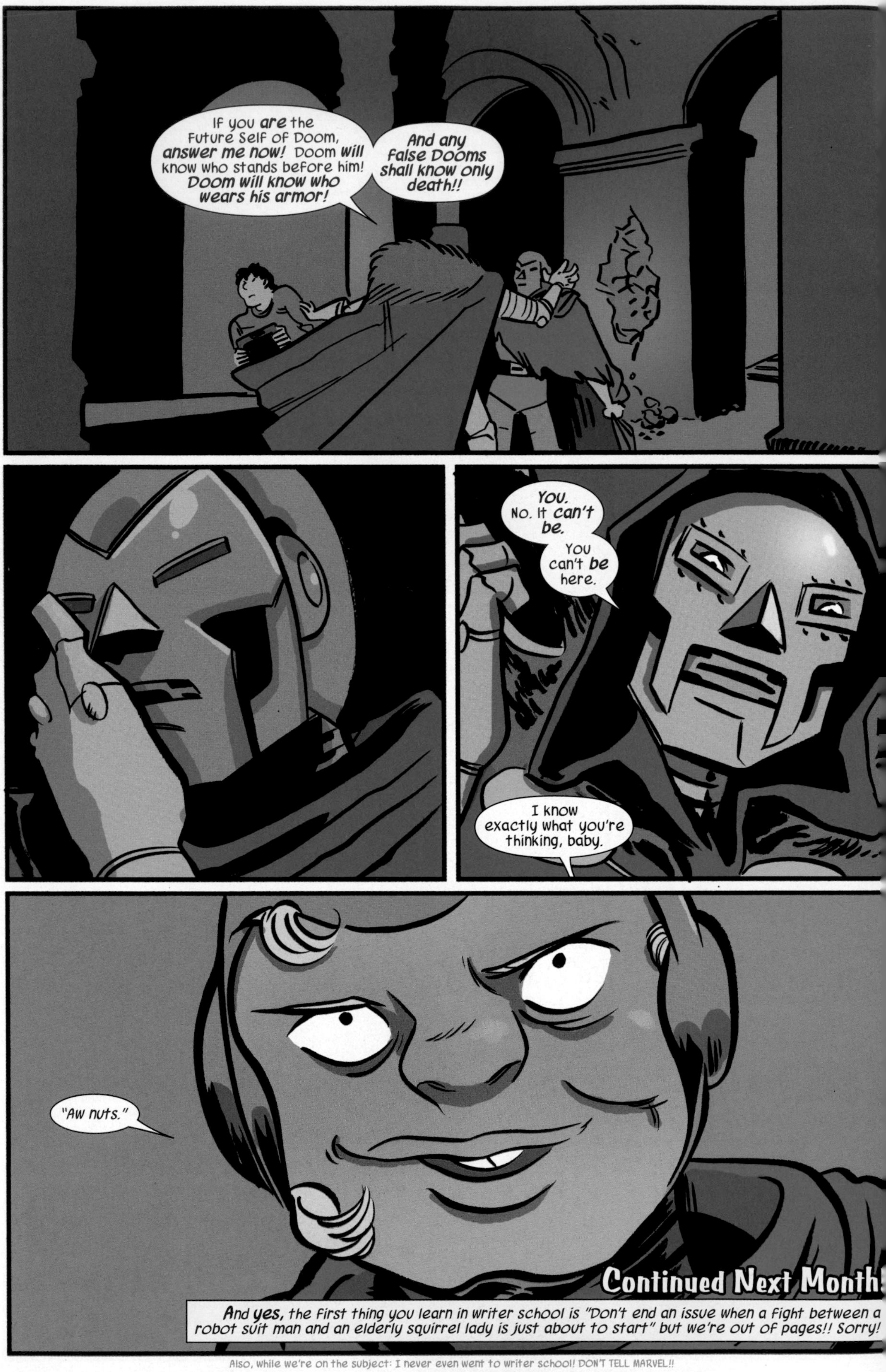
If you are the Future Self of Doom, answer me now! Doom will know who stands before him! Doom will know who wears his armor!
And any false Dooms shall know only death!!
You. No. It can't be.
You can't be here.
I know exactly what you're thinking, baby.
"Aw nuts."
Continued Next Month!
And yes, the first thing you learn in writer school is "Don't end an issue when a fight between a robot suit man and an elderly squirrel lady is just about to start" but we're out of pages!! Sorry!

Also, while we're on the subject: I never even went to writer school! DON'T TELL MARVEL!!

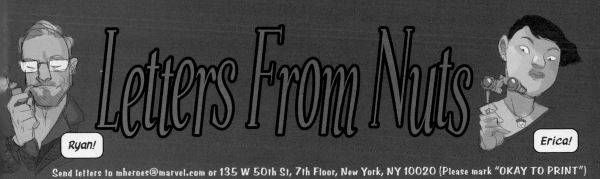

Letters From Nuts

Ryan! Erica!

Send letters to mheroes@marvel.com or 135 W 50th St, 7th Floor, New York, NY 10020 (Please mark "OKAY TO PRINT")

Dear Squirrel Girl Family,
I'm pretty sure I am Squirrel Girl. My name isn't Doreen, but I do go to school for engineering (pretty close to CS) in Boston (a big city like New York). I also have a friend that loves cats, and also crochets (which is just like knitting). However, her cat's name is Crape, not Mew. While my squirrel skillz have not shown themselves yet, I'm sure they will soon. I'll just keep waiting and hanging out at the park with my squirrel friends. I think I've figured out how to say acorn.

Anyways, I just read the second, second issue of the Unbeatable Squirrel Girl and I have to say I thoroughly enjoyed it. I especially liked the clothes Doreen ended up choosing to help her blend in to the '60s (one of my personal favorite decades, I'm listening to Jimi Hendrix as I write this, great choice). She will be my fashion inspiration this weekend for sure!

So I was wondering if you know what kind of music Doreen jams to? I think that would be an important clue to really reveal if I am in fact Squirrel Girl or not.

I've attached an image of myself and my fearless sidekick, Tippy-Toe.

Tippy toe and I are getting excited

Best,
Squirrel Girl… I mean, Emily

RYAN: This is a great costume, dang! So great. I am also big into the idea that you're living the SG lifestyle so completely that really our comic is just Emily fan fiction. For music, Erica and I actually make a playlist that's half music we listen to and half music Doreen does: if you look up "Music to Marvel By: Squirrel Girl" you will find it! I warn you:

it contains only the tightest of jams and the sickest of beats. FUN FACT: this story was originally going to have SG be sent back to the 1950s, but Erica pointed out that a) everyone goes to the '50s, and b) the '60s had way more fun fashions anyway. And she was correct! Also the '60s ended up working a lot better for the story anyway, so GOOD WORK, ERICA. Good work spotting my bad ideas and making them good.
ERICA: Ryan, everyone does the '50s. Like EVERYONE. I know you wanted to do Back To The Future, but we're not meeting anyone's grandparents so we can go to ANY TIME WE WANT.

Hello all,
It both makes me lol and makes me sad that the cover says 'Only our second #1 this year!'…
But I digress. I'm writing because I just have to ask:
When Brain Drain says "And so after the Canadian tundra released its frozen grasp up on me," is that a reference to his appearances in Alpha Flight?
Because that would be so so so cool to me.
Mik Bonnett
Canberra, Australia

R: Yep! I wanted to work in this dude's history, even if I was retconning it I MEAN FIXING IT at the same time.

Dear Ryan and Erica,
Congratulations on surviving Secret Wars! I'll admit that I was a bit worried about how Squirrel Girl and her friends would fare in the "All-New, All Different" era of Marvel Comics, but after reading The Unbeatable Squirrel Girl #1 No. 2, I'm glad to see that this corner of the Marvel Universe hasn't changed too much. Squirrel Girl is still the funniest, most optimistic, most butt-kicking and nut-eating comic on the market today!
I've been a fan since Issue #1 No. 1. I love how Doreen uses her wits and her charming personality to defeat the bad guys. I mean, this is the hero who literally defeated Galactus by using the Power of Friendship—and it was awesome! And speaking of friends, I love how Nancy and Doreen are super tight. No matter what super villain or complex algorithm Squirrel Girl finds herself up against, Nancy, Mew, and Nancy's knitting needles have got her back. I can't wait to see what kinds of shenanigans they'll get into next! It was great to see Nancy get her moment in the spotlight in Asgard. Will we get to see another Nancy-centric issue again soon? And what's the deal with Chipmunk Hunk? Do I sense a budding romance for our favorite squirrel-themed super hero?

By the way, speaking of Doreen and Nancy, I love their new haircuts! As always, Erica, you are knocking it out of the park with the artwork. And Ryan's jokes have had me busting a gut laughing in every single issue so far. As I keep telling all my comics-reading friends, "Hey, remember when comics were fun? Remember how great that was? Then you should be reading Squirrel Girl! Seriously!"
Keep on rockin' it, Squirrel Gang!
R Evans
Tacoma, WA
p.s. Nice leaning on the fourth wall re: Squirrel Girl's backstory. "Doreen is medically and legally distinct from being a mutant, and I can never take this back," eh? I see what you did there.
p.p.s. What are the odds of a Squirrel Girl/Ms. Marvel team-up? Or even better: Squirrel Girl and Groot vs. the Termite-inator?

R: Aw thanks, man! This was super flattering to read. I really like Nancy too, and I think you were probably happy with how much Nancy there was in the last couple issues! There's less of her in this issue, but that's only because I didn't get your letter in time. So let's say that every scene that she DOESN'T appear in during this issue, it's only because she was just out of frame, only nobody comments on that for some reason. I'm sure that won't cause any continuity problems at all!
p.s.: The deal with Chipmunk Hunk is that he is a hunk who has all the powers of a chipmunk. I thought that was pretty clear??

Dear Ryan and Erica,
Your series has made Squirrel Girl my favorite hero of all time! I love that she is smart and powerful, but also goofy and sassy. The writing is snappy and hilarious, and makes me laugh out loud every issue. I adore your cute art style, especially the body diversity that shows up in the different characters. Can't wait to see more of Squirrel Girl and Tippy's adventures! I have included photos of me in my Unbeatable Squirrel Girl costume. And thank you guys so much for an Unbeatable Comic!

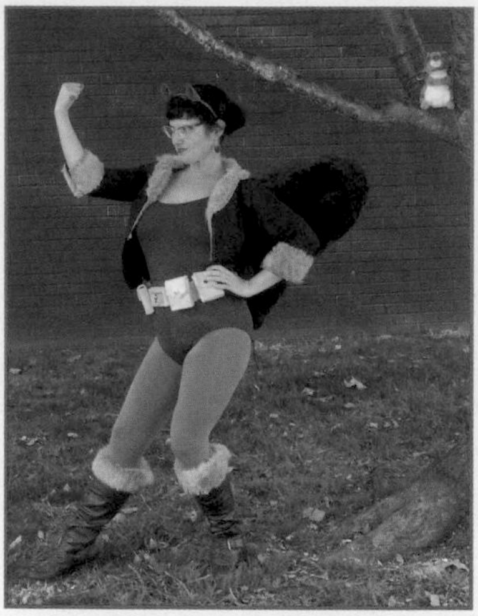

Sincerely,
Amanda Kindler

R: Amanda, your costume is spot-on! Amazing. I'm sincerely impressed! And now we've gone and given her a new costume, but it's our intention that she keeps them both around and uses them at different times and for different reasons: I figure that jacket probably gets hot if you do too much running around in it. Hey, does that jacket get hot if you do too much running around in it?

E: That jacket probably does get too hot. The new costume was based on tennis dresses that I saw at a sneaker store that was doing some big tennis-related promotion. And I liked the idea that it's this cute little girl dress but also 100% useful for running around in the heat.

Dear Ryan and Erica,

I just finished reading your new second issue, and it looks like Volume 2 of The Unbeatable Squirrel Girl is off and running. I look forward to seeing where your time travel story is headed; Dr. Doom has already appeared and I can only wonder if Doreen will become entangled in any of the timelines involving Kang / Rama-Tut / Immortus.

It was fun to see Doreen adjust to 1962. I've enclosed a Marvel Comics Group house ad from that year. As an old Silver Ager, I love how The Unbeatable Squirrel Girl logo uses a typeface virtually identical to that used on the Amazing Adult Fantasy and Fantastic Four comics of yesteryear. Who, pray tell, designed your logo? Please thank and congratulate him/her on my behalf.

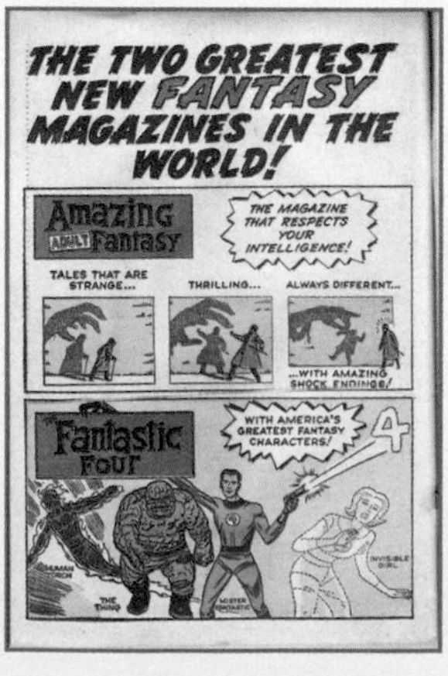
THE TWO GREATEST NEW FANTASY MAGAZINES IN THE WORLD!
Amazing ADULT Fantasy
THE MAGAZINE THAT RESPECTS YOUR INTELLIGENCE!
TALES THAT ARE STRANGE...
THRILLING...
ALWAYS DIFFERENT...
...WITH AMAZING SHOCK ENDINGS!
Fantastic Four
WITH AMERICA'S GREATEST FANTASY CHARACTERS!
4

Excelsior!

Charles Hoffman
Van Nuys, CA

R: Oh man, I never even realized the similar type treatment to Amazing ADULT Fantasy (what a title that was) but I hope we can carry on its tradition of being The Magazine That Respects Your Intelligence! Our logo was done by Mike Allred, who you don't need me to tell you is AMAZING, and whose work you can check out on SILVER SURFER AS WE SPEAK (ps: it's really good).

E: DON'T EVEN GET ME STARTED ON HOW BAD I WANT TO DRAW KANG.

Dear Ryan and Erica,

Hey guys! I'm loving the new series, and I'm trying to get some of my friends into it. The trouble is, they don't think Squirrel Girl is important enough to care about. Do you have any advice on how to change their minds?

Oscar Lee

R: Oh this is an easy one! Grab one of our issues and tape over its cover with a piece of paper upon which you have written "VERY IMPORTANT DOCUMENTS!!!!!!". They will be drawn to it like a moth to flame, or more appropriately, like a ground-dwelling squirrel to other ground-dwelling squirrels (ground-dwelling squirrels are generally social animals, while tree-dwelling squirrels are more solitary). P.S.: guess what? That was a very important squirrel fact that your friends who only care about important things should be made aware of!!

Hello, Team SG! I just wanted to say thank you for making such a wonderful comic. Doreen and Nancy are both so relatable and inspirational. Every single issue makes me laugh and smile, mostly from Ryan's dorky comments. Erica, I absolutely adore how you draw Doreen. She's not the overused stereotype of enormous breasts and unrealistic waistline. She looks like a realistic representation of a college student, and she helps me feel better about my own appearance. Keep up the great work, you two!

Sam
Colorado

R: Hey Sam, thanks! I think I've mentioned this before, but the character of SG really came into focus for me when Erica sent over her early sketches: they had such life and humor and confidence in them that I was like, oh, OKAY, I know who this person is! DONE. And I like how Erica draws different body types in our book because I think it's great when you can look inside a comic and see someone who looks like you. I'm glad you agree!

E: Thanks! It's not really something I thought about too much except that in most of her older appearances the joke was that she was the most unassuming and sometimes dorky looking character who nobody could think was UNBEATABLE. Also I just like when characters who are more physical are a little thicker--makes me think I can't take them out by sitting on them.

Dear Ryan and Erica.

The Unbeatable Squirrel Girl is the first comic that my 7 year old daughter Riley re
and every month we eagerly await the ne
issue to read at bedtime. Riley is such a hu
fan of Doreen that she dressed up as her f
Halloween. Here are some photos of her (wi
Tippy-Toe)

Mike Dav

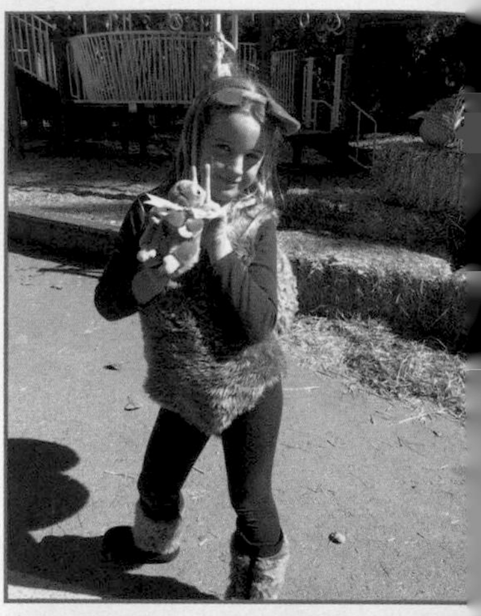

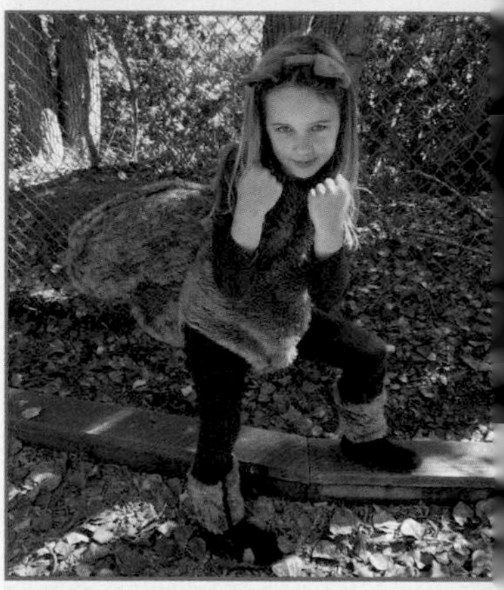

R: Riley, I'll tell you one thing: you costume is amazing and you've got th attitude down COLD. I hope you enjoyed thi issue! Now since you read these at bedtime I guess it's TIME FOR SLEEP. Here's a fu fact about sleep: we don't really know wh it happens! Scientists think that maybe i helps our brains and/or bodies recharg and recover, but we can't yet say for sure Basically, ask a scientist for the reason wh people sleep, and they'll say "because the get real sleepy." Amazing!

Dear Ryan & Erica,

Thank you so much for your work on Th Unbeatable Squirrel Girl! There's not a lot o books that I pick up on Wednesdays that m wife wants to read too. Now, we share th adventures of Doreen and the gang together And we've become an even closer couple.

I can't remember where I heard it first, bu I know there was talk sometime ago abou Kristen Schaal being on the short list t portray SG in the MCU. Reading issue 1, all could hear was her voice for Miss Green.

Ryan, did you have anyone in mind whe pennig the script?

Erica, is Squirrel Girl's mug modeled afte anyone in particular?

R & E, how would you guys feel abou Kristen playing the role? Or whom else woul

ɔu cast if not her?
Thanks again for a wonderful read!

Take care,
Todd A. Davis
Greenville, SC
@MrToddADavis

R: I didn't have anyone in mind for SG when I was writing her, o, but I can see Kristen Schaal being a good fit! I've also heard eople suggest Ellie Kemper in a sort of "Unbreakable Squirrel irl" pitch and I can totally see that too. ComicsAlliance suggested lae Whitman for Doreen and Vicky Jeudy for Nancy (and Eugene utz for Kraven) earlier this year and I was like, yes, yes, please.

The bad news is we don't get to say who gets cast in movies (or ven which characters show up in movies) but clearly SOMEONE oes, and hopefully that person likes comics! HELLO, person who ecides to put Squirrel Girl in a movie and who is reading this etters page right now! In my opinion, you should decide to do that ning you're currently considering!!

E: I didn't have anyone in mind when I started. Now, I'd like ɔ see Jennifer Lawrence in the role since she's known for being oofy, is an action hero and has those cheeks! She's also in the "if ou think that's fat then I don't even know" category.

ollege-Educated Squirrel Girl Folks,

I decided to give my Statistics class the included question on an ssignment I'll be handing out today. Surely, you all can determine ne answers!

Stephen Davidson
Danville, VA

R: AMAZING. Also, if you are a student in Stephen's class who as picked up this comic to find out the correct answers (thank ou! I hope you enjoyed it!), you should know that I'm not gonna ust GIVE you them, but I'll remind you you're simply looking for he ratio of the standard deviation to the mean! No sweat!

E: I...went to art school.

Come back next month for #5, the exciting conclusion! (Old Lady Squirrel Girl is even more awesome than you're no doubt already imagining her to be!)

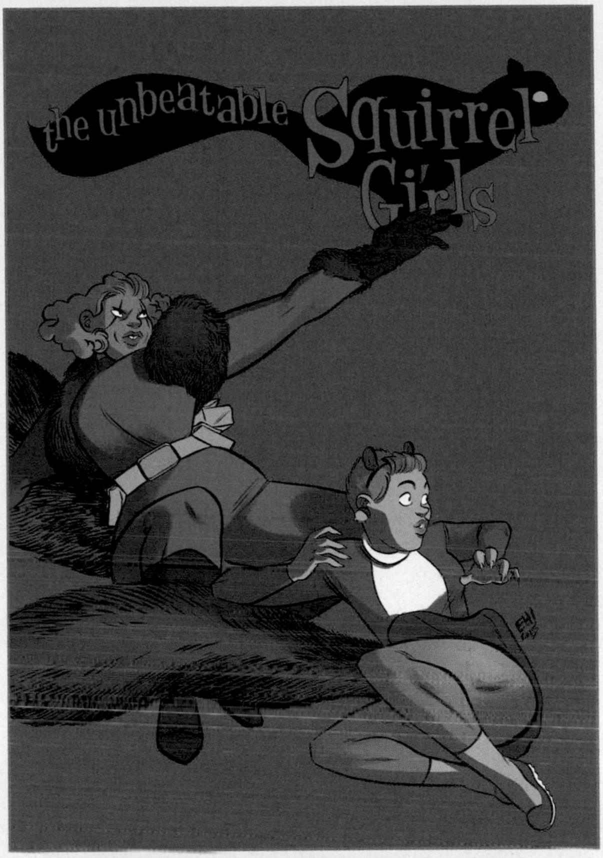
the unbeatable Squirrel Girls

10. Squirrel Girl and her friends are preparing a huge Arbor Day celebration (like we all do) and they have decided to go out and collect nuts for the big bash rather than spend money buying them. They also hold a friendly competition to see who has more invitees show up at the party because all parties are in actuality a celebration of friendship. The below table lists how many nuts each party planner collects and how many invitees of each planner attends the party. Find the coefficient of variation of the number of collected nuts as well as for the number of attending invitees. Also, read THE UNBEATABLE SQUIRREL GIRL. Unless you hate art, fun, friendship, laughing, being entertained, and words.

Party Planner	Number of Nuts Collected	Number of Attending Invitees
Squirrel Girl – 50% squirrel, 100% girl	578	34
Tippy Toe – 100% squirrel	3,916	4
Nancy Whitehead – 100% girl	110	42
Koi Boi – 0% squirrel, 0% girl	6	2
Chipmunk Hunk – the rhyming squirrel names were taken	488	19

Attention, Squirrel Scouts! Make sure to check out our production blog, **unbeatablesquirrelgirl.tumblr.com**, where we post behind-the-scenes stuff on how the book gets made, along with all sorts of cool things *you* make: fanart, cosplay, whatever!

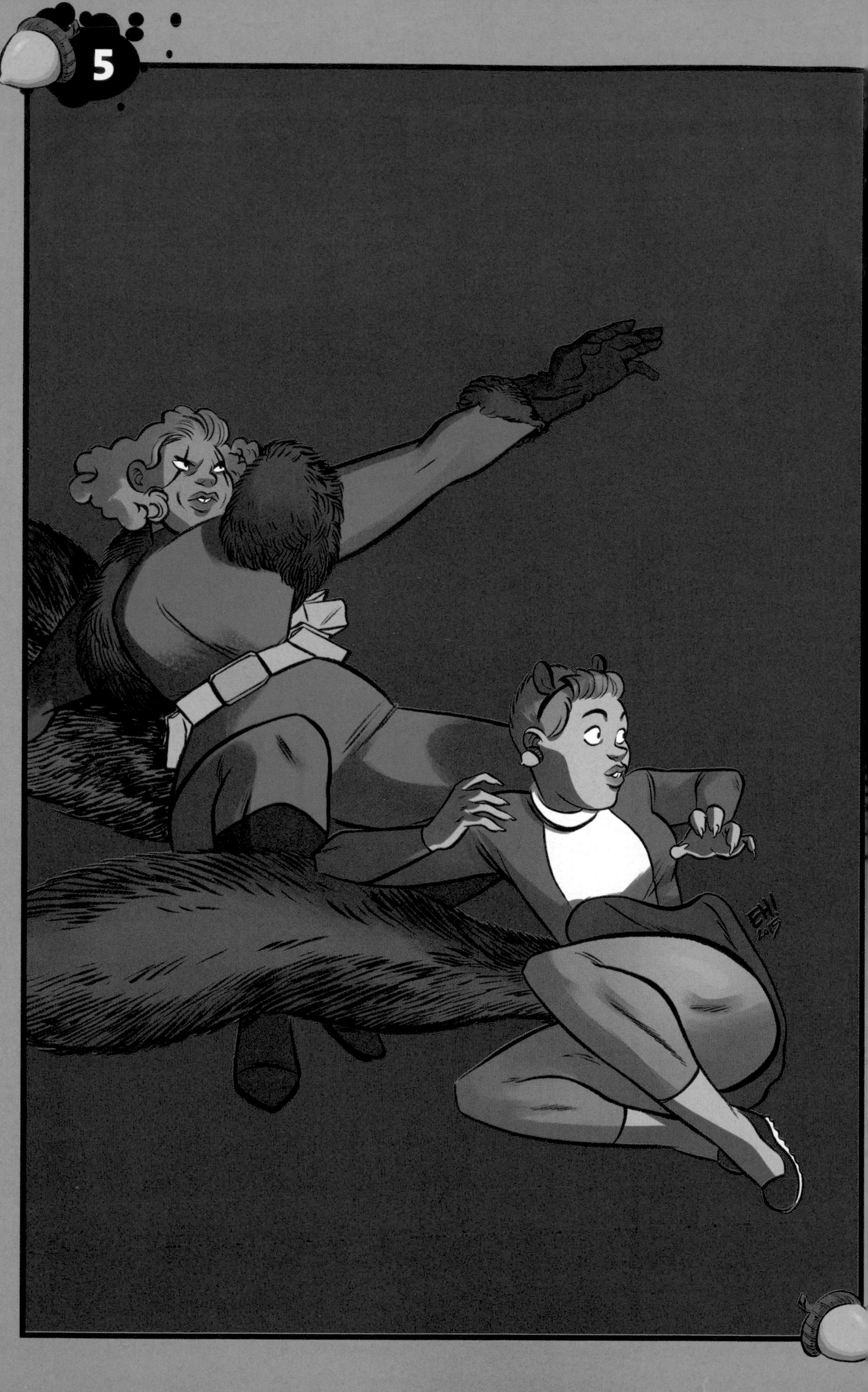
5

Doreen Green isn't just a second-year computer science student: she secretly also has all the powers of both squirrel and girl! She uses her amazing abilities to fight crime **and** be as awesome as possible. You know her as...**The Unbeatable Squirrel Girl!** Find out what she's been up to, with...

Squirrel Girl *in a nutshell*

[X] URGENT

WHILE YOU WERE OUT

To **The United Nations**

From **Squirrel Girl**

Of **The East Coast Squirrel Girls**

[X] TELEPHONED   [ ] PLEASE CALL

[ ] CAME TO SEE YOU   [ ] WILL CALL AGAIN

[X] WANTS TO SEE YOU   [ ] RETURNED YOUR CALL

Message Um, I warned y'all that Doctor Doom came back in time to the '60s (ie: RIGHT NOW) and what did you do? NOTHING. So me and my friends ~~invented EMP generators~~ found some EMP generators lying around and tried to stop him, but it didn't work! SO THANKS FOR NOTHING, THE UNITED NATIONS!

[X] URGENT

WHILE YOU WERE OUT

To **The United Nations**

From **Squirrel Girl**

Of **The same woman who sent the last note**

[X] TELEPHONED   [X] PLEASE CALL

[ ] CAME TO SEE YOU   [ ] WILL CALL AGAIN

[ ] WANTS TO SEE YOU   [ ] RETURNED YOUR CALL

Message Oh and, AND, Doom also built DOOMBOTS (robot duplicates of himself) and programmed them using a weird "DOOMssembly" language he invented, so if we lose and he takes over the world then all I can tell you about it is that the commands are all variants of "DOOM" and it looks like a real pain to program in, tbh

---

[X] URGENT

WHILE YOU WERE OUT

To **The United Nations**

From **Squirrel Girl**

Of **how do you not know me yet, sheesh**

[ ] TELEPHONED   [ ] PLEASE CALL

[ ] CAME TO SEE YOU   [ ] WILL CALL AGAIN

[X] WANTS TO SEE YOU   [ ] RETURNED YOUR CALL

Message Also this guy Cody came back in time from the future (ie: MY present) with an older me!! Haha YEP I'M FROM THE FUTURE and wasn't even born in the '60s!! I don't even mind telling you United Nations guys anymore, because nobody even READS these notes even though I put them up really nicely on your stupid bulletin board!!

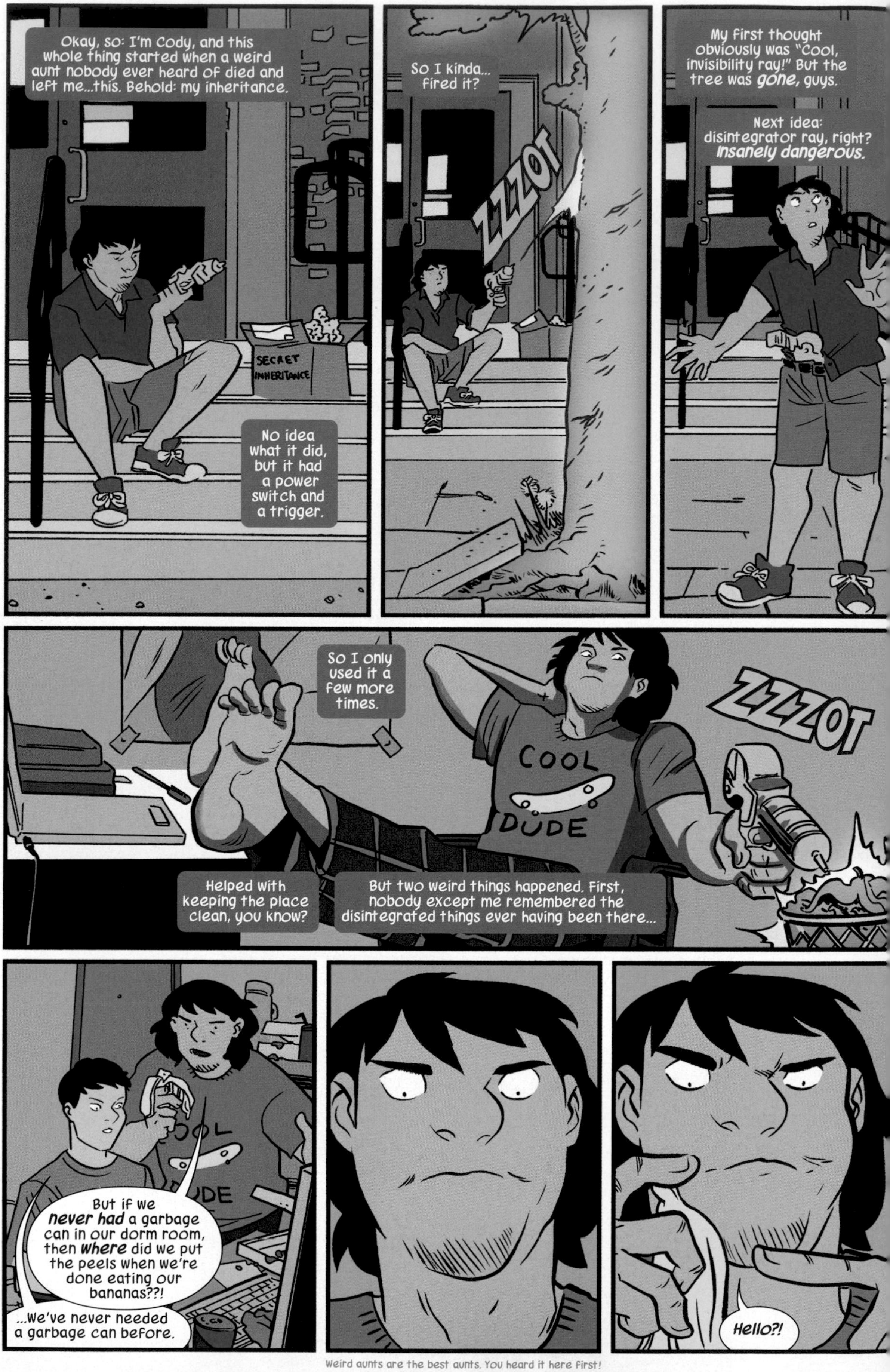

Okay, so: I'm Cody, and this whole thing started when a weird aunt nobody ever heard of died and left me...this. Behold: my inheritance.
SECRET INHERITANCE
No idea what it did, but it had a power switch and a trigger.
So I kinda... fired it?
ZZZOT
My first thought obviously was "Cool, invisibility ray!" But the tree was gone, guys.
Next idea: disintegrator ray, right? Insanely dangerous.
So I only used it a few more times.
ZZZOT
COOL DUDE
Helped with keeping the place clean, you know?
But two weird things happened. First, nobody except me remembered the disintegrated things ever having been there...
But if we never had a garbage can in our dorm room, then where did we put the peels when we're done eating our bananas??!
...We've never needed a garbage can before.
Hello?!

Weird aunts are the best aunts. You heard it here first!

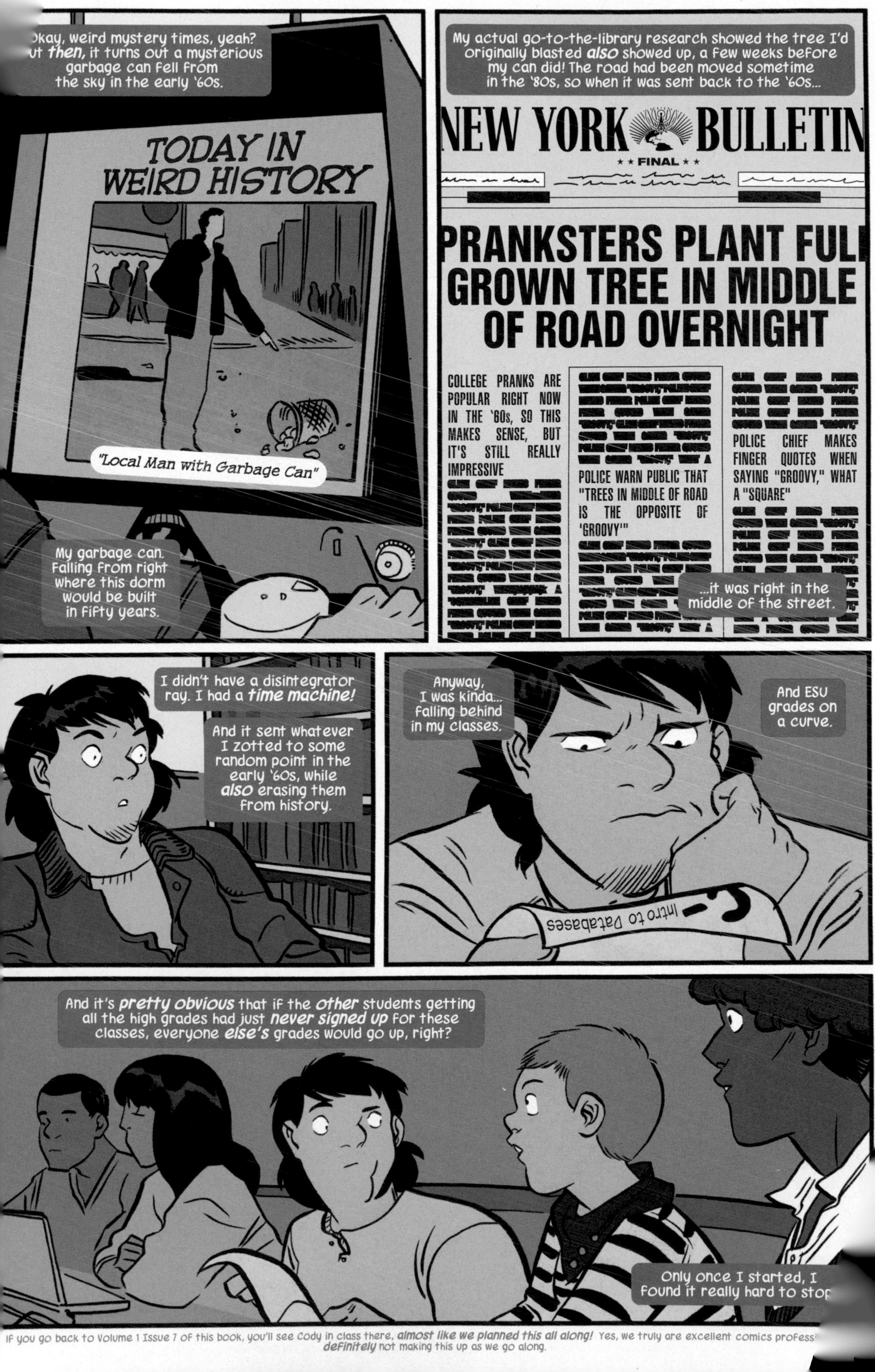
Okay, weird mystery times, yeah? ut *then*, it turns out a mysterious garbage can fell from the sky in the early '60s.
TODAY IN WEIRD HISTORY
"Local Man with Garbage Can"
My garbage can. Falling from right where this dorm would be built in fifty years.
My actual go-to-the-library research showed the tree I'd originally blasted *also* showed up, a few weeks before my can did! The road had been moved sometime in the '80s, so when it was sent back to the '60s...
NEW YORK BULLETIN
FINAL
PRANKSTERS PLANT FULL GROWN TREE IN MIDDLE OF ROAD OVERNIGHT
COLLEGE PRANKS ARE POPULAR RIGHT NOW IN THE '60s, SO THIS MAKES SENSE, BUT IT'S STILL REALLY IMPRESSIVE
POLICE WARN PUBLIC THAT "TREES IN MIDDLE OF ROAD IS THE OPPOSITE OF 'GROOVY'"
POLICE CHIEF MAKES FINGER QUOTES WHEN SAYING "GROOVY," WHAT A "SQUARE"
...it was right in the middle of the street.
I didn't have a disintegrator ray. I had a *time machine!*
And it sent whatever I zotted to some random point in the early '60s, while *also* erasing them from history.
Anyway, I was kinda... falling behind in my classes.
And ESU grades on a curve.
Intro to Databases
And it's *pretty obvious* that if the *other* students getting all the high grades had just *never signed up* for these classes, everyone *else's* grades would go up, right?
Only once I started, I found it really hard to stop

If you go back to Volume 1 Issue 7 of this book, you'll see Cody in class there, *almost like we planned this all along!* Yes, we truly are excellent comics profess *definitely* not making this up as we go along.

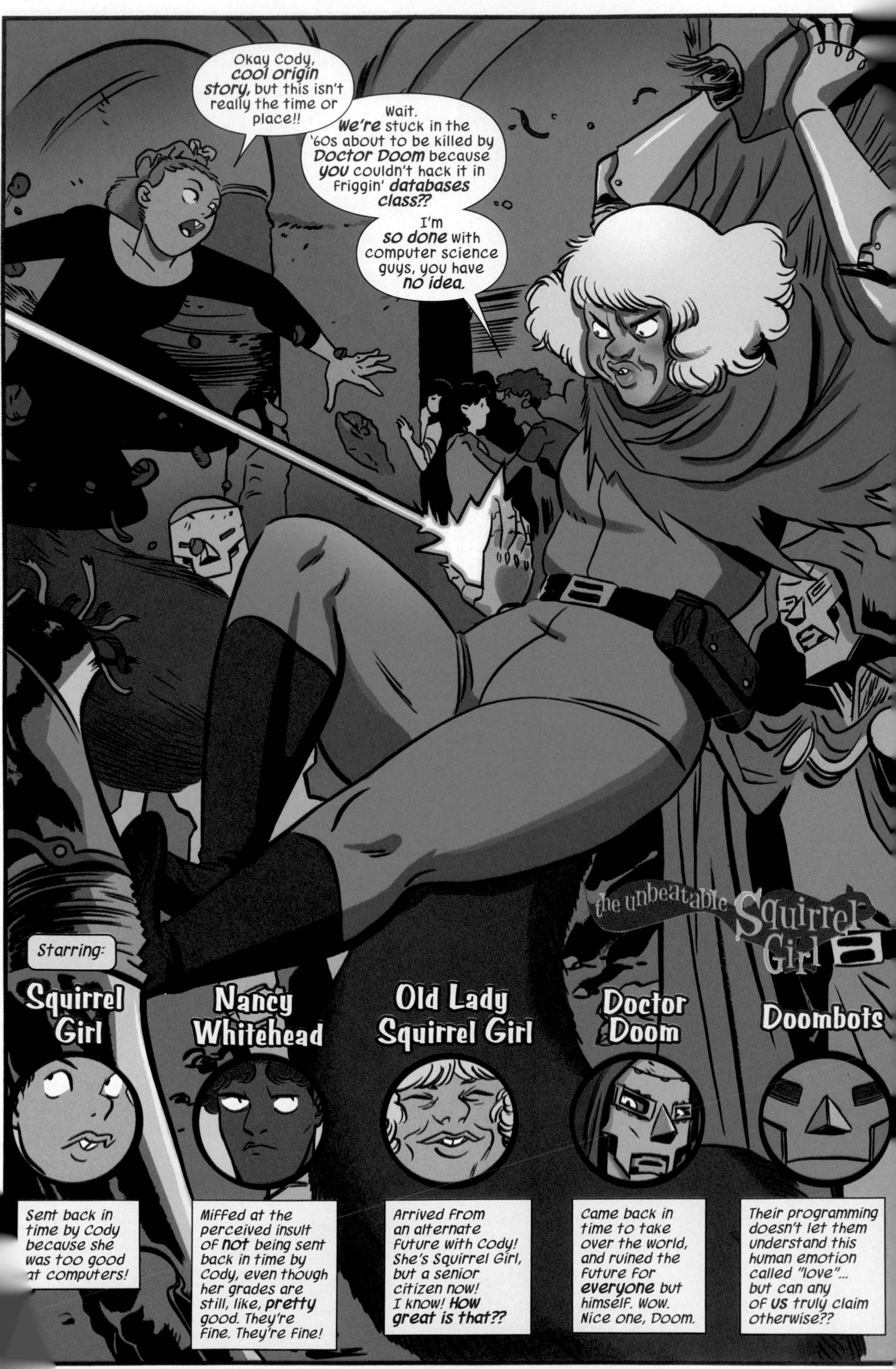
Okay Cody, cool origin story, but this isn't really the time or place!!
Wait. We're stuck in the '60s about to be killed by Doctor Doom because you couldn't hack it in friggin' databases class??
I'm so done with computer science guys, you have no idea.
the unbeatable Squirrel Girl
Starring:
Squirrel Girl
Nancy Whitehead
Old Lady Squirrel Girl
Doctor Doom
Doombots
Sent back in time by Cody because she was too good at computers!
Miffed at the perceived insult of not being sent back in time by Cody, even though her grades are still, like, pretty good. They're fine. They're fine!
Arrived from an alternate future with Cody! She's Squirrel Girl, but a senior citizen now! I know! How great is that??
Came back in time to take over the world, and ruined the future for everyone but himself. Wow. Nice one, Doom.
Their programming doesn't let them understand this human emotion called "love"... but can any of us truly claim otherwise??

rring: Tippy-Toe, who is upset her character photo didn't make the cut, and who says it would've been a shot of her holding up a tiny dumbbell, only with acorns at its ends instead of weights. Dang, Tippy, that's actually super cute! Now I'm upset too!

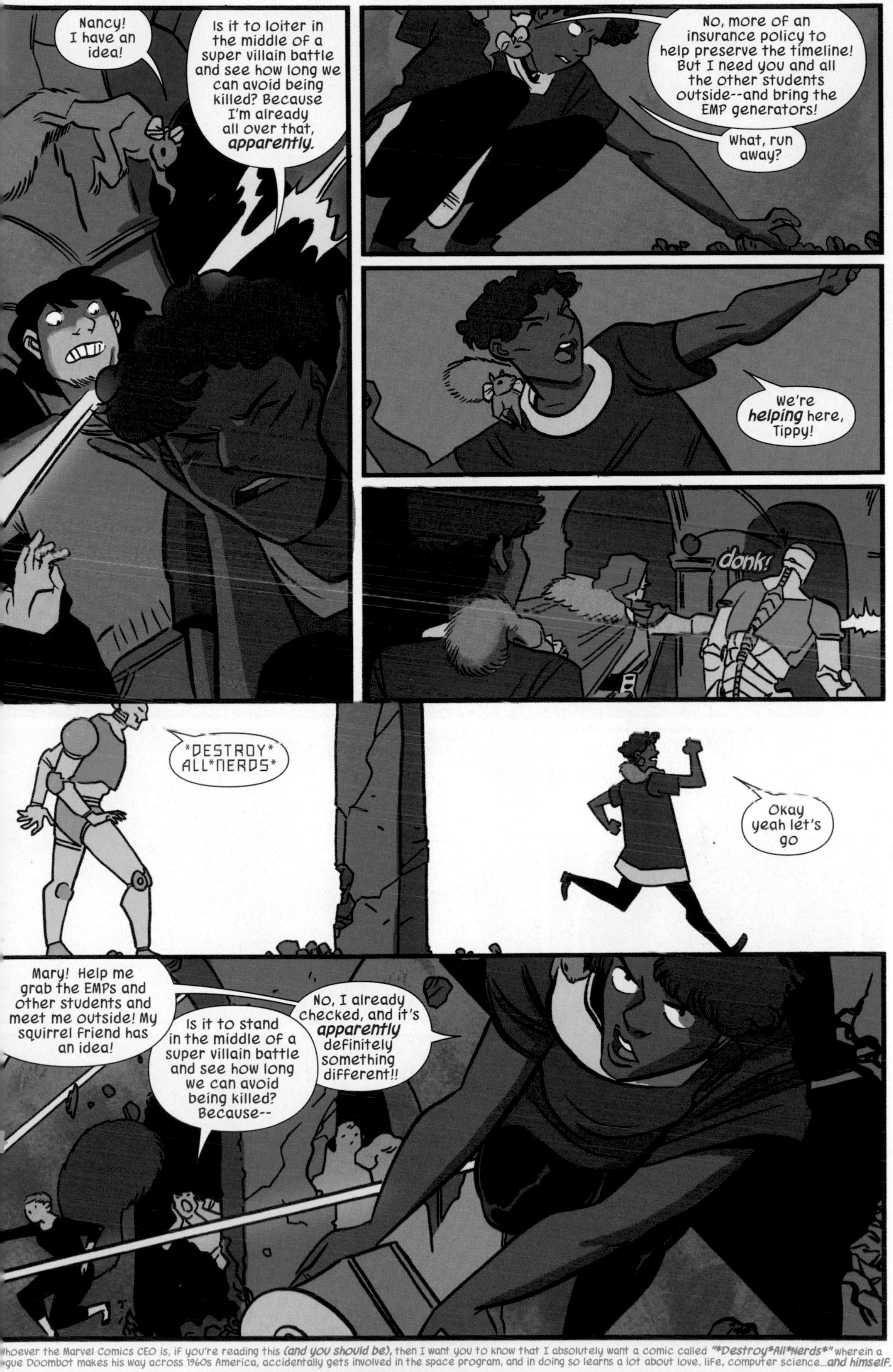
Nancy! I have an idea!
Is it to loiter in the middle of a super villain battle and see how long we can avoid being killed? Because I'm already all over that, apparently.
No, more of an insurance policy to help preserve the timeline! But I need you and all the other students outside--and bring the EMP generators!
What, run away?
We're helping here, Tippy!
donk!
DESTROY ALL*NERDS*
Okay yeah let's go
Mary! Help me grab the EMPs and other students and meet me outside! My squirrel friend has an idea!
Is it to stand in the middle of a super villain battle and see how long we can avoid being killed? Because--
No, I already checked, and it's apparently definitely something different!!

Whoever the Marvel Comics CEO is, if you're reading this *(and you should be)*, then I want you to know that I absolutely want a comic called *"*Destroy*All*Nerds*"* wherein a rogue Doombot makes his way across 1960s America, accidentally gets involved in the space program, and in doing so learns a lot about love, life, computer science... *and himself.*

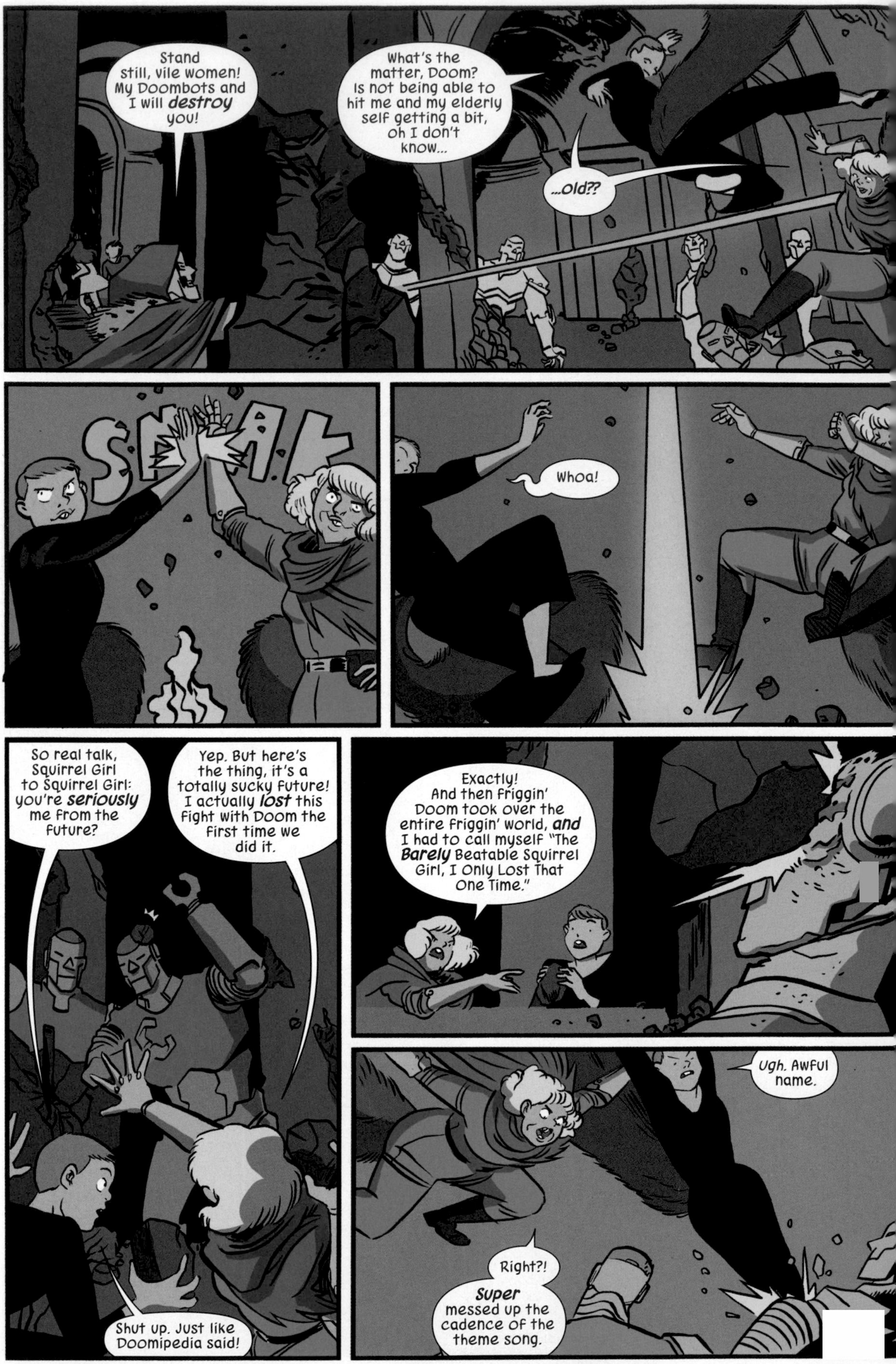
Stand still, vile women! My Doombots and I will destroy you!
What's the matter, Doom? Is not being able to hit me and my elderly self getting a bit, oh I don't know...
...old??
SNAK
Whoa!
So real talk, Squirrel Girl to Squirrel Girl: you're seriously me from the future?
Yep. But here's the thing, it's a totally sucky future! I actually lost this fight with Doom the first time we did it.
Shut up. Just like Doomipedia said!
Exactly! And then friggin' Doom took over the entire friggin' world, and I had to call myself "The Barely Beatable Squirrel Girl, I Only Lost That One Time."
Ugh. Awful name.
Right?! Super messed up the cadence of the theme song.

Squirrel Girl, Squirrel Girl / Let's not beat / Squirrel Girl / Did she lose? / On-ly once / And it was / To a dunce / Hey there! Sick burns on Doctor Doom

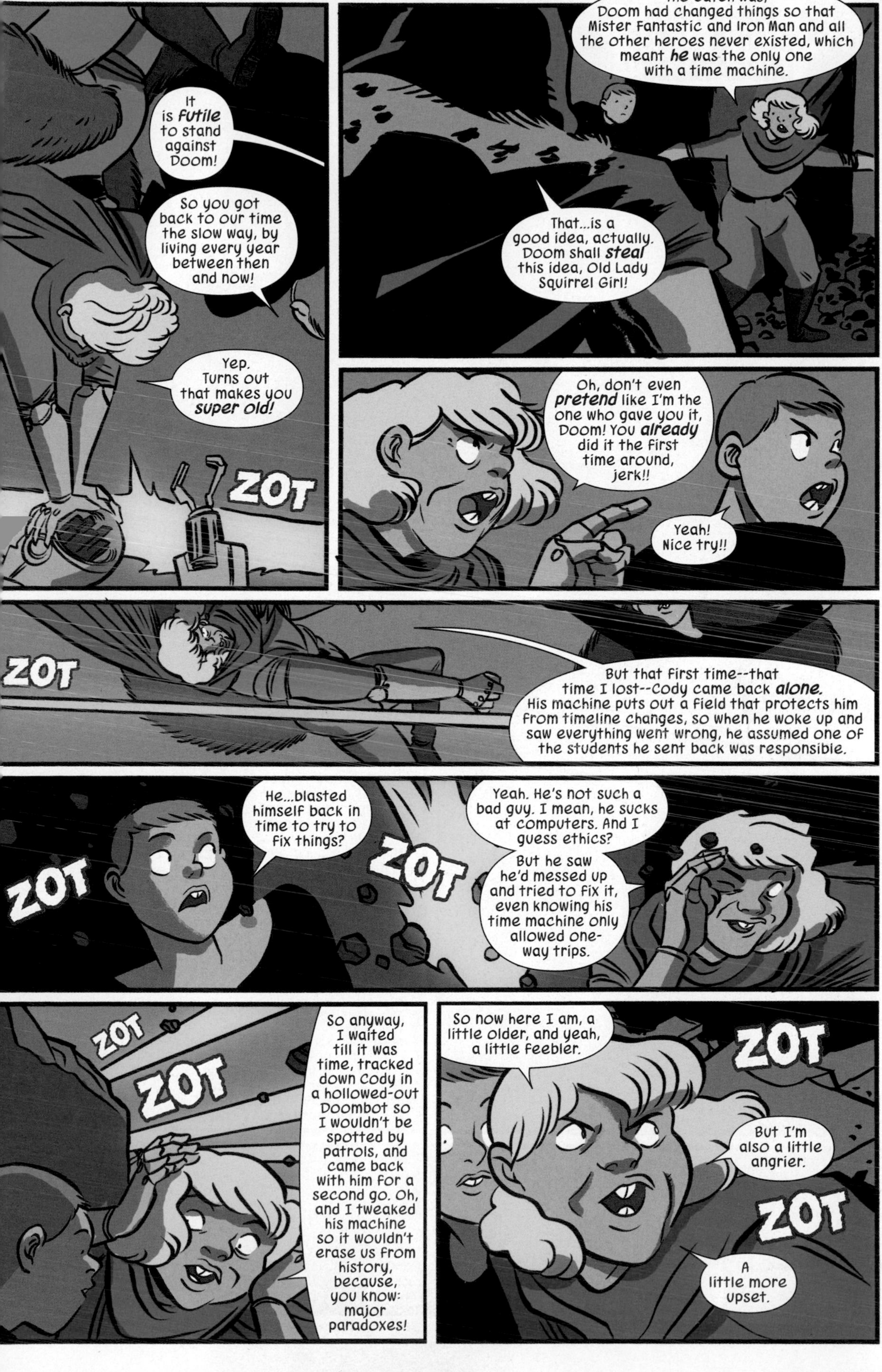
It is futile to stand against Doom!
So you got back to our time the slow way, by living every year between then and now!
Yep. Turns out that makes you super old!
ZOT
The catch was, Doom had changed things so that Mister Fantastic and Iron Man and all the other heroes never existed, which meant he was the only one with a time machine.
That...is a good idea, actually. Doom shall steal this idea, Old Lady Squirrel Girl!
Oh, don't even pretend like I'm the one who gave you it, Doom! You already did it the first time around, jerk!!
Yeah! Nice try!!
ZOT
But that first time--that time I lost--Cody came back alone. His machine puts out a field that protects him from timeline changes, so when he woke up and saw everything went wrong, he assumed one of the students he sent back was responsible.
ZOT
He...blasted himself back in time to try to fix things?
ZOT
Yeah. He's not such a bad guy. I mean, he sucks at computers. And I guess ethics?
But he saw he'd messed up and tried to fix it, even knowing his time machine only allowed one-way trips.
ZOT
ZOT
So anyway, I waited till it was time, tracked down Cody in a hollowed-out Doombot so I wouldn't be spotted by patrols, and came back with him for a second go. Oh, and I tweaked his machine so it wouldn't erase us from history, because, you know: major paradoxes!
So now here I am, a little older, and yeah, a little feebler.
ZOT
But I'm also a little angrier.
ZOT
A little more upset.

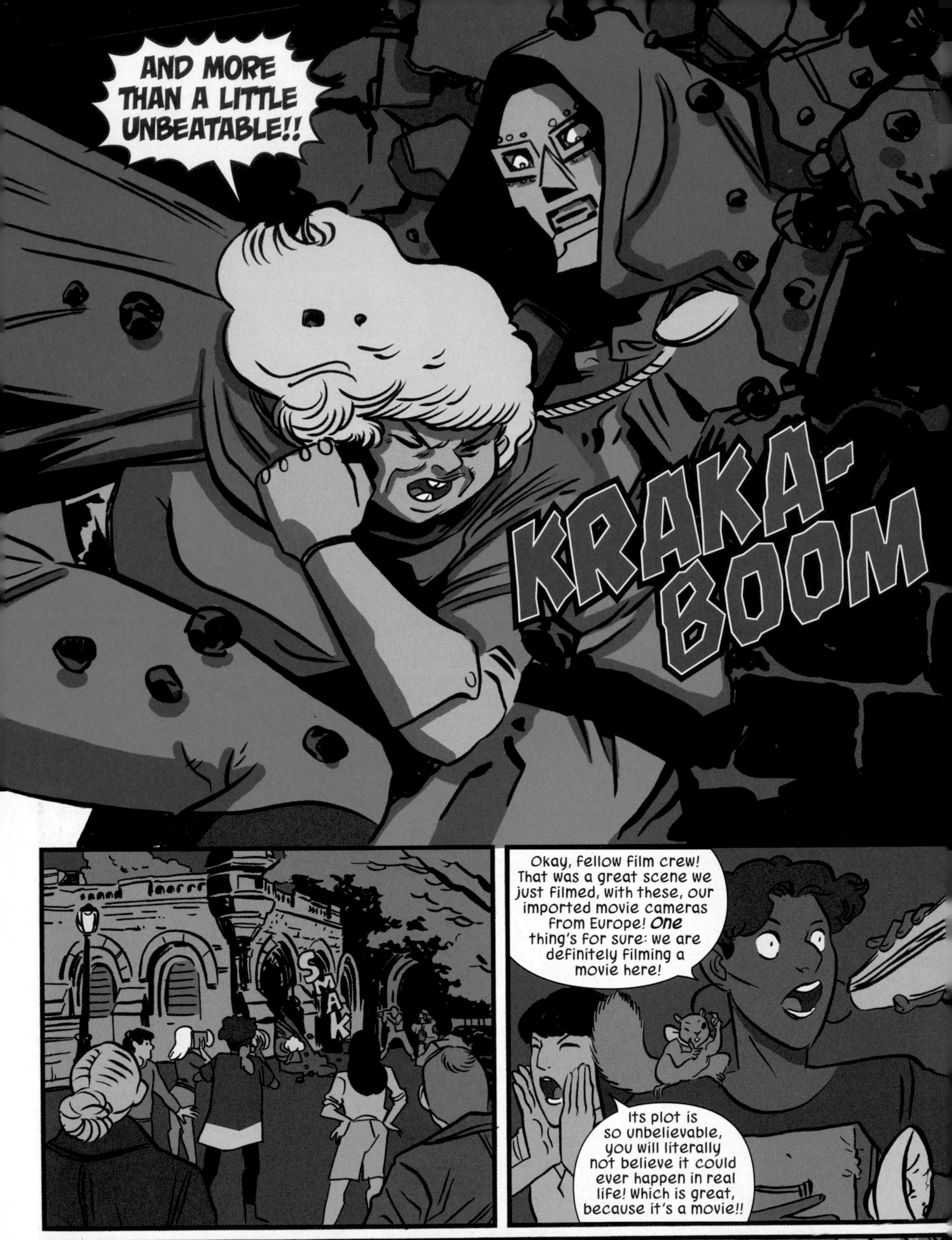
AND MORE THAN A LITTLE UNBEATABLE!!
KRAKA-BOOM
SMAK
Okay, fellow film crew! That was a great scene we just filmed, with these, our imported movie cameras from Europe! *One* thing's for sure: we are definitely filming a movie here!
Its plot is so unbelievable, you will literally not believe it could ever happen in real life! Which is great, because it's a movie!!
You couldn't beat me in your *prime,* Old Lady Squirrel Girl, and yet you dare to stand against *Doom* in these, your *sunset years?*
Such breathtaking egoism.

Tippy's "pretend we're filming a movie so nobody suspects we're from the future" plan is pretty good, especially when you consider that it was thought up by an actual squirr

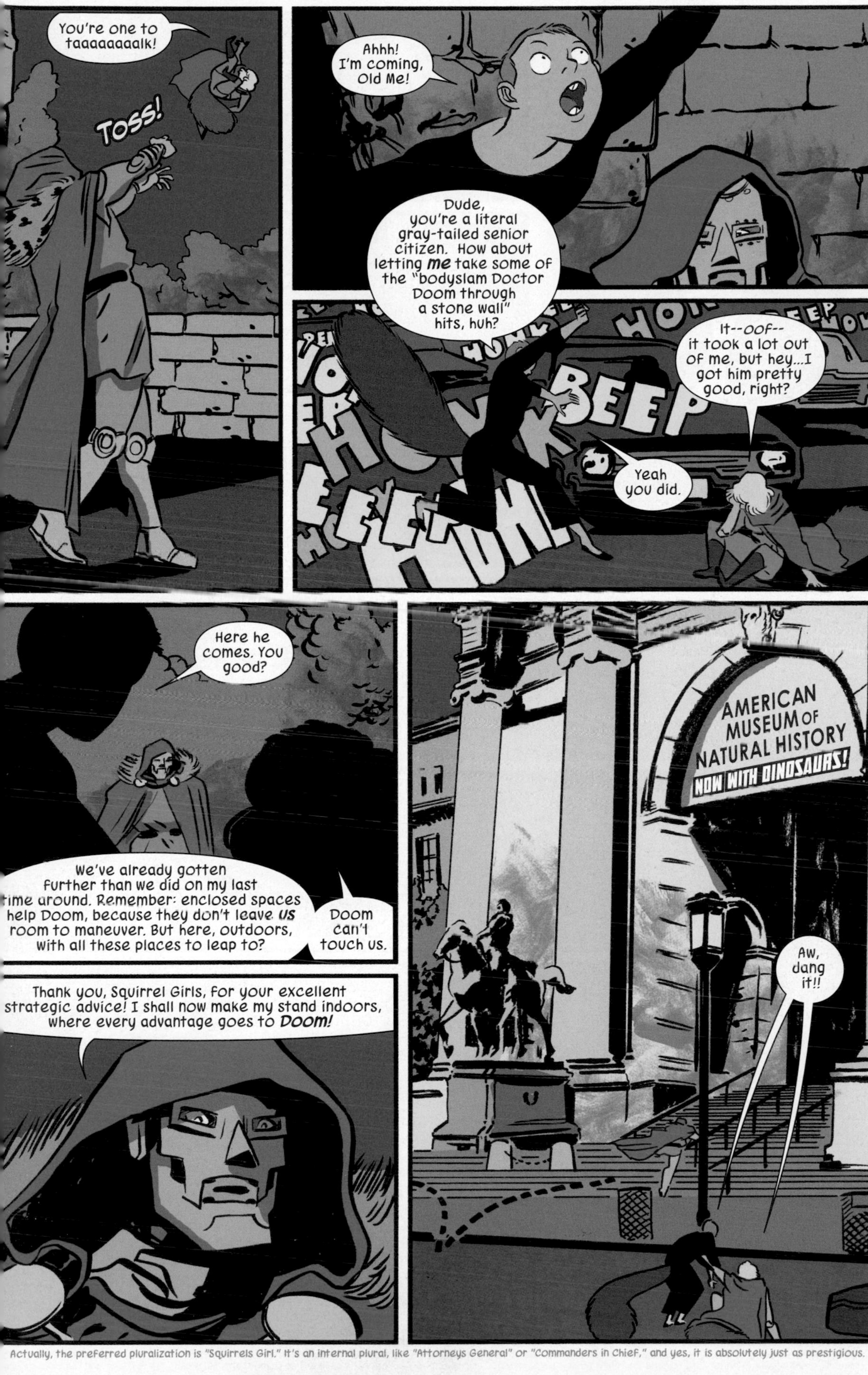
You're one to taaaaaaaalk!
TOSS!
Ahhh! I'm coming, Old Me!
Dude, you're a literal gray-tailed senior citizen. How about letting *me* take some of the "bodyslam Doctor Doom through a stone wall" hits, huh?
It--*OOF*-- it took a lot out of me, but hey...I got him pretty good, right?
Yeah you did.
BEEP
Here he comes. You good?
We've already gotten further than we did on my last time around. Remember: enclosed spaces help Doom, because they don't leave *US* room to maneuver. But here, outdoors, with all these places to leap to?
Doom can't touch us.
Thank you, Squirrel Girls, for your excellent strategic advice! I shall now make my stand indoors, where every advantage goes to *DOOM!*
AMERICAN MUSEUM OF NATURAL HISTORY
NOW WITH DINOSAURS!
Aw, dang it!!

Actually, the preferred pluralization is "Squirrels Girl." It's an internal plural, like "Attorneys General" or "Commanders in Chief," and yes, it is absolutely just as prestigious.

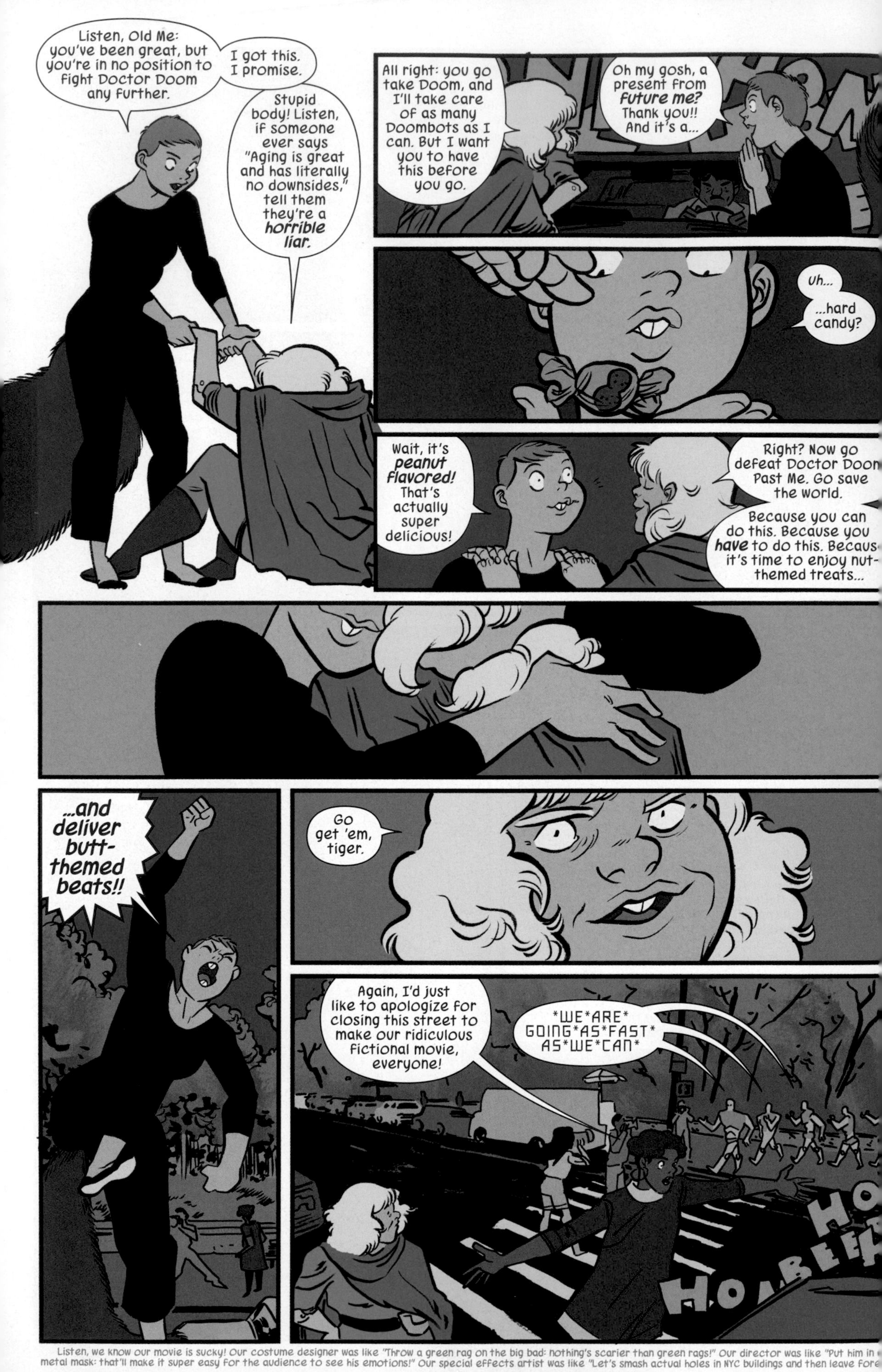

Listen, Old Me: you've been great, but you're in no position to fight Doctor Doom any further.
I got this. I promise.
Stupid body! Listen, if someone ever says "Aging is great and has literally no downsides," tell them they're a ***horrible liar.***
All right: you go take Doom, and I'll take care of as many Doombots as I can. But I want you to have this before you go.
Oh my gosh, a present from ***future me?*** Thank you!! And it's a...
Uh...
...hard candy?
Wait, it's ***peanut flavored!*** That's actually super delicious!
Right? Now go defeat Doctor Doom Past Me. Go save the world.
Because you can do this. Because you ***have*** to do this. Because it's time to enjoy nut-themed treats...
...and deliver butt-themed beats!!
Go get 'em, tiger.
Again, I'd just like to apologize for closing this street to make our ridiculous fictional movie, everyone!
*WE*ARE*GOING*AS*FAST*AS*WE*CAN*

Listen, we know our movie is sucky! Our costume designer was like "Throw a green rag on the big bad: nothing's scarier than green rags!" Our director was like "Put him in a metal mask: that'll make it super easy for the audience to see his emotions!" Our special effects artist was like "Let's smash actual holes in NYC buildings and then leave fore

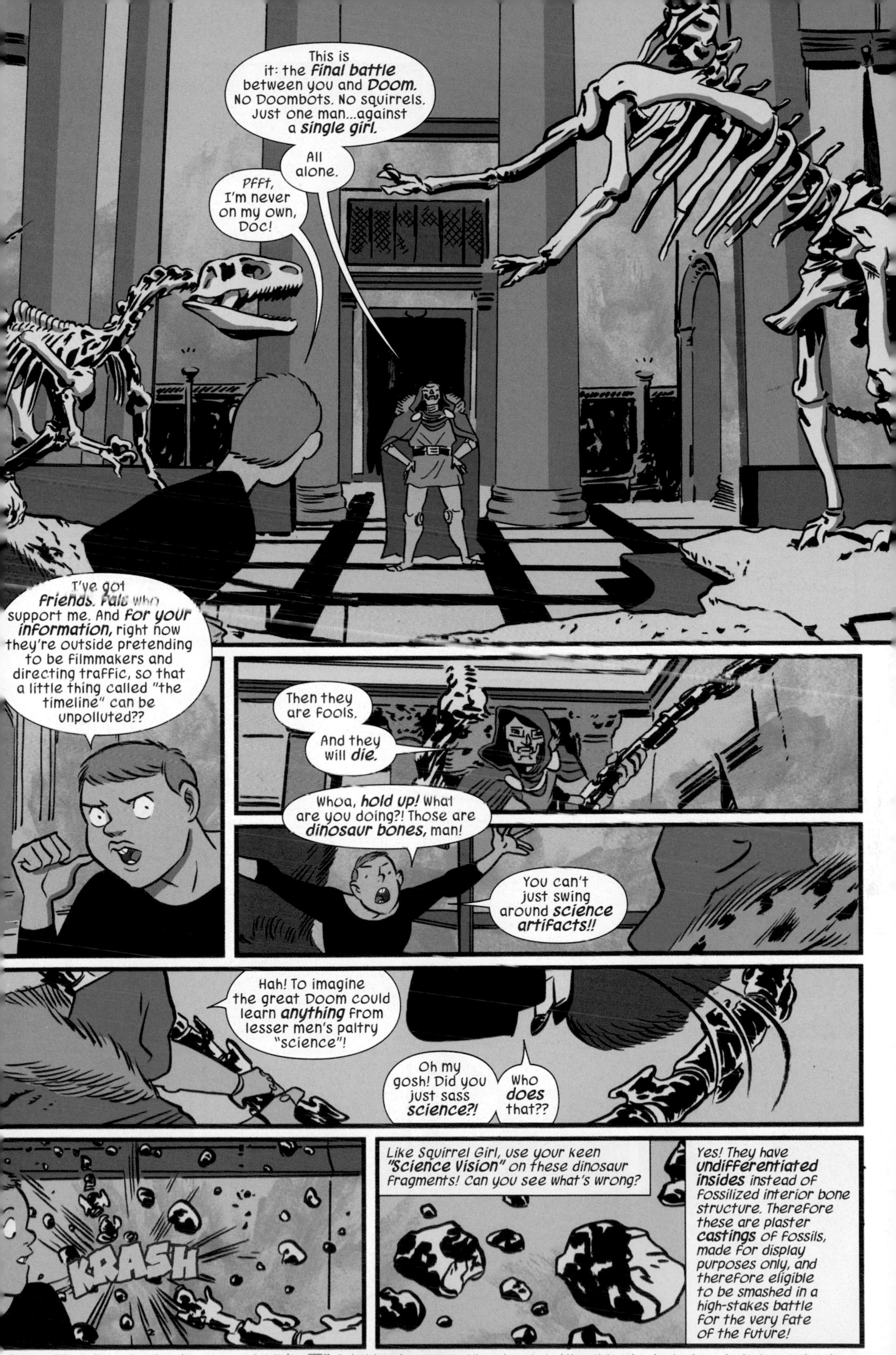
This is it: the final battle between you and Doom. No Doombots. No squirrels. Just one man...against a single girl.
All alone.
Pfft, I'm never on my own, Doc!
I've got friends. Pals who support me. And for your information, right now they're outside pretending to be filmmakers and directing traffic, so that a little thing called "the timeline" can be unpolluted??
Then they are fools.
And they will die.
Whoa, hold up! What are you doing?! Those are dinosaur bones, man!
You can't just swing around science artifacts!!
Hah! To imagine the great Doom could learn anything from lesser men's paltry "science"!
Oh my gosh! Did you just sass science?!
Who does that??
KRASH
Like Squirrel Girl, use your keen "Science Vision" on these dinosaur fragments! Can you see what's wrong?
Yes! They have undifferentiated insides instead of fossilized interior bone structure. Therefore these are plaster castings of fossils, made for display purposes only, and therefore eligible to be smashed in a high-stakes battle for the very fate of the future!

Science Vision isn't a squirrel-based super-power, but it *is* a *STEM* student-based super-power! It can be unlocked through learning about science, technology, engineering, and/or math.

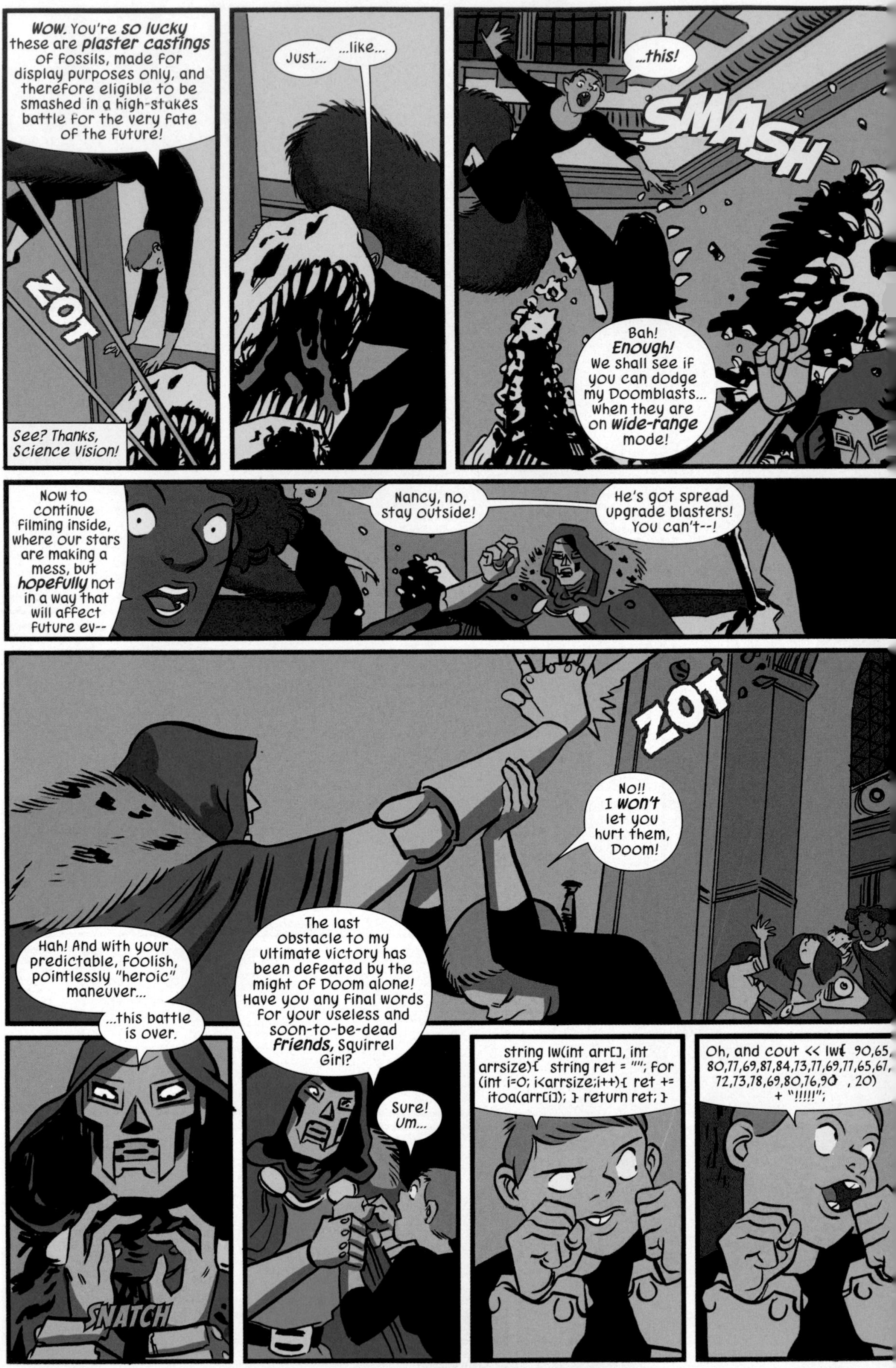

WOW. You're so lucky these are plaster castings of fossils, made for display purposes only, and therefore eligible to be smashed in a high-stakes battle for the very fate of the future!
ZOT
See? Thanks, Science Vision!
Just...
...like...
...this!
SMASH
Bah! Enough! We shall see if you can dodge my Doomblasts... when they are on wide-range mode!
Now to continue filming inside, where our stars are making a mess, but hopefully not in a way that will affect future ev--
Nancy, no, stay outside!
He's got spread upgrade blasters! You can't--!
ZOT
No!! I won't let you hurt them, Doom!
Hah! And with your predictable, foolish, pointlessly "heroic" maneuver...
...this battle is over.
SNATCH
The last obstacle to my ultimate victory has been defeated by the might of Doom alone! Have you any final words for your useless and soon-to-be-dead friends, Squirrel Girl?
Sure! Um...
string lw(int arr[], int arrsize){ string ret = ""; for (int i=0; i<arrsize;i++){ ret += itoa(arr[i]); } return ret; }
Oh, and cout << lw(90,65, 80,77,69,87,84,73,77,69,77,65,67, 72,73,78,69,80,76,90 , 20) + "!!!!!";

Those of us who can run C++ programs in our heads are going *"Oh dang!!"* right now, while the rest of us are saying "Man, I could run that program in my head if I wanted to," looking around, and then quickly turning the page to see what happens.

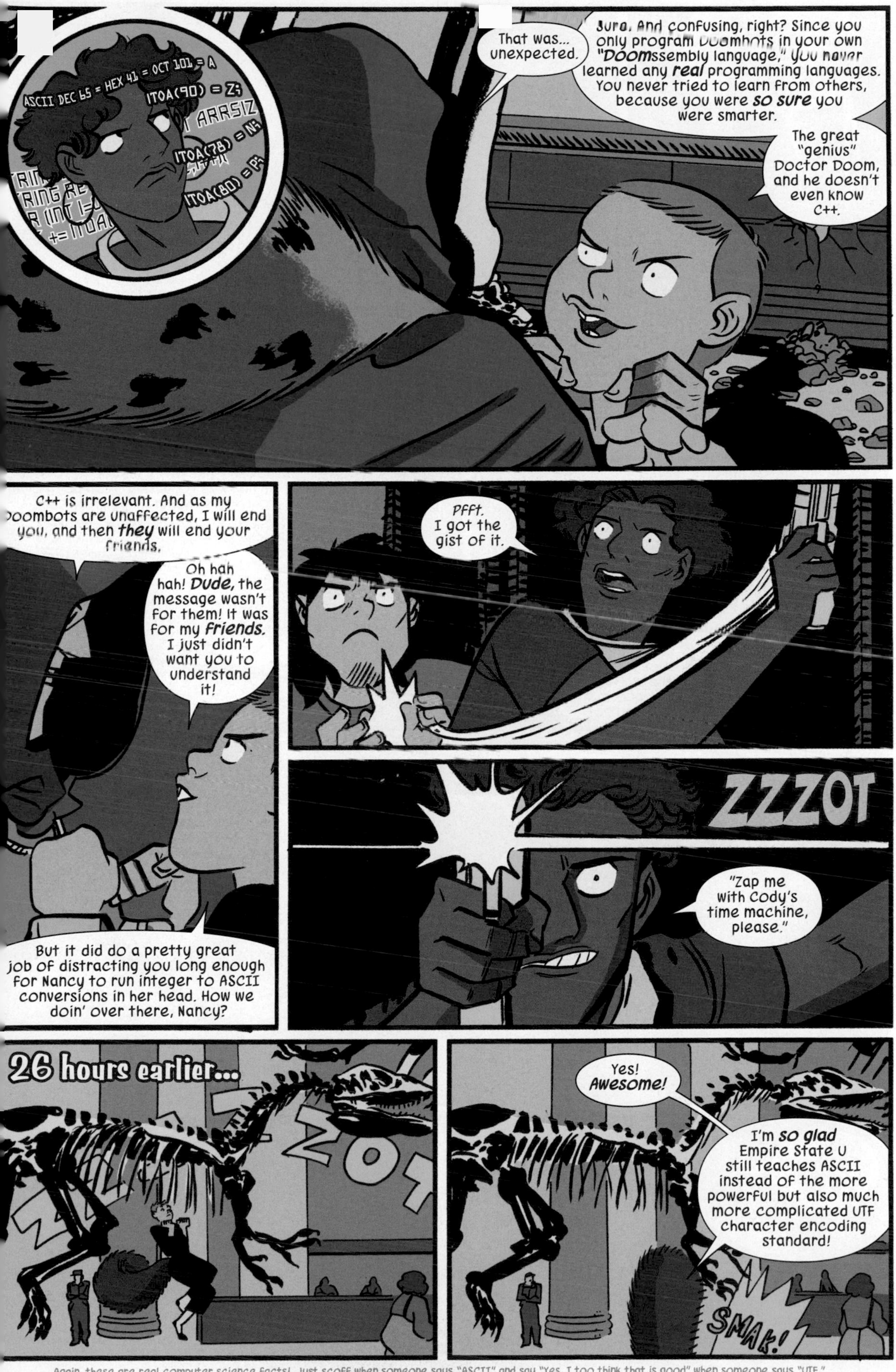
ASCII DEC 65 = HEX 41 = OCT 101 = A
ITOA(90) = Z;
ITOA(78) = N;
ITOA(80) = P;
That was... unexpected.
Sure. And confusing, right? Since you only program Doombots in your own "DOOMssembly language," you never learned any real programming languages. You never tried to learn from others, because you were so sure you were smarter.
The great "genius" Doctor Doom, and he doesn't even know C++.
C++ is irrelevant. And as my Doombots are unaffected, I will end you, and then they will end your friends.
Oh hah hah! Dude, the message wasn't for them! It was for my friends. I just didn't want you to understand it!
But it did do a pretty great job of distracting you long enough for Nancy to run integer to ASCII conversions in her head. How we doin' over there, Nancy?
Pfft. I got the gist of it.
ZZZOT
"Zap me with Cody's time machine, please."
26 hours earlier...
ZOT
Yes! Awesome!
I'm so glad Empire State U still teaches ASCII instead of the more powerful but also much more complicated UTF character encoding standard!
SMAK!

Again, these are real computer science facts! Just scoff when someone says "ASCII" and say "Yes, I too think that is good" when someone says "UTF," and you will *absolutely* pass as a computer scientist.

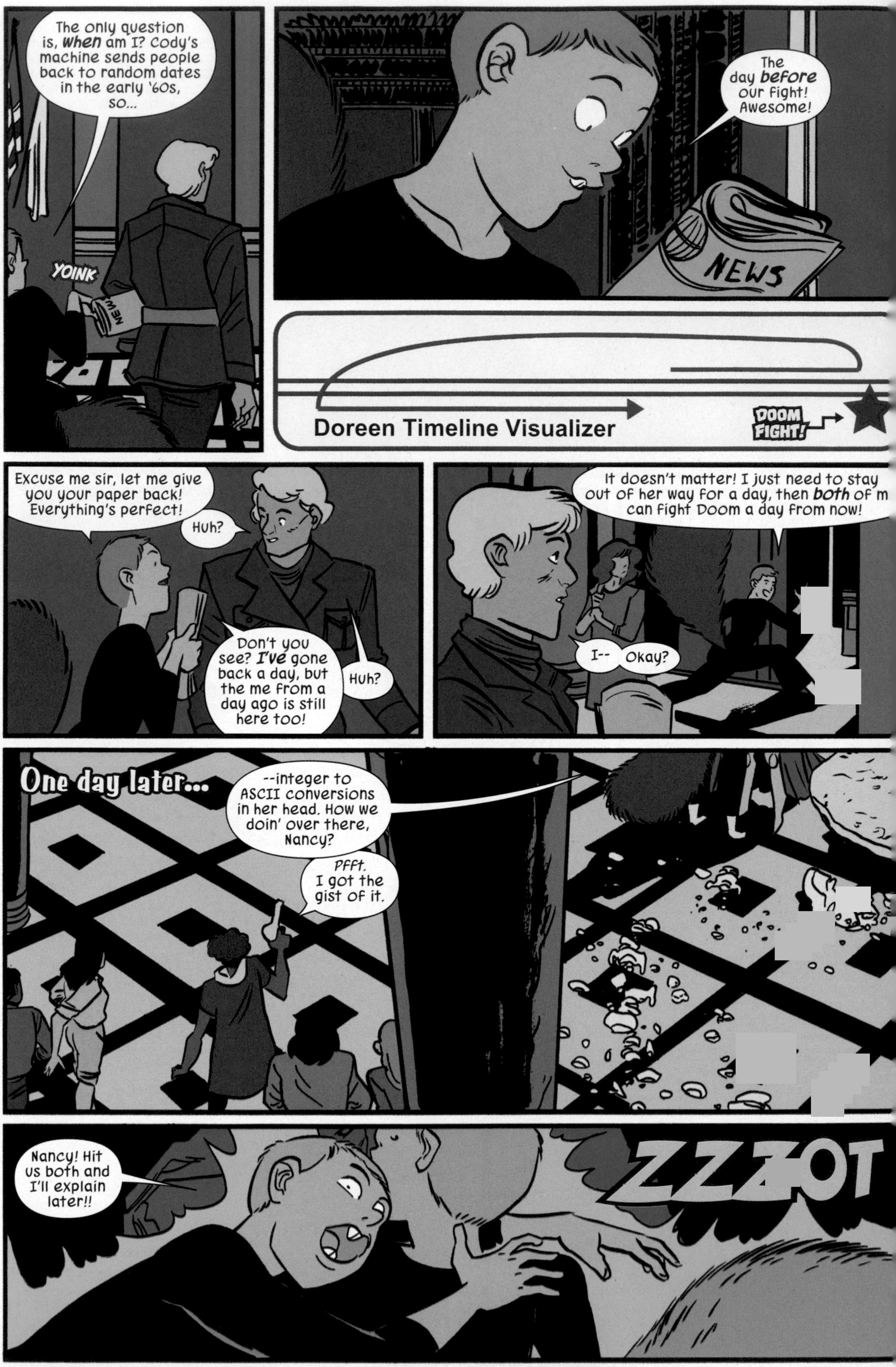

The only question is, *when* am I? Cody's machine sends people back to random dates in the early '60s, so...
YOINK
NEWS
The day *before* our fight! Awesome!
NEWS
Doreen Timeline Visualizer
DOOM FIGHT!
Excuse me sir, let me give you your paper back! Everything's perfect!
Huh?
Don't you see? *I've* gone back a day, but the me from a day ago is still here too!
Huh?
It doesn't matter! I just need to stay out of her way for a day, then *both* of m can fight Doom a day from now!
I--
Okay?
One day later...
--integer to ASCII conversions in her head. How we doin' over there, Nancy?
Pfft. I got the gist of it.
Nancy! Hit us both and I'll explain later!!
ZZZOT

This businessman will never appear in this comic again, so here is his entire backstory: his name is "Pete McFleet" and his interests include business, spreadsheets, and the business of spreadsheets. Fare thee well, Pete McFleet!

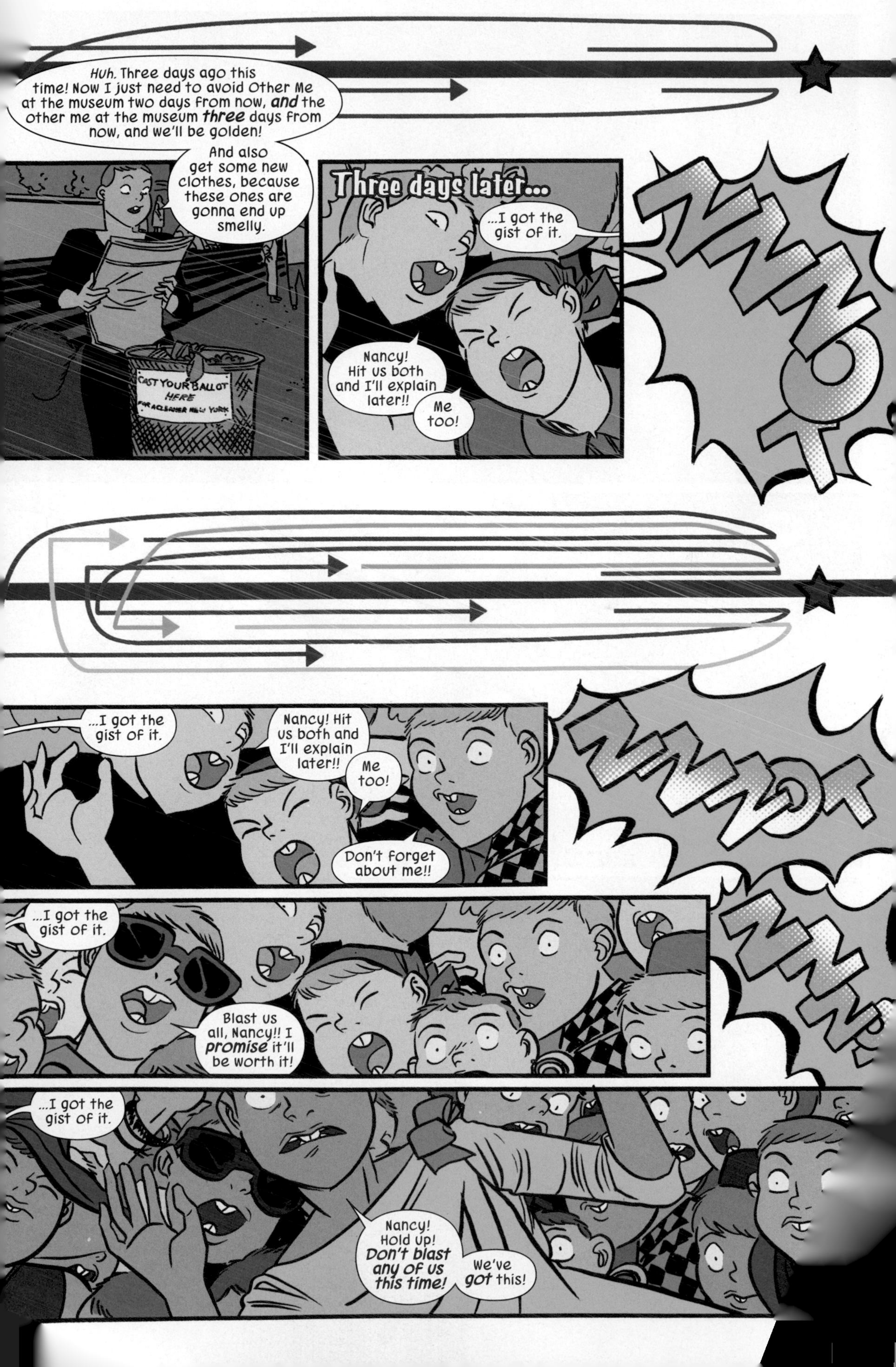
Huh. Three days ago this time! Now I just need to avoid Other Me at the museum two days from now, and the other me at the museum three days from now, and we'll be golden!
And also get some new clothes, because these ones are gonna end up smelly.
CAST YOUR BALLOT HERE FOR A CLEANER NEW YORK
Three days later...
...I got the gist of it.
Nancy! Hit us both and I'll explain later!!
Me too!
NNNOT
...I got the gist of it.
Nancy! Hit us both and I'll explain later!!
Me too!
Don't forget about me!!
NNNOT
...I got the gist of it.
Blast us all, Nancy!! I promise it'll be worth it!
...I got the gist of it.
Nancy! Hold up! Don't blast any of us this time!
We've got this!

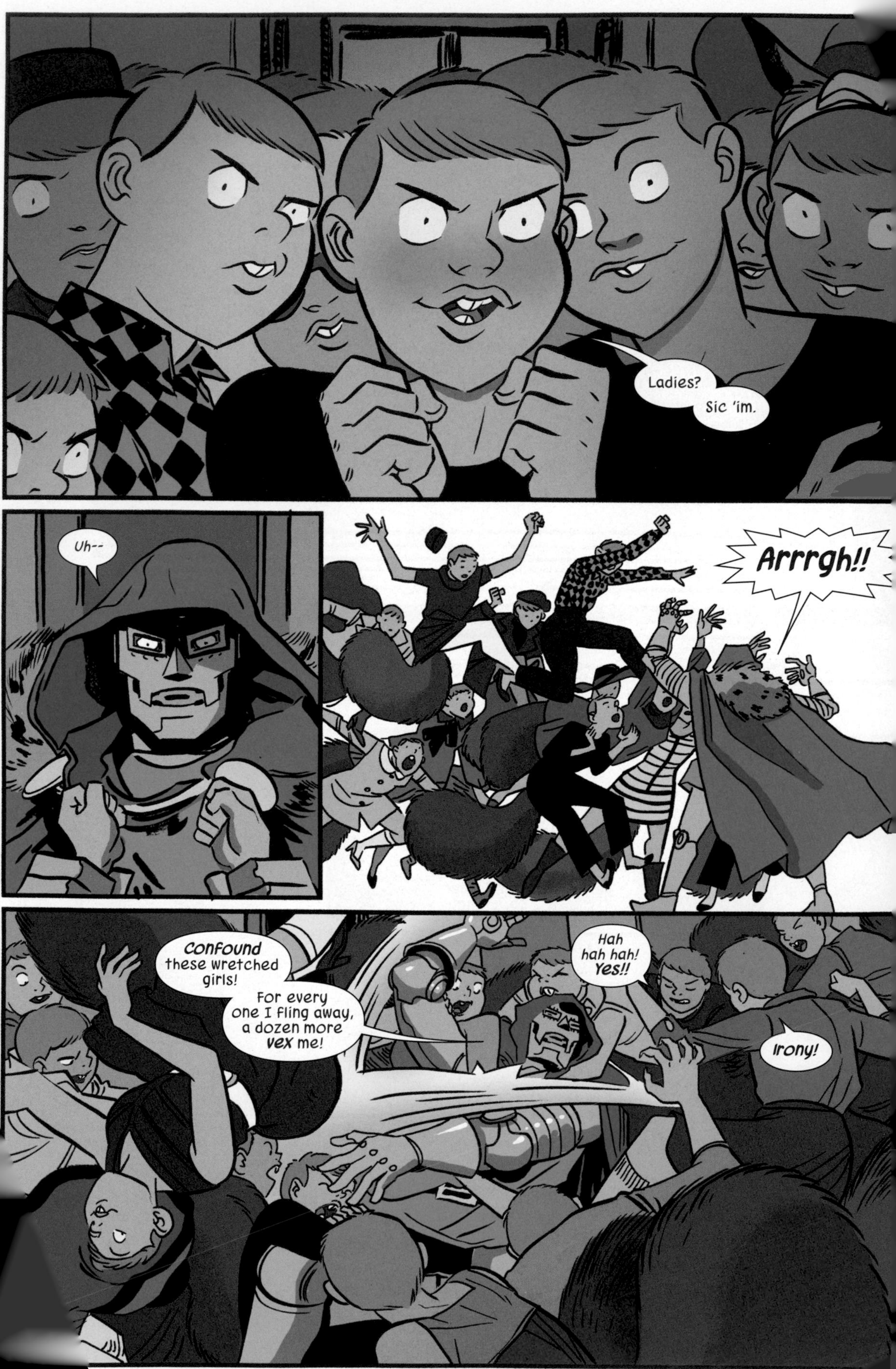
Ladies?
Sic 'im.
Uh--
Arrrgh!!
Confound these wretched girls!
For every one I fling away, a dozen more vex me!
Hah hah hah! Yes!!
Irony!

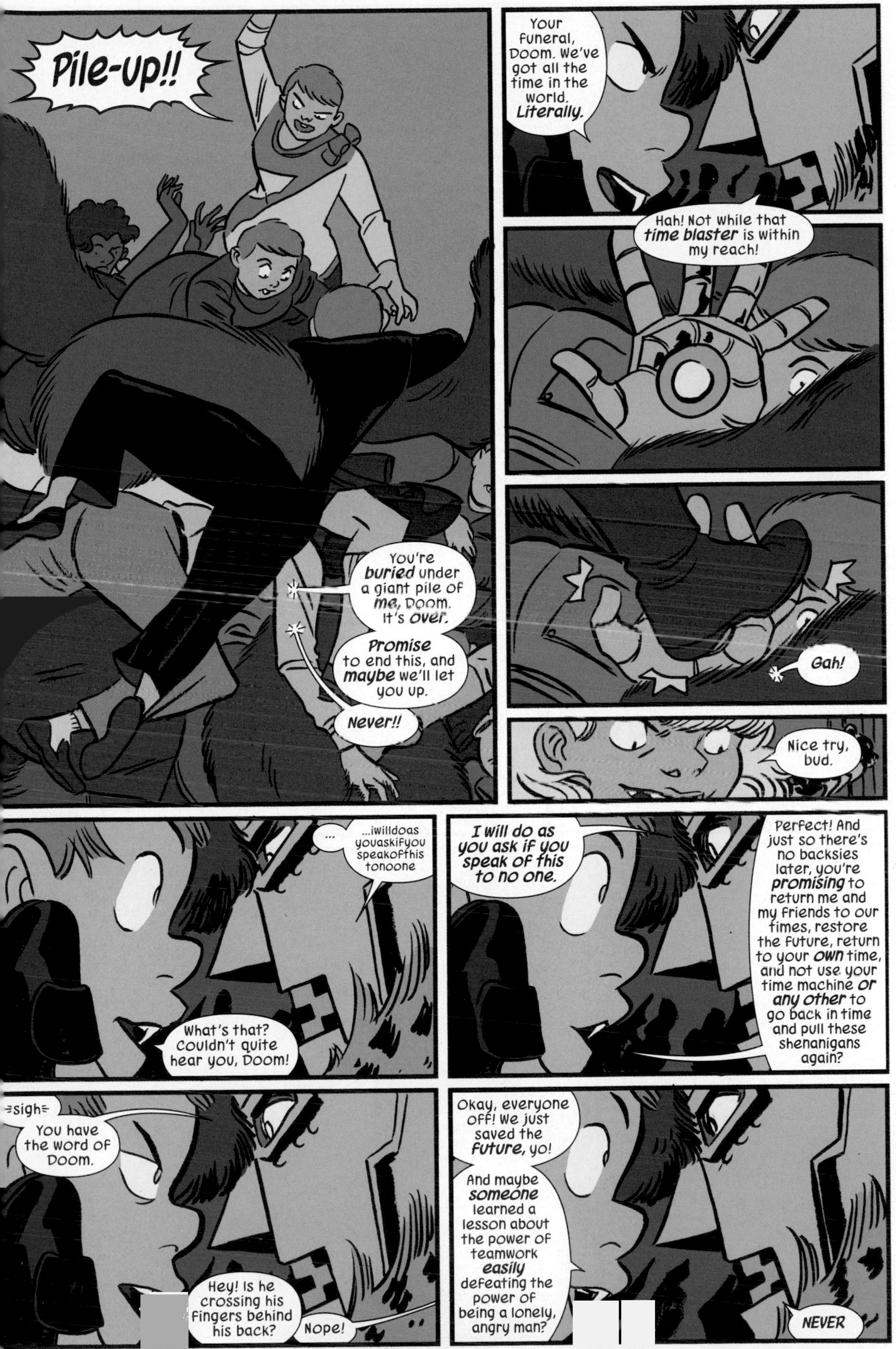
Pile-up!!
You're buried under a giant pile of me, Doom. It's over.
Promise to end this, and maybe we'll let you up.
Never!!
Your funeral, Doom. We've got all the time in the world. Literally.
Hah! Not while that time blaster is within my reach!
Gah!
Nice try, bud.
...
...iwilldoas youaskifyou speakofthis tonoone
What's that? Couldn't quite hear you, Doom!
I will do as you ask if you speak of this to no one.
Perfect! And just so there's no backsies later, you're promising to return me and my friends to our times, restore the future, return to your own time, and not use your time machine or any other to go back in time and pull these shenanigans again?
=sigh=
You have the word of Doom.
Hey! Is he crossing his fingers behind his back?
Nope!
Okay, everyone off! We just saved the future, yo!
And maybe someone learned a lesson about the power of teamwork easily defeating the power of being a lonely, angry man?
NEVER

Sorry there weren't any captions on the last couple pages: I was still thinking about Pete McFleet! It's like, why would a businessman who loves *spreadsheets* go to the dinosaur exhibit...in the middle of a workday? I'll tell you what I think: I think Pete's a mass of contradictions and untold nuance, and I think he feels things very deeply. I hope he's doing well.

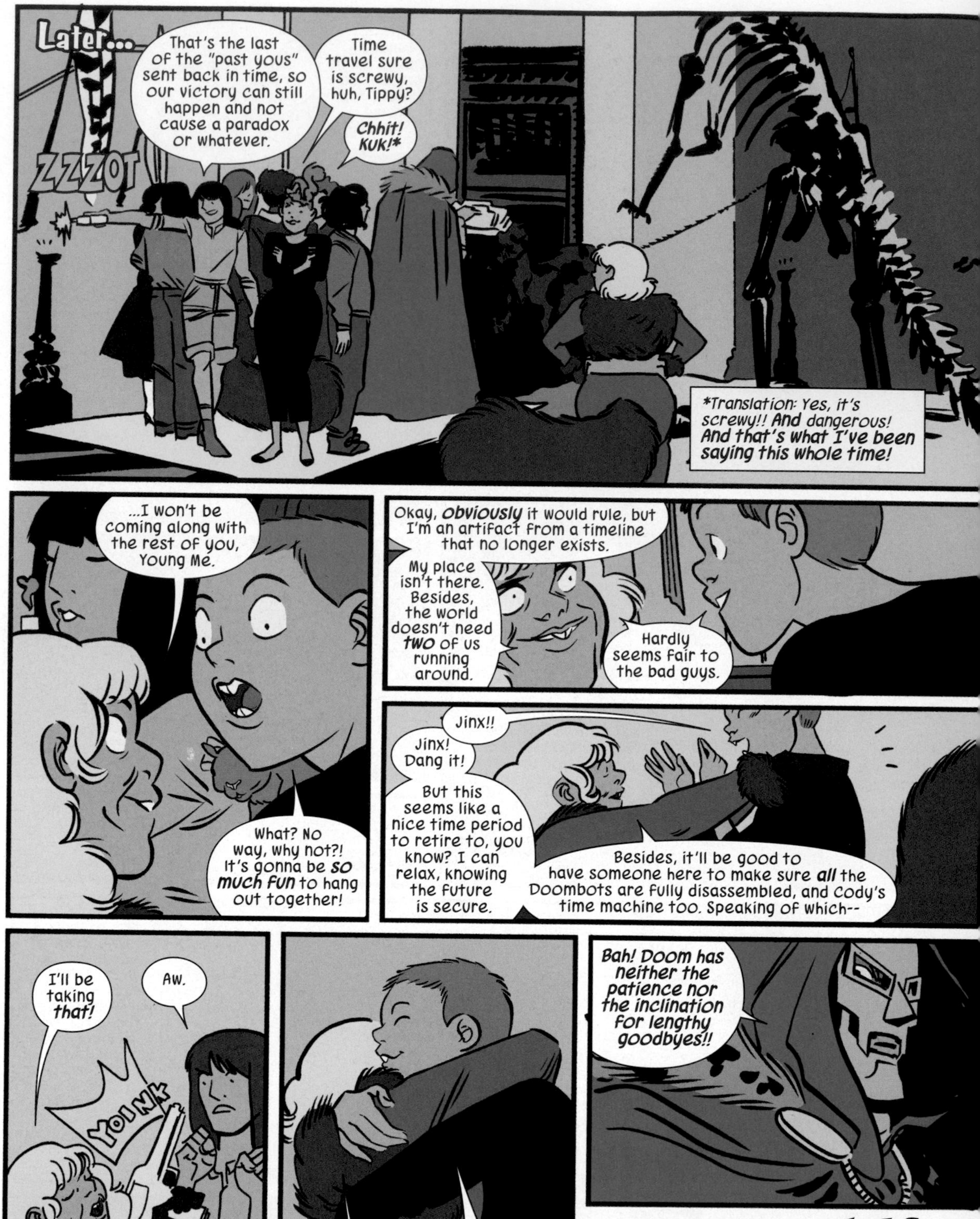
Later...
That's the last of the "past yous" sent back in time, so our victory can still happen and not cause a paradox or whatever.
Time travel sure is screwy, huh, Tippy?
Chhit! KUK!*
ZZZOT
*Translation: Yes, it's screwy!! And dangerous! And that's what I've been saying this whole time!
...I won't be coming along with the rest of you, Young Me.
What? No way, why not?! It's gonna be so much fun to hang out together!
Okay, obviously it would rule, but I'm an artifact from a timeline that no longer exists.
My place isn't there. Besides, the world doesn't need two of us running around.
Hardly seems fair to the bad guys.
Jinx!!
Jinx! Dang it!
But this seems like a nice time period to retire to, you know? I can relax, knowing the future is secure.
Besides, it'll be good to have someone here to make sure all the Doombots are fully disassembled, and Cody's time machine too. Speaking of which--
I'll be taking that!
Aw.
YOINK
I'm gonna miss you, Old Alternate-Timeline Me. I'm glad we turned out awesome.
Never any doubt about that. After all...look how great I was at your age.
Bah! Doom has neither the patience nor the inclination for lengthy goodbyes!!
KRA-KA-KOOM

Doom has neither the time, nor the patience, nor the inclination, nor the desire, nor the instinct, nor the impulse to express the unvarnished and raw if often unexpressed emotions that can often be found in a lengthy goodbye! *Begone!!*

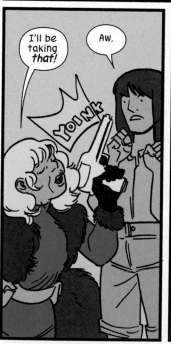

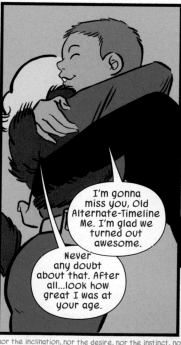

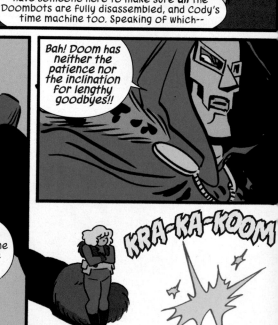

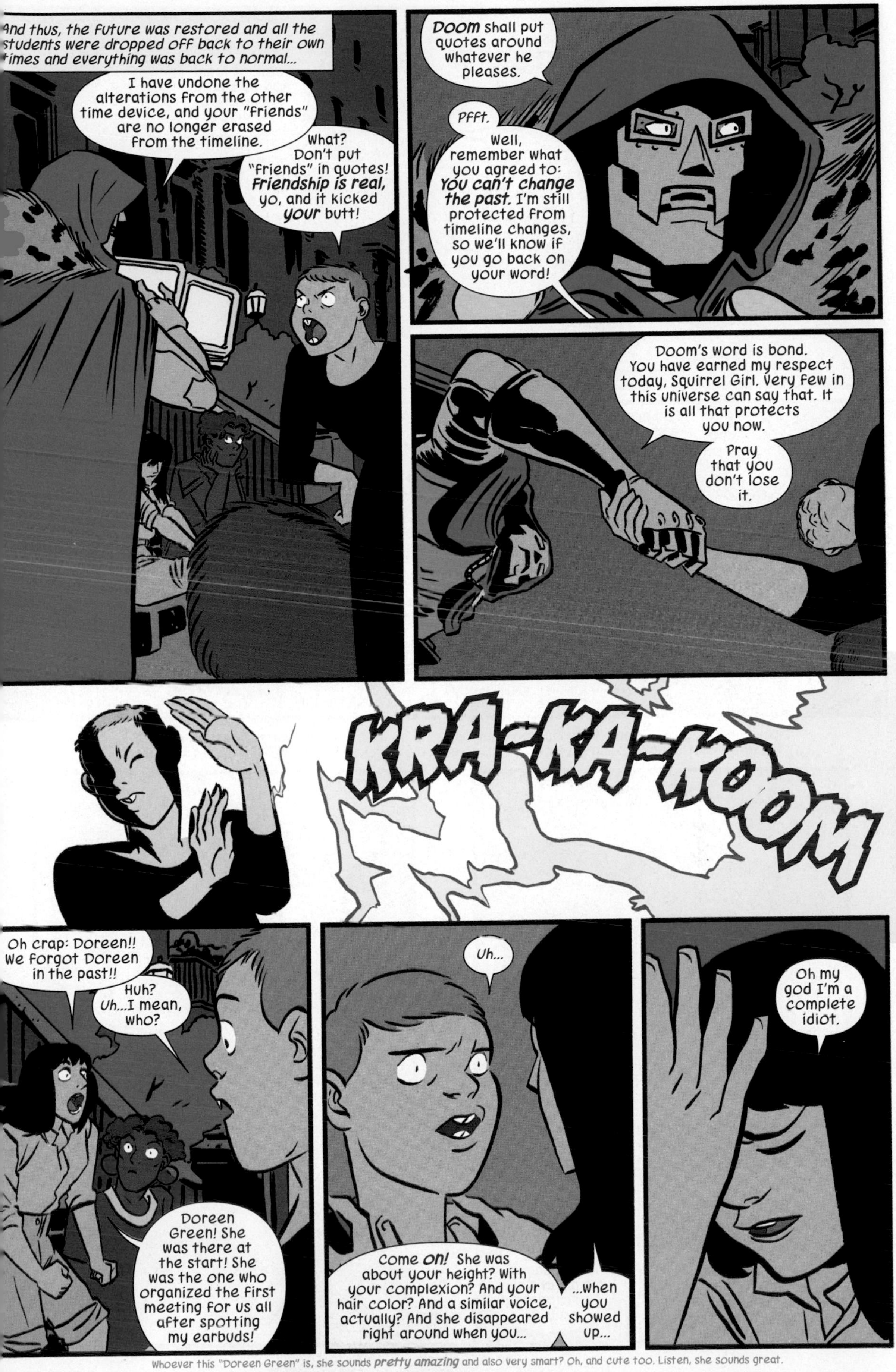
And thus, the future was restored and all the students were dropped off back to their own times and everything was back to normal...
I have undone the alterations from the other time device, and your "friends" are no longer erased from the timeline.
What? Don't put "friends" in quotes! Friendship is real, yo, and it kicked your butt!
Doom shall put quotes around whatever he pleases.
Pfft.
Well, remember what you agreed to: You can't change the past. I'm still protected from timeline changes, so we'll know if you go back on your word!
Doom's word is bond. You have earned my respect today, Squirrel Girl. Very few in this universe can say that. It is all that protects you now.
Pray that you don't lose it.
KRA-KA-KOOM
Oh crap: Doreen!! We forgot Doreen in the past!!
Huh? Uh...I mean, who?
Doreen Green! She was there at the start! She was the one who organized the first meeting for us all after spotting my earbuds!
Uh...
Come on! She was about your height? With your complexion? And your hair color? And a similar voice, actually? And she disappeared right around when you...
...when you showed up...
Oh my god I'm a complete idiot.

Whoever this "Doreen Green" is, she sounds *pretty amazing* and also very smart? Oh, and cute too. Listen, she sounds great.

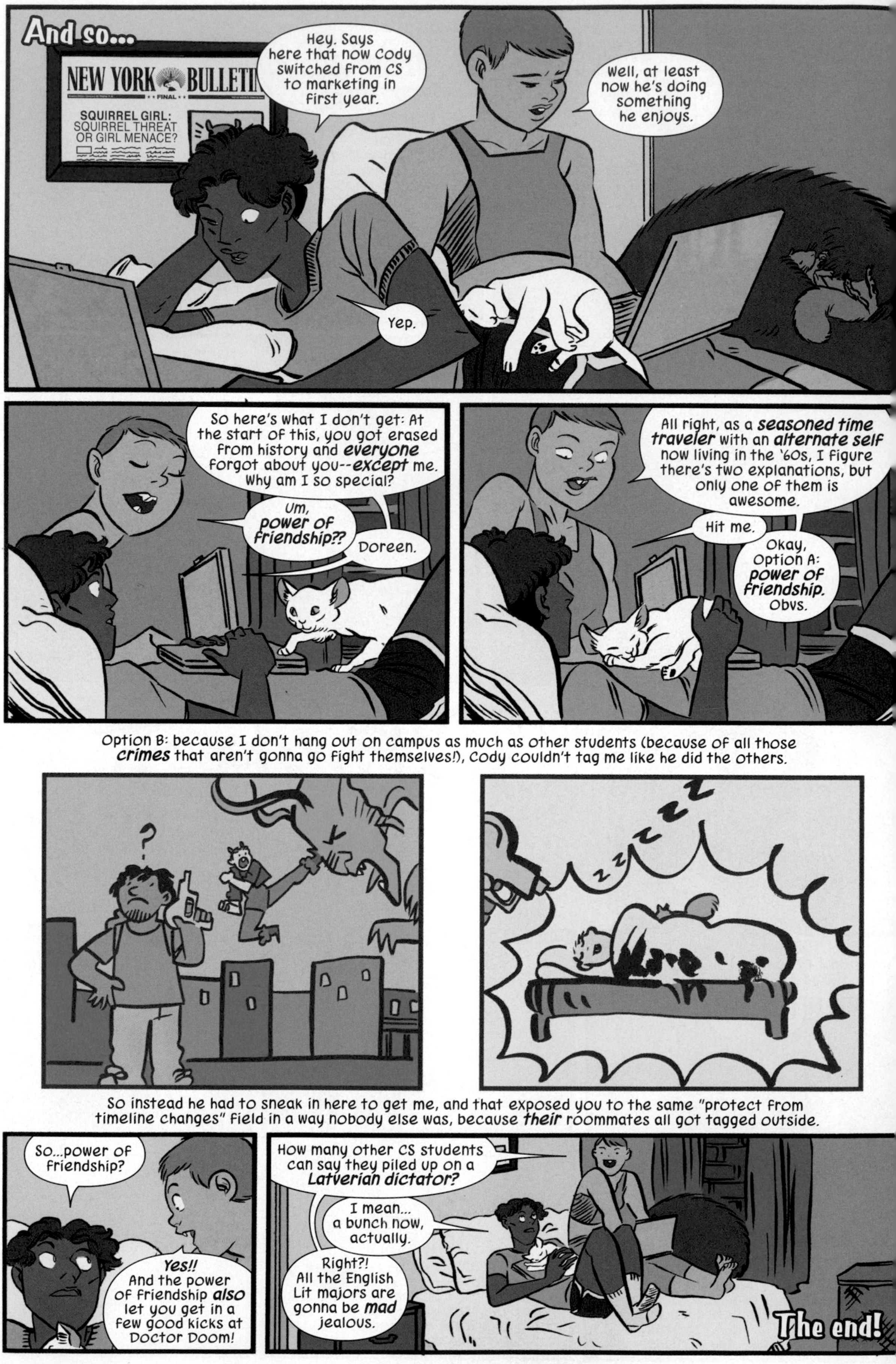

And so...
NEW YORK BULLETIN
SQUIRREL GIRL: SQUIRREL THREAT OR GIRL MENACE?
Hey. Says here that now Cody switched from CS to marketing in first year.
Well, at least now he's doing something he enjoys.
Yep.
So here's what I don't get: At the start of this, you got erased from history and everyone forgot about you--except me. Why am I so special?
Um, power of friendship??
Doreen.
All right, as a seasoned time traveler with an alternate self now living in the '60s, I figure there's two explanations, but only one of them is awesome.
Hit me.
Okay, Option A: power of friendship. Obvs.
Option B: because I don't hang out on campus as much as other students (because of all those crimes that aren't gonna go fight themselves!), Cody couldn't tag me like he did the others.
?
ZZZZZZ
So instead he had to sneak in here to get me, and that exposed you to the same "protect from timeline changes" field in a way nobody else was, because their roommates all got tagged outside.
So...power of friendship?
Yes!! And the power of friendship also let you get in a few good kicks at Doctor Doom!
How many other CS students can say they piled up on a Latverian dictator?
I mean... a bunch now, actually.
Right?! All the English Lit majors are gonna be mad jealous.
The end!

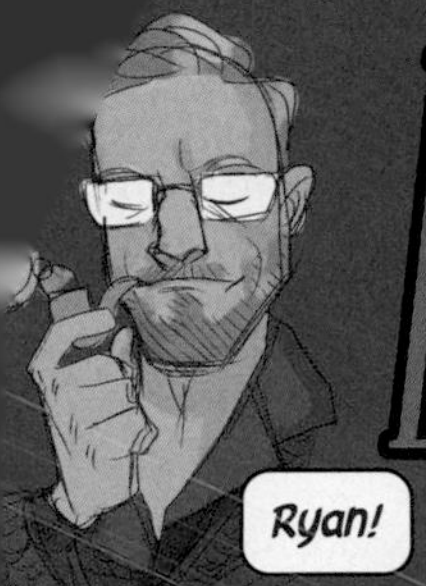
Ryan!

Letters From Nuts

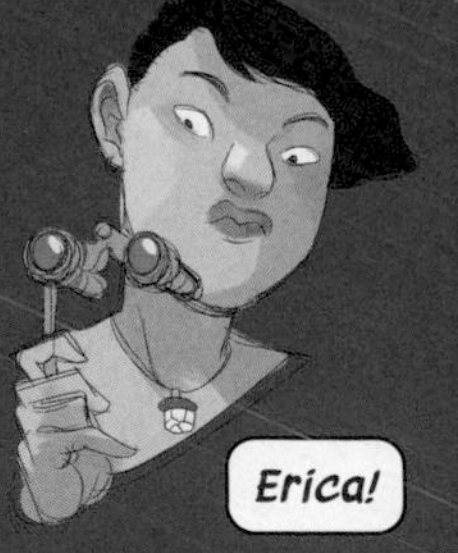
Erica!

Send letters to mheroes@marvel.com or 135 W 50th St, 7th Floor, New York, NY 10020 (Please mark "OKAY TO PRINT")

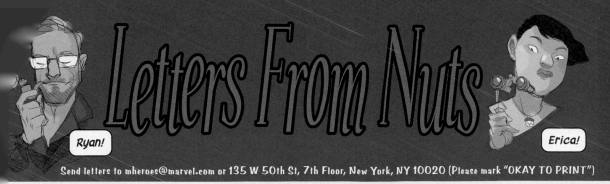

Dearest Squirrel Girl team,

I just wanted to drop you guys a line about how amazing this series has been, from issue 1. It can be difficult to find comics that read so well with my five-year-old daughter, but you guys have made it easy. Squirrel Girl has a proud, prominent place in her short box, and "nuts" and "butts" a prominent place in her vocabulary, so thanks I guess? Anyway, issue 4 in particular was a big hit with her and the very next morning she made me staple some paper together so she could start creating her own comics. So keep up the good work!

Cheers,
Alexander and Zoe Burns

PS: Zoe found Galactus to be "very silly," so maybe up your game in the villain department?

RYAN: Haha, that is amazing! AMAZING. And I'm super glad we could inspire Zoe to make her own comics. Comics is my favorite medium and the more people playing in it the better! If our legacy can be "got lots of people into comics, while at the same time getting lots of people into the word 'butts,'" I will be a very happy man.

ERICA: From now on we will only stick to the very serious villains like Rhino, the Rhino. Also I am now working on ways to get more butts into this comic.

P.S. A friend of mine who just came back from visiting family told me that an (adult) relative of hers only JUST learned that girls can read comics, so I'm glad we're getting the word out earlier now!

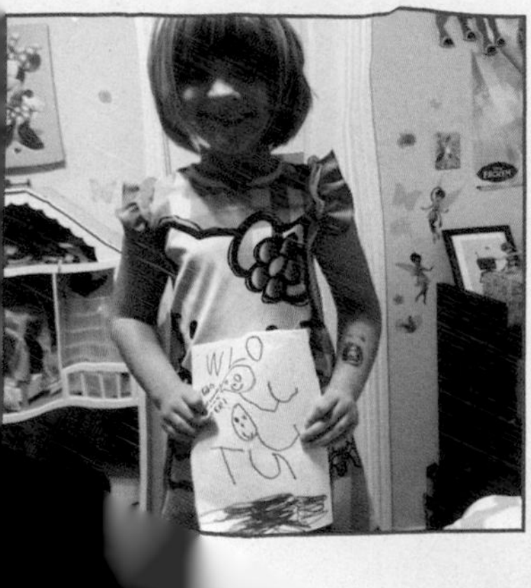

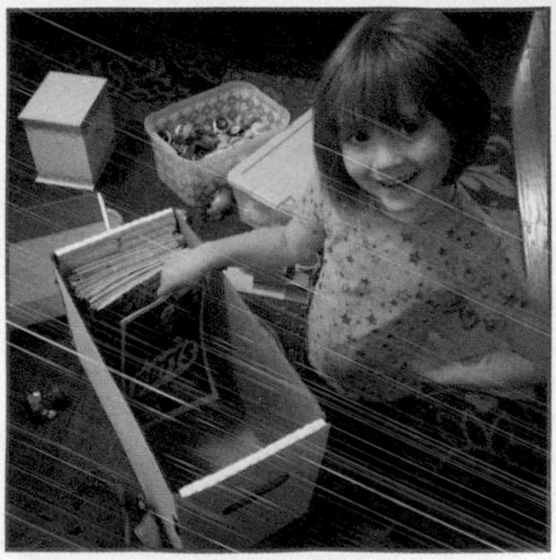

Hello,

I have been a fan of Squirrel Girl for a long time, and I love what you have done with the book. The writing, art, lettering, and coloring, it all matches the tone of the character wonderfully. Keep up the excellent work! Just some questions:

Will Monkey Joe ever make a return from the dead? Will Doreen ever check in with her former teammates in the GLA and see what they have been up to recently? Will she get new villains, maybe take on squirrel hunters? (Or would that be too serious? Maybe make it in tone with comics that took on political issues of the '60s and '70s, though, with a Doreen twist?)

Anyway, happy Squirrel Appreciation Day (Jan 21st), and thanks for the stories.

Paul

R: Guess who didn't know about Squirrel Appreciation Day until just recently, when January 21st rolled around? THIS GUY. We run Squirrel Girl's Twitter account, @unbeatablesg (also, yes, all those Twitter accounts in the recap pages are real, SURPRISE), and that day it was just a million people tagging her with photos of squirrels. It was... kinda the best??

Anyway, in answer to your questions, one of them at least is a yes! But... WHICH ONE?? It's probably the GLA one; Erica's big into seeing Flatman come back. She put a scarf in his likeness on the cover of issue 5 like it wasn't even a big deal!!

E: I learned about Squirrel Appreciation Day about two weeks prior to the 21st because of Cute Overload, may it rest in peace. Anyway, am I allowed to say this? I don't know, I didn't consult with anyone [It's fine, Erica, you can say anything you want! Go ahead! – Wil], but I'm going to pretty firmly say that Monkey Joe is staying the way he is [Wait, what?!? – Wil]. I think I've said it before, but even just going past the whole problem with bringing the dead back, I think as maybe the only super hero to stay dead (and he WAS a full card-carrying member of the GLA, so he's totes a real super hero), his death is the most poignant and important of any super hero. So to sum up, Monkey Joe > most other heroes.

Hey guys!

I can't really add anything on top of the praise I've been reading in your letters column but allow me to throw this out there: If ever there's a Squirrel Girl cartoon, I think Kristen Schaal should do the voice. I already hear her in my head whenever I read the comic, so why not make it official?

Keep up the solid work,

Vrej H.
Brossard, Quebec

R: Thank you! My typical go-to answer to "who should voice-act a character" is "Patrick Stewart" -- regardless of who the character i -- and I'm afraid I must stand firm that choice here. Whenever you r the comic, please imagine D using Patty Stew's stentorian to is definitely a reasonable thing

That said, Kristen Schaal w solid understudy!

E: My vote is Alison Bri has such a good "friend screaming transition. Schaal in mind for Tipp to Schaal's voice scree

paradoxes right now, actually.

Dear Ryan and Erica,

My 10-year-old daughter has gone nuts for Squirrel Girl! She was just outside singing the Squirrel Girl theme song to a squirrel in the tree. It's great to have a comic that has hooked the whole family. Keep up the great work!

Here is a picture of her wearing her Squirrel Girl shirt, holding her Deadpool's Guide to Super Villains trading cards that she made herself, and her stuffed toy Tippy-Toe, and she is wearing a Squirrel Girl headband she also made herself.

Amy (and young Squirrel Girl superfan)

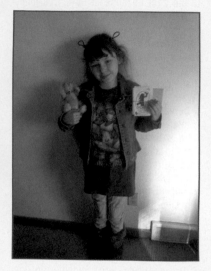

R: Amy, your daughter is SUPER GREAT, and I love her Deadpool cards. If Squirrel Girl got de-aged into a 10-year-old girl, I think your daughter would be a dead ringer for her! And yes, I know that this implies that a de-aged Doreen would go around wearing a Squirrel Girl t-shirt. I feel like that fits her personality -- kinda perfectly, actually??

E: I love this. This is great. Seeing people make their own Deadpool cards is one of my favorite things.

Dear Erica & Ryan,

I don't remember when or how I ...ed up the first issue of SQUIRREL ... but I can tell you I've never put it ... Doreen's ability to defuse potential ... into friendship is the best ability ... the Avengers are underutilizing ...ngness). Maybe Mr. Ultron ... been persuaded to value humanity by sharing some hearty laughs over a cup of tea and candied pecans (seriously, Avengers, a prerequisite Squirrel Essentials 101 course). With that being said, I wanted to thank your team and all my fellow fans of Squirrel Girl for ensuring her a place on comic store shelves. Doreen Green adds the much needed joy and sunshine into my otherwise exhausting graduate student life!!!

Forever A Squirrel Girl Fan,

Brandy Heath
Syracuse, NY

R: Aw, thank you, Brandy! I'm stoked that we can end out a column that has lots of "my child loves your comic!" letters with a "I am a grad student and I love your comic too!" letter. When I was a grad student I was not a particularly great grad student, because I spent most of my free time writing comics instead of researching the class-based productivity of light verb expressions like "take a walk" and "give a smile," like I was supposed to be doing. So I'm glad I can kinda make up for that by having our comics HELP you in your studies by giving you a break from your work!

P.S.: In case you're interested, turns out they ARE productive, and to find out more, look up "Computational Measures of the Acceptibility of Light Verb Constructions by Ryan North" to find my Masters thesis on the matter! It took me three years, so I am absolutely justified in giving it a shout out on the letters page of our talking squirrel comic.

E: I only have four years of higher education under my belt, which is probably okay considering I really only use my BFA in film to tweet about old movies that aren't very good. At any rate, I'm glad we can help you take a break. It'll make your work that much better! As a serial workaholic, I know what I'm talking about here!

Okay, everybody, thanks again for reading and writing in -- keep the letters and photos coming! And hey, come back next month for "Animal House" Part One, kicking off our two-part crossover with HOWARD THE DUCK! The creative team of HOWARD, writer Chip Zdarsky and artist Joe Quinones, will be joining us, and then we'll be joining them on HOWARD THE DUCK #6 a few weeks later!

Want some teases? Here you... Learn the origin of Squirrel Girl's n... costume! Witness the return of Krave... driving his new Kra-Van! And watch Doreen and Howard throw garbage a... each other! It's truly gonna be a story for the ages!!!

USG#5 Michael Cho variant:

the unbeatable
SQUIRREL GIRL

USG #6 cover:

the unbeatable Squirrel Girl

Howard the Duck #6 cover:

HOWARD the DUCK

...Scouts! Make sure to check out our production *blog*, **unbeatablesquirrelgirl.tumblr.com**, where we post behind-the-sc... stuff on how the book gets made, along with *all sorts* of cool things *you* make: fanart, cosplay, whatever!

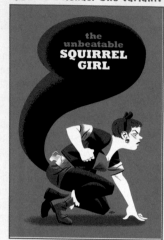

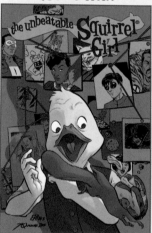

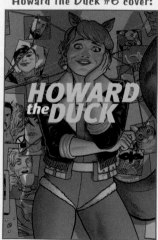

Meanwhile, in the past...

To think that the great **Doctor Doom** could suffer **any** defeat at the claws of **Squirrel Girl** is too insulting-- too **ignominious**-- to consider!

All the better that, by the time this hour is out, it will **never** have taken place! For while Doom **did** make promises about his **own** time traveling...

...he made **no** such promises for his **Doombots!**

Come, Doombots, to my **time platform!** I shall send **you** back in time, where your new mission will be to **aid** your master in his battle against that vile woman!

Defeat the Squirrel Girl, or you shall **all** be reduced to debris, nothing more than worthless metal s--

--crap.

Squirrel Girl.

Blast you, Squirrel Girl!

Blaaast youuu, Squiiiirrrel Giiiirl!

Blaaaaaaassssssst youuuuuuuuuuuuu!!

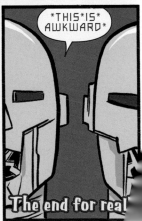

*THIS*IS* AWKWARD*

The end for real

Afterwards Old Lady Squirrel Girl lived happily ever after until she eventually died of old age, which is a pretty good way to go, assuming you have to. And in her will she left the time blaster to Cody, so everything would work out as it was supposed to! Oh snap she was the weird aunt all along, oh snap!!

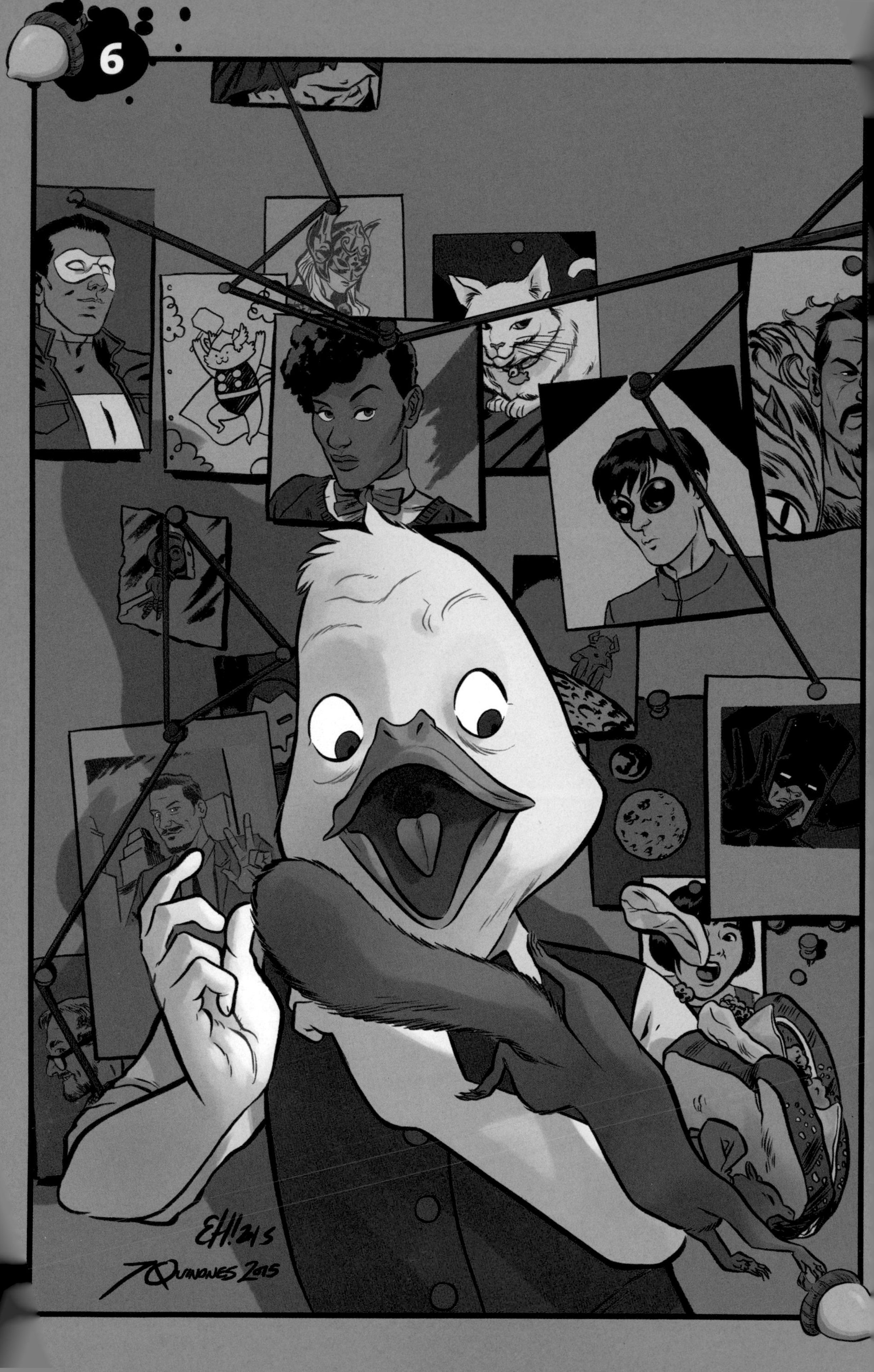
6
EH!21s
JQuiñones 2015

Doreen Green isn't just a first-year computer science student: she secretly also has all the powers of both squirrel and girl! She uses her amazing abilities to fight crime **and** be as awesome as possible. You know her as...The Unbeatable Squirrel Girl! Let's catch up with what she's been up to until now, with...

Squirrel Girl in a nutshell

Nancy W. @sewwiththeflo
That's right. You are reading the tweets of a first-year computer science GRADUATE, friends and neighbors. 2nd year, here I come.

Nancy W. @sewwiththeflo
But first: a summer break filled with knitting, Mew, knitting, Mew, movies, knitting, and Mew.

Squirrel Girl @unbeatablesg
@sewwiththeflo OMG Nancy that sounds super great!! make it a double

Nancy W. @sewwiththeflo
@unbeatablesg Yes! It sure does! Thank you for taking an INEXPLICABLE INTEREST IN ME, RANDOM SUPER HERO!!

Squirrel Girl @unbeatablesg
@starkmantony Hey Tony!! You don't have a secret identity--do you think that's something other super heroes should try? Seems easier tbh

Tony Stark @starkmantony ✓
@unbeatablesg Who says I don't have a secret identity? ;P

Squirrel Girl @unbeatablesg
@starkmantony omg did you just type out a winky smiley with its tongue hanging out

Squirrel Girl @unbeatablesg
@starkmantony did a founding member of the avengers and platinum-elite ceo just send me a ;P

Tony Stark @starkmantony ✓
@unbeatablesg No. Obviously I am too important a person to have done that. It must have been my secretary, who sent it by accident.

Squirrel Girl @unbeatablesg
@starkmantony your secretary. who handles chatting online for you. who reads your messages and then takes your dictated responses.

Tony Stark @starkmantony ✓
@unbeatablesg Tell her yes, Jarvis, and let's leave it there. Stop typing, Jarvis. There's no reason for you to be typing. Jarvis.

Squirrel Girl @unbeatablesg
@starkmantony hahaha NICE TRY ,P ;P ;P

Howard The Duck @imhowatrd
thids siote is badf!!@ how comr thisd wax the onhyl namr lefy

Howard The Duck @imhowatrd
anf its hardf top tyhpe wi8tghy feqaythers anbyewayh!1 whyt wolujd anyon e ujse thyis stu[id sitew

Squirrel Girl @unbeatablesg
@imhowatrd You should talk to the Hulk! The fact that @HULKYSMASHY was the only name left for HIM just serves to increase his anger too!!

HULK @HULKYSMASHY
@unbeatablesg @imhowatrd HULK ALSO GET ANGRY THAT WE CAN SEND MAN TO MOON BUT SOMEHOW CAN'T FILTER OUT PEOPLE SASSING HULK ON THIS SITE??

HULK @HULKYSMASHY
@unbeatablesg @imhowatrd HULK DOESN'T NEED RANDOS TELLING HIM OFF!!!! HULK SMASH ENOUGH KEYBOARDS ALREADY!!!

HULK @HULKYSMASHY
@unbeatablesg @imhowatrd ARGH!! HJGIHBDA,N'K',KNGDS'HJRWPO98Y43POUEQ IU'

Squirrel Girl @unbeatablesg
@HULKYSMASHY @imhowatrd It's okay big guy! They don't know the REAL you, remember!!

Howard The Duck @imhowatrd
@unbeatablesg @HULKYSMASHY i donlt kmow anyt of youi perople

search! 🔍

#kraVAN

#kraVAN

#kraVAN

#kraVAN

#kraVAN

#kraVAN4life

Ryan North with
Chip Zdarsky - writers
Erica Henderson - artist
Chip again - trading card artist
Joe Quinones - van art, *uh,* artist
Rico Renzi - color artist
Travis Lanham - letterer & production
Erica Henderson with
Joe Quinones - cover artists
Erica Henderson with
Chip Zdarsky; Tradd Moore
& Matthew Wilson;
Kamome Shirahama -
variant cover artists
Chris Robinson - ex-asst. editor
Charles Beacham - new asst. editor
Wil Moss - editor
Tom Brevoort - executive editor
Axel Alonso - editor in chief
Joe Quesada - chief creative officer
Dan Buckley - publisher
Alan Fine - exec. producer

Oh, and if it strikes terror into the cowardly and superstitious hearts of criminals, all the better! So to summarize: practical, cute, reduces criminals to a state of quivering and abject terror, useful pockets and/or belt. Got it, Chip?

Is this...do you do this in every issue? Does Marvel pay more for these?

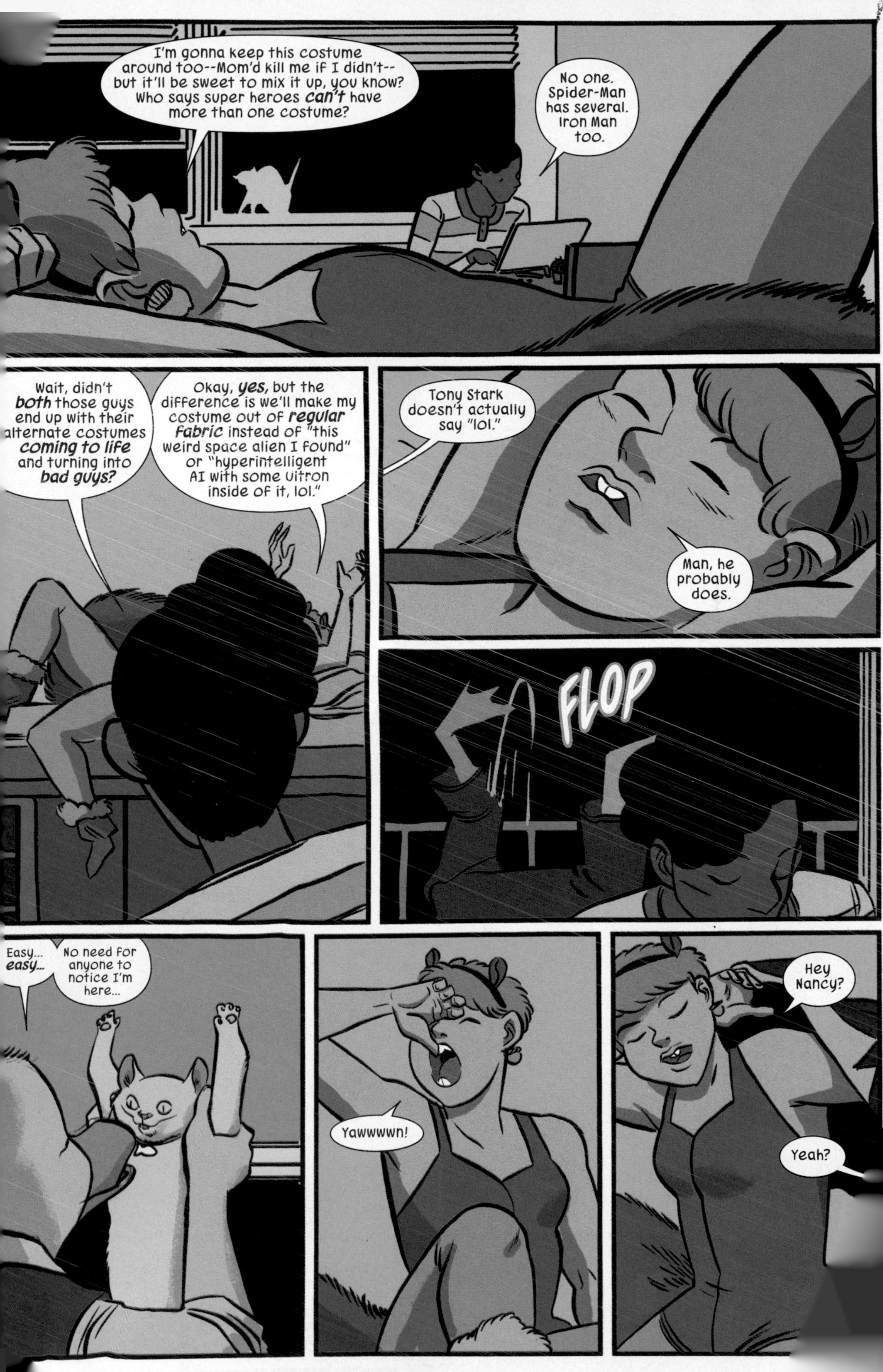

I'm gonna keep this costume around too--Mom'd kill me if I didn't--but it'll be sweet to mix it up, you know? Who says super heroes *can't* have more than one costume?
No one. Spider-Man has several. Iron Man too.
Wait, didn't *both* those guys end up with their alternate costumes *coming to life* and turning into *bad guys?*
Okay, *yes,* but the difference is we'll make my costume out of *regular fabric* instead of "this weird space alien I found" or "hyperintelligent AI with some Ultron inside of it, lol."
Tony Stark doesn't actually say "lol."
Man, he probably does.
FLOP
Easy... *easy...*
No need for anyone to notice I'm here...
Yawwwwn!
Hey Nancy?
Yeah?

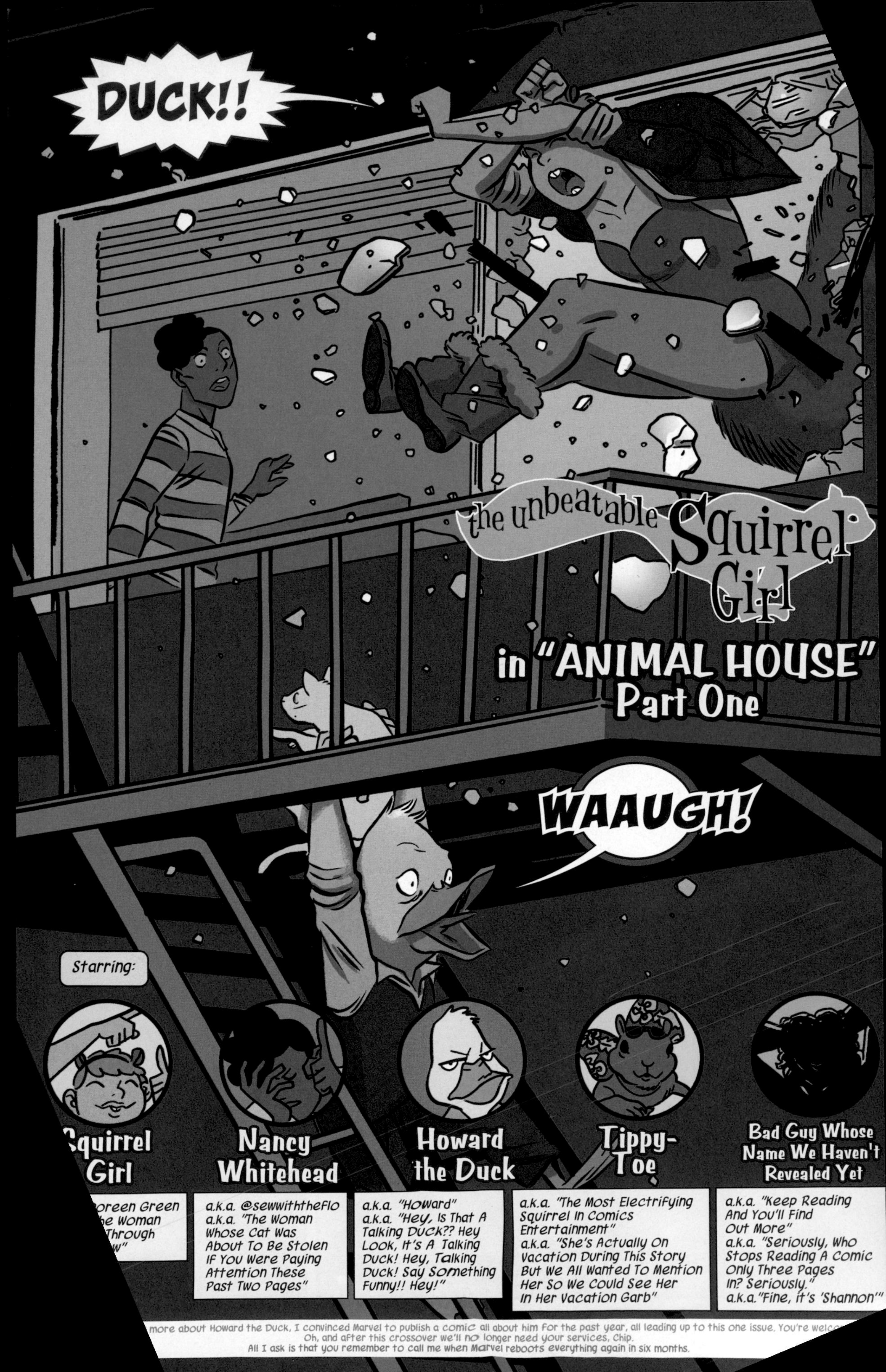

DUCK!!
the unbeatable Squirrel Girl
in "ANIMAL HOUSE"
Part One
WAAUGH!
Starring:
Squirrel Girl
oreen Green
he Woman
Through
w"
Nancy Whitehead
a.k.a. @sewwiththeflo
a.k.a. "The Woman Whose Cat Was About To Be Stolen If You Were Paying Attention These Past Two Pages"
Howard the Duck
a.k.a. "Howard"
a.k.a. "Hey, Is That A Talking DUCK?? Hey Look, It's A Talking Duck! Hey, Talking Duck! Say Something Funny!! Hey!"
Tippy-Toe
a.k.a. "The Most Electrifying Squirrel In Comics Entertainment"
a.k.a. "She's Actually On Vacation During This Story But We All Wanted To Mention Her So We Could See Her In Her Vacation Garb"
Bad Guy Whose Name We Haven't Revealed Yet
a.k.a. "Keep Reading And You'll Find Out More"
a.k.a. "Seriously, Who Stops Reading A Comic Only Three Pages In? Seriously."
a.k.a."Fine, it's 'Shannon'"
more about Howard the Duck, I convinced Marvel to publish a comic all about him for the past year, all leading up to this one issue. You're welco
Oh, and after this crossover we'll no longer need your services, Chip.
All I ask is that you remember to call me when Marvel reboots everything again in six months.

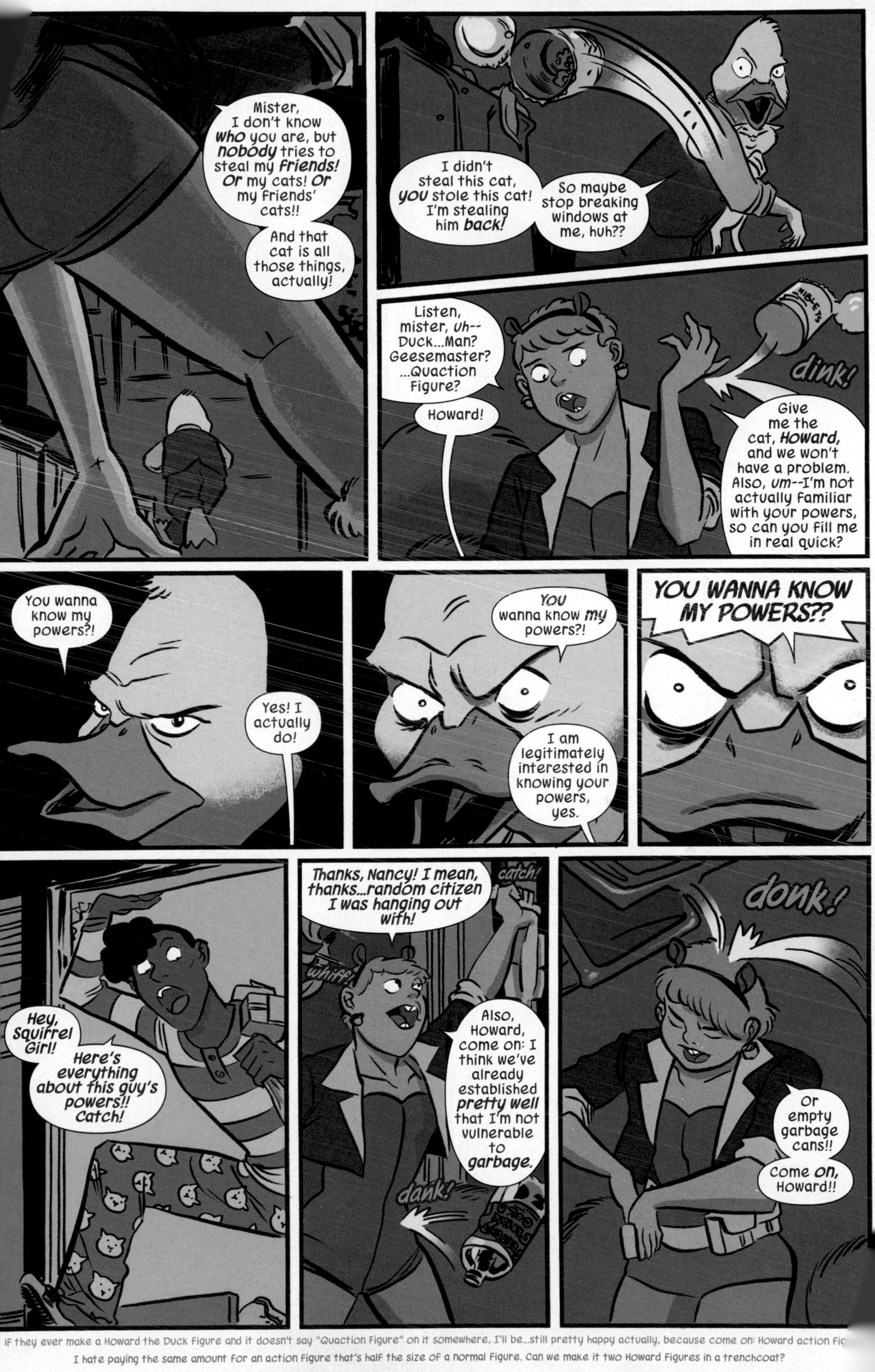
Mister, I don't know *who* you are, but *nobody* tries to steal my *friends!* *Or* my cats! *Or* my friends' cats!!
And that cat is all those things, actually!
I didn't steal this cat, *YOU* stole this cat! I'm stealing him *back!*
So maybe stop breaking windows at me, huh??
Listen, mister, *uh*-- Duck...Man? Geesemaster? ...Quaction Figure?
Howard!
dink!
Give me the cat, *Howard,* and we won't have a problem. Also, *um*--I'm not actually familiar with your powers, so can you fill me in real quick?
You wanna know my powers?!
Yes! I actually do!
YOU wanna know *my* powers?!
I am legitimately interested in knowing your powers, yes.
YOU WANNA KNOW MY POWERS??
Hey, Squirrel Girl!
Here's everything about this guy's powers!! Catch!
Thanks, Nancy! I mean, thanks...random citizen I was hanging out with!
catch!
whiff!
Also, Howard, come on: I think we've already established *pretty well* that I'm not vulnerable to *garbage.*
dank!
donk!
Or empty garbage cans!!
Come *on,* Howard!!

If they ever make a Howard the Duck figure and it doesn't say "Quaction Figure" on it somewhere, I'll be...still pretty happy actually, because come on: Howard action fi
I hate paying the same amount for an action figure that's half the size of a normal figure. Can we make it two Howard figures in a trenchcoat?

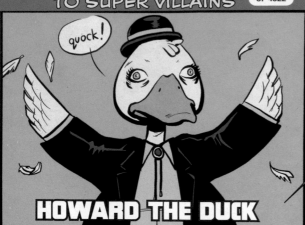

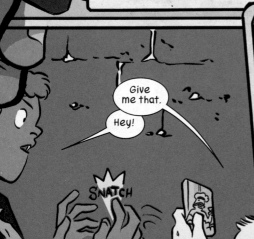

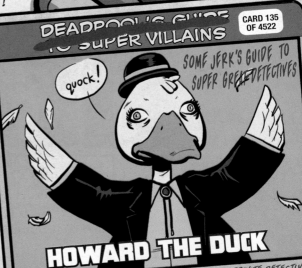

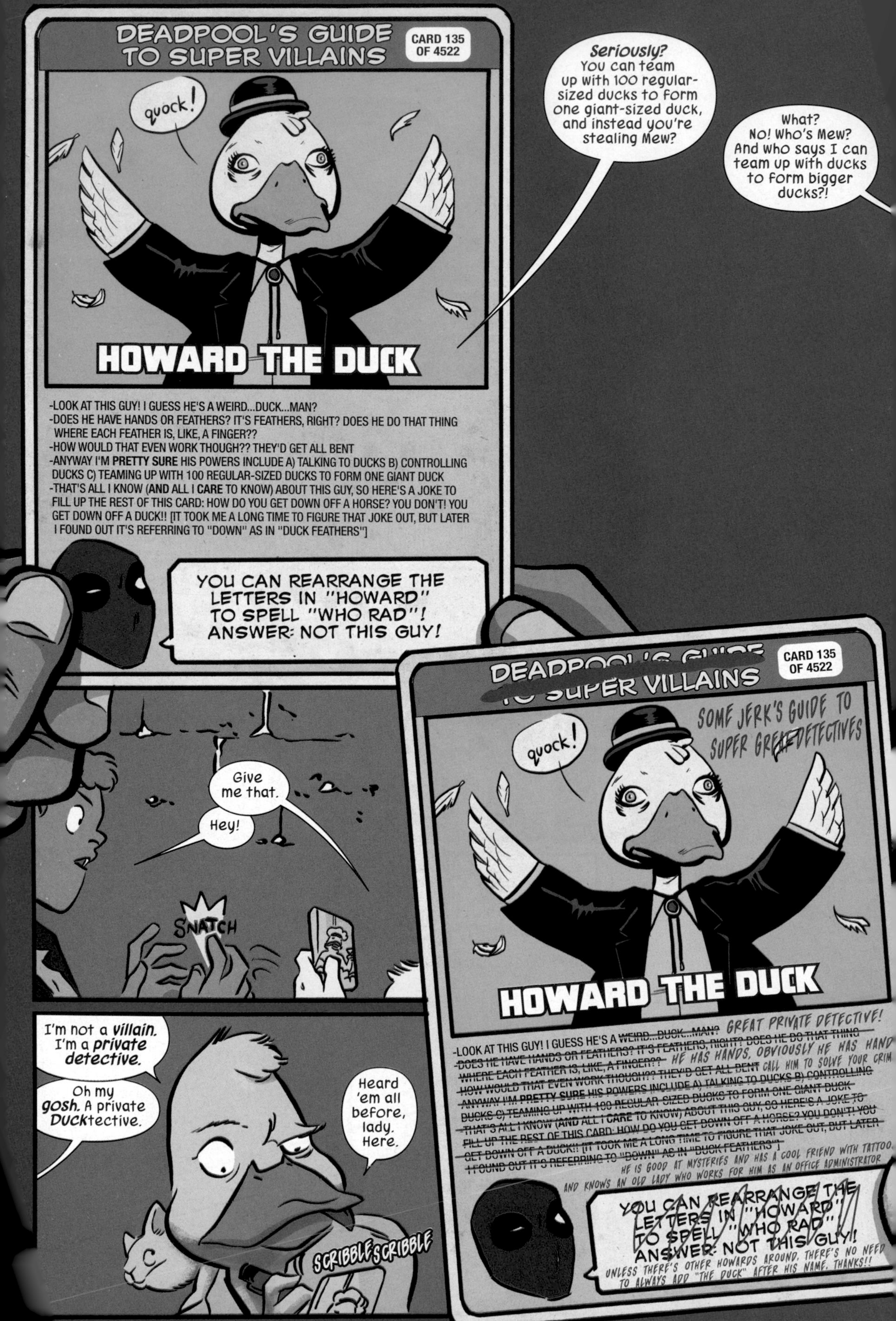
DEADPOOL'S GUIDE TO SUPER VILLAINS
CARD 135 OF 4522
quock!
HOWARD THE DUCK
-LOOK AT THIS GUY! I GUESS HE'S A WEIRD...DUCK...MAN?
-DOES HE HAVE HANDS OR FEATHERS? IT'S FEATHERS, RIGHT? DOES HE DO THAT THING WHERE EACH FEATHER IS, LIKE, A FINGER??
-HOW WOULD THAT EVEN WORK THOUGH?? THEY'D GET ALL BENT
-ANYWAY I'M PRETTY SURE HIS POWERS INCLUDE A) TALKING TO DUCKS B) CONTROLLING DUCKS C) TEAMING UP WITH 100 REGULAR-SIZED DUCKS TO FORM ONE GIANT DUCK
-THAT'S ALL I KNOW (AND ALL I CARE TO KNOW) ABOUT THIS GUY, SO HERE'S A JOKE TO FILL UP THE REST OF THIS CARD: HOW DO YOU GET DOWN OFF A HORSE? YOU DON'T! YOU GET DOWN OFF A DUCK!! [IT TOOK ME A LONG TIME TO FIGURE THAT JOKE OUT, BUT LATER I FOUND OUT IT'S REFERRING TO "DOWN" AS IN "DUCK FEATHERS"]
YOU CAN REARRANGE THE LETTERS IN "HOWARD" TO SPELL "WHO RAD"! ANSWER: NOT THIS GUY!
Seriously? You can team up with 100 regular-sized ducks to form one giant-sized duck, and instead you're stealing Mew?
What? No! Who's Mew? And who says I can team up with ducks to form bigger ducks?!
Give me that.
Hey!
SNATCH
I'm not a villain. I'm a private detective.
Oh my gosh. A private Ducktective.
Heard 'em all before, lady. Here.
SCRIBBLE SCRIBBLE
DEADPOOL'S GUIDE TO SUPER VILLAINS
CARD 135 OF 4522
SOME JERK'S GUIDE TO SUPER GREAT DETECTIVES
quock!
HOWARD THE DUCK
-LOOK AT THIS GUY! I GUESS HE'S A WEIRD...DUCK...MAN? GREAT PRIVATE DETECTIVE!
-DOES HE HAVE HANDS OR FEATHERS? IT'S FEATHERS, RIGHT? DOES HE DO THAT THING WHERE EACH FEATHER IS, LIKE, A FINGER?? HE HAS HANDS, OBVIOUSLY HE HAS HAND
-HOW WOULD THAT EVEN WORK THOUGH?? THEY'D GET ALL BENT CALL HIM TO SOLVE YOUR CRIM
-ANYWAY I'M PRETTY SURE HIS POWERS INCLUDE A) TALKING TO DUCKS B) CONTROLLING DUCKS C) TEAMING UP WITH 100 REGULAR-SIZED DUCKS TO FORM ONE GIANT DUCK
-THAT'S ALL I KNOW (AND ALL I CARE TO KNOW) ABOUT THIS GUY, SO HERE'S A JOKE TO FILL UP THE REST OF THIS CARD: HOW DO YOU GET DOWN OFF A HORSE? YOU DON'T! YOU GET DOWN OFF A DUCK!! [IT TOOK ME A LONG TIME TO FIGURE THAT JOKE OUT, BUT LATER I FOUND OUT IT'S REFERRING TO "DOWN" AS IN "DUCK FEATHERS"]
HE IS GOOD AT MYSTERIES AND HAS A COOL FRIEND WITH TATTOO. AND KNOWS AN OLD LADY WHO WORKS FOR HIM AS AN OFFICE ADMINISTRATOR
YOU CAN REARRANGE THE LETTERS IN "HOWARD" TO SPELL "WHO RAD"! ANSWER: NOT THIS GUY!
UNLESS THERE'S OTHER HOWARDS AROUND, THERE'S NO NEED TO ALWAYS ADD "THE DUCK" AFTER HIS NAME. THANKS!!

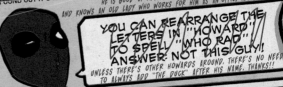

're wondering why Howard's card is number 135, 135 is the sum of 40 plus 34 plus 61, and those numbers make up an ASCII-art duck. ***OBSERVE:*** ("=

("= ((ha ha see what i did there ha ha

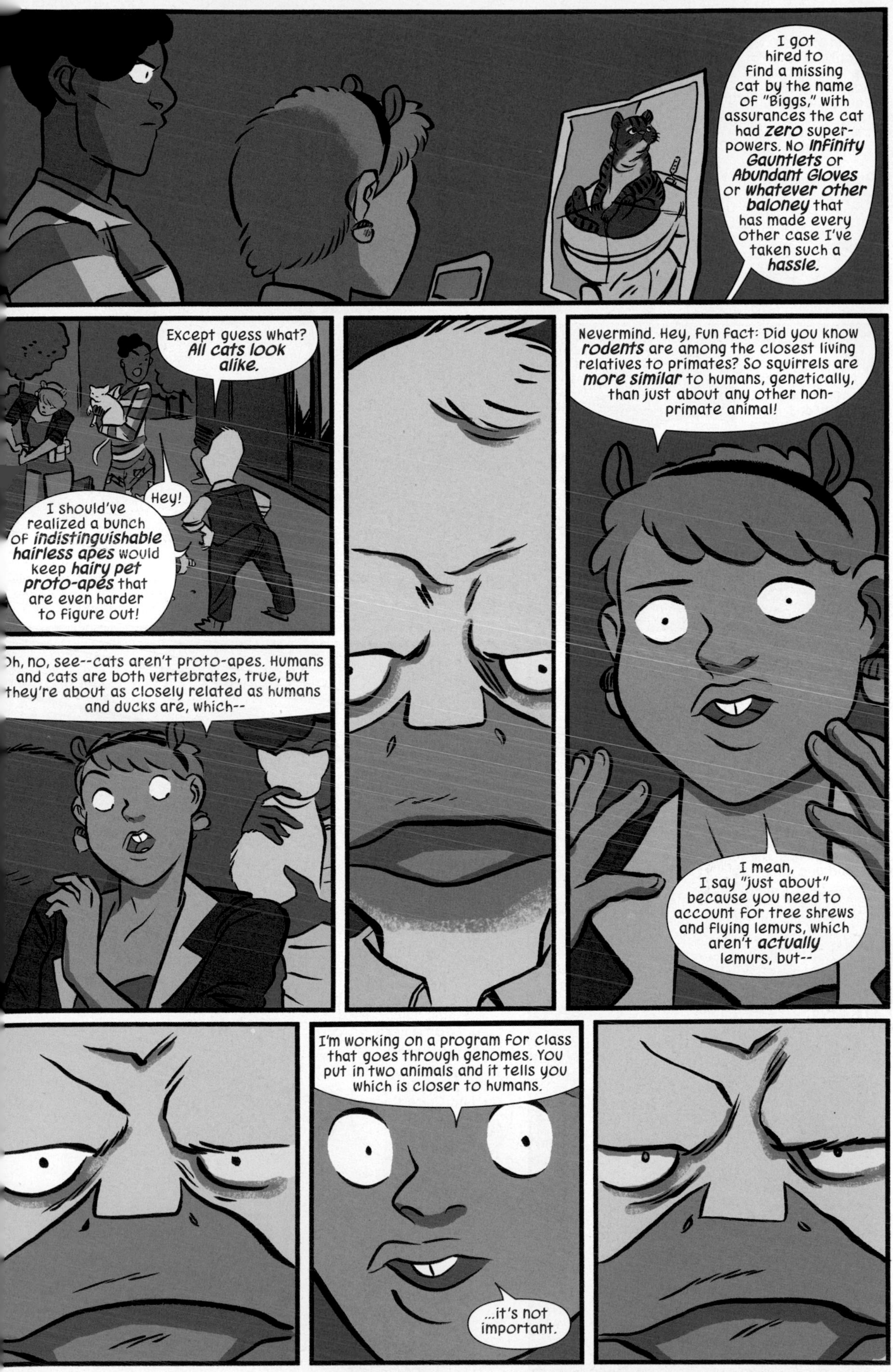
I got hired to find a missing cat by the name of "Biggs," with assurances the cat had **zero** superpowers. No **Infinity Gauntlets** or **Abundant Gloves** or **whatever other baloney** that has made every other case I've taken such a **hassle.**
Except guess what? **All cats look alike.**
Hey!
I should've realized a bunch of **indistinguishable hairless apes** would keep **hairy pet proto-apes** that are even harder to figure out!
Oh, no, see--cats aren't proto-apes. Humans and cats are both vertebrates, true, but they're about as closely related as humans and ducks are, which--
Nevermind. Hey, fun fact: Did you know **rodents** are among the closest living relatives to primates? So squirrels are **more similar** to humans, genetically, than just about any other non-primate animal!
I mean, I say "just about" because you need to account for tree shrews and flying lemurs, which aren't **actually** lemurs, but--
I'm working on a program for class that goes through genomes. You put in two animals and it tells you which is closer to humans.
...it's not important.

SCIENCE CORNER: Actually, humans and ducks diverged when mammals and birds did (pre-dinosaurs), but humans and cats diverged later as mammals diversified. So humans actually share **more** genes with cats than they do with ducks. Sorry, Howard.

Um, **actually,** humans are **very** different from cats and ducks. Citation: my own eyes.

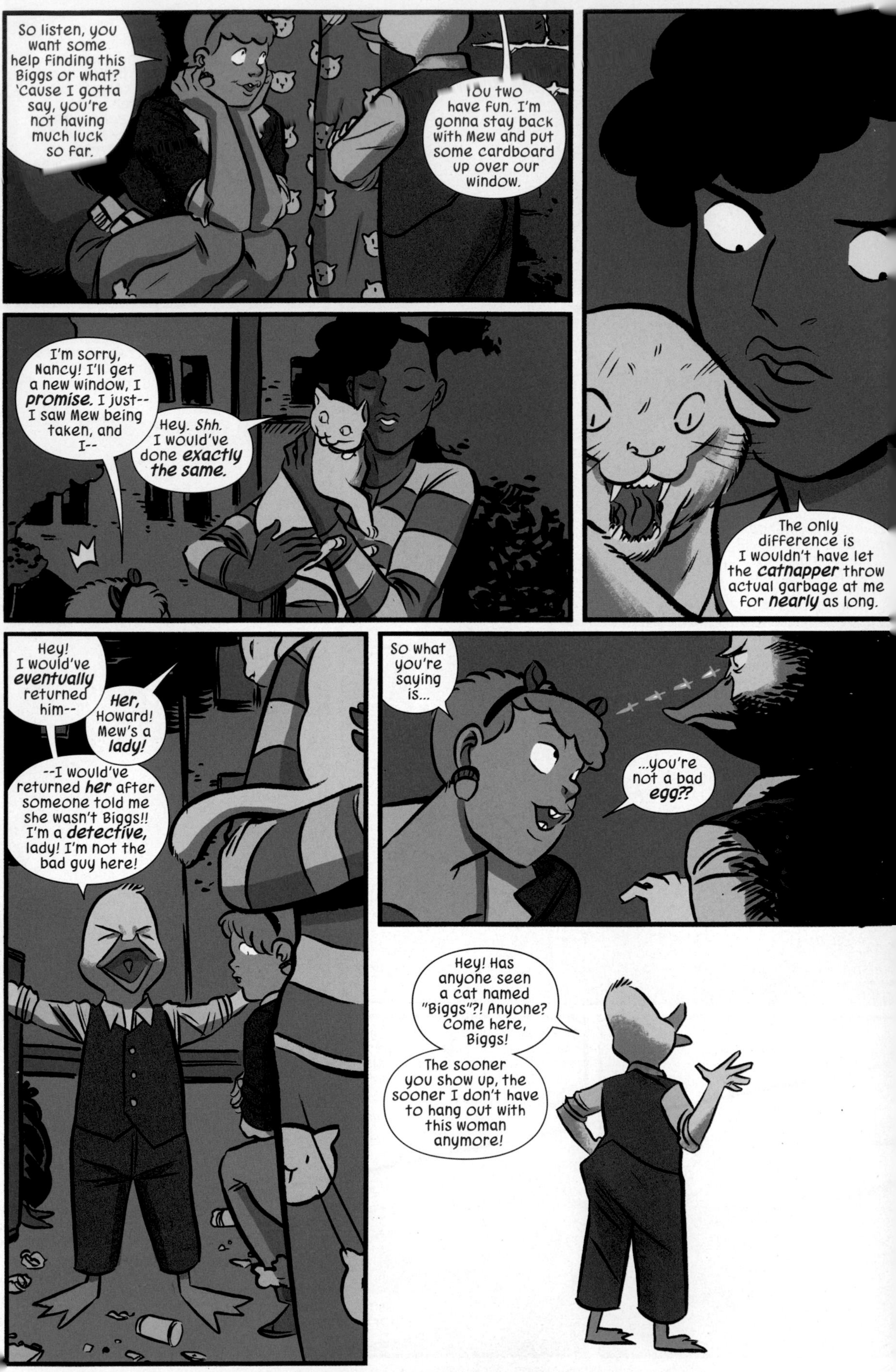

So listen, you want some help finding this Biggs or what? 'Cause I gotta say, you're not having much luck so far.
You two have fun. I'm gonna stay back with Mew and put some cardboard up over our window.
I'm sorry, Nancy! I'll get a new window, I promise. I just-- I saw Mew being taken, and I--
Hey. Shh. I would've done exactly the same.
The only difference is I wouldn't have let the catnapper throw actual garbage at me for nearly as long.
Hey! I would've eventually returned him--
Her, Howard! Mew's a lady!
--I would've returned her after someone told me she wasn't Biggs!! I'm a detective, lady! I'm not the bad guy here!
So what you're saying is...
...you're not a bad egg??
Hey! Has anyone seen a cat named "Biggs"?! Anyone? Come here, Biggs!
The sooner you show up, the sooner I don't have to hang out with this woman anymore!

I'm sorry, Howard, I thought you'd like the duck puns! I'm big into the nut puns myself, so I just assumed. You might even say nut puns are...me in a *nutshell?*
Ugh I didn't realize this was a crossover with the *PUN*isher.

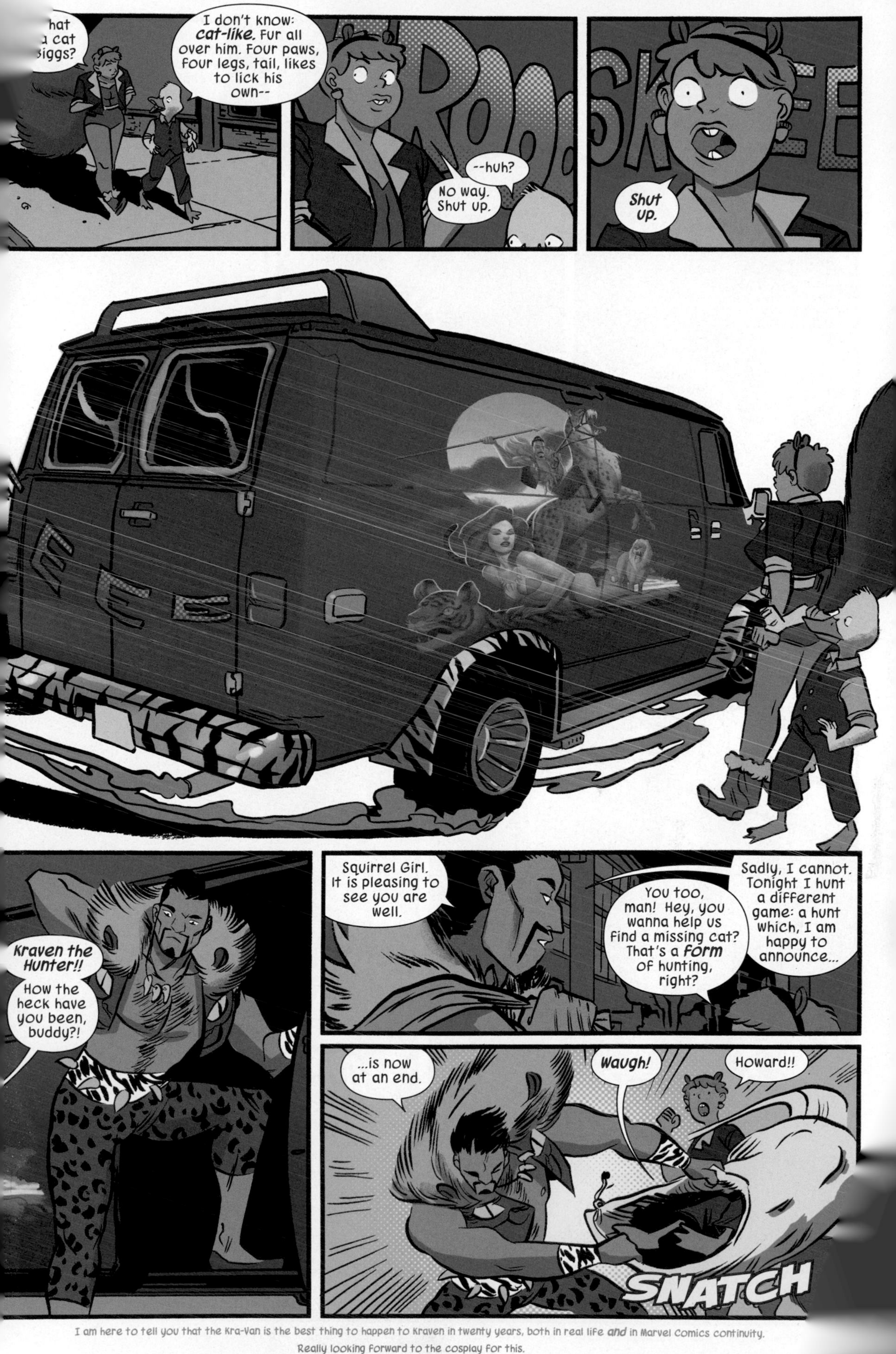

I don't know: *cat-like.* Fur all over him. Four paws, four legs, tail, likes to lick his own--
--huh?
No way. Shut up.
Shut up.
Kraven the Hunter!! How the heck have you been, buddy?!
Squirrel Girl. It is pleasing to see you are well.
You too, man! Hey, you wanna help us find a missing cat? That's a *form* of hunting, right?
Sadly, I cannot. Tonight I hunt a different game: a hunt which, I am happy to announce...
...is now at an end.
Waugh!
Howard!!
SNATCH

I am here to tell you that the Kra-Van is the best thing to happen to Kraven in twenty years, both in real life *and* in Marvel Comics continuity. Really looking forward to the cosplay for this.

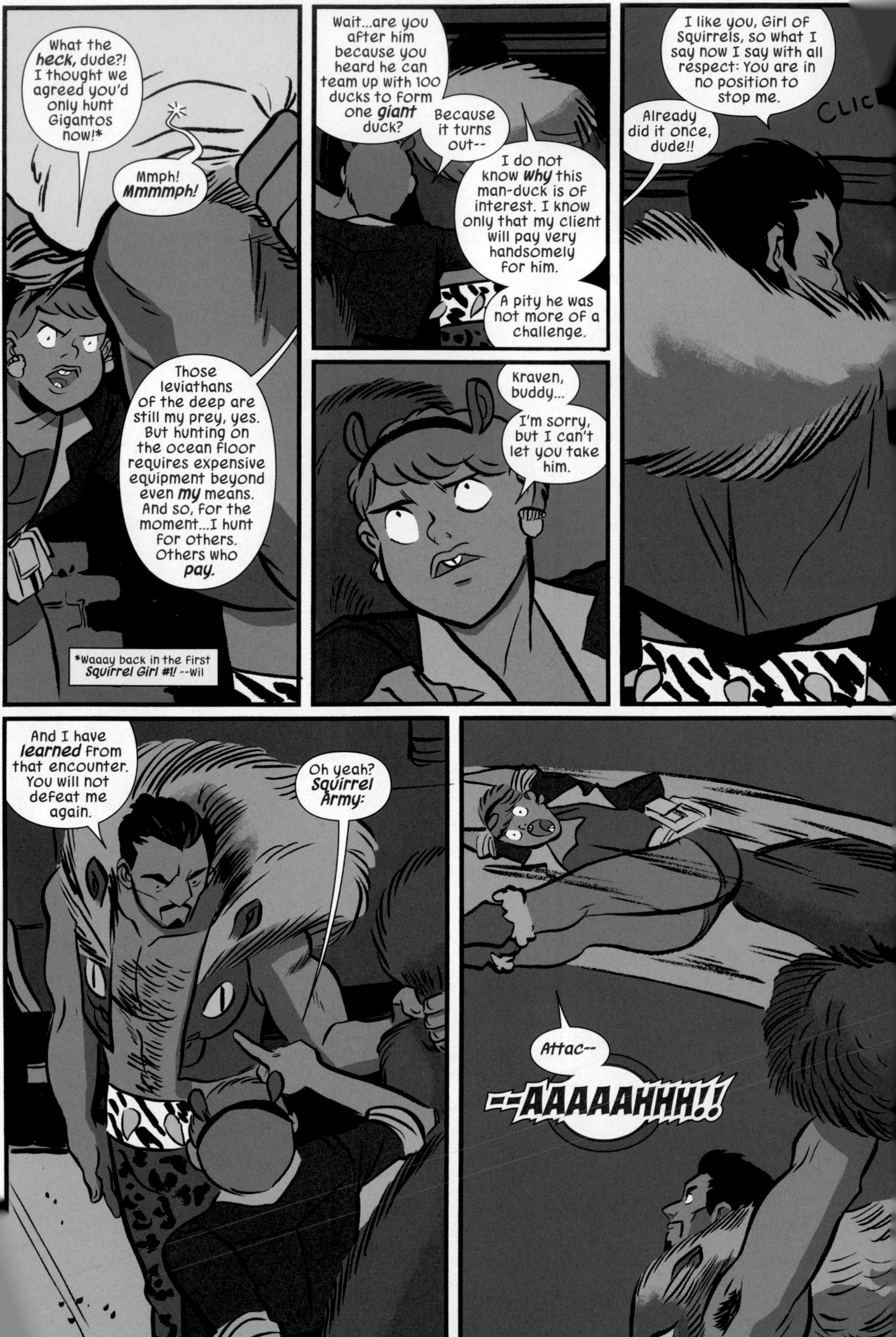
What the heck, dude?! I thought we agreed you'd only hunt Gigantos now!*
Mmph! Mmmmph!
Those leviathans of the deep are still my prey, yes. But hunting on the ocean floor requires expensive equipment beyond even my means. And so, for the moment...I hunt for others. Others who pay.
*Waaay back in the first Squirrel Girl #1! --Wil
Wait...are you after him because you heard he can team up with 100 ducks to form one giant duck?
Because it turns out--
I do not know why this man-duck is of interest. I know only that my client will pay very handsomely for him.
A pity he was not more of a challenge.
Kraven, buddy...
I'm sorry, but I can't let you take him.
I like you, Girl of Squirrels, so what I say now I say with all respect: You are in no position to stop me.
Already did it once, dude!!
CLICK
And I have learned from that encounter. You will not defeat me again.
Oh yeah? Squirrel Army:
Attac--
--AAAAAHHH!!

nearby squirrels are all: *"attacaaaaahhhh"?* That's not an actual command! Squirrel Girl must've gotten distracted while talking to us. Well, as we were, I guess. ok.

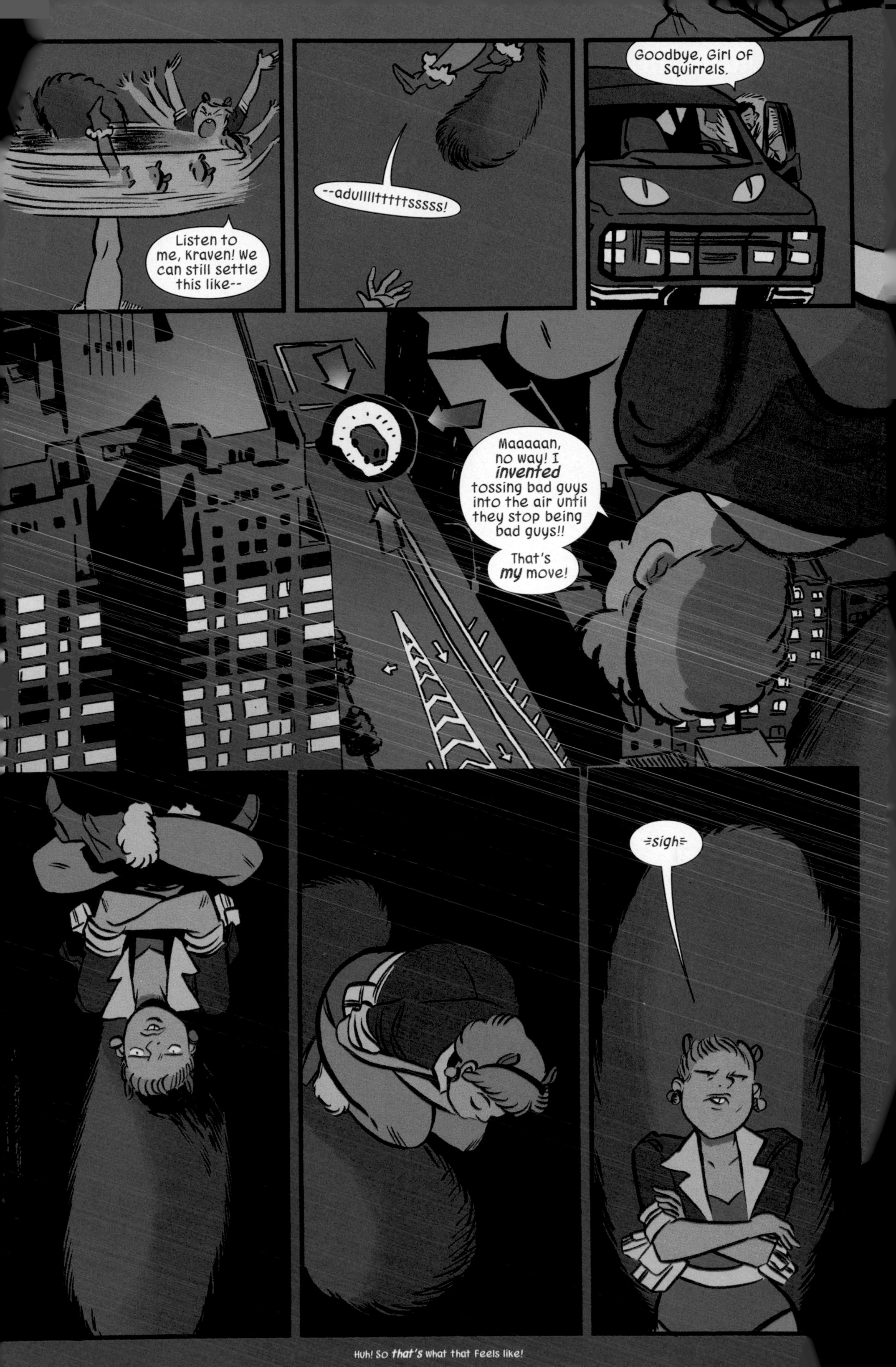
Listen to me, Kraven! We can still settle this like--
--adulllltttttsssss!
Goodbye, Girl of Squirrels.
Maaaaan, no way! I *invented* tossing bad guys into the air until they stop being bad guys!!
That's *my* move!
=sigh=
Huh! So *that's* what that feels like!
I would be so conflicted, 'cause I'm in a battle, but being tossed into the air would be so much fun!

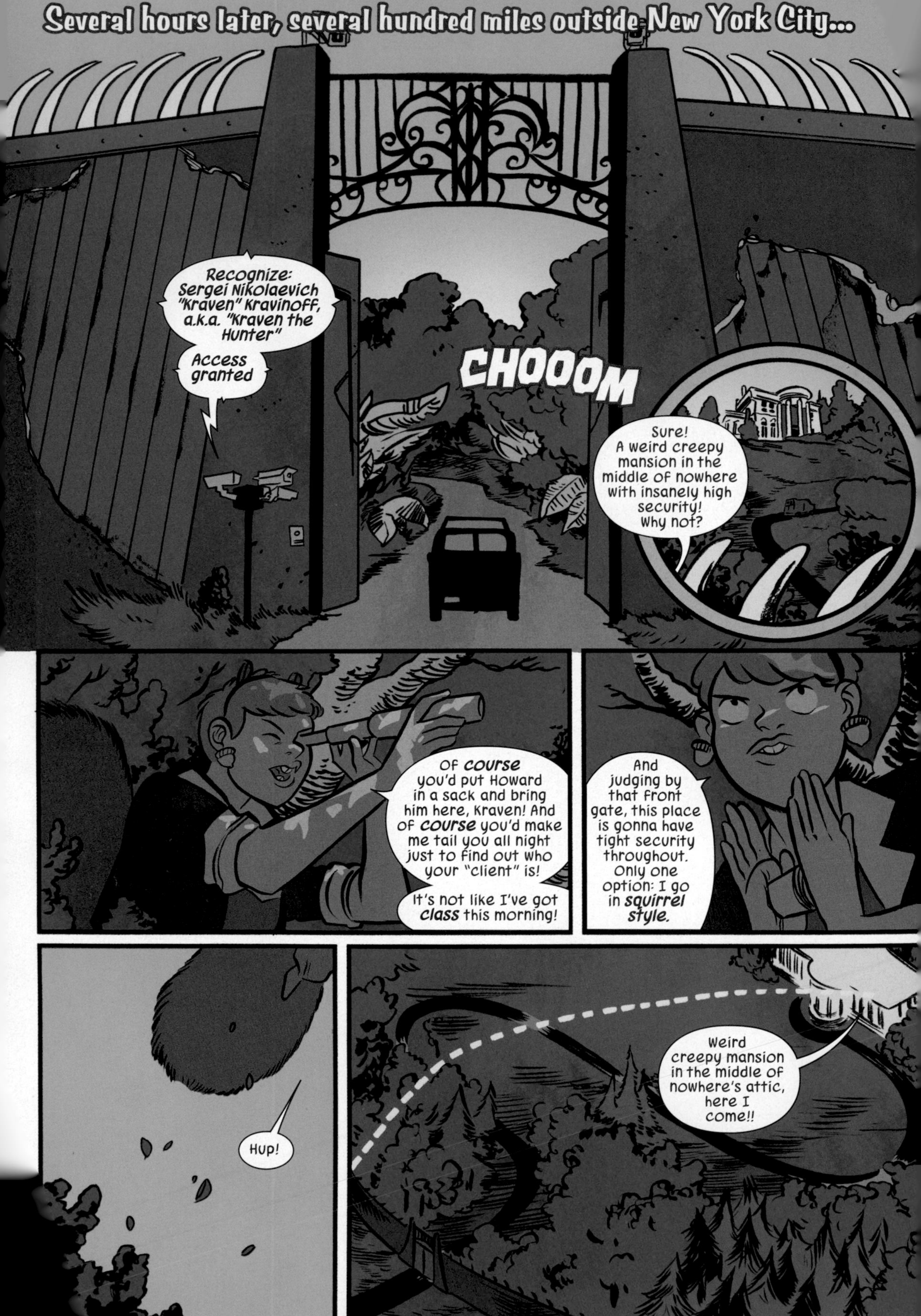
Several hours later, several hundred miles outside New York City...
Recognize: Sergei Nikolaevich "Kraven" Kravinoff, a.k.a. "Kraven the Hunter"
Access granted
CHOOOM
Sure! A weird creepy mansion in the middle of nowhere with insanely high security! Why not?
Of course you'd put Howard in a sack and bring him here, Kraven! And of course you'd make me tail you all night just to find out who your "client" is!
It's not like I've got class this morning!
And judging by that front gate, this place is gonna have tight security throughout. Only one option: I go in squirrel style.
Hup!
Weird creepy mansion in the middle of nowhere's attic, here I come!!

ed about Doreen Green missing class too, but don't worry: she reads ahead, so when she has to miss class like this, she doesn't fall too far behind. Thanks, Doreen! Now we can all enjoy the rest of this comic without worrying.

Hm. I heard she just skims.

Shannon Sugarbaker will not tolerate anyone in the room being more of a Southern Belle than her and that is all you need to know about Shannon Sugarbaker.
It's why I *cannot* be in the same room with Shannon Sugarbaker.

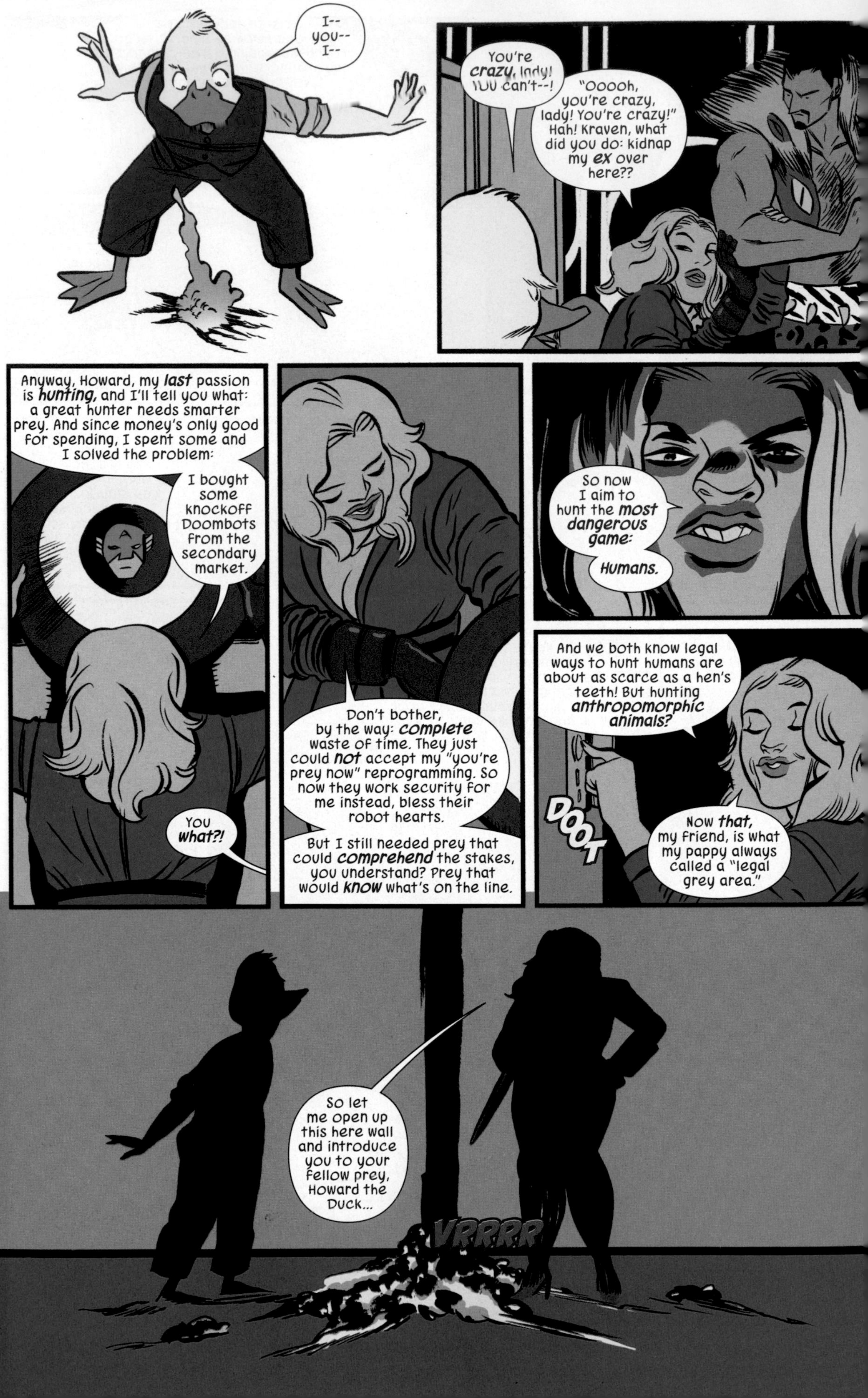
I-- you-- I--
You're crazy, lady! YOU can't--!
"Ooooh, you're crazy, lady! You're crazy!" Hah! Kraven, what did you do: kidnap my ex over here??
Anyway, Howard, my last passion is hunting, and I'll tell you what: a great hunter needs smarter prey. And since money's only good for spending, I spent some and I solved the problem:
I bought some knockoff Doombots from the secondary market.
You what?!
Don't bother, by the way: complete waste of time. They just could not accept my "you're prey now" reprogramming. So now they work security for me instead, bless their robot hearts.
But I still needed prey that could comprehend the stakes, you understand? Prey that would know what's on the line.
So now I aim to hunt the most dangerous game:
Humans.
And we both know legal ways to hunt humans are about as scarce as a hen's teeth! But hunting anthropomorphic animals?
DOOT
Now that, my friend, is what my pappy always called a "legal grey area."
So let me open up this here wall and introduce you to your fellow prey, Howard the Duck...
VRRRR

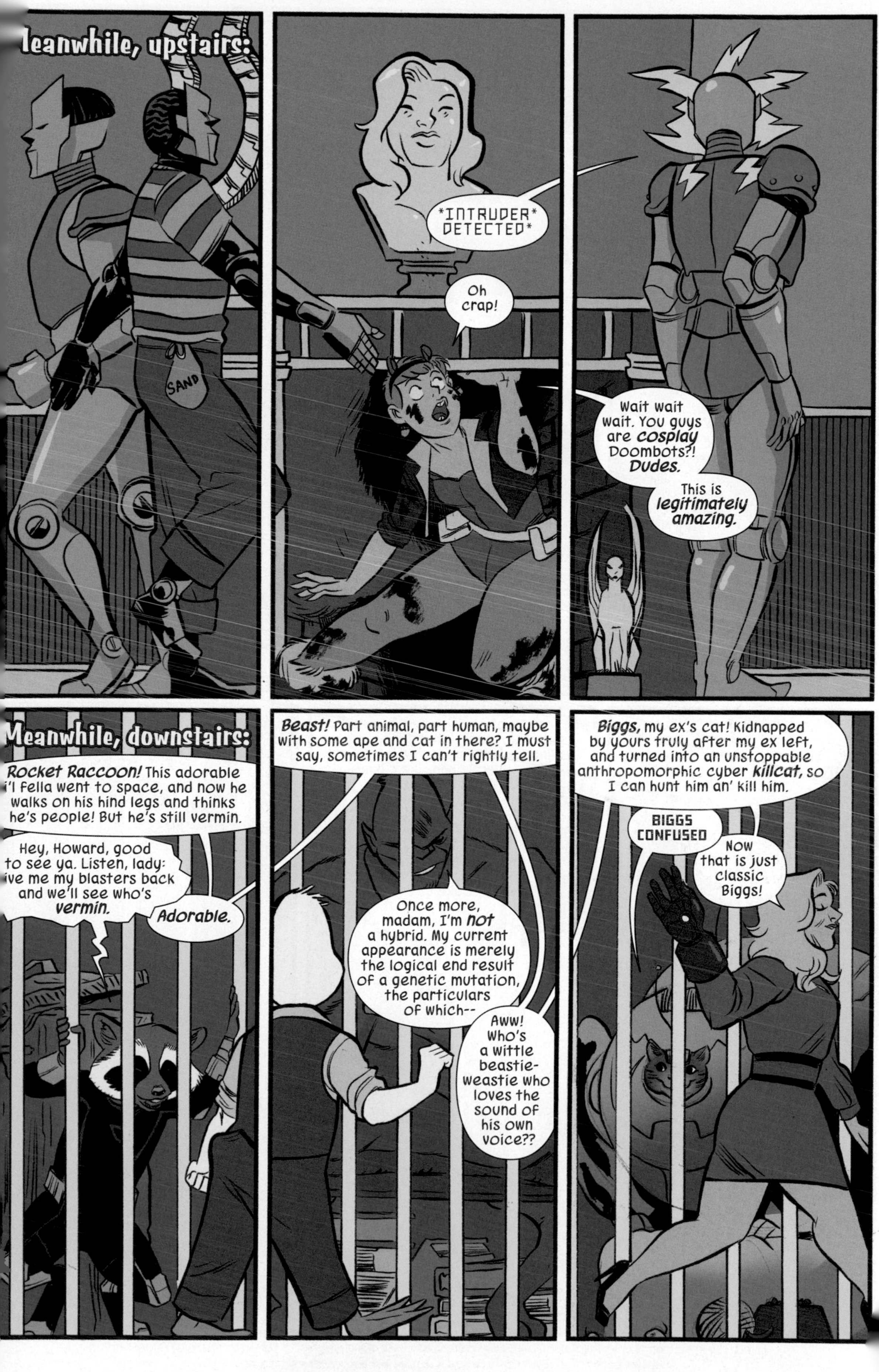

leanwhile, upstairs:
SAND
INTRUDER DETECTED*
Oh crap!
Wait wait wait. You guys are cosplay Doombots?! Dudes.
This is legitimately amazing.
Meanwhile, downstairs:
Rocket Raccoon! This adorable 'l fella went to space, and now he walks on his hind legs and thinks he's people! But he's still vermin.
Hey, Howard, good to see ya. Listen, lady: ive me my blasters back and we'll see who's vermin.
Adorable.
Beast! Part animal, part human, maybe with some ape and cat in there? I must say, sometimes I can't rightly tell.
Once more, madam, I'm not a hybrid. My current appearance is merely the logical end result of a genetic mutation, the particulars of which--
Aww! Who's a wittle beastie-weastie who loves the sound of his own voice??
Biggs, my ex's cat! Kidnapped by yours truly after my ex left, and turned into an unstoppable anthropomorphic cyber killcat, so I can hunt him an' kill him.
BIGGS CONFUSED
Now that is just classic Biggs!

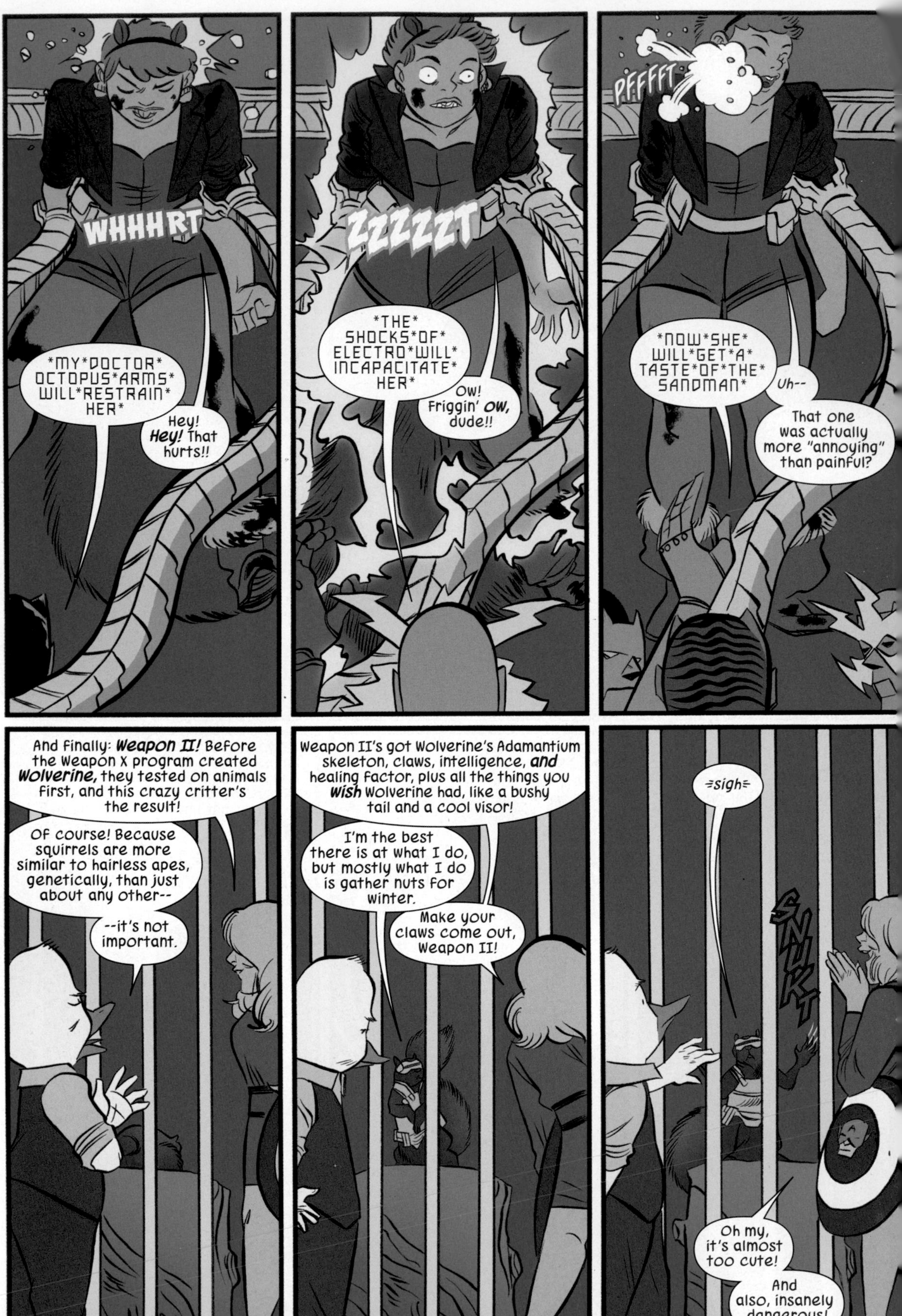
WHHHRT
*MY*DOCTOR*
OCTOPUS*ARMS*
WILL*RESTRAIN*
HER*
Hey! Hey! That hurts!!
ZZZZZT
THE
SHOCKS*OF*
ELECTRO*WILL*
INCAPACITATE*
HER*
Ow! Friggin' OW, dude!!
PFFFFT
*NOW*SHE*
WILL*GET*A*
TASTE*OF*THE*
SANDMAN*
Uh--
That one was actually more "annoying" than painful?
And finally: Weapon II! Before the Weapon X program created Wolverine, they tested on animals first, and this crazy critter's the result!
Of course! Because squirrels are more similar to hairless apes, genetically, than just about any other--
--it's not important.
Weapon II's got Wolverine's Adamantium skeleton, claws, intelligence, and healing factor, plus all the things you wish Wolverine had, like a bushy tail and a cool visor!
I'm the best there is at what I do, but mostly what I do is gather nuts for winter.
Make your claws come out, Weapon II!
sigh
SNIKT
Oh my, it's almost too cute!
And also, insanely dangerous!

*THERE*CAN*BE*NO*ESCAPE*/*MY*SAND*WAS*PROGRAMMED*TO*BE*COARSE*AND*ROUGH*AND*IRRITATING*AND*TO*GET*EVERYWHERE*

SCIENCE CORNER: Interesting sand fact: sand is actually just dirt but different I guess!

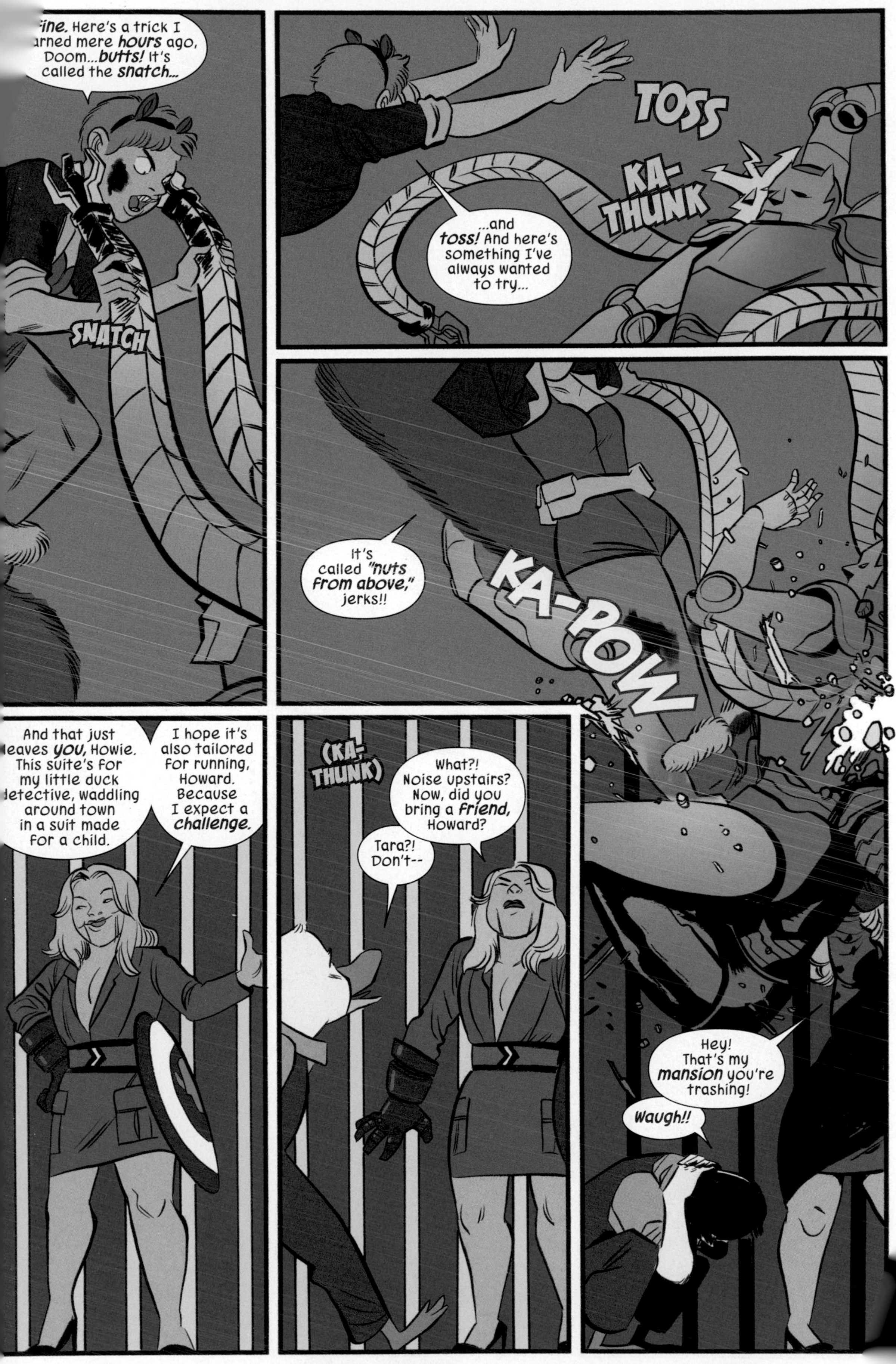
Fine. Here's a trick I learned mere hours ago, Doom...butts! It's called the snatch...
SNATCH
TOSS
KA-THUNK
...and toss! And here's something I've always wanted to try...
It's called "nuts from above," jerks!!
KA-POW
And that just leaves you, Howie. This suite's for my little duck detective, waddling around town in a suit made for a child.
I hope it's also tailored for running, Howard. Because I expect a challenge.
(KA-THUNK)
What?! Noise upstairs? Now, did you bring a friend, Howard?
Tara?! Don't--
Hey! That's my mansion you're trashing!
Waugh!!

I didn't ask Chip if it was canon that Howard buys his suits from the children's section, but I feel pretty confident that I am 100% correct

Um, *children* buy their suits from the *Howard* section, *Ryan.*

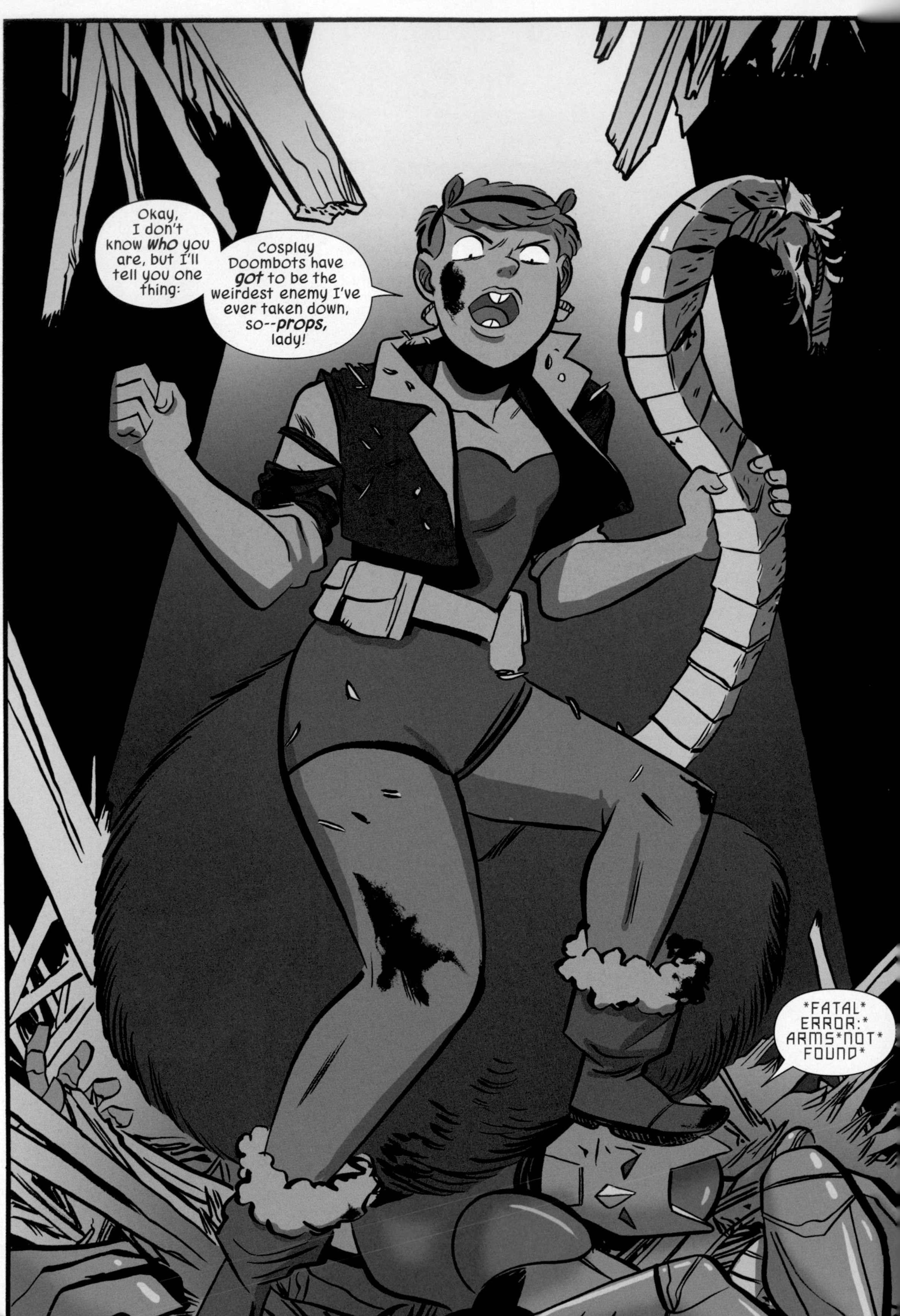
Okay, I don't know who you are, but I'll tell you one thing:
Cosplay Doombots have got to be the weirdest enemy I've ever taken down, so--props, lady!
FATAL ERROR:* ARMS*NOT* FOUND*

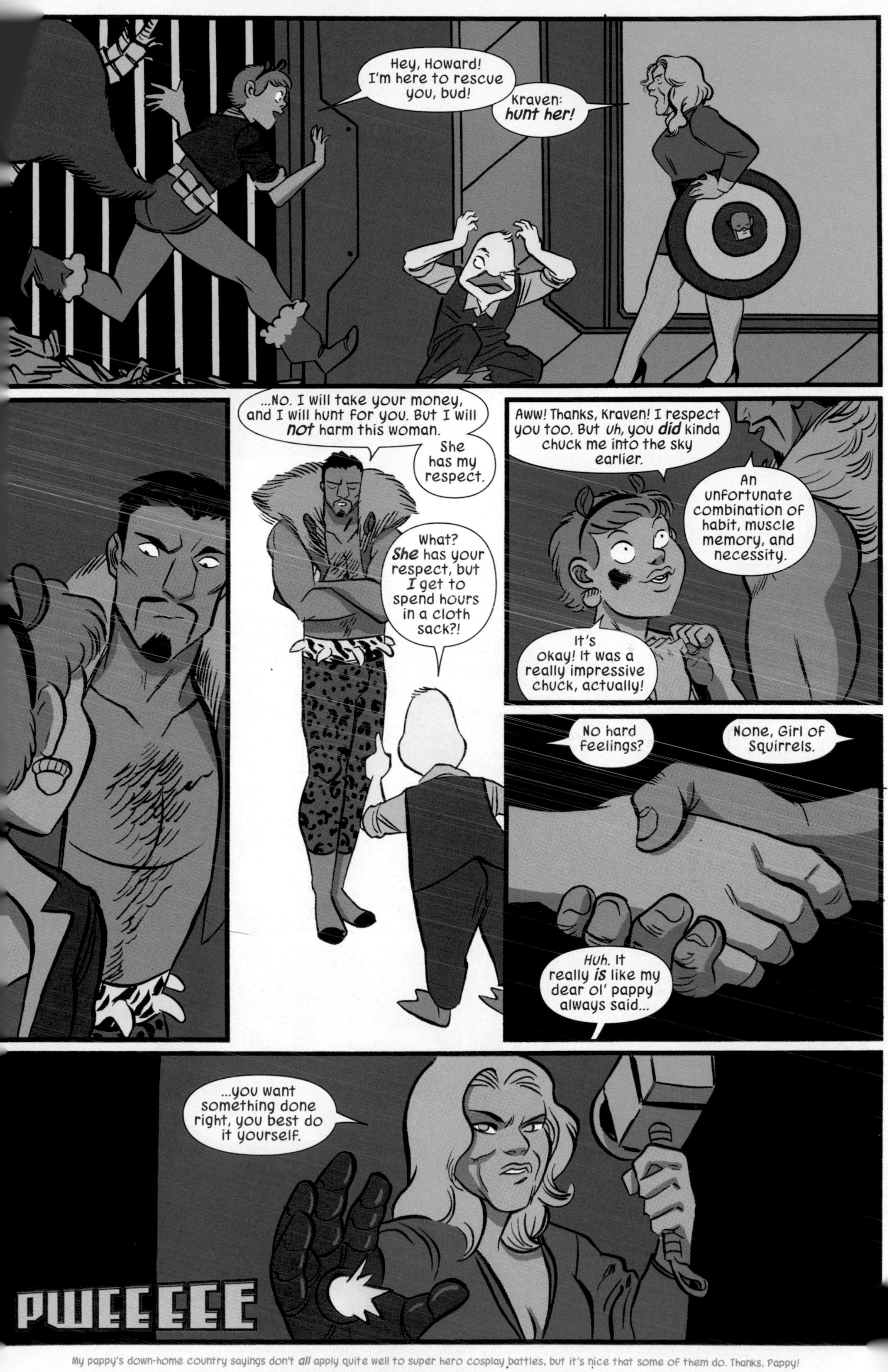
Hey, Howard! I'm here to rescue you, bud!
Kraven: hunt her!
...No. I will take your money, and I will hunt for you. But I will not harm this woman.
She has my respect.
What? She has your respect, but I get to spend hours in a cloth sack?!
Aww! Thanks, Kraven! I respect you too. But uh, you did kinda chuck me into the sky earlier.
An unfortunate combination of habit, muscle memory, and necessity.
It's okay! It was a really impressive chuck, actually!
No hard feelings?
None, Girl of Squirrels.
Huh. It really is like my dear ol' pappy always said...
...you want something done right, you best do it yourself.
PWEEEEE

My pappy's down-home country sayings don't *all* apply quite well to super hero cosplay battles, but it's nice that some of them do. Thanks, Pappy!
Um, if you want something done right, you hire a person who specializes in the task that needs completing. Your pappy needs to be corrected.

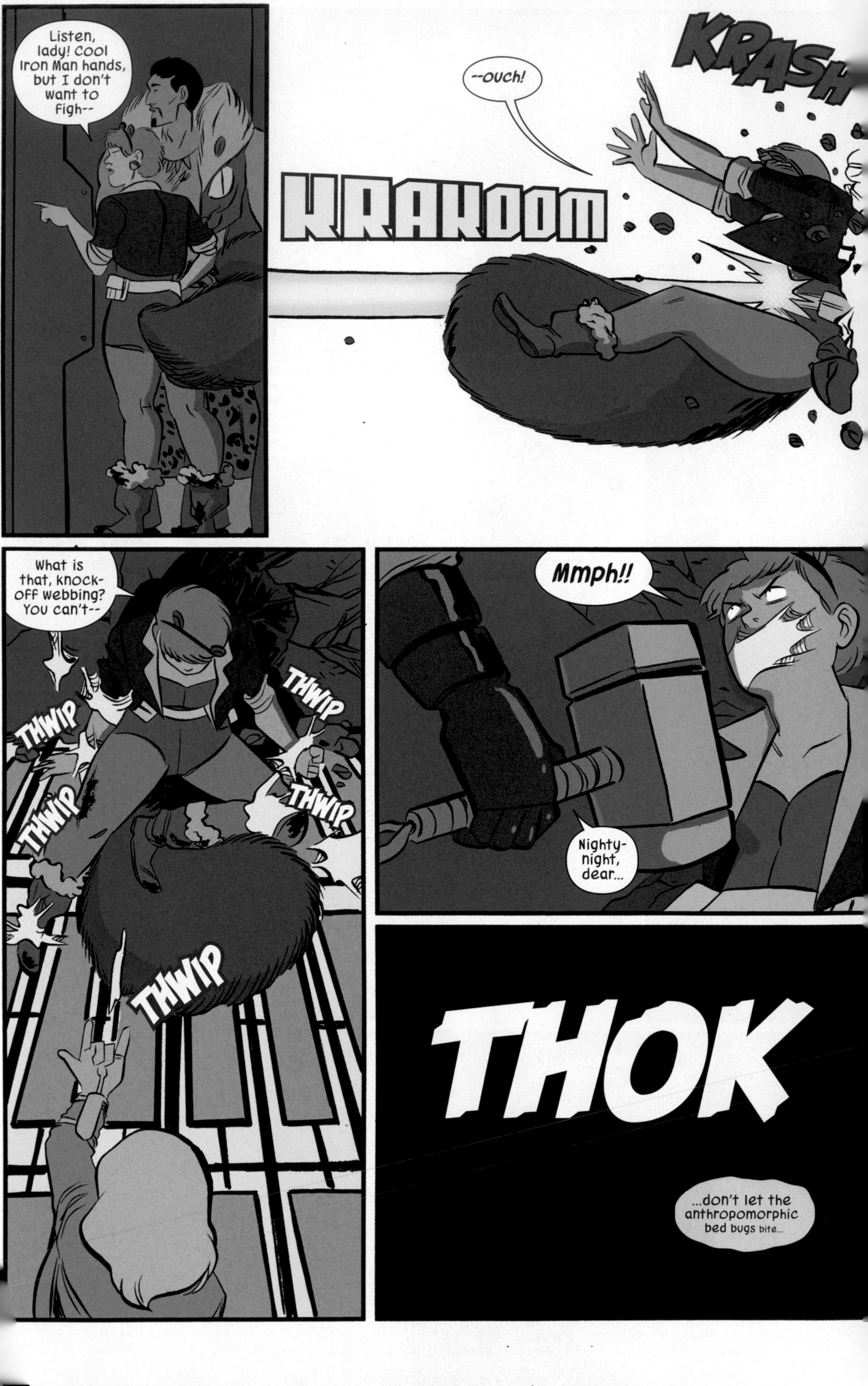
Listen, lady! Cool Iron Man hands, but I don't want to figh--
--ouch!
KRAKOOM
KRASH
What is that, knock-off webbing? You can't--
THWIP
THWIP
THWIP
THWIP
THWIP
Mmph!!
Nighty-night, dear...
THOK
...don't let the anthropomorphic bed bugs bite...

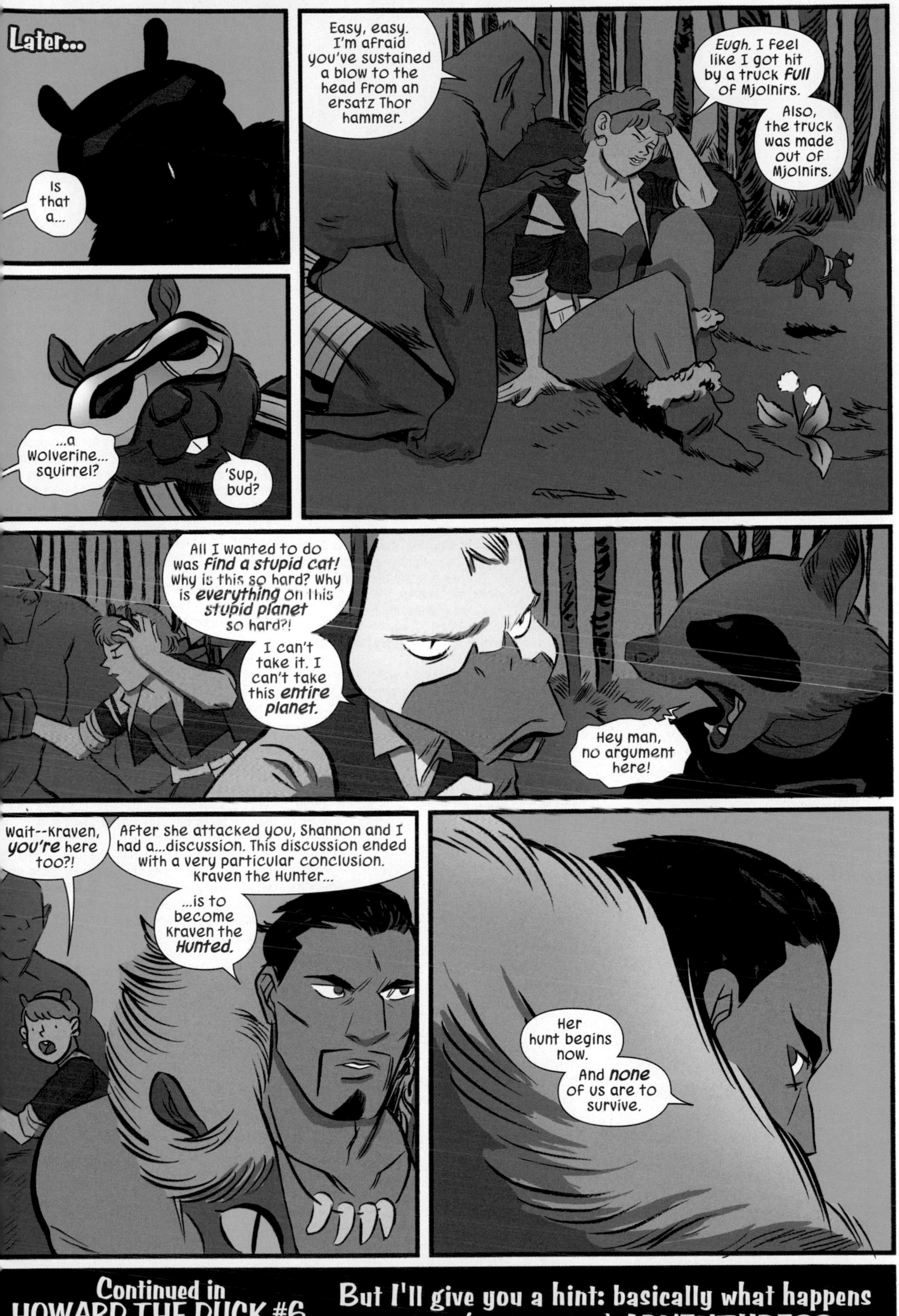
Later...
Is that a...
...a Wolverine... squirrel?
'Sup, bud?
Easy, easy. I'm afraid you've sustained a blow to the head from an ersatz Thor hammer.
Eugh. I feel like I got hit by a truck FULL of Mjolnirs.
Also, the truck was made out of Mjolnirs.
All I wanted to do was find a stupid cat! Why is this so hard? Why is everything on this stupid planet so hard?!
I can't take it. I can't take this entire planet.
Hey man, no argument here!
Wait--Kraven, you're here too?!
After she attacked you, Shannon and I had a...discussion. This discussion ended with a very particular conclusion. Kraven the Hunter...
...is to become Kraven the Hunted.
Her hunt begins now.
And none of us are to survive.

Continued in HOWARD THE DUCK #6, out next month!

But I'll give you a hint: basically what happens in it is (spoiler alert) ADVENTURE??

Also: cosplay. Lots of cosplay.
I'm cosplaying right now! It's as a guy who forgot that he now has to write a whole *Howard the Duck* comic!!

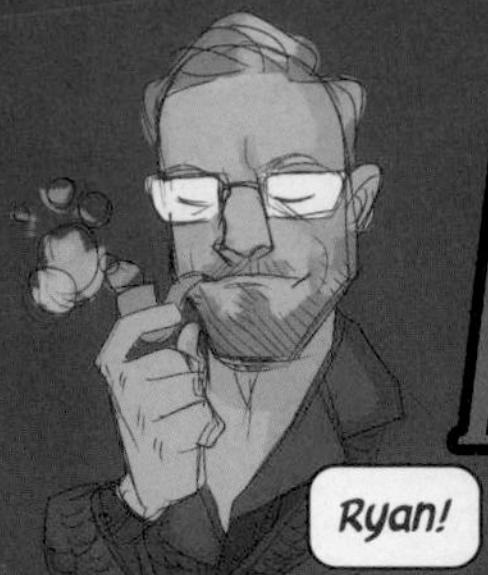
Ryan!

Letters From Nuts

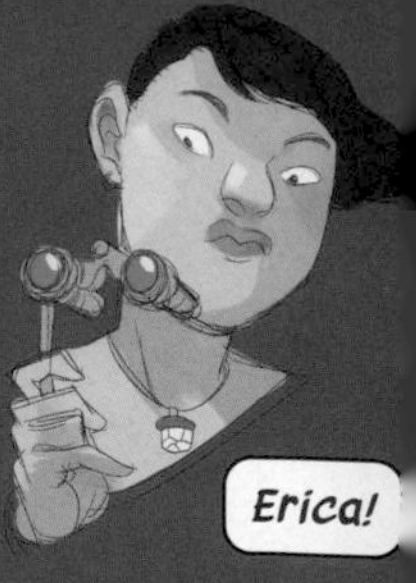
Erica!

Send letters to mheroes@marvel.com or 135 W 50th St, 7th Floor, New York, NY 10020 (Please mark "OKAY TO PRINT

Hey everybody! How'd you like the first part of our crossover with HOWARD THE DUCK? Special thanks to the HOWARD creative team -- Chip Zdarsky & Joe Quinones -- for helping us with this issue. Join us as we go help them tell the second half of this story next month in HOWARD THE DUCK #6! But hey, first let's get to your letters!

Dear Squirrel Girl,

We like you. You're funny! We read your comic every month. Daddy puts the next comic on the calendar so we can count until the day. We have read every single one of your books and comic books. We share them with our friends! We share them with Eva and Bella (our cousins), and now they read them, too! We share them with Tyler, too. He's our Sunday School teacher. He borrows them every Sunday morning, and gives them back in a week. He thinks you are funny, too.

We just read Issue 5, and it was cool. And funny. Our favorite part was when all you girls vexed Doctor Doom. It was just like when your squirrel friends did last time!

We love dressing up! For Halloween we were YOU and COMMANDER KEEN! And we went to Kapow and met Captain America and Luigi, and Tippy-Toe beat up the Red Skull! This happened for real. We have pictures.

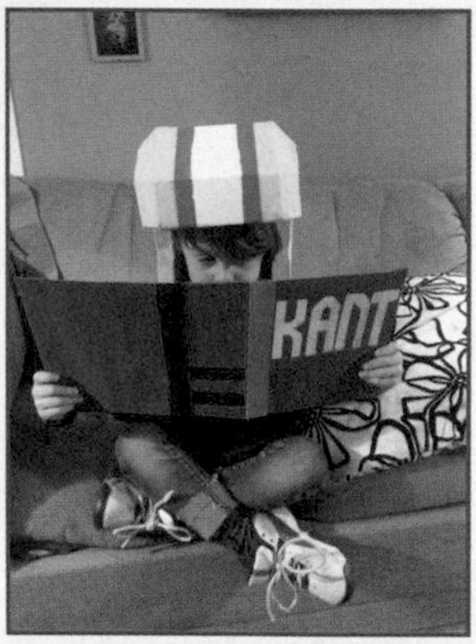
KANT

I (Elijah) like to read SQUIRREL GIRL when I pretend to read Kant.

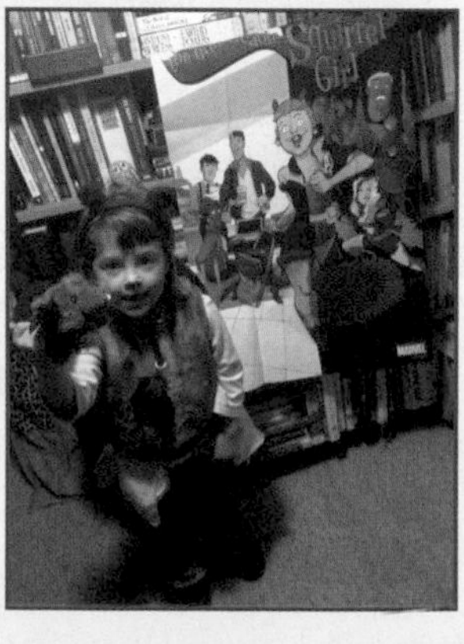

Wally at Kapow says I (Grace) am the biggest Squirrel Girl fan in town, so he gave me the poster to keep!

Love from,
The Unbeatable Twins, Elijah and Grace
(we are five-and-a-half)

RYAN: Aw, that's super great! ESPECIALLY the Commander Keen costume, because I am a Keen fan from way back. Did you know that if you let Keen sit around in Pyramid of the Moons in Keen 4, he'll eventually moon the camera? I played this game LITERALLY 20 YEARS AGO and I still remember that fact.

Anyway, in non-mooning news, I loved your costumes, and the fact that you like our comics AND share them with your friends! This is super great and I bet your friends think you're the coolest for doing that. If I had a friend that loaned me comics, I would be all "Thanks, friend! You ARE the coolest!" and my friend would be all "Yes, obviously I am the coolest friend, due to all these comics I am sharing" and they would be telling the TRUTH.

ERICA: I would also like a moment to geek out over Commander Keen. Do you guys even have a computer that can run those games? Were they re-released? Oh my god, somebody please tell me. I ALSO PLAYED THIS GAME 20 YEARS AGO AND THINK ABOUT IT ALL THE TIME.

You guys got the Squirrel Girl poster!!! That's exciting because I haven't seen that many around. This seems like a fun house to be in. I'm pretty jealous.

Consistently the best book on the racks, I absolutely love what Ryan and Erica are doing with Squirrel Girl. Issue 4 had three brilliant ideas of how to use a time machine to defeat Dr Doom, the third being best of all, and a gorgeous nod to Secret Squirrel with Doreen's sleuthing disguise ensemble. Hey, given that this story was set in the 60s, maybe the creators of Secret Squirrel actually got their idea from seeing Doreen's outfit, which makes for crazy bootstrapping paradox.

We also got an excellent fight with Dr Doom, where in keeping with the book's philosophy that talking with the antagonist can produce better results than fists and power beams, there's a conversation that sparkles with ideas and humour. I mean, when was the last time anyone saw Maslow's Hierarchy in a superhero fight? Plus we learned what Dr Doom thinks of Galactus, and of course Doom's ego is such that he even looks down on Galactus.

It is so refreshing and inspiring to pick up a comic book that uses the medium to the fullest (what other medium could pull off the 'can you spot Doom grinding a rail' gag, or the footnotes?) and also just delights and revels in the idea of having superpowers and the joy that they can bring.

It might have been easy to conceive of a comic book that was an antidote to all the grim, dark, angsty stuff around but to pull off a series that does that whilst showing true love and respect to the tradition of comics and real fondness for the characters is a different matter entirely.

It is a true joy to pick up this comic, thanks for sharing it with us.

Andrew Pack,
Brighton, England

R: Thanks, Andrew! I think it helps th everyone involved in the book really loves comi as a medium, so we're here to have the mo fun we can have. Comics is a terrific way to t stories! Prose is fine I GUESS if there's no artis around, but we all know the REAL medium write like Chaucer and Shakespeare wished they cou have worked in, if only they could've drawn bette

E: This has been way more fun to work on th I ever thought it would be. I think I've mention this before, but nobody on the team really kne one another (Wil and I had exchanged three six emails, Rico and I had said a few words each other), but I think it all really clicked. We a wanted the same things and have a similar sen of humor. It's been a great ride.

"Steve Rogers called me 'Son.'" That line had m literally rolling on the floor laughing! I can't tell y what a delight the Squirrel Girl book is. Like a lot long-time readers, I like a lot of fun in my comic so I really appreciate what you do. Oh, and I tota caught the "Secret Squirrel" nod in #4. What a gre and appropriate easter egg! I love the art, Erica, ar Ryan, keep making me laugh!

Thank
Brian Langlo

R: I didn't mention it in the answer to the la letter because I thought I could get away with but the jig is up! The Secret Squirrel referenc was ALL ERICA. I just wrote her in a trenchco and fedora, and Erica was like "Ryan, this ca be done better." The best part was, there real WERE hats sold like that in the time period. remember Erica found photo reference. Mode fashion really needs to up its game! I want glasses hat, STAT.

E: I honestly don't even remember how I foun sunglasses hats. I really don't. I purposely looke up when Secret Squirrel debuted because I mig not have done the outfit if it weren't from the '60 Then I looked up '60s versions of the things h wore. #obsessive

Okay, Marvel people, I know this is a lor shot, but hear me out: We need to bring Netflix Unbreakable Kimmy Schmidt into the Marv universe, and Squirrel Girl can make it happen.

Picture this: Kimmy shows up for her first da of class at Empire State University (Normal Clas for People with Normal Lives 101, natch), only find herself seated next to Doreen Green. The hit it off immediately as the two most upbeat ar enthusiastic accumulations of organic matter in th history of the universe. Kimmy can immediately ta to Tippy-Toe. She takes on the super hero monik of Camel Damsel and joins Squirrel Girl in her que to rid New York City of jerks who suck.

And the theme song...

Un-BEATable!
She's a squirrel, DANGIT.
It's a MIRACLE!

haos in the streets. Productivity plummets all-time lows as frenzied excitement for this ssover obliterates work attendance and throws e stock market into an irreparable downward piral. Civilization as we know it ceases to exist. On econd thought, this might not be a great idea. Sorry brought it up.

Zack Miller
Brooklyn, NY

R: Just on the off chance that multinational orporation Marvel/Disney is waiting for MY ermission to make this happen, this is me saying: nake this happen! Marvel, get Netflix on the hone! I don't know if they have phones, actually! Marvel, send Netflix a DM on Twitter!!

ley Ryan, Erica and the rest of the team!

I want to start off by saying how much I'm njoying USG -- I've been a fan of Doreen for over 20 years and it's easily my favorite comic so far this entury! My girlfriend Jo and I eagerly await each new issue every month.

Like you guys, I'm dismayed at the lack of nerchandise featuring Squirrel Girl, so I decided o take matters into my own hands... I made a custom SG Marvel Legends action figure, complete with custom packaging! She's super-posable, has a real (fake) fur tail (that's also super-posable) and ncludes 7 of her squirrels, including Tippy-Toe!

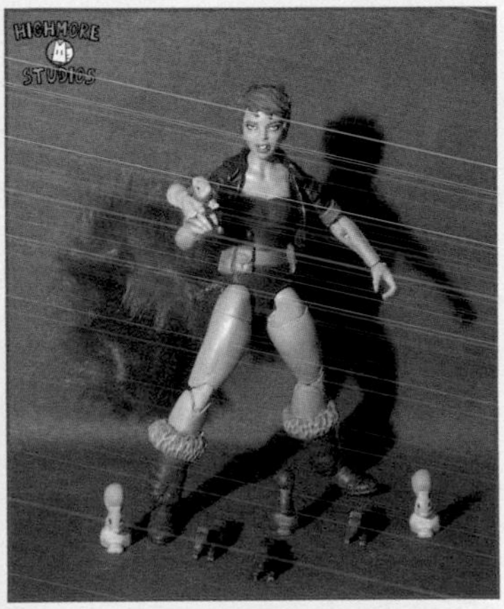
HIGHMORE
STUDIOS

Keep up the squirrelly good work!
Matt Beahan

R: Matt, I LOVE YOUR ACTION FIGURE. It's so great! We did that action figure variant cover for #3 and my first words to our editor were "YES HELLO CAN THIS BE A REAL THING PLEASE THANKS IN ADVANCE." It's my understanding that action figures take much longer to produce than talking squirrel comic books, though, so I don't think we're gonna see much OFFICIAL merchandise for a while – but I hold out hope for a figure someday that even approaches how cool this is!!

E: OH MY GOD. I LOVE IT. Did you make the Tippy? Did you get it from another set? I love it so much.

Dear Team Squirrel Girl,

Hi, I'm Tabby, and I truly love The Unbeatable Squirrel Girl! I've been collecting pieces for a costume to wear to a comic convention, so I could meet Rico Renzi, and show it off to him. Unfortunately I got real sick, and had to go to the hospital for a while. I ended up with a feeding tube, but I wasn't going to let that stop me from going to the convention and meeting Rico. The convention was the day after I got home from the hospital, but I let my mother know I would go nuts if she didn't take me.

With my sidekick Tippy-Toe (really my sister Abigail), I made it to the convention and met Rico. He was awesome, and super friendly and signed posters for the both of us. I've included a picture. I'm still fighting to get better, but we are unbeatable just like Squirrel Girl!

Love Tabby!

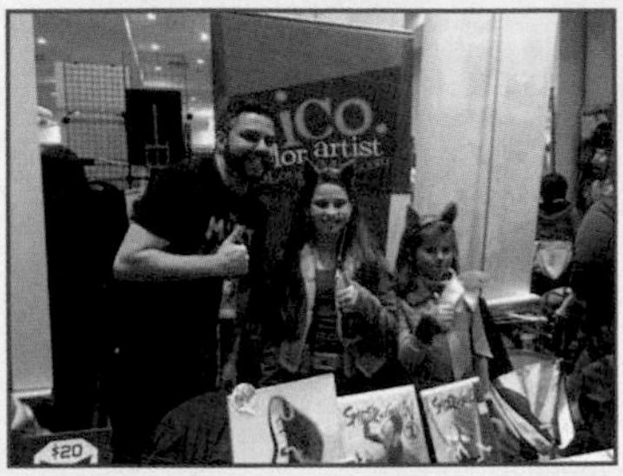

R: Aw, Tabby are you the best? IT SEEMS LIKELY. Rico told us about this and he was super excited that you made it out! Both your and Abigail's costumes are terrific, and I'm really glad you were well enough for a day at the comics show, and I hope you feel better soon! I was on a feeding tube once and it was not as fun as it sounded (free food through a tube? SIGN ME UP). I know that you are as unbeatable as your costume is awesome, which is to say: extremely.

E: Agh. You're tougher than I am. The worst I've had is an appendectomy, so they let me eat after a day or two. I'm glad you could make it out after you put all that work in! Great costume!

I have been loving the adventures of Doreen, from vol. 1 and now vol. 2. I particularly enjoy the Computer Science references, and how Doreen and her friends are so excited about their academic studies. Warms this old professor's heart.

But it's a reference in issue 4 that only an "old" professor would get that motivates my letter. When Doreen needs to sneak up and secretly spy on Castle Doom in Central Park, she is dressed as... Secret Squirrel! I LOVED that show when it first aired in 1965 (did I mention the 'old' part?). Now want guest appearances from Morocco Mole, or at least Scott Lang dressed as Atom Ant.

If Doreen or Nancy need any help with their other science courses (hey - you don't just take classes in your major while at college), they should feel free to drop me a line.

I don't have any photos of me dressed like Squirrel Girl, but I do have a drawing (by Gene Ha!) of me as Ryan from the letter column graphic.

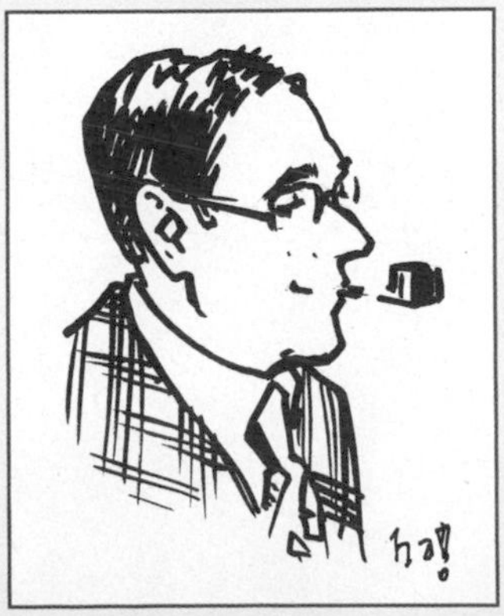

Off to eat nuts.

Your Friendly Neighborhood Physics Professor,
Jim Kakalios
Taylor Distinguished Professor
School of Physics and Astronomy
The University of Minnesota
Minneapolis, MN 55455

R: Jim, it is amazing to hear from you, because I HAVE READ YOUR BOOK. It's called The Physics of Superheroes and I think of it every time Doreen leaps over NYC and lands like it isn't even a thing. As you can tell, I studied it extremely carefully.

And I love that you have a drawing (by Gene Ha!) of you as ME from our letters page! That is amazing and I would've never expected to live in a world where this is the case. I'm super stoked you like our comics!

E: Morocco Moleman? Huckleberry Havok? Ah, too bad we don't have the rights to those guys.

Next:

You gotta read HOWARD THE DUCK #6, on sale next month, for the rest of this story!

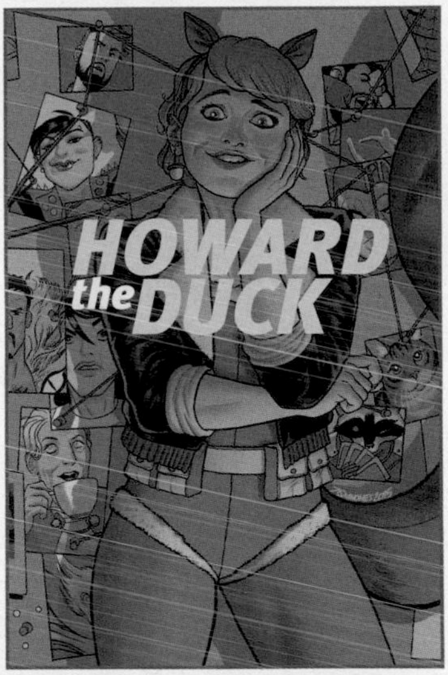
HOWARD
the DUCK

And then after that come back here for an insanely awesome new story where YOU call the shots!

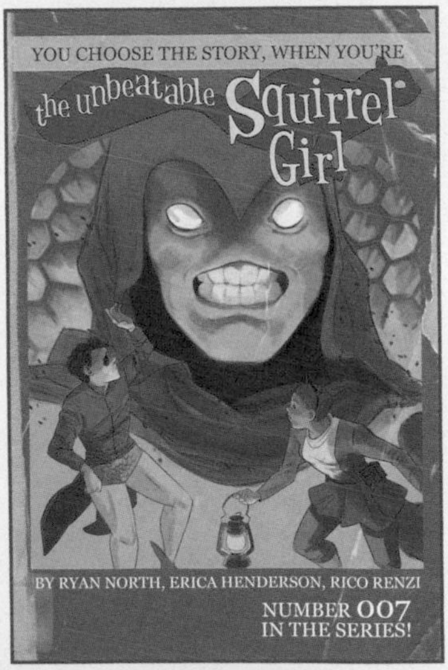
YOU CHOOSE THE STORY, WHEN YOU'RE
the unbeatable Squirrel Girl
BY RYAN NORTH, ERICA HENDERSON, RICO RENZI
NUMBER 007
IN THE SERIES!

Attention, Squirrel Scouts! Make sure to check out our production blog, **unbeatablesquirrelgirl.tumblr.com**, where we post behind-the-scenes stuff on how the book gets made, along with all sorts of cool things *you* make: fanart, cosplay, whatever!

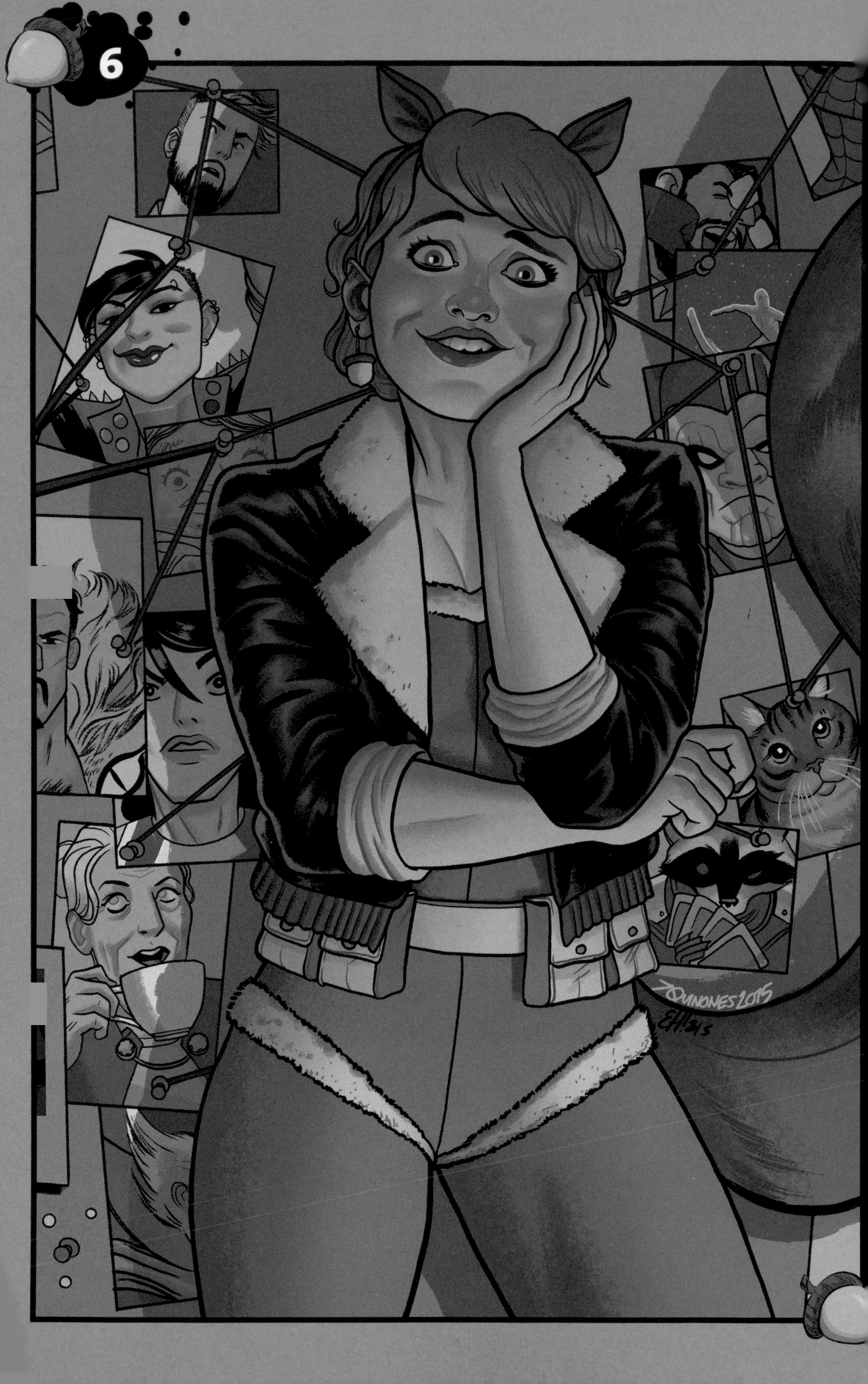

HOWARD the DUCK

HEY, HOPEFULLY THIS ISN'T NEWS TO YOU, BUT THIS ISSUE RIGHT HERE IS PART TWO OF A TWO-PART STORY THAT BEGAN IN **THE UNBEATABLE SQUIRREL GIRL #6!** HOWARD DOES A PRETTY GOOD JOB ON THE NEXT PAGE OF SUMMARIZING WHAT HAPPENED IN THAT ISSUE, BUT STILL, **U.S.G.** IS REALLY GOOD, YOU SHOULD TRACK THAT ISSUE DOWN. (AND YES YOU **CAN** TRUST THIS TOTALLY UNBIASED RECAPPER!)

ANYWAY, HERE'S SOME ADDITIONAL HOWARD-CENTRIC CONTEXT FOR THIS ISSUE, OKAY?

EVER SINCE THE START OF THIS NEW VOLUME, HOWARD'S HAD WHAT APPEARS TO BE A CYBORG CAT FOR A PET. WHAT IS **UP** WITH THAT CAT? FIND OUT IN THIS VERY ISSUE, WHICH TAKES PLACE BETWEEN THIS VOLUME AND THE LAST ONE. (I KNOW, I KNOW-- COMICS!)

HUH. GUESS THERE WASN'T A WHOLE LOTTA CONTEXT TO SHARE ACTUALLY. YOU'RE FREE TO GO!

CHIP ZDARSKY with RYAN NORTH
WRITERS
JOE QUINONES
PENCILER
JOE RIVERA, MARC DEERING, JOE QUINONES
INKERS
JOE QUINONES & JORDAN GIBSON
COLORISTS
TRAVIS LANHAM
LETTERER & PRODUCTION
CHARLES BEACHAM
ASSISTANT EDITOR
WIL MOSS
EDITOR
TOM BREVOORT
EXECUTIVE EDITOR
CHIP ZDARSKY
RECAP PAGE ARTIST

HOWARD THE DUCK CREATED BY **STEVE GERBER & VAL MAYERIK**

JOE QUINONES with ERICA HENDERSON
COVER ARTISTS
JOE QUINONES & PAOLO RIVERA; TRADD MOORE & MATTHEW WILSON
VARIANT COVER ARTISTS
AXEL ALONSO EDITOR IN CHIEF **JOE QUESADA** CHIEF CREATIVE OFFICER
DAN BUCKLEY PUBLISHER **ALAN FINE** EXECUTIVE PRODUCER

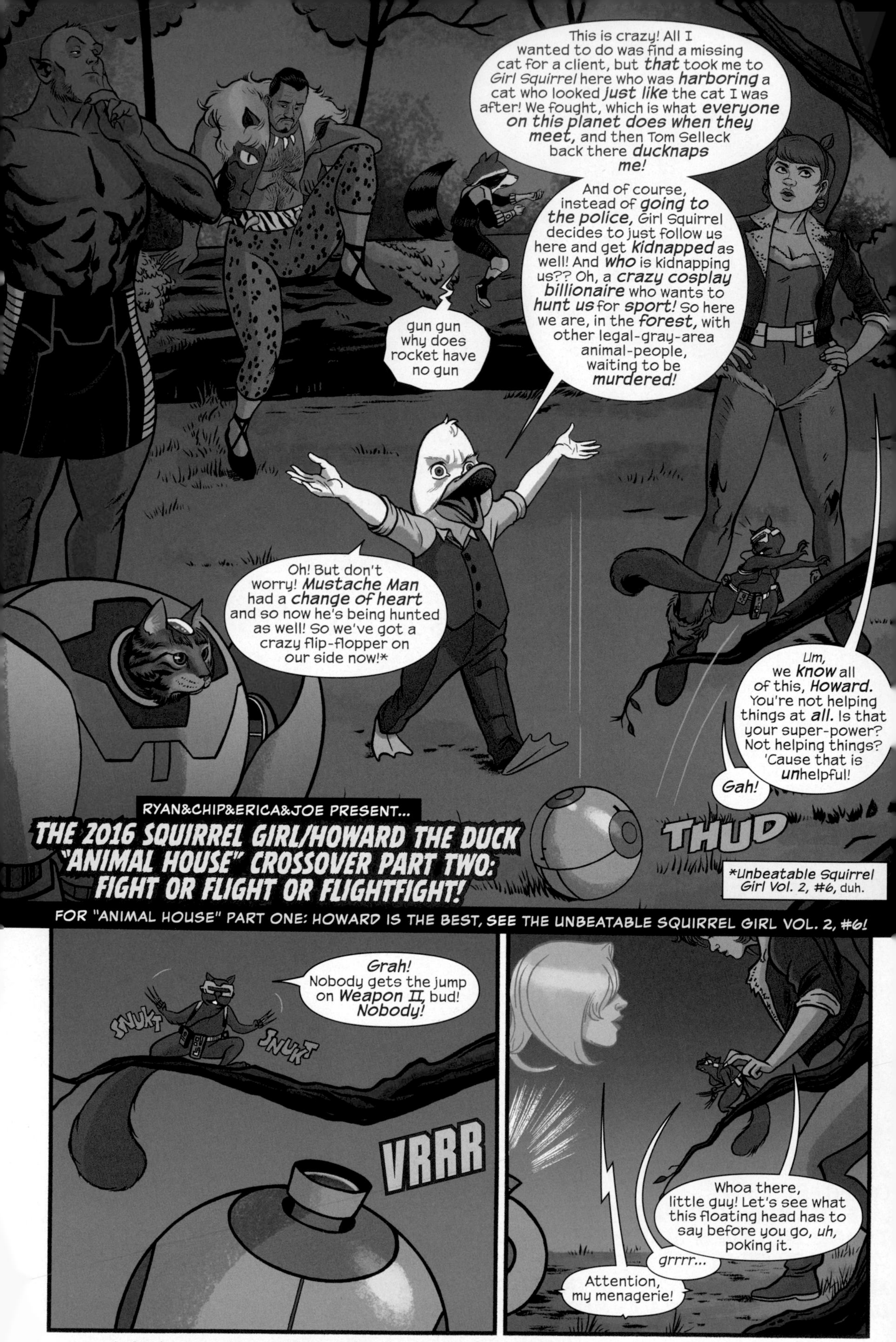
This is crazy! All I wanted to do was find a missing cat for a client, but *that* took me to *Girl Squirrel* here who was *harboring* a cat who looked *just like* the cat I was after! We fought, which is what *everyone on this planet does when they meet,* and then Tom Selleck back there *ducknaps me!*
gun gun why does rocket have no gun
And of course, instead of *going to the police,* Girl Squirrel decides to just follow us here and get *kidnapped* as well! And *who* is kidnapping us?? Oh, a *crazy cosplay billionaire* who wants to *hunt us* for *sport!* So here we are, in the *forest,* with other legal-gray-area animal-people, waiting to be *murdered!*
Oh! But don't worry! *Mustache Man* had a *change of heart* and so now he's being hunted as well! So we've got a crazy flip-flopper on our side now!*
Um, we *know* all of this, *Howard.* You're not helping things at *all.* Is that your super-power? Not helping things? 'Cause that is *un*helpful!
Gah!
THUD
RYAN&CHIP&ERICA&JOE PRESENT...
THE 2016 SQUIRREL GIRL/HOWARD THE DUCK "ANIMAL HOUSE" CROSSOVER PART TWO: FIGHT OR FLIGHT OR FLIGHTFIGHT!
Unbeatable Squirrel Girl Vol. 2, #6, duh.
FOR "ANIMAL HOUSE" PART ONE: HOWARD IS THE BEST, SEE THE UNBEATABLE SQUIRREL GIRL VOL. 2, #6!
Grah! Nobody gets the jump on *Weapon II,* bud! *Nobody!*
SNUKT
SNUKT
VRRR
Whoa there, little guy! Let's see what this floating head has to say before you go, *uh,* poking it.
grrrr...
Attention, my menagerie!

So, Ryan does these weird "alt text" things in *Squirrel Girl* to prove that they're not just about "mainstream text," I guess. Cool stuff, guys! And if you're here from *Squirrel Girl,* you should know normally Chip *doesn't* do this text at the bottom, so if you look at the other issues, you'll just be disappointed!! Okay bye

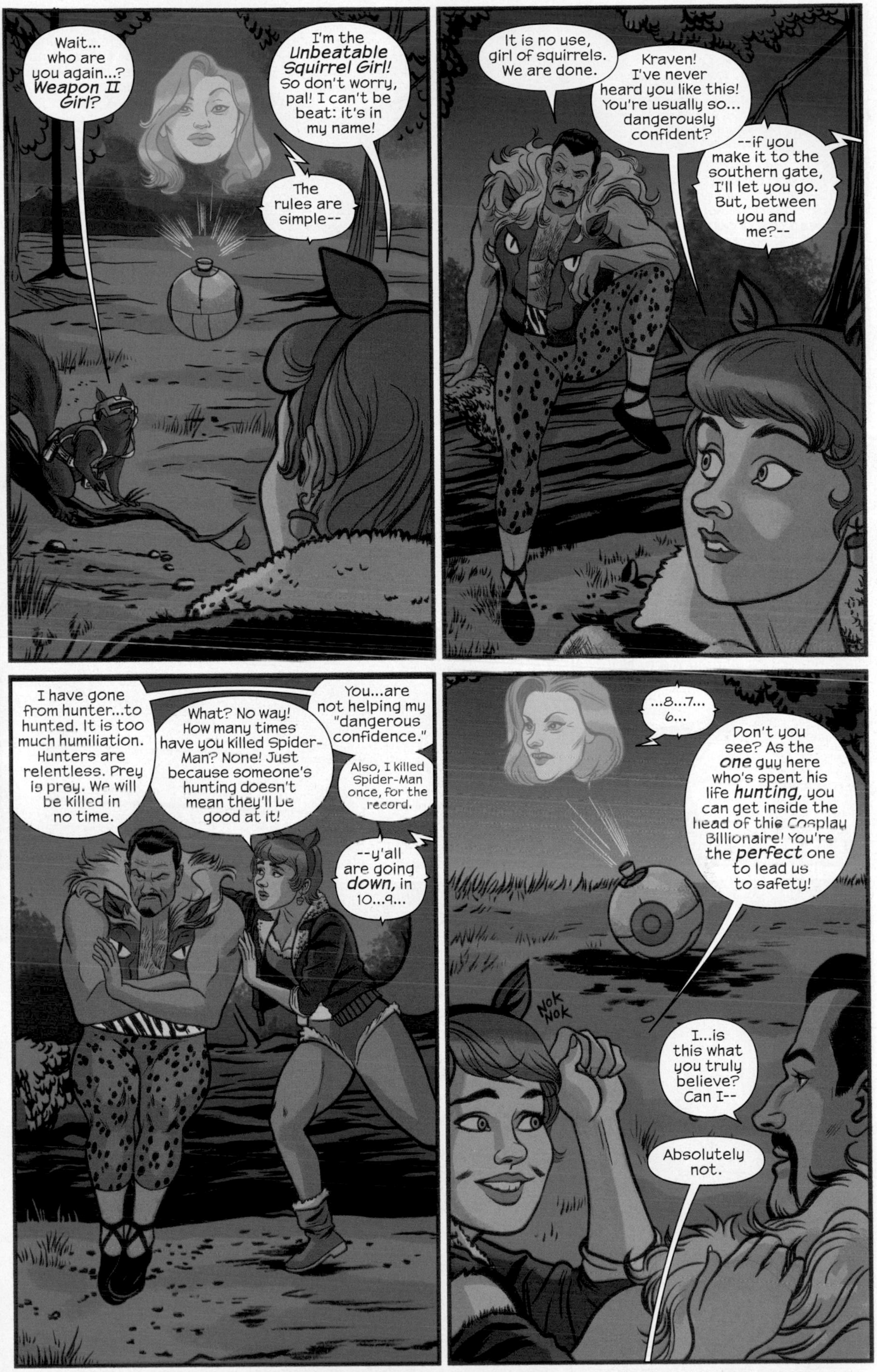

Wait... who are you again...? *Weapon II Girl*?
I'm the *Unbeatable Squirrel Girl!* So don't worry, pal! I can't be beat: it's in my name!
The rules are simple--
It is no use, girl of squirrels. We are done.
Kraven! I've never heard you like this! You're usually so... dangerously confident?
--if you make it to the southern gate, I'll let you go. But, between you and me?--
I have gone from hunter...to hunted. It is too much humiliation. Hunters are relentless. Prey is prey. We will be killed in no time.
What? No way! How many times have you killed Spider-Man? None! Just because someone's hunting doesn't mean they'll be good at it!
You...are not helping my "dangerous confidence."
Also, I killed Spider-Man once, for the record.
--y'all are going *down,* in 10...9...
...8...7... 6...
Don't you see? As the *one* guy here who's spent his life *hunting,* you can get inside the head of this Cosplay Billionaire! You're the *perfect* one to lead us to safety!
NOK NOK
I...is this what you truly believe? Can I--
Absolutely not.

Weapon II was in the same program as the old ***Wolverine,*** who was ***Weapon X!*** You probably thought that was just an "X" and not a "10"! Funny story: Professor Xavier actually named the X-Men ***"Ten-Men,"*** because he wanted ten guys on the team, but nobody got it so he just let people believe it was X-Men.

Now ***that's*** a tenhilarating addition to Marvel canon!

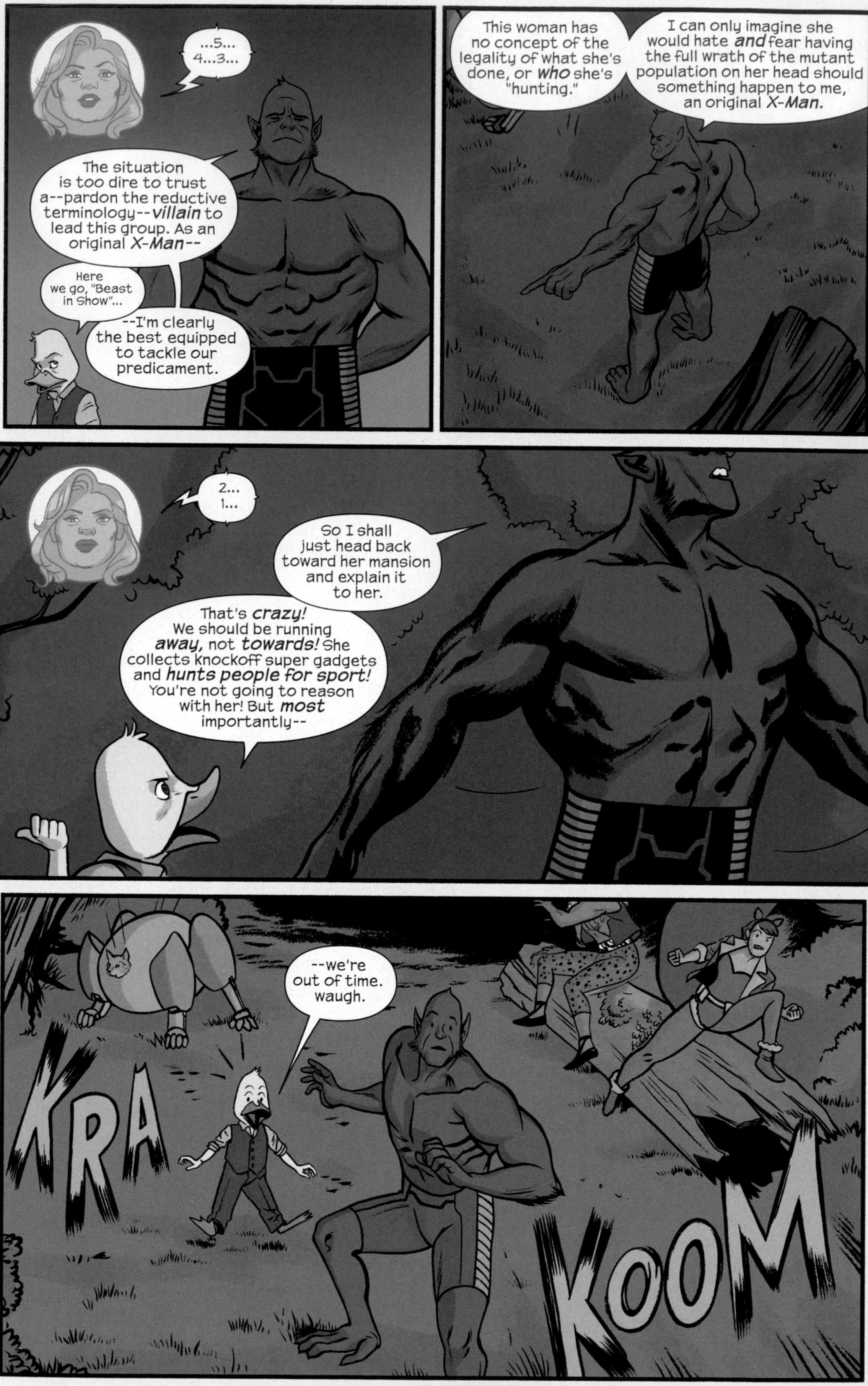
...5... 4...3...
The situation is too dire to trust a--pardon the reductive terminology--*villain* to lead this group. As an original *X-Man*--
Here we go, "Beast in Show"...
--I'm clearly the best equipped to tackle our predicament.
This woman has no concept of the legality of what she's done, or *who* she's "hunting."
I can only imagine she would hate *and* fear having the full wrath of the mutant population on her head should something happen to me, an original *X-Man.*
2... 1...
So I shall just head back toward her mansion and explain it to her.
That's *crazy!* We should be running *away,* not *towards!* She collects knockoff super gadgets and *hunts people for sport!* You're not going to reason with her! But *most* importantly--
--we're out of time. waugh.
KRA
KOOM

Don't call yourself ***Beast*** if you're super smart and want people to listen to you! Take a page from ***Mr. Fantastic.*** Who wouldn't listen to a ***Mr. Fantastic?*** Even ***Dr. Doom*** knew he should let people know he's a ***doctor*** in his name.

Thought you could ever only have a character say "...we're out of time" in a time travel story? ***Think again.***

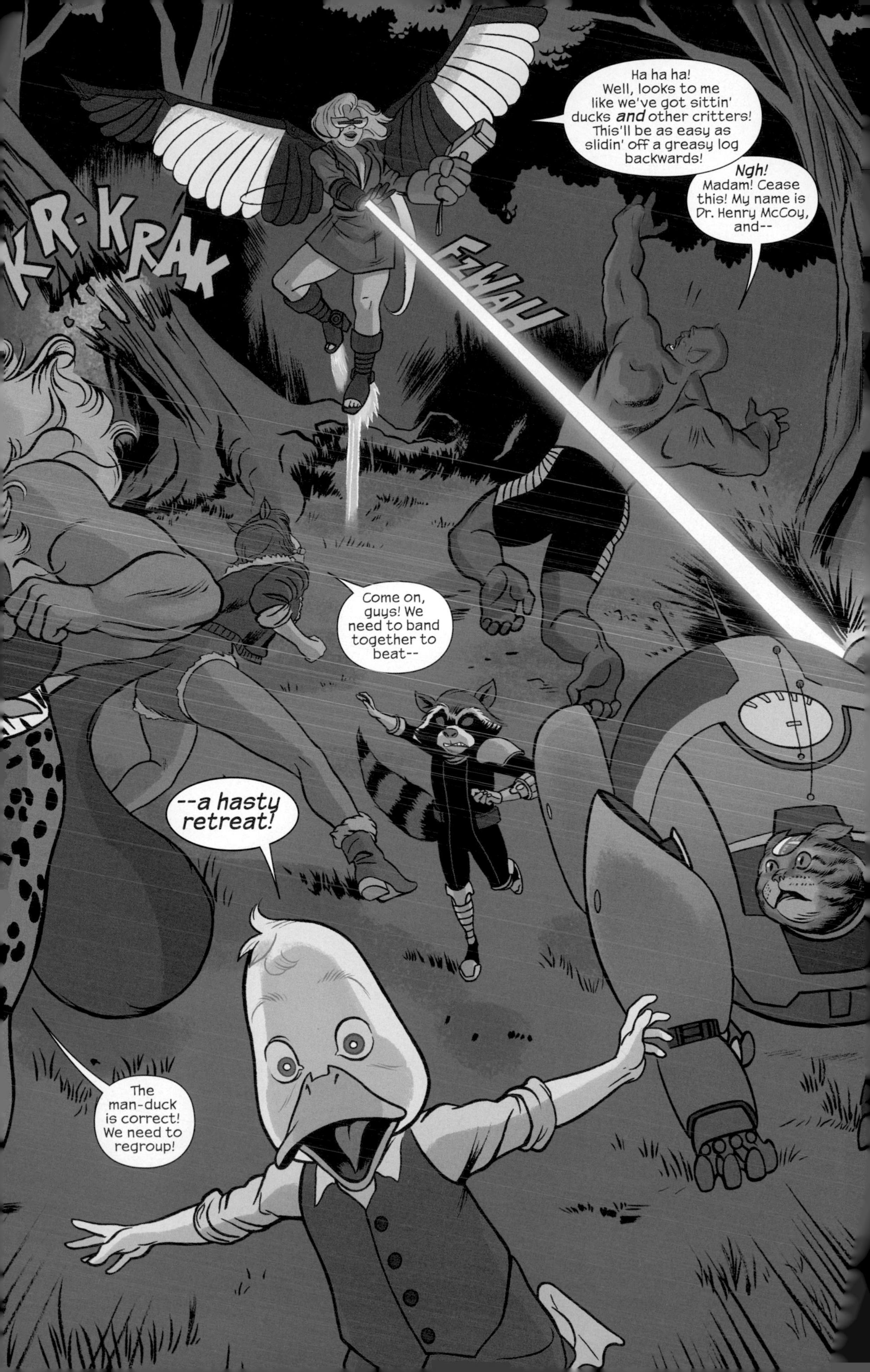

Ha ha ha! Well, looks to me like we've got sittin' ducks *and* other critters! This'll be as easy as slidin' off a greasy log backwards!
KR-KRAK
FZWAH
Ngh! Madam! Cease this! My name is Dr. Henry McCoy, and--
Come on, guys! We need to band together to beat--
--a hasty retreat!
The man-duck is correct! We need to regroup!

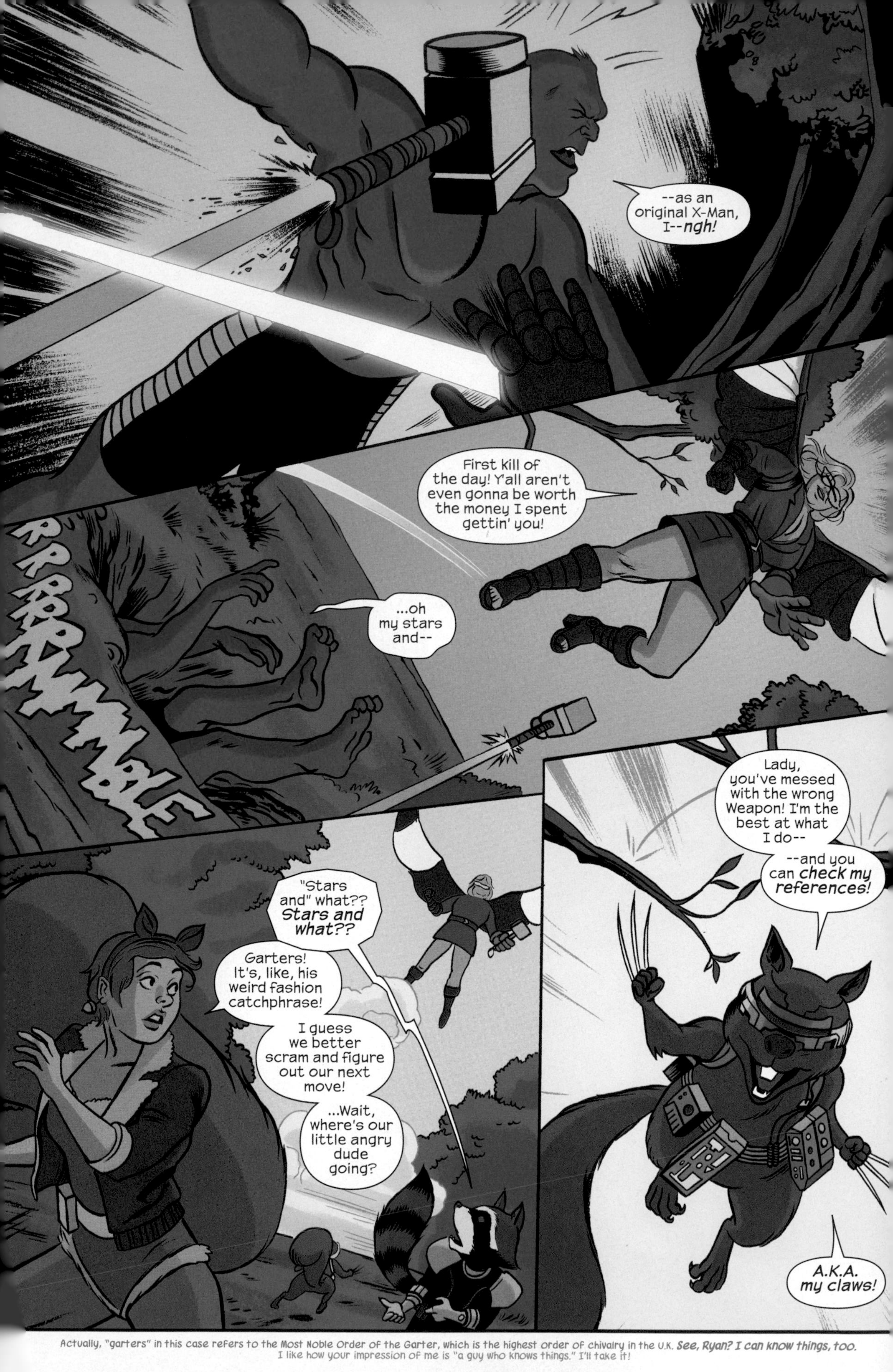
--as an original X-Man, I--ngh!
First kill of the day! Y'all aren't even gonna be worth the money I spent gettin' you!
...oh my stars and--
"Stars and" what?? Stars and what??
Garters! It's, like, his weird fashion catchphrase!
I guess we better scram and figure out our next move!
...Wait, where's our little angry dude going?
Lady, you've messed with the wrong Weapon! I'm the best at what I do--
--and you can check my references!
A.K.A. my claws!

Actually, "garters" in this case refers to the Most Noble Order of the Garter, which is the highest order of chivalry in the U.K. *See, Ryan? I can know things, too.*
I like how your impression of me is "a guy who knows things." I'll take it!

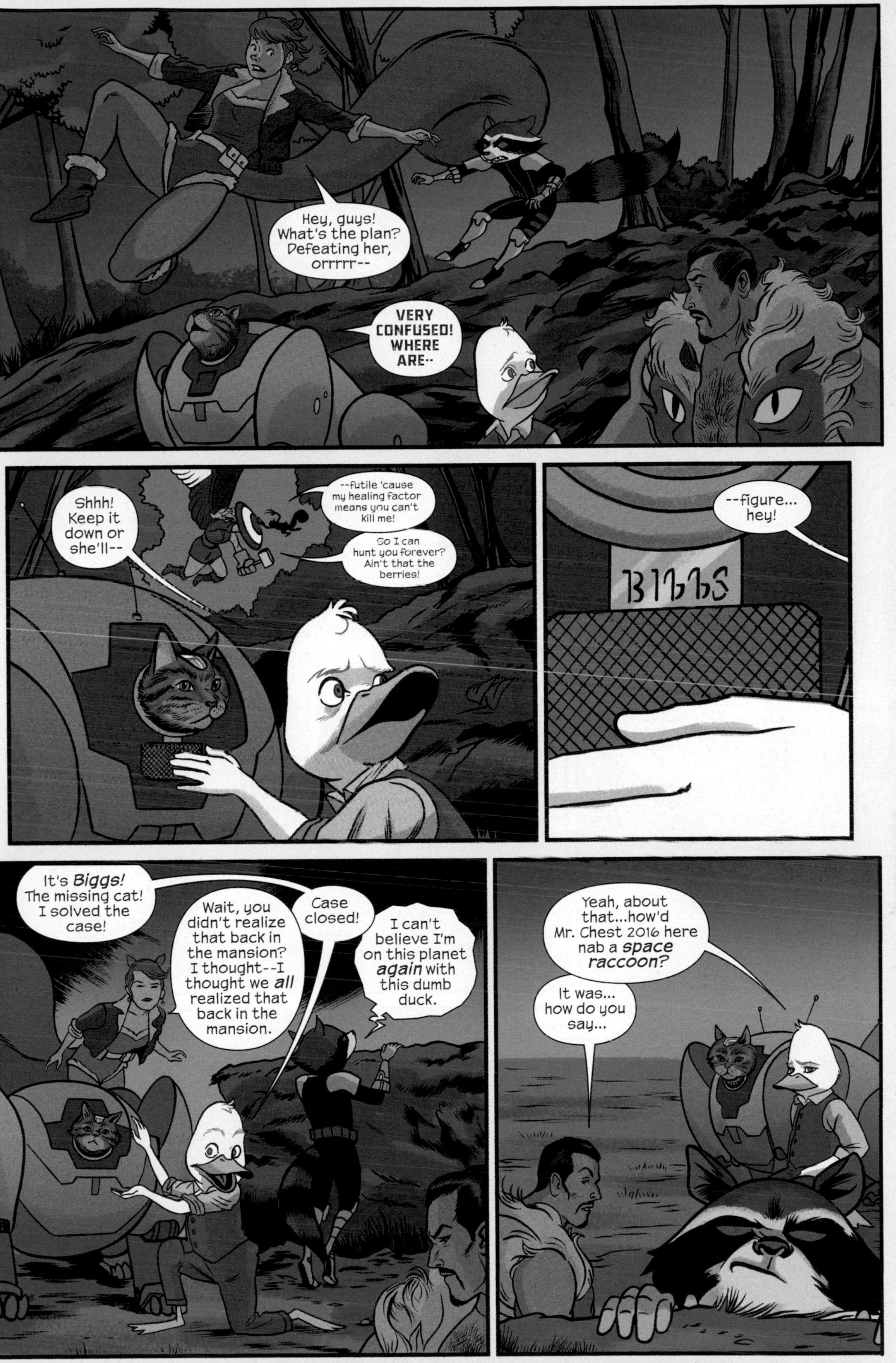
Hey, guys! What's the plan? Defeating her, orrrrr--
VERY CONFUSED! WHERE ARE--
Shhh! Keep it down or she'll--
--futile 'cause my healing factor means you can't kill me!
So I can hunt you forever? Ain't that the berries!
--figure... hey!
It's *Biggs!* The missing cat! I solved the case!
Case closed!
Wait, you didn't realize that back in the mansion? I thought--I thought we *all* realized that back in the mansion.
I can't believe I'm on this planet *again* with this dumb duck.
Yeah, about that...how'd Mr. Chest 2016 here nab a *space raccoon?*
It was... how do you say...

Ducks actually have excellent vision and can see two, three times farther than humans! But sometimes you can't see the forest for the trees, and Howard is all about complaining about the trees.

As a guy who knows things, I agree.

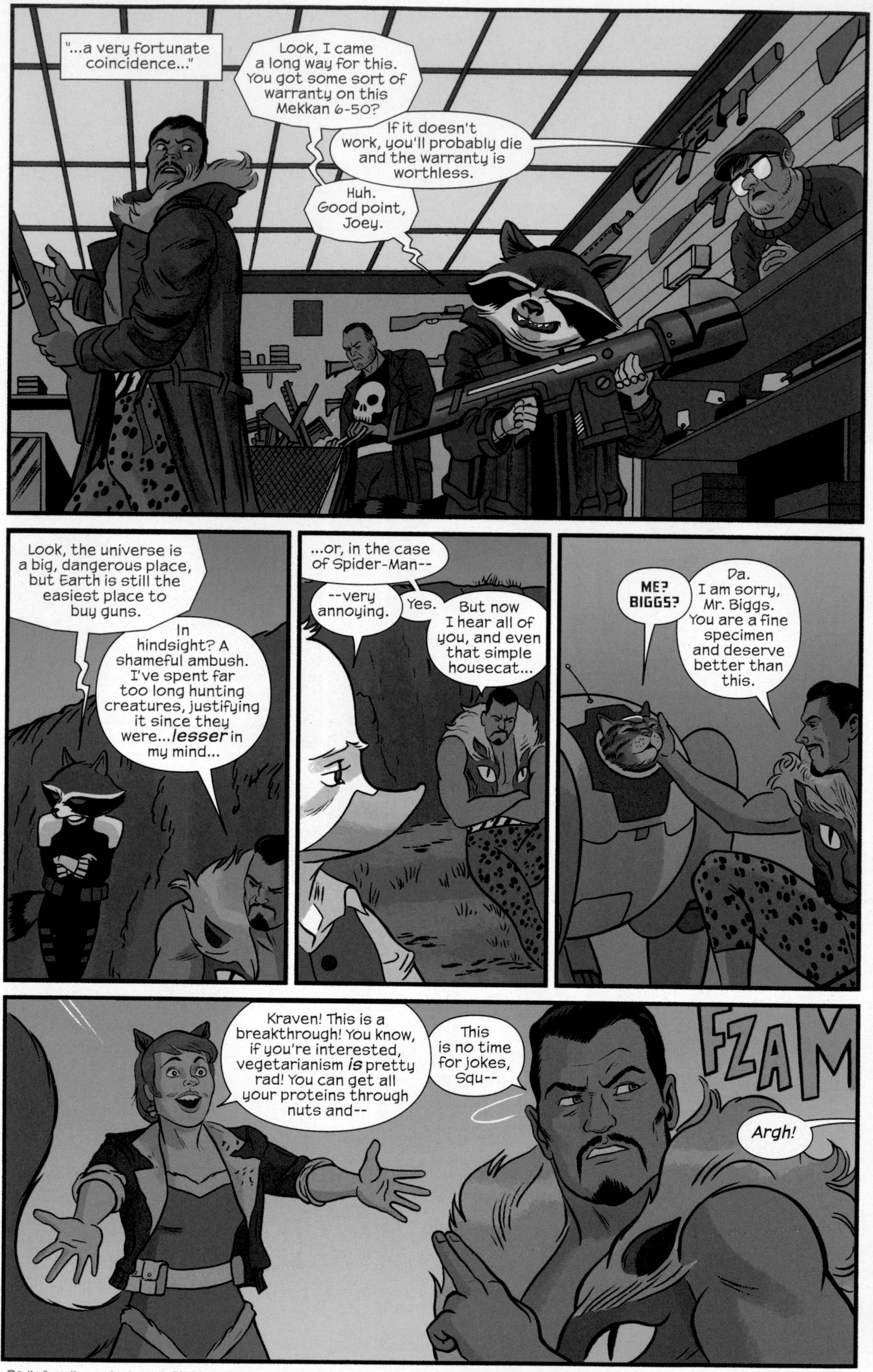
"...a very fortunate coincidence..."
Look, I came a long way for this. You got some sort of warranty on this Mekkan 6-50?
If it doesn't work, you'll probably die and the warranty is worthless.
Huh. Good point, Joey.
Look, the universe is a big, dangerous place, but Earth is still the easiest place to buy guns.
In hindsight? A shameful ambush. I've spent far too long hunting creatures, justifying it since they were...*lesser* in my mind...
...or, in the case of Spider-Man--
--very annoying.
Yes.
But now I hear all of you, and even that simple housecat...
ME? BIGGS?
Da. I am sorry, Mr. Biggs. You are a fine specimen and deserve better than this.
Kraven! This is a breakthrough! You know, if you're interested, vegetarianism *is* pretty rad! You can get all your proteins through nuts and--
This is no time for jokes, Squ--
FZAM
Argh!

Da. My favorite comics trope is ESL characters only saying the simplest words in their native language, like Gambit saying *"Oui"* or *"chere,"* almost as if those are the only foreign words the writer knows? Oh well! *Sayonara!*

Mine's when their speech is only partially translated for dramatic effect. It really gives *un petit quelque chose* to the *mise-en-scène.*

...ngh... my healing factor'll...do its job...like a little...body hospital... and then...

UGH STOP TALKING ABOUT YOUR HEALING FACTOR NOBODY CARES

This ain't over, bud... *urk!*

BRMMMMMMBILLE

Hooookay, so Wolverteeny is down. What now?

Even if we made it to the finish line, there's **no way** she'd just let us go! We'd be back with Avengers and Fantastic Fours and maybe even cops in no time!

Hmm, then our only options are to ambush her here in the woods or head to the mansion. We can then... ugh...call for help...or find something we can use against her.

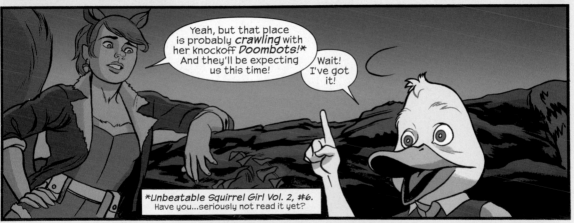

Yeah, but that place is probably *crawling* with her knockoff *Doombots!* * And they'll be expecting us this time!

Wait! I've got it!

*Unbeatable Squirrel Girl Vol. 2, #6. Have you...seriously not read it yet?

And who calls their abilities a "Factor"? That's like me saying my "writing Factor" will finish this script in no time, or Ryan saying "My tall Factor will help me get that can on the top shelf." It's weird, man.
Chip, look, do you want the can or not?

Biggs! Dig a hole!

OKAY.

Uh, Howard? Cats only dig holes when they, uh...you-know-what, and I ***don't*** *want to see this cat's you-know-what...*

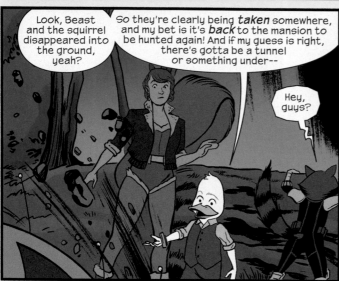

Look, Beast and the squirrel disappeared into the ground, yeah?

So they're clearly being *taken* somewhere, and my bet is it's *back* to the mansion to be hunted again! And if my guess is right, there's gotta be a tunnel or something under--

Hey, guys?

If you have a plan, better get to it pronto, 'cause she's headed our way!

♪ Come out, come out, wherever you are... ♪

Raccoon. Let us hold this glorious hunter off and buy our comrades time to infiltrate! Here--I have used my hunting factor to craft these!

Uhhh... thanks?

Whoa. Really? That's pretty cool, guys! Okay, well-- we'll save everyone, don't worry!

Hey! Lady! Why don't you try picking on someone your own size!

THE HUNTED IS NOW ONCE AGAIN THE HUNTER!! HA HA!!

*Poop. That's what cats do. They poop. ~Chipipedia!
Uh, I'm gonna call "chiptation needed" on that one.*

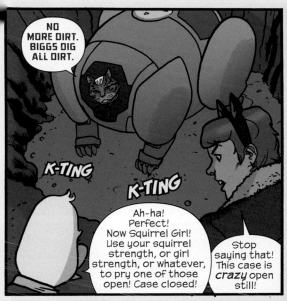

NO MORE DIRT. BIGGS DIG ALL DIRT.
K-TING
K-TING
Ah-ha! Perfect! Now Squirrel Girl! Use your squirrel strength, or girl strength, or whatever, to pry one of those open! Case closed!
Stop saying that! This case is *crazy* open still!
Hnnnh!
Perfect!
Sorry, Biggs. You're too big for the hole! Can you try to hold off the mean lady while we save the day?
OKAY DELICIOUS BIRD.
POP
All right! *Now* where do we go?
Uh, I was kind of hoping there'd be a map down here, like in a parking garage or something.
A little help?
I don't think there's a map, dude. And I'm prettttty sure this place isn't covered by Starksearch Street View.
Hey, you never know unless you try!
Oh.
My.
Gosh! Cosplay lady took our weapons, missed your *phone,* and you had it on you this whole *time?* And you didn't think to *call* someone for *help??*
I didn't *think* of it! The same way *you* didn't think to call the cops before *you* were captured *too!*
I'll contact Spider-Man now, *okay?* I text him, you know! *All the time!*
Hmm. No signal.
Of *course* not! We're undergr--
CHK-WHRRR

Always use Safesearch with Starksearch. Just trust me.
Spider-Man set up an autoreply to send "lol no way!!" to every text Howard sends, and he hasn't noticed yet. It's been months.

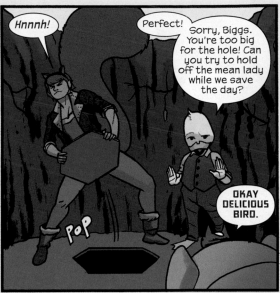

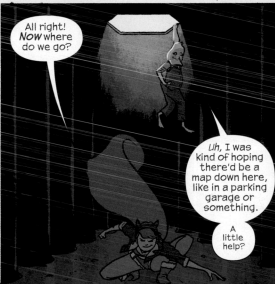

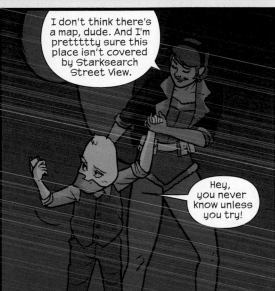

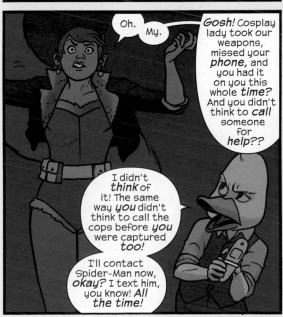

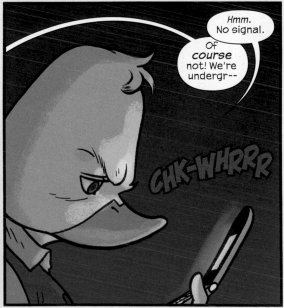

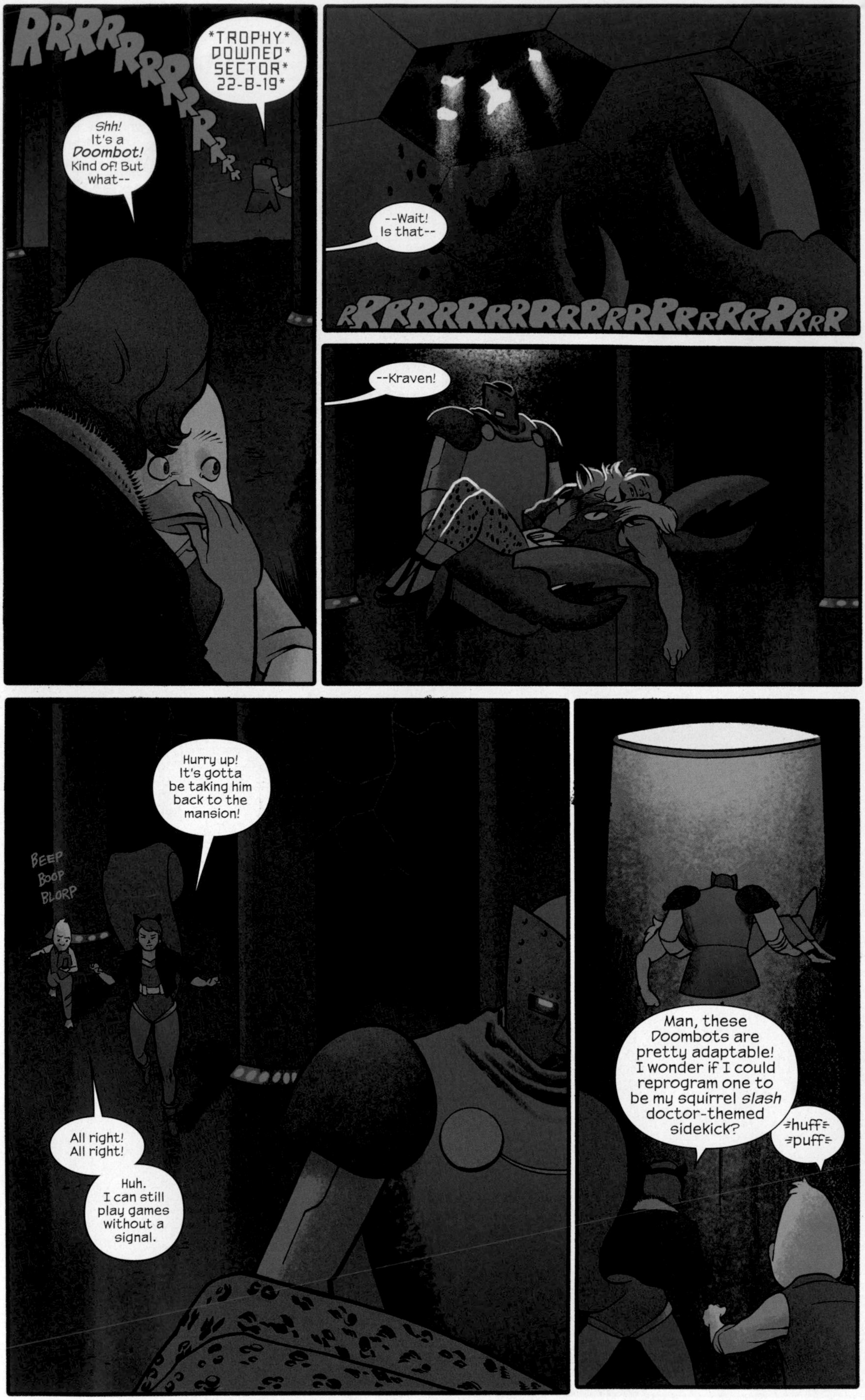
RRRRRRRRRRRRRRRRRkk
TROPHY DOWNED* SECTOR* 22-B-19*
Shh! It's a Doombot! Kind of! But what--
--Wait! Is that--
RRRRRRRRRRRRRRRRRRRRRRRRRR
--Kraven!
Hurry up! It's gotta be taking him back to the mansion!
BEEP BOOP BLORP
All right! All right!
Huh. I can still play games without a signal.
Man, these Doombots are pretty adaptable! I wonder if I could reprogram one to be my squirrel *slash* doctor-themed sidekick?
=huff= =puff=

Think about it, Ryan. If you ***don't*** go for it, I'm going to make one Howard's sidekick: ***Dr. Plume.***
Wow. I ***really*** should've read ***Howard the Duck*** before agreeing to this crossover.

* Unbeatable Squirrel Girl Vol. 1, #4.

**He *will* in *Very Beatable Howard the Duck* Vol. 2, #4, which hasn't happened yet but you've already read it 'cause Make Mine Marvel.

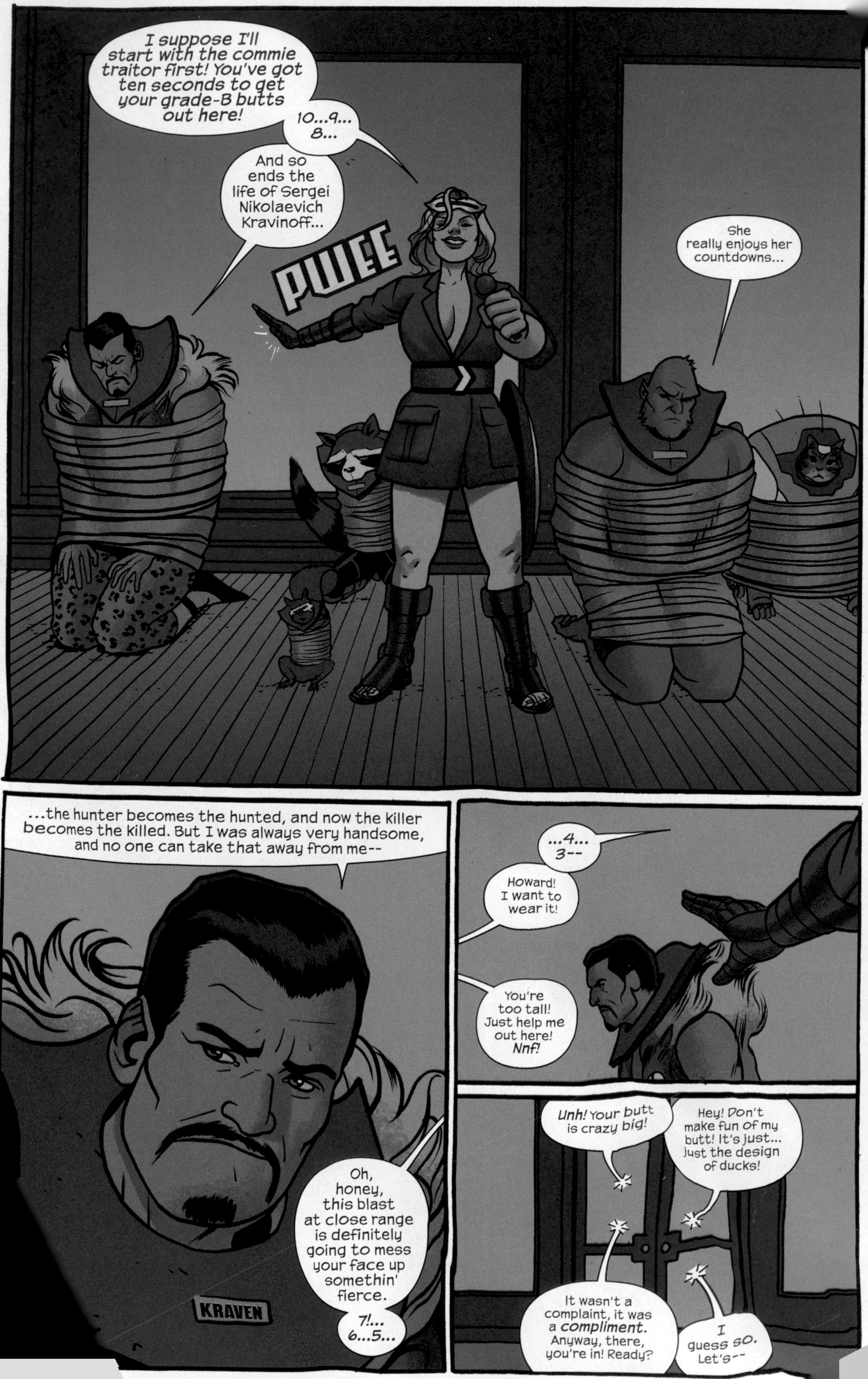
I suppose I'll start with the commie traitor first! You've got ten seconds to get your grade-B butts out here!
10...9... 8...
And so ends the life of Sergei Nikolaevich Kravinoff...
PWEE
She really enjoys her countdowns...
...the hunter becomes the hunted, and now the killer becomes the killed. But I was always very handsome, and no one can take that away from me--
Oh, honey, this blast at close range is definitely going to mess your face up somethin' fierce.
7!... 6...5...
KRAVEN
...4... 3--
Howard! I want to wear it!
You're too tall! Just help me out here! *Nnf!*
Unh! Your butt is crazy big!
Hey! Don't make fun of my butt! It's just... just the design of ducks!
It wasn't a complaint, it was a ***compliment.*** Anyway, there, you're in! Ready?
I guess so. Let's--

before and he was even a ghost for a while! Imagine a ghost hunter skulking around hunting the living? It would be like the op ghostbuster, and pretty cool. ***Call me, Hollywood.***

Hollywood, my idea is like *Chip's,* only better because it's ***also*** like ***Die Hard.*** Call me first.

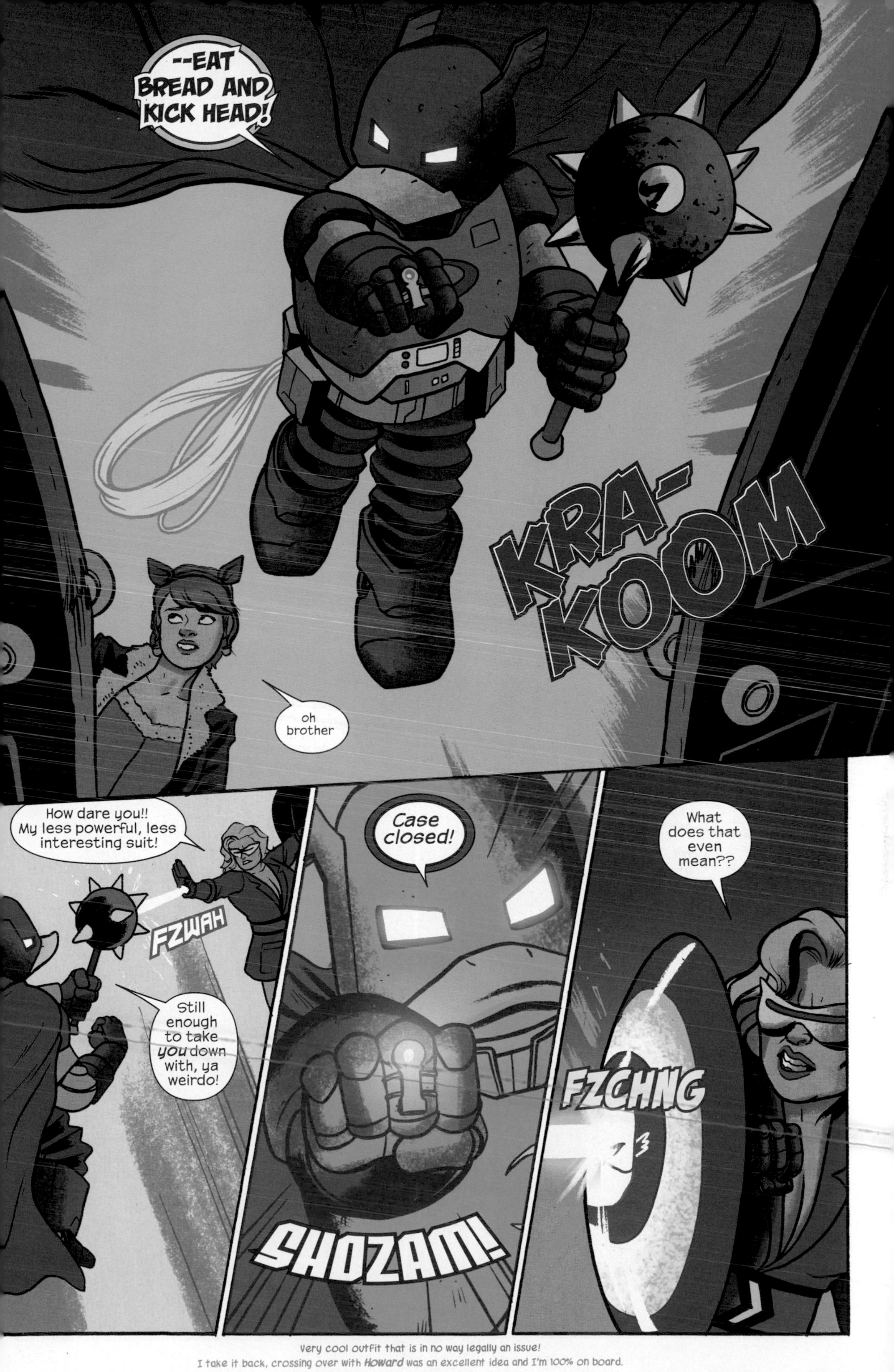
--EAT BREAD AND KICK HEAD!
KRA-KOOM
oh brother
How dare you!! My less powerful, less interesting suit!
FZWAH
Still enough to take *you* down with, ya weirdo!
Case closed!
SHOZAM!
What does that even mean??
FZCHNG

Very cool outfit that is in no way legally an issue!
I take it back, crossing over with ***Howard*** was an excellent idea and I'm 100% on board.

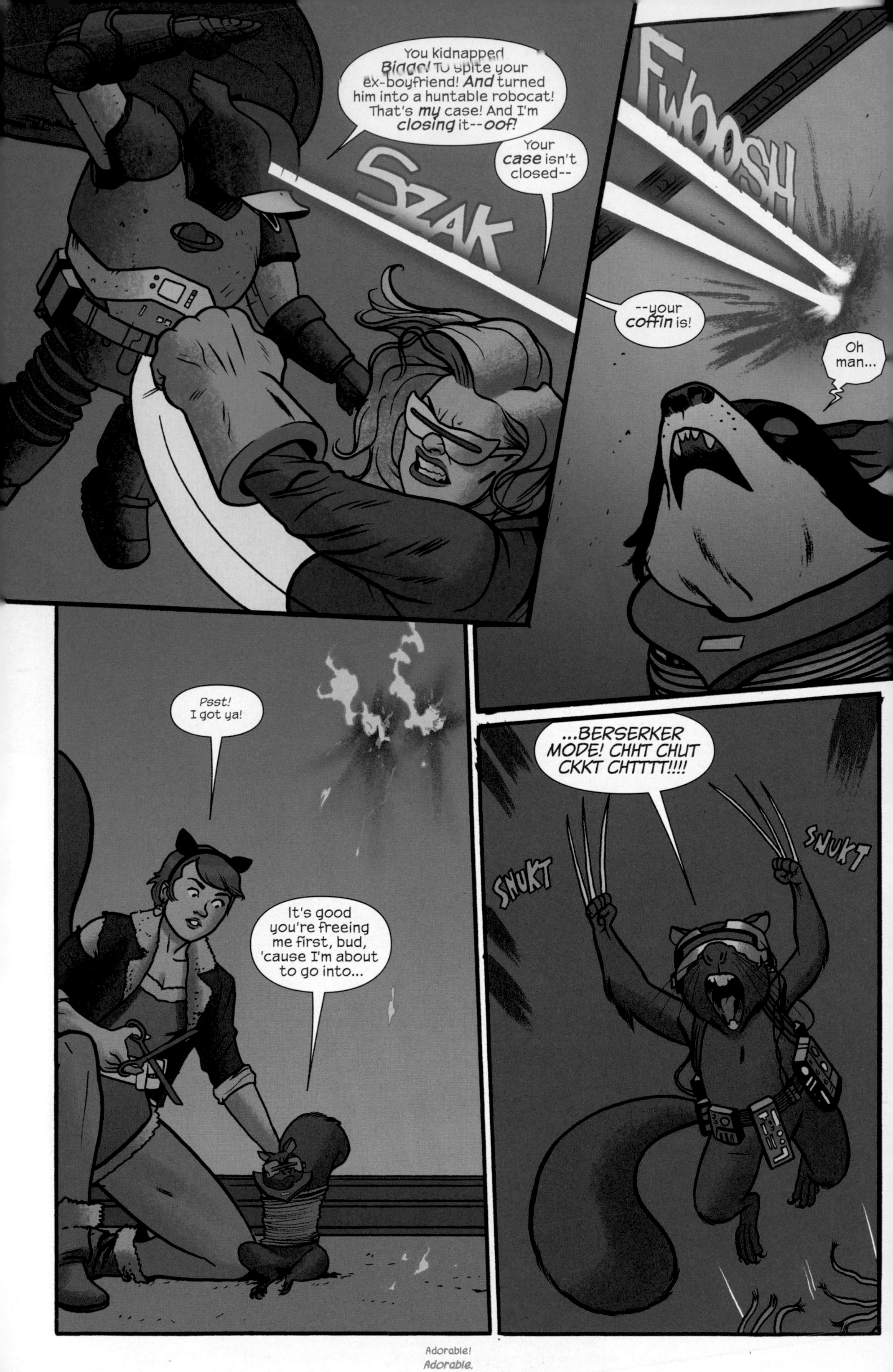
You kidnapped Bingo! To spite your ex-boyfriend! And turned him into a huntable robocat! That's my case! And I'm closing it--oof!
SZAK
Your case isn't closed--
FWOOSH
--your coffin is!
Oh man...
Psst! I got ya!
It's good you're freeing me first, bud, 'cause I'm about to go into...
...BERSERKER MODE! CHHT CHUT CKKT CHTTTT!!!!
SNUKT
SNUKT

Adorable!
Adorable.

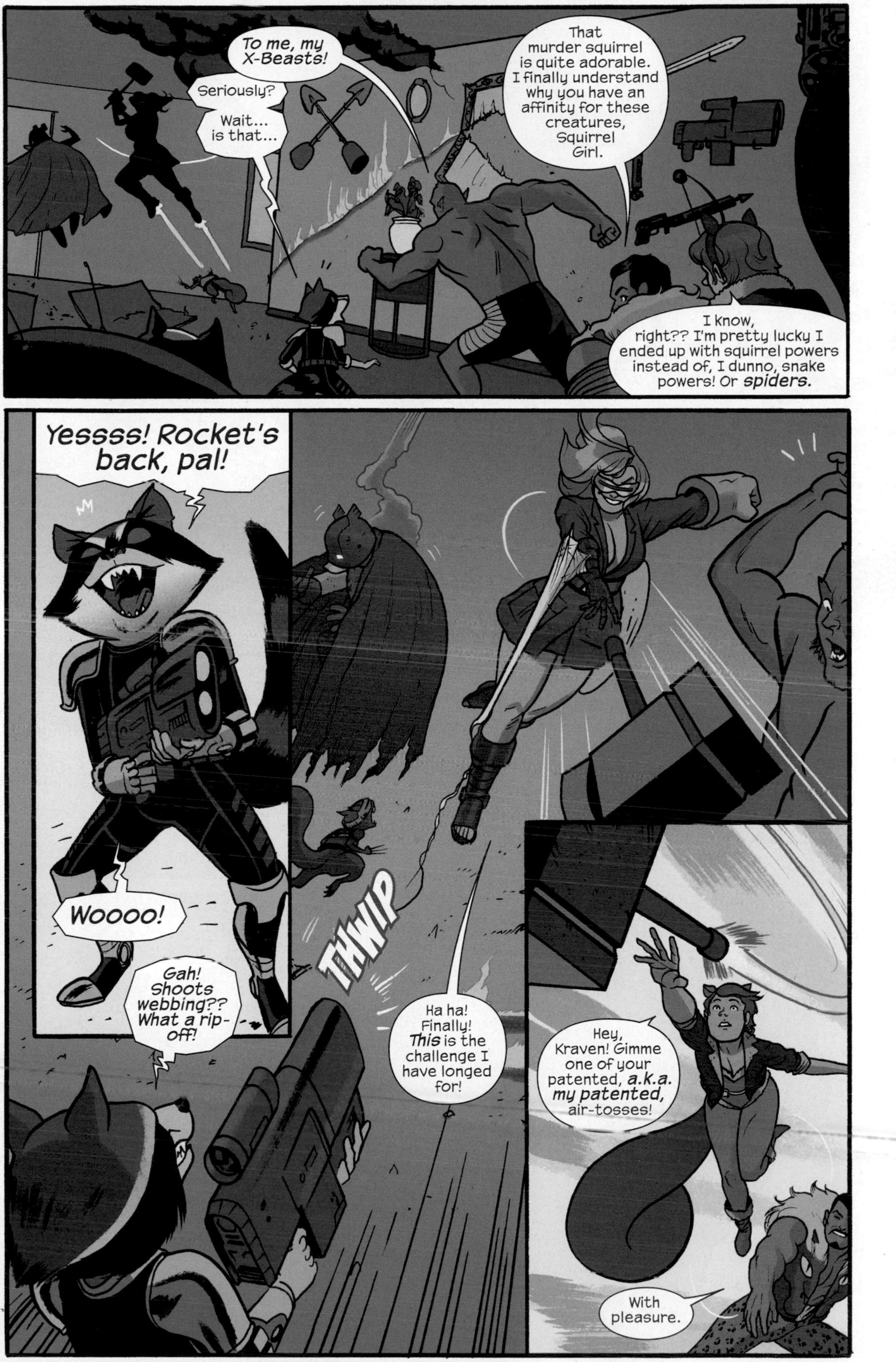

To me, my X-Beasts!
Seriously?
Wait... is that...
That murder squirrel is quite adorable. I finally understand why you have an affinity for these creatures, Squirrel Girl.
I know, right?? I'm pretty lucky I ended up with squirrel powers instead of, I dunno, snake powers! Or spiders.
Yessss! Rocket's back, pal!
Woooo!
Gah! Shoots webbing?? What a rip-off!
THWIP
Ha ha! Finally! This is the challenge I have longed for!
Hey, Kraven! Gimme one of your patented, a.k.a. my patented, air-tosses!
With pleasure.

Snake Girl. There's *another* one for you, *Hollywood!*
I'm more into the idea of a woman who can talk to spiders, and lives in a house full of spiders, and spiders do whatever she says, and she's always covered in spiders. *Nobody would ever mess with her.*

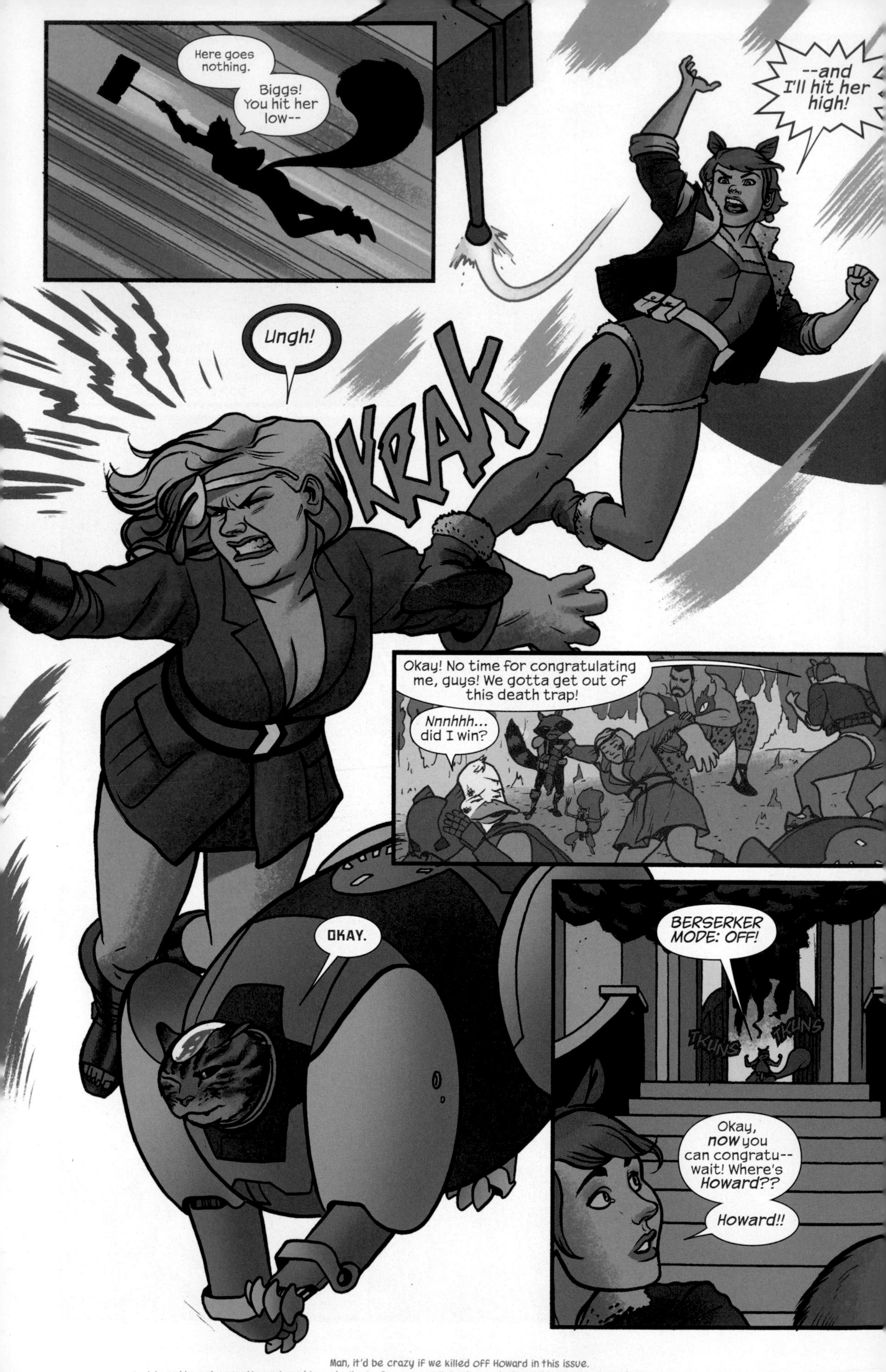
Here goes nothing.
Biggs! You hit her low--
--and I'll hit her high!
Ungh!
KRAK
Okay! No time for congratulating me, guys! We gotta get out of this death trap!
Nnnhhh... did I win?
OKAY.
BERSERKER MODE: OFF!
TKUNS
TKUNS
Okay, **NOW** you can congratu-- wait! Where's Howard??
Howard!!

Man, it'd be crazy if we killed off Howard in this issue.
Just have him get secretly replaced by a duplicate from a parallel universe before this crossover ends. It'll work out great, I promise.

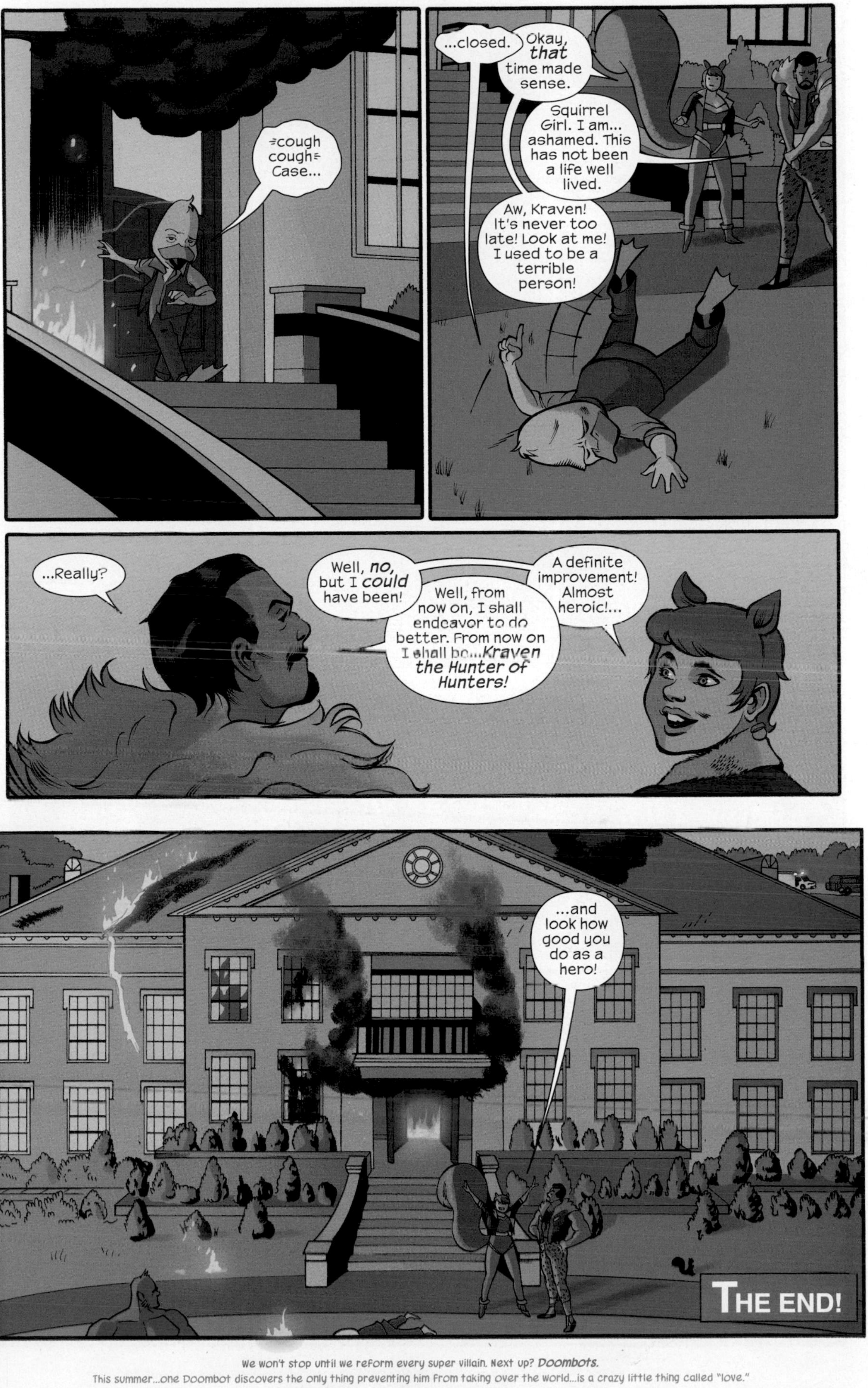

=cough cough= Case...
...closed.
Okay, *that* time made sense.
Squirrel Girl. I am... ashamed. This has not been a life well lived.
Aw, Kraven! It's never too late! Look at me! I used to be a terrible person!
...Really?
Well, *no,* but I *could* have been!
Well, from now on, I shall endeavor to do better. From now on I shall be...*Kraven the Hunter of Hunters!*
A definite improvement! Almost heroic!...
...and look how good you do as a hero!
THE END!

We won't stop until we reform every super villain. Next up? *Doombots.*
This summer...one Doombot discovers the only thing preventing him from taking over the world...is a crazy little thing called "love."

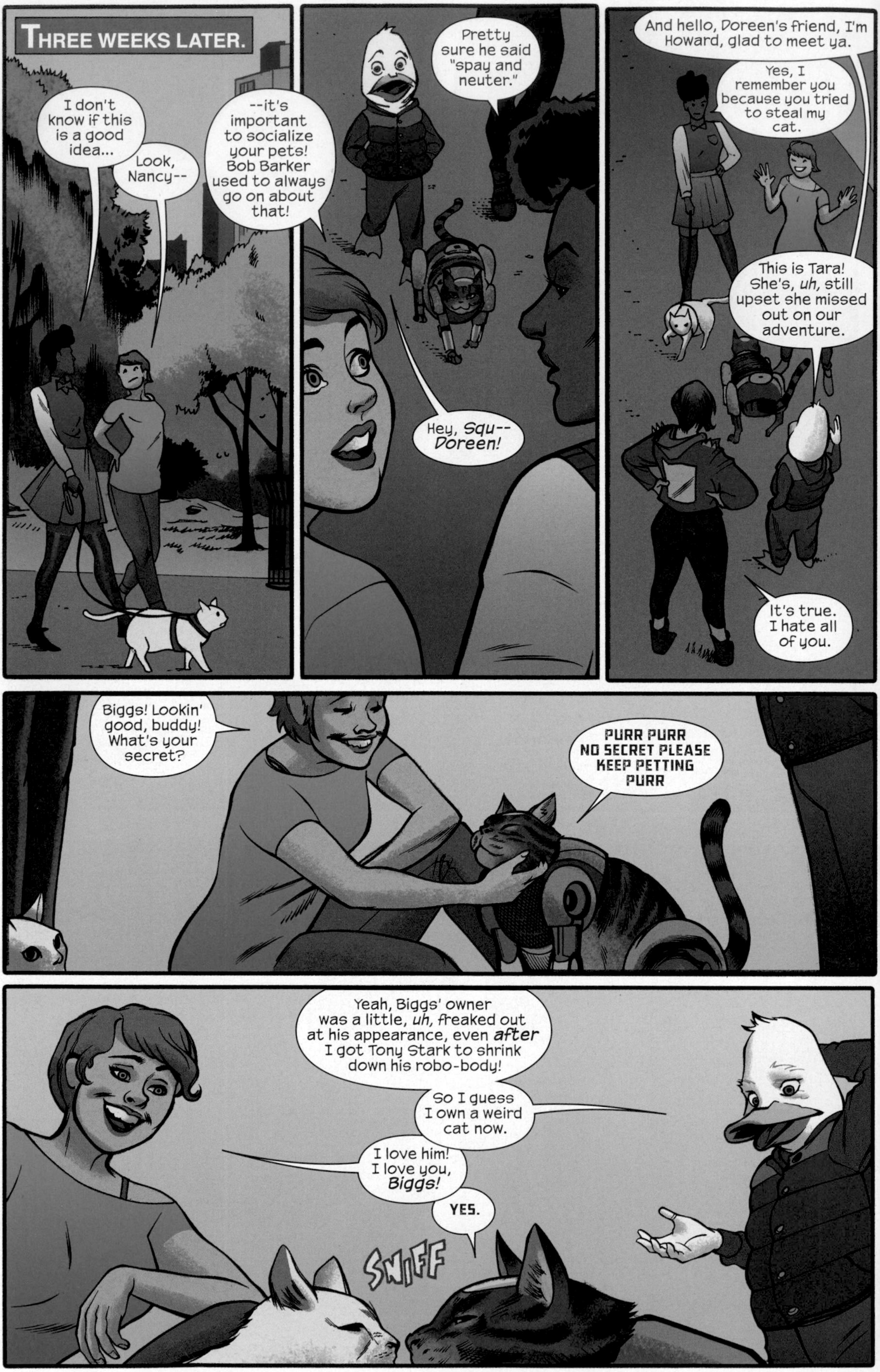
THREE WEEKS LATER.
I don't know if this is a good idea...
Look, Nancy--
--it's important to socialize your pets! Bob Barker used to always go on about that!
Pretty sure he said "spay and neuter."
Hey, *Squ--* *Doreen!*
And hello, Doreen's friend, I'm Howard, glad to meet ya.
Yes, I remember you because you tried to steal my cat.
This is Tara! She's, *uh,* still upset she missed out on our adventure.
It's true. I hate all of you.
Biggs! Lookin' good, buddy! What's your secret?
PURR PURR NO SECRET PLEASE KEEP PETTING PURR
Yeah, Biggs' owner was a little, *uh,* freaked out at his appearance, even ***after*** I got Tony Stark to shrink down his robo-body!
So I guess I own a weird cat now.
I love him! I love you, *Biggs!*
YES.
SNIFF

Yes.
That other cat is named "Mew" and she appears in ***several Squirrel Girl*** issues. That's right. ***Our*** comic has cats, ***too.***

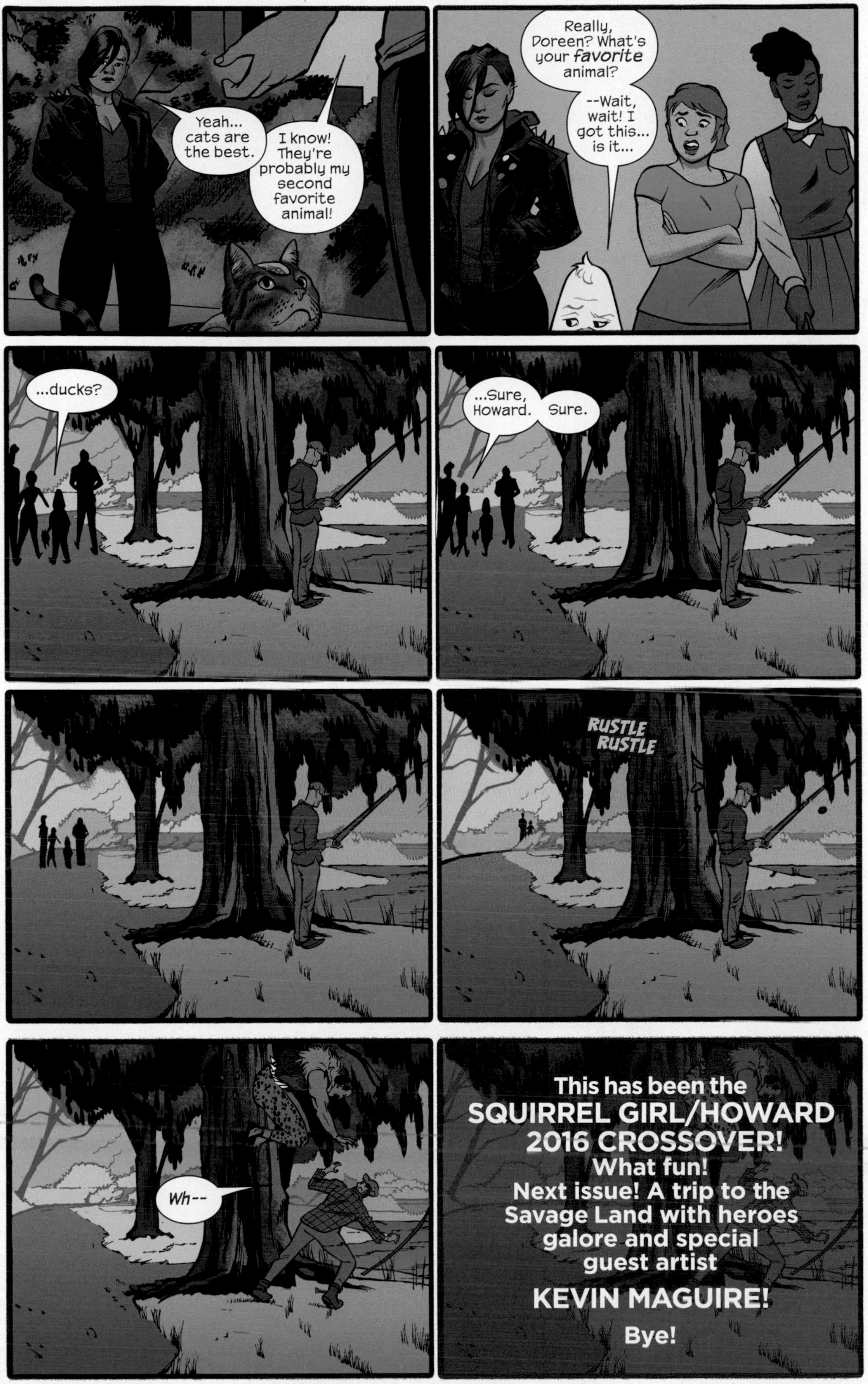
Yeah... cats are the best.
I know! They're probably my second favorite animal!
Really, Doreen? What's your favorite animal?
--Wait, wait! I got this... is it...
...ducks?
...Sure, Howard.
Sure.
RUSTLE RUSTLE
Wh--
This has been the SQUIRREL GIRL/HOWARD 2016 CROSSOVER! What fun! Next issue! A trip to the Savage Land with heroes galore and special guest artist KEVIN MAGUIRE! Bye!

I never wanted this to end. Except I only get paid when it ends.
Chip, it was fun to help you out and write some little words beneath your comic about a talking duck who is mad at things.

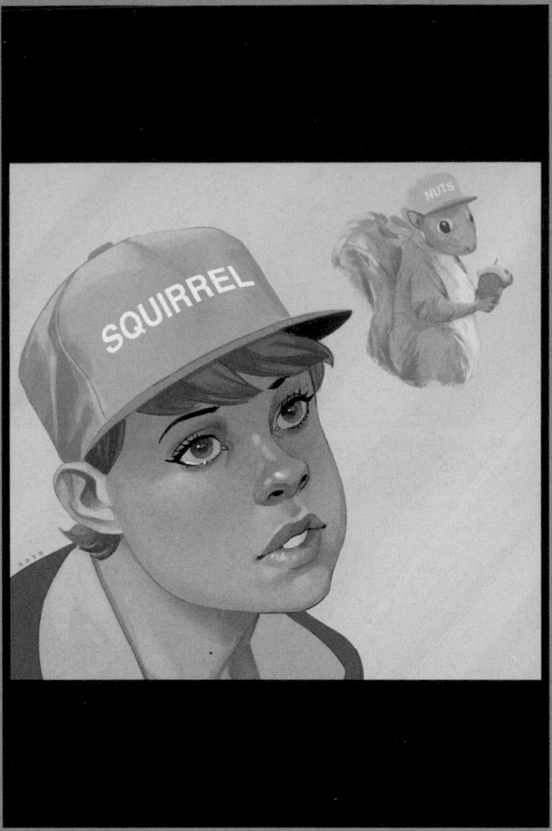
NUTS
SQUIRREL

#1 HIP-HOP VARIANT
BY PHIL NOTO

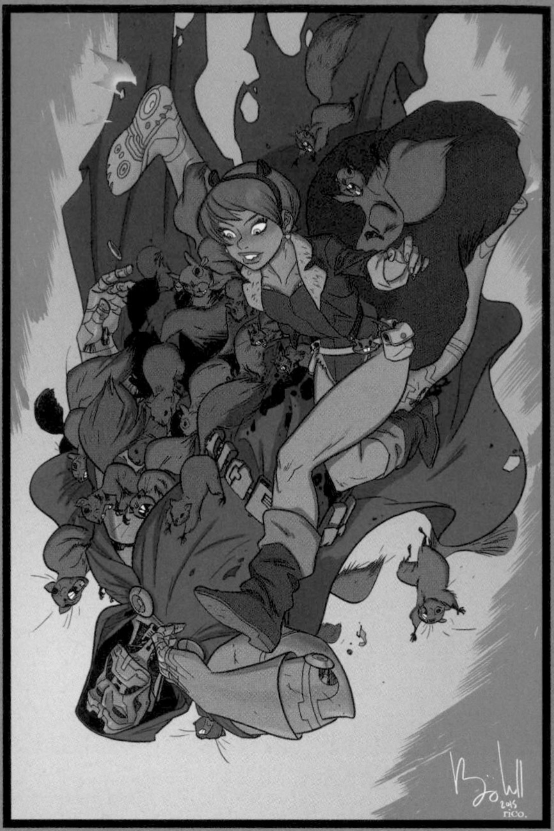

#1 VARIANT
BY BEN CALDWELL & RICO RENZI

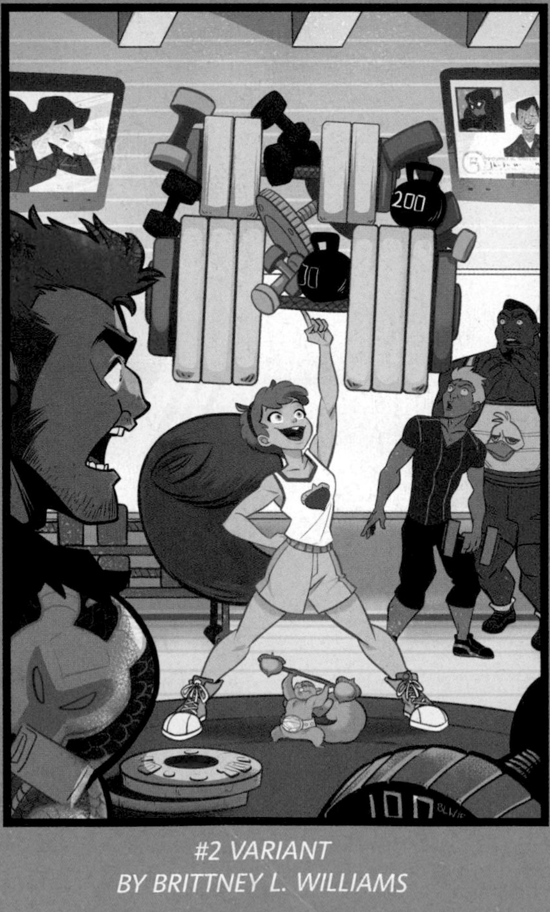
200

#2 VARIANT
BY BRITTNEY L. WILLIAMS

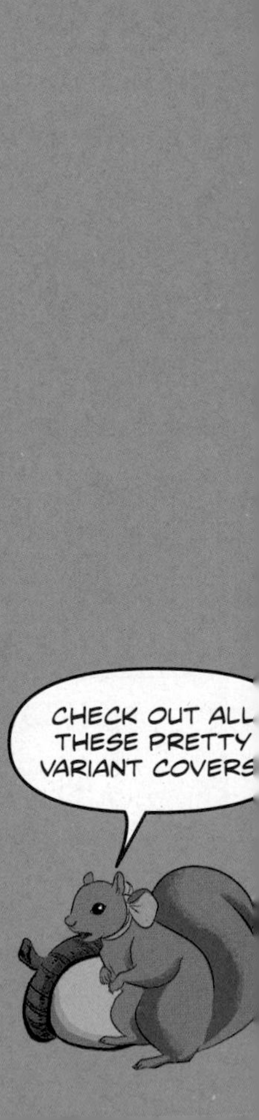
CHECK OUT ALL THESE PRETTY VARIANT COVERS

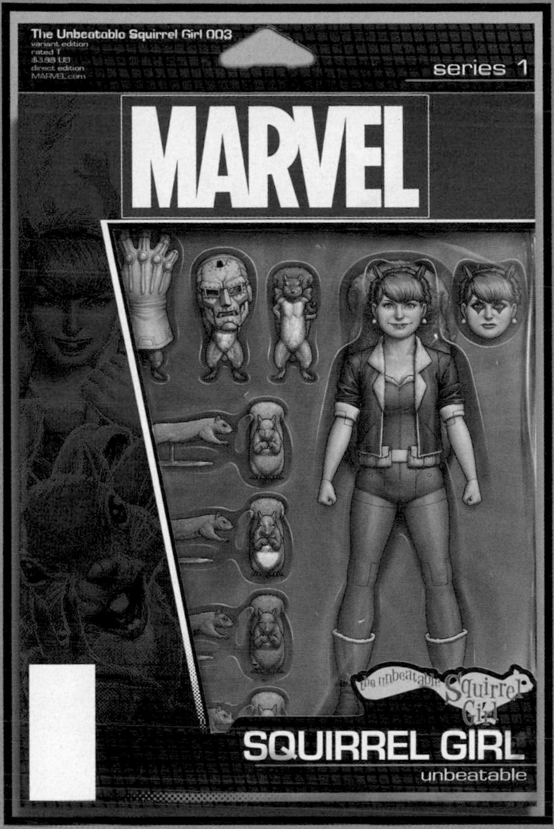
The Unbeatable Squirrel Girl 003
series 1
MARVEL
the unbeatable Squirrel Girl
SQUIRREL GIRL
unbeatable

#3 ACTION FIGURE VARIANT
BY JOHN TYLER CHRISTOPHER

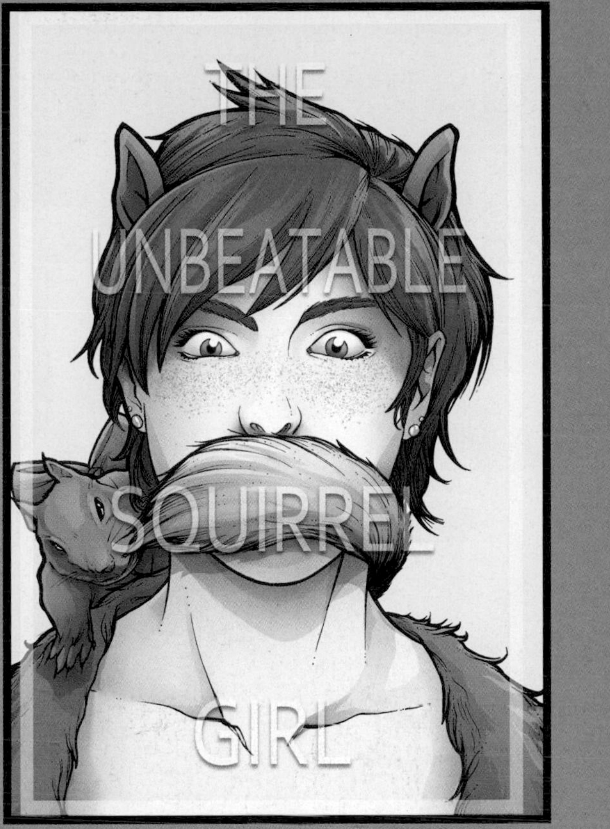
THE
UNBEATABLE
SQUIRREL
GIRL

#3 VARIANT
BY MATT WAITE

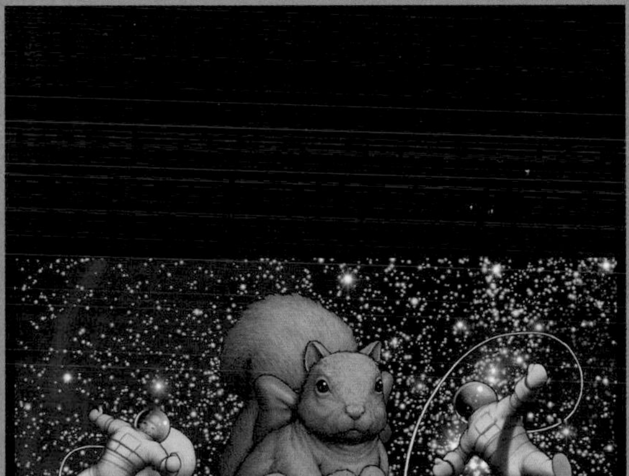

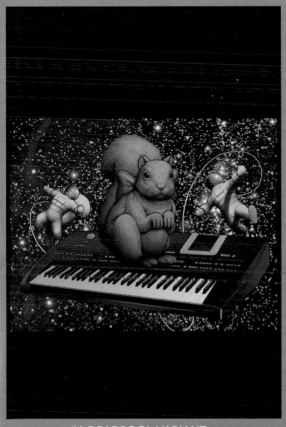

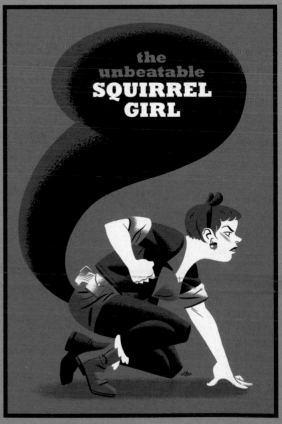

#4 DEADPOOL VARIANT
BY JOHN TYLER CHRISTOPHER

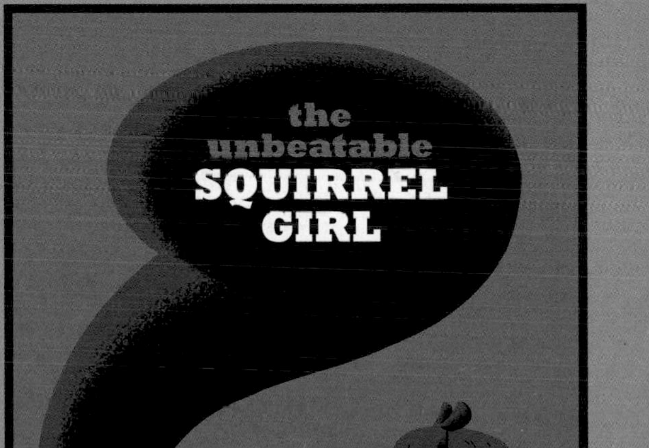
the
unbeatable
SQUIRREL
GIRL

#5 VARIANT
BY MICHAEL CHO

UNBEATABLE SQUIRREL GIRL #6 & HOWARD THE DUCK #6 *COMBINED VARIANTS*
BY TRADD MOORE & MATTHEW WILSON

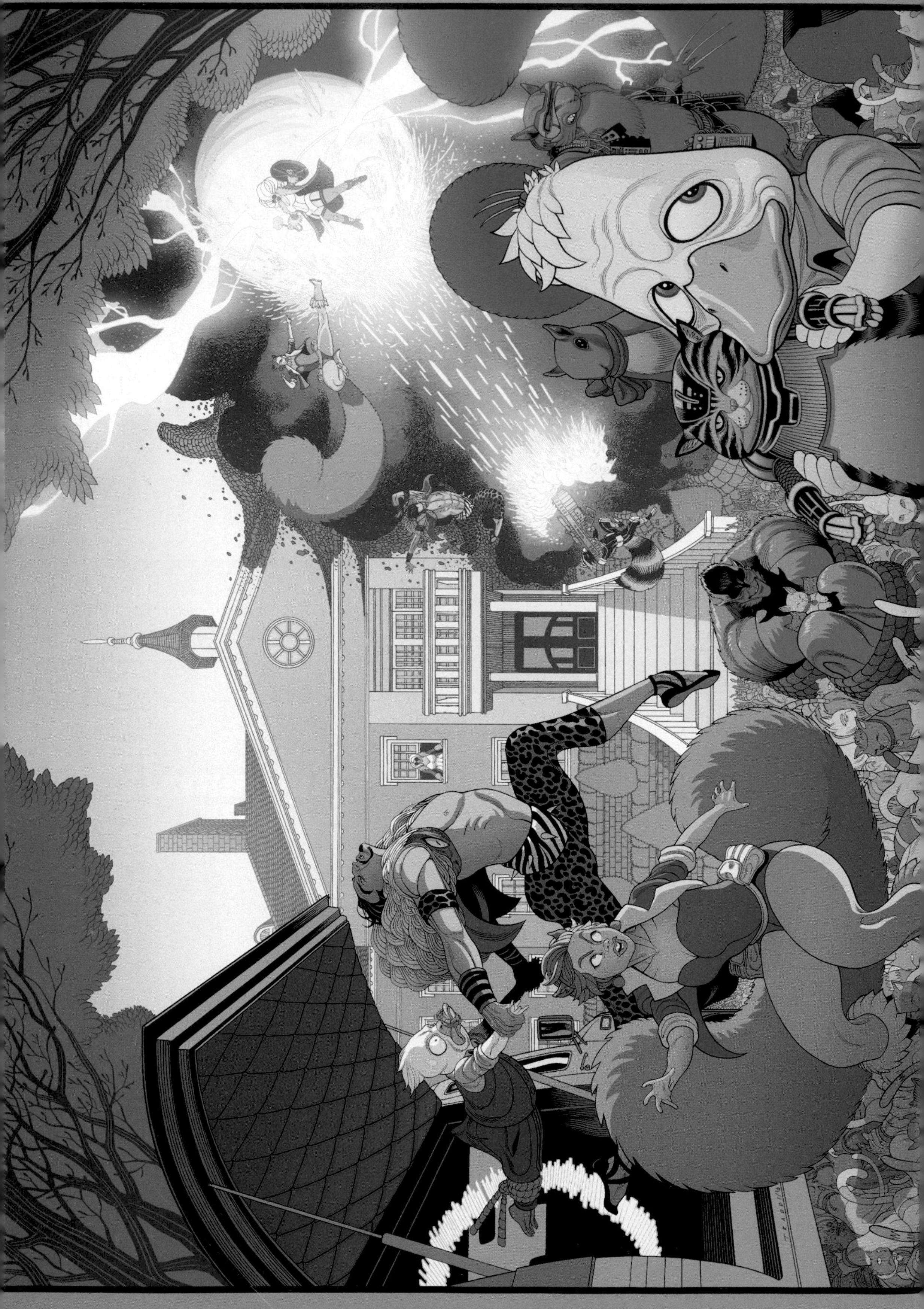